Democratization in Africa:
Progress and Retreat

A *Journal of Democracy* Book

•

Published under the auspices of
the International Forum for Democratic Studies

Democratization in Africa: Progress and Retreat

Second Edition

Edited by
Larry Diamond and Marc F. Plattner

The Johns Hopkins University Press
Baltimore

9 8 7 6 5 4 3 2 1

Chapters in this volume appeared in the following issues of the *Journal of Democracy:*
chapter 22, April 2007; chapters 5, 6, 8, and 17, July 2007; chapter 9, October 2007,
chapters 11 and 12, January 2008; chapters 1, 2, 3, and 4, April 2008; chapters 15 and
18, July 2008; chapters 7, 14, and 24, October 2008; chapter 10, April 2009; chapters 16,
19, and 23, October 2009. For all reproduction rights, please contact the Johns Hopkins
University Press.

The Johns Hopkins University Press
2715 North Charles Street
Baltimore, Maryland 21218-4363
www.press.jhu.edu

Library of Congress Cataloging-in-Publication Data

Democratization in Africa: progress and retreat / [edited by] Larry Diamond, Marc F. Plattner. — 2nd ed.
    p. cm. — (A Journal of democracy book)
      Includes bibliographical references and index.
      ISBN-13: 978-0-8018-9483-1 (hardcover : alk. paper)
      ISBN-10: 0-8018-9483-2 (hardcover : alk. paper)
      ISBN-13: 978-0-8018-9484-8 (pbk. : alk. paper)
      ISBN-10: 0-8018-9484-0 (pbk. : alk. paper)
      1. Democracy—Africa 2. Africa—Politics and government—1960–
  I. Diamond, Larry Jay. II. Plattner, Marc F., 1945–

  JQ1879.A15D465 2010
  320.96—dc22

                             2009045033
A catalog record for this book is available from the British Library.

CONTENTS

III. East Africa

IV. Southern and Central Africa

ACKNOWLEDGMENTS

Although this is the second edition of *Democratization in Africa*—the first was published in 1999—all the material that it contains is entirely new. Hence we have given it the subtitle *Progress and Retreat,* both to distinguish it from the earlier edition and to indicate the complex developments that have taken place in recent years. The first edition had appeared about a decade after the third wave of democratization reached Africa's shores in 1990, and it focused on the continent's experience during the immediate post–Cold War period. It is now more than ten years since the publication of that volume. A more up-to-date account was clearly needed, and the appearance of a profusion of recent articles on Africa in the *Journal of Democracy* provided ample material for this wholly new edition.

The volume you hold in your hands significantly expands on the first edition in terms of both the number of chapters and the range of African countries addressed: It includes 21 essays that appeared in the pages of the *Journal of Democracy* between 2007 and 2009, along with previously unpublished essays by Kate Baldwin, Kenneth Good, and Dave Peterson, and a new introduction by Larry Diamond. In addition to fresh treatments of countries covered in the first edition—Ghana, Kenya, Nigeria, South Africa, and Uganda—the second edition includes chapters on Angola, Botswana, the Democratic Republic of the Congo, Liberia, Senegal, Sierra Leone, Somaliland, Tanzania, Zambia, and Zimbabwe. Even with the considerable expansion in the number of themes and countries included here, there remain regrettable gaps in our coverage of a continent as large and as varied as Africa. Nonetheless, some selectivity was essential in order to keep this volume to a manageable size and cost, and we believe that, despite its inevitable limitations, it succeeds in presenting readers with the information and analysis critical to understanding the varied fortunes of democracy in the countries of Africa.

As with the previous books in the *Journal of Democracy* series, this volume would not have been possible without the assistance of a number of organizations and individuals. We are very thankful for our longstanding partnership with the Johns Hopkins University Press, the publisher of the *Journal* and now of more than twenty of our books. Henry Tom in the Books Division has played an essential role since the beginning in developing and guiding our book series, and Bill Breichner and Carol Hamblen in the Journals Division have been unfailingly helpful colleagues.

The Lynde and Harry Bradley Foundation has provided essential financial assistance to the *Journal* since its inception, and we are immensely grateful for its continuing support. We are also deeply indebted to our parent organization, the National Endowment for Democracy. The Endowment's president Carl Gershman and its Board of Directors, now chaired by former House majority leader Richard A. Gephardt, have never faltered in their support of the *Journal,* while at the same time wholly respecting our editorial independence and integrity. Other members of the NED staff have helped us in many ways large and small. We consider ourselves extremely fortunate to function within such an admirable and open-minded institution.

Whatever success we have achieved is in large part due to the efforts of the *Journal* staff. Executive editor Phil Costopoulos and associate editor Tracy Brown worked tirelessly to give the essays collected here the unique mix of accessibility and depth that has always been the aim and—we hope—the hallmark of the *Journal of Democracy*. Managing editor Brent Kallmer ably took charge of the volume's layout and production, and assistant editor Marta Kalabinski juggled an ever-growing array of editorial responsibilities with characteristic competence and flexibility.

Finally, we are pleased to acknowledge the contribution of Dorothy Warner, who, aside from compiling the index with her usual efficiency, provided extremely useful help to Larry Diamond in drafting parts of the Introduction.

INTRODUCTION

Larry Diamond

Over the past two decades, sub-Saharan Africa (hereafter simply "Africa") has been partly transformed by the winds of democratic change. In 1989, the year the Africa volume of *Democracy in Developing Countries* first appeared, there were only three countries in the region that had sustained multiparty democracy for a significant stretch of time: Botswana, the Gambia, and Mauritius, and the Gambia's electoral regime (which had known only one president for nearly thirty years) was swept aside by a military coup in 1994.[1] Most of that book had to be devoted to explaining why the high hopes for democracy that attended the popular movements for independence in the 1950s and 1960s had crashed and burned, and why it had proven so difficult to develop and sustain democracy subsequently.

Through the first three decades of Africa's independence, the story was one of repeated collapses of democracy in countries such as Ghana, Nigeria, and Sudan, and of the noteworthy variety of authoritarian regimes: military, one-party, socialist, and personal dictatorships.[2] By comparison, the controlled political pluralism of Senegal—which at the time was often called "semidemocratic" but which would now be termed less charitably "competitive authoritarian"—looked quite liberal. In fact, Senegal in the 1980s was one of the more democratic countries in Africa, even though it was quite clearly not a democracy. The same was true for Zimbabwe, which was sometimes mistakenly labeled a democracy in that period. Indeed, back in the 1980s, democracies were so thin on the ground in Africa that some observers tried to stretch the term to apply to the one-party Kenyan and Tanzanian regimes, of which one could at least say that a significant number of legislators lost their bids for reelection.

By the time the first edition of this book (much more limited in scope) was published in 1999, the situation had changed dramatically.[3] In fact, it was the events of 1989—the fall of the Berlin Wall and the implosion of the socialist model—that provided the catalyst. Two events in February 1990—the seizure of governing power by civil society from the one-party dictatorship of Mathieu Kérékou in Benin, and the release of Nelson Mandela and the unbanning of the African National Congress in South Africa—marked the beginning of a "second liberation" in Africa (though as Crawford Young noted, it was actually the third wave of efforts to inaugurate democracy in Africa).[4] Coincidentally, in that same month, as South Africa was finally beginning to turn away from repression and racial exclusion in favor of a negotiated transition to democracy, the Constituent Assembly of Namibia (which as South West Africa had been ruled for seven decades by the white minority regime in South Africa) approved a liberal-democratic constitution under which the country gained independence the following month. Nearly two decades later, Benin, Namibia, and South Africa all remain comparatively stable and free democracies.

The democratic wave of the 1990s left few African states untouched. As Michael Bratton noted in the first edition of this book, by 1997's end only four of sub-Saharan Africa's four-dozen states had failed to hold a competitive multiparty national election.[5] Two of those four, Nigeria and Zaire (later redubbed the Democratic Republic of Congo or DRC), did so in 1999 and 2006, respectively. This left Somalia and Swaziland as the only holdouts. Of course, as the essays in this volume (and those in our first edition) note, many of Africa's new competitive elections were deeply flawed and even blatantly rigged. But the mere fact that dictators felt compelled to legalize opposition parties and permit at least a semblance of multiparty competition represented a sea change in the postindependence politics of Africa. Moreover, as Staffan Lindberg has shown, repeated competitive elections in Africa improved democracy's prospects *even when the electoral process was less than free and fair*. Even flawed elections worked as a force for democracy, Lindberg argues, by extending the scope for freedom, enhancing democratic values and awareness among citizens, and stimulating the growth of civic organizations and independent media organs.[6]

At the time of this writing in late 2009, a glance at Africa's political landscape brings to view both democracy on the march and democracy in retreat. On the hopeful side, there are three more electoral democracies in Africa (making a current total of twenty) than there were when the first edition of this book was published a decade ago. Levels of freedom have also continued to improve. Back in 1974, the average score on political rights and civil liberties across Africa was 5.5 on the Freedom House scale (where a score of 1 indicates most free and 7 most repressive). By 2000, that score had improved substantially to 4.4, and eight years later it had further improved to 4.2. Moreover, democracy has either held its own or improved in a number of African countries, as symbolized by the second alternation of power in Ghana at the end of 2008, following a closely fought presidential election. Ghana is one of eight African countries whose scores on political rights and civil liberties identify them as relatively liberal democracies (see Table on page xxvi). Perhaps most remarkable is the continuation of democracy in Sierra Leone and Liberia despite the immense devastation—physical, political, and psychological—wrought by brutal civil wars in those small West African countries.

Recent years, however, have also seen negative trends, including five outright reversals of democracy. In Nigeria and Kenya, ruling parties have brazenly rigged national elections—in the latter case plunging the country into paroxysms of postelectoral violence. Similarly, democracy was strangled in 2009 by the elected president in Niger, Mamadou Tandja, when he shut down parliament and arrested political opponents in order to extend his term in office. A military coup overthrew a weak, fledgling democracy in Mauritania, while a military-backed popular rebellion displaced an elected government in Madagascar. And in many more African countries that are classified by Freedom House as electoral democracies, the electoral playing field is so tilted and civil liberties are so severely restricted that the accuracy of the "democratic" label falls into question. Steven Levitsky and Lucan Way argue that the systematic electoral advantages in access to resources and the mass media enjoyed by ruling parties in Botswana, Malawi, Mali, Mozambique, Namibia, Senegal, and Zambia mean that all are misclassified when referred to as democracies.[7] Although most moderately knowledgeable observers of African politics and development would be surprised to learn that Botswana is not a democracy, that is in fact what Kenneth Good suggests in his chapter here, which documents a striking deterioration in civil liberties and the rule of law in that country. If we were to eliminate from the "democratic" category all the regimes that Levitsky and Way regard as examples of competitive authoritarianism, the share of regimes in Africa that are rightly classed as belonging to the ranks of the world's democracies would fall from 42 percent to barely a quarter.

Even if we hold to the classification scheme in the Table, many African democracies are of low quality, with political competition, freedom, and the rule of law all degraded by widespread corruption and clientelism as well as the underlying syndrome of "big man" politics. Comparative experience from around the globe tells us that unless effective institutions arise to bring these problems gradually under control, democracies will remain fragile and liable to reversal, whether by soldiers, ruling parties, or presidents themselves. Although conditions placed on aid by the established democracies as well as international pressures of a more general sort do tend to limit the scope for blatant authoritarian reversals—as evidenced in the virtual disappearance of formal military rule as a regime type in Africa—such restraining factors are far less effective at discouraging even slightly subtler manipulations of the democratic form. Moreover, as Richard Joseph notes in our opening chapter, the arrival of China as a major aid donor, investor, and geopolitical player in Africa has given a new lease on life to authoritarian regimes that now have in Beijing an alternative political patron whom they can play off against the West.

Thus, two decades after competitive politics swept the continent, Africa witnesses contradictory political trends: democratic progress and retreat. As we see in the pages that follow, there are important (and, for Africa, historic) positive trends. As Daniel Posner and Daniel Young show in chapter 5, Africa's politics have grown less violent and more institutionalized since 1990, with elections becoming a much more frequent vehicle for changes of government, and more presidents abiding by term limits than eviscerating them. Even where elections remain unfair and rulers abusive, African civil societies are becoming more vigorous, experienced, and committed to democratic norms, challenging constitutional violations and demanding political accountability. Perhaps most significant, as Michael Bratton shows in chapter 9, a large share of the citizenry in country after country across Africa has come to demand democracy. Moreover, about half of all Africans surveyed also reject all feasible authoritarian options. The problem is that these democratic citizens quite correctly perceive their respective governments' failures to supply as much democracy as the people want.

A "Frontier" and Its Discontents

In the opening essay to this volume, Richard Joseph sets the tone for many of our contributors by depicting sub-Saharan Africa as a "frontier" region. Despite centuries of contact with the more developed world, Africa still features not only the great opportunities of a newly "discovered" region, but also the very considerable risks. Africa is attracting growing equity investment, heightened economic interest from China, and global capital institutions seeking to foster entrepreneurship in hopes of generating new wealth. On the side of the ledger where risks are tallied, however, appear many factors that give investors and other observers pause. The ongoing tension in African nations between personal rule and democracy—Joseph calls this a "struggle between two rival types of institutions"—has left the continent in a state of uncertainty. A few promising exceptions aside, Joseph (like a number of our other contributors) sees personal rule as a lurking danger that lies perennially in wait for nearly all African regimes. Although Joseph notes some encouraging trends toward more respect for the rule of law, he concludes that "the struggle to cross the frontier from personal rule to rule-based governance is still far from over in much of Africa." Then too, even in Africa's more successful democracies, the threat posed by corruption looms large. The firm consolidation of democracy's key institutional bulwarks—reliable electoral systems, a free press, an independent judiciary, strong legislatures, and a vibrant civil society—continues to prove elusive across much of the continent. Yet Joseph remains confident that these very institutions, helped by donors and aided by new technologies and advances in communication, may yet blossom even under harsh conditions.

In chapter 2, H. Kwasi Prempeh cautions that despite some evidence of increased checks on the executive (for instance, 33 African states now have presidential term limits), Africa's imperial presidencies survive, "term-limited but not tamed." Though conditions "on the ground" may appear less repressive, "power in the African state . . . continues to rest with the president." More often than not, the president, not the legislature, introduces new laws simply by proclamation. This system, once defended by many observers as necessary in postcolonial nations beset by ethnic or regional tensions, has nevertheless been a failure, and resulted in "strong presidents atop weak states." Yet paradoxically, even those who have dared to challenge the continent's strong presidents have made few true changes. Instead of reforming the system, challengers such as Zambia's Frederick Chiluba have merely "re-formed" a new authoritarian regime. The solution, Prempeh insists, lies only in the development of stronger countervailing institutions, particularly legislatures, to thwart presidential ambitions. While acknowledging the uphill struggle for legislatures, weakened not only by traditions of deference to the president but also by a lack of fiscal authority and rampant patronage and corruption, Prempeh recommends constitutional remedies. With as much precision as possible, written constitutions must place limits on cabinet posts, appointment criteria, and the prosecutorial powers of presidents. Additionally, urges Prempeh, political parties should become more democratic with respect to their own internal procedures, including their methods of nominating candidates for office. As for the third branch of government, he points again to constitutional innovations that will strengthen the judiciary as a means of kicking the props out from beneath the edifice of African authoritarianism.

If Africa's legislatures are the best hope for providing the needed check on Africa's "big men," it is worth examining those among the continent's lawmaking bodies that have become, in Joel Barkan's words, "significant institutions of countervailing power." Looking at the track record of six nations (Benin, Ghana, Kenya, Senegal, South Africa, and Uganda), chapter 3 considers the future of legislatures in Africa. The unique functions of any true legislature—representative decision making, writing and passing laws, overseeing the executive branch, and constituent service—are, at best, in tension with one another. In agrarian and rural societies, the last function looms largest, because local interests often determine whether a legislator is reelected. Hence Barkan suggests changing the incentives facing African lawmakers so that they spend more time on national and not just local questions. Years of one-party rule have left most African legislatures hollow and dysfunctional. Legislators too often seek office solely for power or patronage opportunities, or are so poorly paid that they become ripe for corruption. As the rules in some countries have evolved toward allowing multiparty competition and granting legislators adequate resources, "coalitions for change" have begun to emerge. These coalitions, comprising reformers and opportunists alike, have begun to use technology and private-sector entrepreneurial skills to alter the system. The goal is to make constitutional changes that "tip the balance" away from the president toward a more balanced government. Such gains as there have been on behalf of this laudable effort have been uneven and highly qualified, however, as well as limited thus far mostly to Kenya, South Africa, and Uganda.

Across Africa, the chief obstacle to an assertive parliament is a powerful president. In chapter 4, Larry Diamond examines the ongoing pull of two trends in African societies. One trend leads toward democratization, while the other points to personal rule. Although the number of African democracies has risen dramatically in the past two decades, only one of Africa's larger countries (South Africa) is a democracy. But if one considers how unlikely democracy had seemed in some of the smaller, poorer nations, and in countries such as Burundi, where violence had been rampant, even incremental progress can appear remarkable. Despite its persistence in some states, one-party rule is on the decline. Here Diamond credits international donors and African publics with pushing for greater accountability in the form of free, regular, and genuinely contested elections. Still more significant than elections, says Diamond, are indicators that point to the growth of civil society. With the help of foreign donors, Africa is developing a core of civic associations that are not only helping their members to build the skills and patience needed for democracy, but are also helping other associations to advance the cause of democracy itself. Helped by digital and cellular technology, independent media are emerging. Surveys show that more Africans than ever want democracy and are willing to be patient in awaiting its results.

Sadly, however, the glacial pace at which those results are arriving may try that patience sorely. Surveys that measure the quality of governance still put Africa (South Africa excepted) below even the Middle East and South Asia. Despite appearances to the contrary, Africa's neopatrimonial systems are alive and well, characterized by personalized, unaccountable power concentrated in the executive. Several of Africa's "big men" have been in power for decades. Only steady empowerment of civil society will, over the long term, lead to the kind of countervailing institutions that can sustain self-government. In this effort, Diamond encourages international donors to provide support and encouragement for these vital, though fledgling, institutions.

Since independence, democratic rules and institutions have often been formally in place in Africa, but they have been largely ignored. In chapter 5, Posner and Young cite the example of Nigeria's recent denial of a third term to President Olusegun Obasanjo as evidence that "the formal rules of the game [in Africa] are beginning to matter." These rules have "displaced violence as the primary source of constraints on executive behavior." Increasingly, it is not coups but elections or term limits that have sent presidents packing. Posner and Young acknowledge the corruption and violence that still too often surround African elections, but they draw encouragement from evidence that these same elections are becoming more intensely contested and harder to rig. The new rules have not made it less likely that incumbents will win, but the rules have made it more likely that incumbents will at least have to stand the test of a fairly free election. When the end of their allotted two consecutive terms arrived, half the presidents in Posner and Young's study chose to step down, while the other half attempted to change the rules to permit themselves another term. Some of them succeeded, including Uganda's Yoweri Museveni and the late Omar Bongo of Gabon, who died of natural causes in mid-2009 while in the midst of his forty-second straight year in office. Those who failed to overcome term limits included Zambia's President Chiluba as well as Bakili Muzuli of Malawi. Thus, though the pattern of long-serving executives in Africa is alive and well, the means of retaining executive power are clearly changing.

With the "big men" now holding power more or less "by the rules," can it be that the military coup is on the decline in Africa? John F. Clark takes up this question in chapter 6. More pointedly, Clark asks, given the powerful incentives for military leaders to seek political control by violent means, why do coups *not* happen more often in many African states? Clark ponders whether the apparent decline in military coups since the 1990s is a function of a change in the external constraints on military leaders, or should be ascribed instead to a change in the political consciousness of the leaders themselves. His analysis leads him to emphasize the latter explanation. Drawing on Bratton and Nicolas van de Walle's work on democratic transitions and using Freedom House data, Clark identifies a liberalization trajectory for 21 African states during the 1990s and early 2000s. He then examines whether or not those states experienced military interventions. Clark concludes that democratic legitimacy makes military coups less likely, but by no means serves as perfect insulation. Military coups appear likely "in states that start down a path of liberalization but then give way to 'democratic backsliding'" (especially when they have a history of military rule). In seeking to improve legitimacy, it is as important for regimes to make some economic progress and retain public order as it is to hold free elections.

In chapter 7, Peter Lewis takes up the thorny problem of the relationship between political reform and economic regeneration. Hopes that the democratic revolutions in the 1990s would revive Africa's economies have so far been disappointed. Though some macroeconomic indicators have been on the rise, most people in most countries have not seen their own living standards improve. Examining the data, Lewis finds some evidence that, over the past decade, Africa's democracies have recorded faster economic growth than their autocratic neighbors. He notes as well that "Africa's democracies attain better Human Development scores than the region's nondemocratic countries." This advantage erodes when looking at change over time, however, and his key finding emphasizes "the limited progress in popular welfare among all African countries." Sounding a common theme of this book, Lewis stresses that the depth of democracy matters. Nations that combine democratic forms with an everyday political mire of neopatrimonialism have little incentive to improve the lot of individual citizens. In particular, when the ruling party stays in power over many legislative terms—as has been the case in Nigeria, South Africa, and Tanzania, for example—the opposition can do little to change deep-seated patterns of clientelism. The weakness of both civil society and the state and the pervasiveness of corruption also impede progress. Africa, Lewis concludes, needs better-trained government leaders who care more about reform, stronger oppositions and civic organizations, and more effective corruption-fighting institutions. Still, Lewis cites the Afrobarometer measures of citizen patience, both with democracy and with sluggish economic improvements, as hopeful signs that Africans will not turn away from democracy.

Democracy, one could say, is still making its own case on the African continent. In chapter 8, Michael Bratton addresses the success of that case as measured through the public-opinion polling data compiled by the Afrobarometer. His aim is to determine whether it is the formal (legal and constitutional) or the informal (actual power relations as experienced by most citizens) institutions that most shape the perception of democracy. Chief among the informal institutions in Africa are the classic three pillars of neopatrimonial rule: corruption, clientelism, and presidentialism. Bratton acknowledges that both formal and informal institutions shape the people's outlook toward political matters, but he asks which matters more to most people.

The Afrobarometer data show that the proportion of Africans who favor democracy is growing. In countries where elections have brought about a change in the ruling group (Ghana, Kenya, and Senegal), support is the highest, but overall 62 percent of Africans prefer democracy to any other kind of government, and nearly 75 percent reject military rule. Slightly more than half reject all three authoritarian alternatives when these are put to them. The survey shows, promisingly, that most Africans are willing to accept democracy even with some flaws, though in most of the surveys the share of citizens who profess themselves satisfied with the way that democracy works in their own country has been declining. Democracy as an idea is doing well in Africa—there is sufficient *demand*; it is the *supply* that remains uncertain. Although an overwhelming majority of Africans prefer competitive elections, only minorities believe that elections will actually remove leaders from office. Nigerians' experience with President Obasanjo's attempt to overthrow term limits was so sour that their expressed unhappiness with democracy's working in their country acted as a downward drag on the whole continent's average democratic-satisfaction score. Yet in nearby (but much smaller) Ghana, an improving electoral commission has likewise made citizens feel more satisfied with their country's democracy. And Africans, the survey shows, are demanding more than free and fair elections; they also want their leaders to be responsive to citizens' needs as well as accountable for both behavior in office and policy outcomes. Corruption in particular is "clearly corrosive to democracy," especially when "political elites monopolize available resources." Despite the unevenness of their experience, however, Africans still express hope for the future of democracy in their own countries.

West Africa: Many Countries, Many Paths

The remainder of this volume examines the strengths and weaknesses of democracy in individual countries, starting with those in West Africa. In chapter 9, Rotimi Suberu takes up the troubling case of Nigeria and its deeply flawed April 2007 national elections. Having failed to extend his limited term of office, President Obasanjo tried other means to retain power: first, by handpicking his party's next candidate, the frail Umaru Yar'Adua; by using police and security forces to intimidate the opposition; and then by politicizing the Independent National Election Commission. Add armed party thugs to the police and security forces, and it is hardly surprising that nearly three-hundred Nigerians lost their lives to election-related violence. Suberu laments the corruption of the electoral process and the missed opportunity that this represented for Nigeria, which had seen and encouraged elections in other African nations. Echoing Peter Lewis, Suberu notes that despite rising national wealth due to rising prices for petroleum exports, average Nigerians are still very poor, and that this, coupled with disgust at the electoral process, has somewhat soured the country on democracy. Although there are a few bright spots—local elections that ended in wins for the opposition, hope for judicial review of election travesties, and some evidence of power-sharing—overall, this election was a setback not only for Nigeria but for the larger cause of democracy in Africa. Still, Suberu notes, challenges to the election results have remained largely peaceful and followed institutional channels, while the new president has at least said all the right things about correcting the institutional side of the electoral process. The hope is that legal and administrative reforms might make this kind of electoral disaster less likely to happen again.

From Ghana, the news for democracy is more encouraging. In chapter 10, E. Gyimah-Boadi recounts the December 2008 national elections and the peaceful January 2009 handoff of power from defeated incumbents to a victorious opposition. The voting ushered in the second rotation of power between ruling parties in eight years, thereby securing

Ghana's status as a beacon of democracy in Africa. But even in Ghana, a smooth election cannot be taken for granted. Both the ruling New Patriotic Party (NPP) and the opposition National Democratic Congress (NDC) had their difficulties: The former appeared to many to be corrupt and elitist, while the latter was hampered by a lackluster presidential candidate and a lack of funds. The parties competed against each other on a more or less level playing field, and by African standards this was a contest of issues, not personalities, at least through the first round of voting. Voter intimidation and outright violence marred the December 7 first round, however, and escalated in the second round three weeks later. The tense days between the end of the voting and the announcement of the results saw more violent clashes. In the end, the NPP's Nana Akufo-Addo conceded to the NDC's John Atta Mills after an extremely close race. Despite all the challenges they faced, the institutions in Ghana held up well. In contrast to Nigeria, it was the independence of the Election Commission that saved the day. Ghana's civil society also held up well and was supported by the international community.

Gyimah-Boadi's hope is that the 2008 election experience will spur Ghana to redouble its efforts to build a truly democratic culture by solidifying key institutions and closing gaps in accountability. Ghana's presidency is still too powerful an office, and as such remains too easily subject to abuse for purposes of patronage and even outright corruption. There are no regulations on campaign spending, and there is little or no transparency in the management of public assets. Public support for democracy remains very high, but a citizenry with poor civic education is still too passive to participate fully in the political process. Gyimah-Boadi cautions the new Mills administration to be mindful of the narrow margin of its victory, which revealed a nearly evenly divided electorate, and to work hard to calm the ethnic and regional tensions that lay behind the razor-thin result. Lastly, the work of election administration too needs ongoing attention, so that the democratic project begun in Ghana may continue to grow.

One need look no further than Senegal for an example of a peaceful transition away from one-party hegemony that has failed to deliver on its promise. In chapter 11, Penda Mbow describes the disappointment of international observers who had hoped that the 2000 victory of long-time oppositionist Abdoulaye Wade, which marked the end of twenty years in power for Abdou Diouf, would be a win for democracy as well. Instead, Senegal has been slouching toward electoral authoritarianism. Wade may have led the opposition for decades, but the political culture that formed him was highly authoritarian, and he has held to that model. Efforts to tame corruption and reform the constitution have largely been symbolic. Wade has manipulated various sources of social influence— labor unions, women's organizations, even religious leaders—to his advantage. He has discouraged what secularism there was in Senegal, and has exaggerated the religious divisions among the largely Sunni Muslim population. Mbow contends that these efforts "hold back the deepening of democracy" by encouraging a heightened religious identity at the expense of citizenship. The deterioration is accelerated by the usual autocratic efforts to weaken civil society, erode civil liberties, constrain the press, corrupt the judiciary, concentrate power in the executive, grab state assets, and coopt or punish opposition. Increasingly, the defeat of Diouf's Socialist Party in 2000 appears not as a genuine political breakthrough to a new type of regime, but a blip on the radar screen, trading one version of single-party hegemony for another, and this time with a hereditary succession looming as the President Wade's son, Karim, amasses ever more power and resources.

In Sierra Leone, by contrast, a once nearly hopeless situation of civil war and political collapse has been transformed, giving that benighted country a new opportunity for democracy, stability, and decent governance. In chapter 12, Christopher Wyrod calls the 2007 vote in Sierra Leone "the freest and most participatory in its history," generating a remarkable number of candidates and impressive voter turnout. A lesson for the rest of Africa may be gleaned from the fact that, after problems with interim elections in 2004, a new and independent National Election Commission was established. By 2007, with UN peacekeepers gone, Sierra Leone ran its own electoral process, redrew district borders, and moved from a proportional to a single-member system. The number of splinter parties fell. In the end, a free and lawful transition saw power pass in orderly fashion from one set of elected civilian leaders to another.

Important challenges linger, of course. First among them is corruption. Sierra Leone remains the world's poorest country, and many of its new leaders have corrupt pasts. President Ernest Bai Koroma has pledged a zero-tolerance policy, but it remains to be seen if he will apply this policy evenly or use it only to punish political opponents. Second, with the national courts still clogged with war-crimes cases and the lower courts in the pockets of local chiefs, access to justice remains unavailable to most citizens. Third, there is little effective press freedom. Unless these grievances are addressed, Sierra Leone may relapse into violence. Thus Wyrod urges that the 2007 election be seen as "a foundation upon which to build, rather than as a set of laurels on which to rest."

The turnaround from bloody conflict to fledgling democracy is perhaps even more extraordinary in Liberia, as Dave Peterson explains in chapter 13. When long-dormant ethnic tensions erupted into civil war in the 1990s, it took international intervention, in the form of a UN-sponsored transitional government and elections, to bring peace back to Liberia. Today, thanks in part to continued international support, Liberia has a freely elected president, a fairly healthy legislature, and a high degree of transparency in its press and civil society. In fact, Peterson sees the country's well-developed civil society, containing some civic institutions that are over a century old, as one of its greatest hopes. Still, Peterson warns of problems ahead. Though there are many institutions in Liberia that work hard to expose and contain corruption, Liberia still ranks alarmingly high on international measures of corruption. The judiciary's chronic weakness compounds this problem. Economic development has also been slow to recover from the civil war, though a fairly robust unofficial economy may mean that ordinary Liberians are doing better than official statistics reveal. Finally, many Liberians (and sympathetic outside observers) understandably worry about the country's capacity to sustain political stability and more responsible governance once the intense interest and support of international donors begins to wane.

East Africa: Forms Without Substance?

Section III examines the emergent democracies of East Africa, beginning with the troubling case of Kenya. As Michael Chege recounts in chapter 14, Kenyans in 2003 appeared to be getting off to a strong start at building democracy. Moving from a Freedom House ranking of Not Free in 1989 to a reformist, coalition-led government following the breakthrough elections of December 2002, Kenya showed signs of political and economic recovery. Yet political reform failed to keep pace with even the modest economic progress that was improving the material lot of average Kenyans. The coalition government's signal failure was its lack of progress at the task of reining in Kenya's infamous levels of corruption. Constitutional struggles in 2005 exacerbated old ethnic rivalries, which reappeared during the 2007 campaign with the opposition Orange Democratic Movement (ODM) adopting the slogan "forty-one tribes against one." Although other issues emerged, ethnic tensions simmered just below the surface of the campaigns run by both the ODM and its rival, the ruling Party of National Unity (PNU). Although election day at year's end went fairly smoothly, the hasty announcement of results—and the conviction on the part of oppositionists that their candidate had been cheated of victory—touched off an explosion of intense riots followed by bloody reprisals. Kenyan leaders averted what could have been even more horrific levels of ethnic violence by quickly negotiating a peace formula, which ushered in a coalition government to share power among parties and ethnic groups. Chege takes note of this, but also insists that if the country wishes to avoid renewed strife in 2012, it will need to make deeper institutional reforms. In particular, Kenya needs constitutional changes to insulate and improve the electoral commission, decentralize power, better protect individual rights, and move from a purely majoritarian electoral system to a partially proportional one.

As Maina Kiai explains in chapter 15, Kenya's 2007 postelection violence—which claimed the lives of more than a thousand people and displaced hundreds of thousands more—was a shock to international observers, given Kenya's status as a refugee haven and tourist destination. During numerous prior national elections, however rigged, Kenya had managed to avoid such a violent reaction. Kiai emphasizes that it is not elections per se but what happens *between* elections that truly determines the political character of a nation. Corruption, a weak and coopted legislature (more than 40 percent of Kenyan MPs serve in the executive branch as ministers or junior ministers), and an inability to confront longstanding ethnic grievances and injustices have damaged Kenya's political culture. Yet Kenyans understand the ballot box's potential to serve as an instrument of peaceful political change. Kiai views the 2008 postelection violence as an understandable, if regrettable, demonstration of Kenyans' "desire to protect their hard-won freedom." But to do this effectively, he maintains, Kenyans must shun violence and pursue a vigorous agenda of institutional reform (not unlike what Chege proposes). For Kiai, the most important reform priorities are to create "competent and independent bodies" to administer elections and fight corruption, as well as a more effective parliament and a "proper justice system, from policing to prisons to the judiciary itself." Finally, Kiai appeals to foreign donors to get tougher with Kenya's politicians, "ensuring that leaders' actions are geared toward bettering the lot of the citizenry rather than enriching themselves."

If the story of Kenya is of a country that briefly got and then quickly lost electoral democracy, Tanzania by contrast has seen a transition to multiparty politics that has yet to overcome the long historical legacy of one-party rule by the Chama Cha Mapinduzi (CCM). In chapter 16, Barak Hoffman and Lindsay Robinson show how the CCM has deftly reconstituted its authoritarian political hegemony in an era of formal but feckless multiparty competition. Unwilling to settle for the "easy explanation" of a weak opposition and a complacent populace, Hoffman and Robinson identify deeper reasons for continued one-party dominance. In the early 1990s, they note, prospects for democracy seemed brighter as the CCM moved from one-party socialism toward pluralist democracy under pressure from international donors. Yet the political reforms proved largely cosmetic, designed to keep the CCM in power. In this they succeeded all too well, and even in popular opinion the CCM holds a preferred place. Although the violent tendencies and fragmentation of Tanzania's opposition parties must bear some blame, it remains true that only the CCM has the funding and authority to stage rallies, give gifts to constituents, and perform the services expected from a major political party. The CCM has done its best to protect itself against losses at the ballot box by stacking electoral formulae and designing ballots to discourage votes for the opposition. When that fails, the threat or blatant exercise of violence has ensured the CCM's ongoing dominance, particularly in the more seriously contested island province of Zanzibar. The press and civil society are likewise intimidated. Thus, the boast made by CCM leader Benjamin Mkapa in 1995 that the party "didn't need to cheat because it was quite certain [it] would win" has been fulfilled time and again in the subsequent fifteen years.

The pattern of creating democratic forms without substance has been perfected in Uganda. In chapter 17, Andrew Mwenda, a Ugandan journalist who has personally experienced the regime's press restrictions, recalls how the early 1990s brought encouraging signs that his long-suffering East African nation would finally tread a path toward better governance. With President Yoweri Museveni having passed his twentieth year in power, however, hopes for democratic reform have long since given way to despair over the entrenchment of yet another corrupt, personalistic African autocracy. In 2004, even democratic forms took a blow when at Museveni's behest Uganda removed term limits for the president, further weakened its parliament, and removed oversight provisions meant to help bar corruption and human-rights abuses. With the judiciary cowering before threats of violence, Museveni now holds "a license for the creation of a presidential monarchy." Any institutional opposition, whether from the press, civil society, or rival politicians, is answered with intimidation, bribery, or brutality. In essence, the state has been "personalized," with the country's armed forces and budgetary resources in the hands of the president, for him to use at will.

Mwenda argues forcefully that foreign donors have made matters worse. Not only has the aid flow not been adjusted as conditions have worsened, but the manner of aid distribution has itself contributed to corruption and government control, while economic "reform" has been manipulated to create more opportunities for patronage. Likewise subject to manipulation have been the "autonomous districts" that Museveni has proliferated in order to prevent any one economic, political, or regional interest from standing up against his personal, military, party, and state authority. Worse still, the wily autocrat has coopted many educated and enterprising Ugandans—the very people who would otherwise be the leaders of civil society—into some role within a ministry, project, or regional government. Despite these forbidding circumstances, Mwenda holds out hope in three areas. First, he argues that foreign donors can stop shielding the regime from democratic forces that would lead to change. Second, he notes that as the number of educated Ugandans grows, there will simply be too many to absorb into fragmented state bureaucracies or NGOs. Third, he posits that rural areas, long the base of whatever popular support the Museveni regime enjoys, may grow weary of supporting a government that is increasingly unable to improve their daily lives.

The view is very different in the Horn of Africa. Seth Kaplan, in chapter 18, describes the thriving democracy in Somaliland, the secessionist northwestern section of Somalia. Independent in nearly all but name since 1991, Somaliland has developed a *beel* (meaning clan or community) system of self-government based on traditional Somali customs. In contrast to neighboring Somalia, which has seen repeated failed attempts to impose order from the top down, this bottom-up approach has worked in Somaliland. Gradually, ethnic loyalties have been nurtured into national loyalties. Critical to the regime's success has been the National Electoral Commission, praised for its high degree of transparency and diligence in tallying votes, critical to ensuring free and fair elections. Somaliland's regime does have troubles, primarily related to enforcement of constitutional provisions. This reflects the culture so frequently observed in African democracies: tepid respect for the rule of law, weak civil society, and strong tribal and traditional ties. Again, as we see throughout much of Africa, Somaliland's legislature lacks powers to check the executive, and the judiciary is underfunded and untrained. While the *beel* system has allowed Somaliland to achieve peace and a measure of democracy largely without foreign intervention or support, the system has also kept Somaliland's government from being truly representative and effective. Notwithstanding these difficulties, Kaplan urges international recognition for an independent Somaliland and commends its example to the international community.

Southern Africa: Democratic Success Stories?

The fourth and final section of the present volume considers democracy's situation in the central and southern parts of the Africa. This region is home to the continent's wealthiest nation, the Republic of South Africa. Probably no other African nation has had more international attention paid not only to its economy, but to its ethnic divisions. Since the first inclusive elections in 1994, South Africa has maintained a high degree of respect for civil liberties, press freedom, and regular free elections. Yet as Steven Friedman explains in chapter 18, one of apartheid's legacies has been the persistent ability of identity politics to exert divisive effects on an electorate in which various ethnic groups remain for the most part geographically separated from one another. Although elections have been free and fair, they have not, within individual districts, been truly competitive. From 1994 until 2009, the ruling African National Congress (ANC) enjoyed an ever-increasing vote share. The resulting assumption of permanency in office on the part of ANC leaders bred a government that lacked incentives for responsiveness and failed to fulfill its own pledge to address this wealthy nation's gnawing problem with poverty among its citizens. Ultimately, what South Africa had was an increasingly isolated government led by a president, Thabo Mbeki, who was unpopular even within his own party. Consequently, in late 2007, the ANC chose a new standard-bearer, Jacob Zuma. The shakeup within the ANC led to the formation of COPE, an ANC splinter party that threatens the ANC's hold on its voter base as never before. At the polls in April 2009, the ANC lost ground, winning overall yet losing its two-thirds majority (enough to change the constitution) in Parliament. Friedman sees this election as a chance for the ANC to grow more responsive, but it remains to be seen whether ANC leadership will take note of this election as a warning or instead see it as another triumph.

South Africa's neighbor to the north, Botswana, has meanwhile offered only the illusion of democracy, Kenneth Good argues in chapter 20. A Freedom House rating of Free masks the reality of superficial (and deteriorating) political pluralism in Botswana. This includes an extremely powerful and increasingly abusive presidency (under the incumbent Ian Khama, son of the founding president), a marginalized legislature, and, despite regular elections, a government that has not changed hands in 44 years. The lack of real political competition has given the reigning Botswana Democratic Party (BDP) no incentive to rein in escalating corruption or to liberalize its oppressive policies toward Botswana's ethnic minorities. Further staining Botswana's liberal international image have been rising numbers of extrajudicial killings, growing state surveillance of communications, and the mounting prominence in government of former high-ranking security officials. The latter are increasingly relied on by President Khama, who spent the first two decades of his professional life in the military before being placed on a fast and virtually uncontested track to presidential power.

Incumbents (whether presidents or parties) enjoy an electoral advantage throughout Africa, and Zambia is no exception. In chapter 21, Kate Baldwin outlines the process by which the ruling MMD party retained its leadership at the polls despite the August 2008 death of its leader, Levy Mwanawasa. The longevity of the MMD's dominance, Baldwin holds, flows not from "an ingenious master plan," but rather is the product of "a series of small decisions and unplanned events." This dominance stems partly from traditional incumbents' advantages in rigging elections or backroom deals, and partly from the MMD's practice of tapping leaders from varying ethnic groups. Thus, in contrast to much of Africa, Zambia has been able to reduce the influence and longevity in office of its "big men." For example, former president Frederick Chiluba was ousted from party leadership as he sought a third term in 2001. Even so, the exit of this or that individual "big man" is meant to serve a system of one-party dominance whose means of support are far from democratic. In both 2001 and 2008, the office of the president was used as a platform for political campaigning. Not only were public funds thus employed for clearly political activity; they were also diverted to enrich various tribal chiefs. In 2008, Acting President Rupiah Banda secured his own electoral prospects by changing the constitutionally required election date and by limiting voter registration. These types of maneuvers, Baldwin holds, do no service to democracy in Zambia, and keep the MMD from being truly accountable to voters.

Did recent elections establish legitimacy and accountability in the nearby Democratic Republic of Congo? Given the history of strife that Herbert Weiss briefly recaps in chapter 22, simply holding the 2006 election in this vast and infrastructure-starved country seems a major accomplishment. Yet the question remains whether this election, as closely supervised and internationally defended as it was, was a true step toward democracy. The constitution's ratification by a narrow popular vote raises questions about the depth of that document's legitimacy. Although turnout was high for both rounds of the presidential and provincial balloting, Weiss argues that most voters were heading to the polls to cast protest votes *against* the parties that had controlled the transitional government, rather than *for* any particular new leadership.

The transitional president, Joseph Kabila, ultimately carried the day after a runoff, but questions of fraud linger, and the polling results bear more than passing traces of the regional and linguistic divisions that have long troubled the DRC. The new government has made no gestures toward including opposition parties (and therefore regions) in its cabinet. Thus, Weiss questions whether the great effort and expense of the DRC elections will result in any positive changes that ordinary Congolese will be able to feel or see.

Chapters 23 and 24 discuss nations that can hardly be called democracies at all. In "Angola's Façade Democracy," Paula Roque underscores the theme that "elections do not a democracy make." The 2008 elections in Angola, in which voters went to the polls for the first time since the end of a 27-year-long civil war in 2002, gave the Popular Movement for the Liberation of Angola (MPLA) more than 80 percent of the vote. The result is that the MPLA now rules virtually unchecked, either politically or by any meaningful civil society or a free press. This has enabled the MPLA to harness state institutions and resources to ensure its continued dominance, while appearing to bow to popular will. The stage was set for the 2008 elections by what happened "between elections," when President Eduardo dos Santos used his powerful office to further emasculate the legislature and intimidate and harass the opposition. Moreover, the opposition failed, in the course of the campaign, to convince Angolans that any of the smaller parties could offer a credible alternative to the MPLA. While Roque holds out hope that the superficial changes made since the election—toward increased civil liberties and decentralization, among others—will plant a seed of democratic progress, there is no question that the road to democracy in Angola runs steeply uphill.

The climb will be even steeper in Zimbabwe. In chapter 24, Michael Bratton and Eldred Masunungure describe the irony in this long-running and increasingly destructive autocracy: Although Robert Mugabe has remained in power for three decades, the oppressive regime is bigger

TABLE—AFRICAN REGIMES IN 2009, BY REGIME TYPE AND FREEDOM HOUSE SCORES

LIBERAL DEMOCRACIES	ELECTORAL DEMOCRACIES	COMPETITIVE AUTHORITARIAN	HEGEMONIC ELECTORAL AUTHORITARIAN	POLITICALLY CLOSED
Cape Verde (1,1)	Lesotho (2,3)	Niger (3,4)	Burkina Faso (5,3)	Cote d'Ivoire (6,5)
Ghana (1,2)	Mali (2,3)	Kenya (4,3)	Gambia (5,4)	Mauritania (6,5)
Mauritius (1,2)	Mozambique (3,3)	Madagascar (4,3)	Ethiopia (5,5)	Swaziland (7,5)
Benin (2,2)	Senegal (3,3)	Tanzania (4,3)	Gabon (6,4)	Eritrea (7,6)
Botswana (2,2)	Seychelles (3,3)	Nigeria (5,4)	Angola (6,5)	Equatorial Guinea (7,7)
Sao Tome & Principe (2,2)	Sierra Leone (3,3)	Uganda (5,4)	Congo, Republic (6,5)	Somalia (7,7)
South Africa (2,2)	Zambia (3,3)	Central African Republic (5,5)	Rwanda (6,5)	Sudan (7,7)
Namibia (2,2)	Comoros (3,4)	Djibouti (5,5)	Togo (6,5)	
-	Liberia (3,4)	Congo, Dem. Republic (6,6)	Cameroon (6,6)	
-	Guinea-Bissau (4,4)	-	Chad (6,6)	-
-	Malawi (4,4)	-	Guinea (7,5)	-
-	Burundi (4,5)	-	Zimbabwe (7,6)	-

Note: Numbers in parentheses are the 2008 Freedom House (FH) scores of political rights and civil liberties, where 1 indicates most free or democratic and 7 most repressive. The framework for classifying regimes and most of the classifications are drawn from Larry Diamond, *The Spirit of Democracy* (New York: Times Books, 2008), Appendix Table 5. Most classifications of countries as democracies (liberal or electoral) follow the Freedom House designations. Liberal democracies are those with a score of 1 or 2 on each of the two scales.

than the "big man" who sits at its head. This is because there are extensive vested interests in continuing the status quo even after the 85-year-old Mugabe passes from the scene. Even though the populace long ago tuned out its message, the ruling ZANU-PF party regards itself as entitled to rule in perpetuity. Threatened by the possibility of an opposition victory in the 2000 constitutional referendum, ZANU-PF struck back with naked force as well as new, restrictive laws designed to limit opposition. Since then, the rulers have sought to perpetuate their hegemony by rigging elections and brutalizing the opposition, led by the Movement for Democratic Change (MDC). The party has coopted the justice and law-enforcement systems, turning them into regime enforcers. ZANU-PF has assumed control of much of the economy, and distributes the spoils to its own leaders. It has also used the challenge in the 2000 election cycle to cement its hold on the military and has since formed the Joint Operations Command (JOC), which mixes the authority of civilian and military rule. In 2008, the JOC used a combination of targeted violence and withholding of food aid to hijack the election for Mugabe. International publicity focusing on these atrocities has further weakened Mugabe's status outside Zimbabwe, but it is doubtful that any promises made to share power with the opposition will have real meaning as long as the military is so intertwined with party authorities. More coherent international pressure "could ultimately go a long way in resolving the country's crisis," but the international actors that matter (including not just the West but South Africa and the Southern African Development Community) remain divided over how to proceed. In any case, real political change would require not just Mugabe's removal but more sweeping institutional reform.

Africa's Democratic Prospects

The chapters in this volume tell fascinating, at times hopeful, but also frequently sobering stories. Africans have grown accustomed to voting, and by every indication they want to do so in elections that are free, fair, open, and meaningful, and with a fair prospect of causing the replacement of rulers and representatives who are not performing. Publics are now more democratically conscious and vigilant than at any time since independence. Legislatures in at least some countries are slowly gaining in institutional strength and confidence, and have on occasion checked the worst excesses of would-be autocratic presidents. Military establishments no longer govern across a wide swath of the continent as they once did, and if in some cases this is only because military officers have donned civilian garb after seizing power, this gesture to constitutionalism is at least a beginning. Politicians who call themselves democrats still too often emulate the overweening practices of the authoritarian big man, but their efforts to establish political hegemony must now confront a more robust and pluralistic civil society—including more diverse and resourceful mass media—than was the case a generation ago. Civil society monitors and advocates are now armed with new information technologies—many of them carried on the platform of low-cost cell phones, whose societal penetration is growing more explosively in Africa than in any other region of the world. These simple devices are becoming powerful tools to monitor elections, report corruption, receive political information, mobilize demonstrations, compare market prices, and thus empower citizens. Moreover, as high-speed Internet access begins to spread in Africa, the independent press is finding a new outlet that evades the old authoritarian constraints on the ability of independent media to print and distribute news and analysis. The proliferation of low-wattage FM radio stations further decentralizes access to information.

Yet, as events in Nigeria, Kenya, Senegal, and Madagascar have illustrated, democratic institutions in Africa cannot be taken for granted.

If, as Kenneth Good shows in his chapter on Botswana, democracy can be diminished and good governance degraded in the one country where these higher political standards were considered by many to have been consolidated, then no democratic experiment in Africa is secure against the temptations of ready riches and the ambitions of emerging autocrats. Only sustained institution building and vigorous oversight by both civil society and the donor community can rein in the relentless dynamics of neopatrimonial politics in Africa. As Richard Joseph warns, rapidly changing international dynamics combined with the regional, tribal, religious, and economic diversity of Africa mean that "the scope for havoc is great." The clear message to donors is that mere forms of democracy, while not to be dismissed, are not enough. If aid is to encourage democracy (or development) in Africa, the donors must not only look as closely as possible at the institutions they wish to encourage, but must also support more vigorously those civic and political actors who are trying to enhance government accountability and level the playing field.

NOTES

1. Larry Diamond, Juan J. Linz, and Seymour Martin Lipset, *Democracy in Developing Countries: Africa* (Boulder, Colo.: Lynne Rienner, 1989).

2. Arguably the most influential book on African regimes during this period was precisely about the varieties of authoritarian personal rule that dominated the politics of the continent. See Robert H. Jackson and Carl G. Rosberg, *Personal Rule in Black Africa: Prince, Autocrat, Prophet, Tyrant* (Berkeley: University of California Press, 1982).

3. Larry Diamond and Marc F. Plattner, eds., *Democratization in Africa* (Baltimore: Johns Hopkins Press, 1999).

4. Crawford Young, "Africa: An Interim Balance Sheet," *Journal of Democracy* 7 (July 1996): 53–68.

5. Michael Bratton, "Second Elections in Africa," *Journal of Democracy* 9 (July 1998): 51–66.

6. Staffan I. Lindberg, "The Surprising Significance of African Elections," *Journal of Democracy* 17 (January 2006): 139–51, and *Democracy and Elections in Africa* (Baltimore: Johns Hopkins University Press, 2006). It is not clear to what extent this effect will hold over time, however, as some African autocracies that have been holding competitive elections (Ethiopia is an example) appear to have learned the dangers of allowing too much space and have recently been moving to clamp down on freedom and competition. Moreover, the effect does not appear to hold across all regions, particularly not the Middle East. For an assessment of the theory, see Staffan I. Lindberg, ed., *Democratization by Elections: A New Mode of Transition* (Baltimore: Johns Hopkins University Press, 2009).

7. They make this case in an essay which, at the time of this writing in late 2009, is scheduled to appear in the January 2010 issue of the *Journal of Democracy*.

I

Progress and Retreat in Africa

1

CHALLENGES OF
A "FRONTIER" REGION

Richard Joseph

Richard Joseph is John Evans Professor of Political Science at Northwestern University and Nonresident Senior Fellow of the Brookings Institution. He is the editor of State, Conflict, and Democracy in Africa *(1999) and coeditor of* Smart Aid for African Development *(2009). This essay originally appeared in the April 2008 issue of the* Journal of Democracy.

From the Cape of Good Hope to the Sahara, and from the Gulf of Guinea to the shores of the Indian Ocean, political and economic life across the African continent today features an interplay of risk, reward, and uncertainty that is well captured by the term "frontier Africa." This term's relevance was suggested to me by the way in which international-finance experts speak of "frontier markets" to denote countries that lack the reliable operating structures of "emerging-market" countries, but which nonetheless yield high profits and show signs of sustained growth and improving economic governance.

Several countries in sub-Saharan Africa, such as Ghana, Mozambique, Nigeria, Tanzania, and Uganda, are now "frontier markets." For the first time in decades, a positive flow of investment capital is entering these countries—and going to sectors other than those devoted to the extraction of natural resources. Where available, local stock markets are producing attractive returns, while annual growth rates of 5 to 7 percent are no longer a rarity. As a consequence, major international-finance companies that long shunned Africa are creating special instruments for equity investments.

Yet as the violence that broke out following Kenya's disputed December 2007 presidential election so powerfully reminds us, the high potential rewards in Africa are counterbalanced by risks that can be just as high. The Kenyan tragedy caps a remarkable wave of change that began almost twenty years ago on the opposite side of the continent, in the small West African state of Benin. By the end of the 1980s, Benin had come to exemplify the economic and political bankruptcy of authoritarian single-party rule in postcolonial Africa. The system was so thoroughly broken that no one wanted to try to fix it—not even France, the former colonial power which remained deeply involved in the politics of its former territories. International financial institutions eventually put aside their unwillingness to interfere in political matters and began pressing Benin's longtime military ruler, Mathieu Kérékou, to mend his ways. The system could not be reformed, however, and had to be jettisoned. For ten remarkable days in February 1990, representatives of civic, religious, and other interest groups met in a national conference that wrested sovereign authority away from Kérékou and initiated a democratic transition.

In the nearly two decades since these seminal events, the "awakening process"[1] has deepened in Benin and a handful of other African countries. Yet as the tragic aftermath of the December 2007 voting in Kenya has shown, governments facing the prospect of a peaceful dismissal by the people can allow the doors of democracy to open further, but such governments can also seek to slam them shut.[2] Since the transformative moment in Benin, systems of personal rule have continued to clash with institutions intended to give expression to the popular will. During the first decade of the *abertura* (opening), Africa matched the post-Soviet world in the rapidity with which liberalizing systems emerged. The following decade, the travails of democracy in Africa mirrored the stalling of democracy worldwide. As many have argued, after the democratic upsurge of the early 1990s, the play of political and socioeconomic forces became too complex to capture under the rubric of the "transition paradigm." I suggested that the resumption of competitive party politics, and the shift from statist to market-oriented economic systems, heralded a "reconfiguration of power" whose outcomes could not be predicted.[3] Today, although we know more about the contours of this reconfiguration, its evolution remains uncertain as illiberal regimes cling to power in economically liberalized systems and as new geopolitical forces come into play.[4]

Few countries illustrate the tortuous trajectory of democracy in Africa better than Benin's much larger and oil-rich eastern neighbor, Nigeria. From 1976 to 1979, the reformist military government of General Olusegun Obasanjo led a gradual transition to civilian rule in this most populous of all African countries. After the armed forces intervened to overthrow the Obasanjo regime's ineffectual civilian successor in December 1983, another fifteen years of military rule ensued, leaving the country in 1998 essentially where it had been two decades earlier. In a quasi-managed process, Obasanjo returned to power as a civilian president in 1999. He then became the first Nigerian president to serve two full constitutional terms and the first to hand power to a civilian successor.

With regard to neither of these Nigerian transitions, however, can we use the adjective "elected" without a host of qualifiers.[5] The national elections held over the last decade (in 1999, 2003, and 2007) became successively less fair, less efficient, and less credible. The 2007 vote kept the ruling People's Democratic Party dominant throughout the federation and elevated to the presidency Umaru Yar'Adua, a little-known former governor of the northern state of Katsina. Among the most hopeful local descriptions of this electoral event is that it could be a case of "muddling forward."[6] What Nigeria and other quasi-democratic African countries greatly need instead of "muddling," however, is a decisive break from the "frontier" character of periodic elections.

Assessments of democracy's prospects in Africa should attend more closely to democracy as more than just a set of rules for managing power struggles among elites. In the context of the great material deprivation of the masses of the people, democracy is an avenue by which their legitimate aspirations for a better future can be expressed and claims for redress made. Abraham Lincoln saw democracy's central qualities as bound up with the principles of freedom, equality, and government by consent that the U.S. Declaration of Independence had laid before "a candid world" in 1776. In 1861, shortly after the beginning of the U.S. Civil War, Lincoln memorably highlighted these principles in his first presidential message to Congress. His words can be echoed in many struggles in Africa today:

> This is essentially a people's contest. . . . it is a struggle for maintaining in the world, that form, and substance of government whose leading object is to elevate the condition of men—to lift artificial weights from all shoulders—to clear the paths for all—to afford all an even start and a fair chance, in the race of life.[7]

China Arrives

Democracy's prospects in Africa cannot be assessed without taking into account China's sweeping engagement across much of the continent over the past decade. At the root of China's involvement is its ever-growing need for natural resources, especially petroleum. With a speed and determination that recall the post-1884 European "scramble for Africa," Chinese state-owned companies have signed long-term contracts for African mineral exports. The Chinese have also quickly moved from refurbishing the statehouses and hometowns of African rulers to contracting to build roads, ports, railways, and even, in the case of Nigeria, a satellite system. China's president and premier have taken turns making high-profile visits to Africa and hosting meetings of African leaders, finance ministers, and development officials. Chinese products have also flowed into African markets, from open-air stalls to contemporary malls, along with thousands of Chinese laborers and small entrepreneurs. Nor has the process been one-way. African merchants hope not only to lure Chinese investment, but also to procure Chinese manufactured products for resale at home. Unhindered by commitments to democracy and human rights, and proceeding under an avowed policy of eschewing involvement in host-country politics, China's growing presence has been complicating prospects for further democratization in Africa.

This is not to say that China's respect for existing political systems has purely negative effects. Chinese officials are prepared to work with whatever political forces and systems exist in each country. In time, the Chinese can be expected to adjust their practices when their investments are criticized for reinforcing corrupt behaviors and exploiting weak legal systems and poorly paid domestic labor. The greater the stakes that China acquires in African countries, the greater the interest that it will take in crafting rules and procedures to safeguard those assets. Finally, China's participation in global institutions, and its accelerating role as an investor in (and not just a trader with) industrialized countries, will enable international and African civil society groups to press China toward compliance with international environmental, labor, and human rights norms.

"Frontier Africa" as a place of dynamic markets involving external actors has, of course, a long history behind it. Explorers, slave traders, imperialists, and colonialists succeeded one another over centuries. Lebanese and other Mediterranean peoples in West Africa, and South Asians in East and Southern Africa, have long conducted high-profit operations using family networks to prosper amid environments marked by weak laws and institutions. Once apartheid ended in 1994, South African businesspeople moved rapidly throughout the continent to buy languishing assets and invest capital in niche markets. These entrepreneurs are now thriving from coast to coast in telecommunications, security services, agriculture, and fast-food outlets.

What defines Africa as a "frontier market" even more today is that core entities of the global capitalist system—and not just mining companies or intrepid ethnic merchants—are bringing African economies into their orbit and generating wealth-creating opportunities for local entrepreneurs and investors. It is, of course, too early to predict the political implications of these rapid developments. At first glance, they appear to be bolstering autocratic rule. Yet that tendency might turn out to be transitory. Over the longer term, the strengthening of the laws, procedures, and institutions necessary for managing private-sector development; the reality of sustained economic growth; the rise of an entrepreneurial bourgeoisie; and the emergence of alternatives to neopatrimonial ways of getting rich could strengthen the bases for more robustly democratic systems.

Christopher Clapham has written insightfully of the "extraversion" of Africa, a continent that has consisted of frontier territories for much of its modern history. He stresses the extent to which African societies, although formally grouped into entities demarcated by international boundaries, continue to be shaped by external forces.[8] These processes have yielded, after half a millennium, an African mosaic of "unfinished states," recalcitrant autocracies, a handful of consolidating democracies, and a large "gray zone" of countries that display a mixture of authoritarian and liberal features.

On top of this, Africa's brief post–Cold War respite from geostrategic machinations has ended. Preventive intervention to contain or forestall radical Islamism is now a major U.S. policy objective in the Horn of Africa and other areas. Since the vast African continent contains large swaths of lightly governed territory, dynamic and expanding Muslim communities, and tens of millions living in poverty, the scope for havoc is great. Counterinsurgency priorities have already had negative consequences for governance in Ethiopia, Somalia, and Uganda. As the United States implements a continental security strategy, including the activation in 2008 of the U.S. military's Africa Command (AFRICOM), concerns about a reprise of the Cold War's negative consequences for democracy have risen. Both African rulers and their opponents must now reckon with intensifying geostrategic considerations in their quest to keep or gain power.

Finally, "frontier Africa" as a term also evokes the weak states, persistent conflicts, and displaced populations that will require international and continental peacekeeping engagements over many years. Warfare, insecurity, and the need for complex, multinational security operations threaten to remain defining characteristics of African life for many years to come.[9] Britain's 2000 to 2002 military intervention in war-torn Sierra Leone was vital to preserving prospects for democracy there; and the UN's assumption of responsibility for bringing peace to Liberia, Côte d'Ivoire, eastern Congo (Kinshasa), and the Darfur region of Sudan likewise implies a series of difficult and prolonged missions. Chad, which has known intermittent warfare for decades, appeared certain to need greater international engagement after insurgent fighters reached the capital, N'Djamena, in early February 2008, and forces from the European Union poised to deploy along the Sudanese border in order to protect refugees.

Law, order, and reliable policing are often in short supply, even in Africa's well-settled cities and countrysides. Frequently, local communities are obliged to take charge of their own safety and governance while holding at bay corrupt, predatory, and ineffective government officials and institutions.[10] In this sense, "frontier Africa" can be found far from lawless border areas between states.[11] Opportunities for the powerful to commit political mischief in these contexts are dismayingly abundant, as the Nigerian and Kenyan elections of 2007 demonstrate. Yet the determination to resist abuses—whether craftily as in the case of Nigeria or cataclysmically as in that of Kenya—is also undiminished.

Beyond Personal Rule?

Following the political openings of the 1990s, newly elected executives moved quickly to shift power away from the people and the other arms of government, and soon began to emulate the recently departed authoritarians when it came to the avid appropriation of public resources. According to the Afrobarometer surveys, sub-Saharan Africa is a place where demand for democracy exceeds supply. Speaking in late 2006 about the poorly prepared elections to be held in his country the following year, Nigerian Nobel laureate Wole Soyinka said presciently that "the Nigerian people have always approached democracy, and the elites have always pushed them back."[12] The struggle for democracy reaches its highest pitch, as in other countries, at the time of national elections. Still unresolved in Africa is the contest between personal rule (typified by the "Big Man" syndrome) and institutions based on the rule of law. The Kenyan electoral tragedy showed, once again, how readily the scales can be tipped between these competing principles of governance.

Africa's emerging democracies have gained ground or been sidetracked depending on whether a given country's political system has evolved to permit the *demos* to act as the ultimate source of political legitimacy. As Robert A. Dahl has written, if "ordinary citizens" cannot "exert a relatively high degree of control over leaders," then the minimal threshold of democracy has not been reached.[13] This democratic promise was postponed in Zimbabwe after voters soundly defeated a February 2000 popular referendum that President Robert Mugabe had arranged for the purpose of extending his regime's powers. Mugabe responded by unleashing land seizures, brutally repressing his opponents, and driving millions into penury and exile. In Kenya, a November 2005 referendum meant to expand the government's powers was decisively defeated. President Mwai Kibaki calmly accepted "the people's choice," and Kenya's economy and democratic system continued to advance rather than decline as in Zimbabwe. Yet just two years later, after the bitterly disputed presidential race between Kibaki and challenger Raila Odinga and its attendant intercommunal strife, Kenya has fallen further away from the threshold of popular control by the *demos* that Dahl identified. It will now take many years to recapture the lost ground, economically as well as politically.

The democratic promise survived attempts to institutionalize personal rule in Malawi and Zambia by elected presidents who sought to overturn constitutional term limits. In Uganda, by contrast, President Yoweri Museveni got away with just such a move, successfully pressing the legislature to eliminate constitutional restrictions on his continuation in power. Then Museveni, much like his former protégé Paul Kagame in Rwanda, began to treat his electoral opponents as traitors. Dismal echoes of these developments resounded in Ethiopia, where almost two-hundred citizens were killed following the 2005 elections, while others, having dared to protest against electoral malfeasance, found themselves jailed and facing treason charges.

Larry Diamond contends that "the political struggle in Africa remains very much a conflict between the rule of law and the rule of a person."[14] I agree, but would go further and describe this struggle as between two rival types of institutionalization. Daniel Posner and Daniel Young have called attention to the progress that Africa has made toward entrenching law-based governance and institutions.[15] Yet they overstate the extent to which the battle against personal rule is being won. Indeed, evidence that the "big man" syndrome is not retreating can be found in the very same issue of the *Journal of Democracy*. There, Andrew Mwenda searingly indicts the autocratic rule that has warped Ugandan political life under Museveni.[16] The battle between rival processes of institutionalization can also be found in other world regions where, as in Africa, the outcome of their duel will strongly affect the prospects for democratic progress.[17]

Posner and Young point to incumbents' losses at the polls, plus failed attempts to erase term limits (most notably in Nigeria), to argue that personal rule is losing ground. "The formal rules of the game," they claim, "are beginning to matter in ways that they previously have not."[18] While the holding of regular multiparty elections and the occasional defeat of incumbents are significant trends, the struggle to cross the frontier from personal rule to rule-based governance is still far from over in much of Africa.

Few African leaders, even in electoral democracies, govern today as committed democrats. Some, such as President Abdoulaye Wade of Senegal, spent many years in opposition sharply criticizing incumbents as undemocratic, only to behave nepotistically and autocratically once they themselves gained power. Contemporary African leaders may govern as autocrats (Meles Zenawi of Ethiopia, Hassan al-Bashir of Sudan, Isaias Afwerki of Eritrea) or as democrats (John Kufuor of Ghana, Amadou Toumani Touré of Mali, Jakaya Kikwete of Tanzania)—or else may oscillate between these two models. Nigeria's Obasanjo is a prime example of the last category. During his 1979 to 1999 stint in the political wilderness, including four years as a prisoner of brutal dictator Sani Abacha, Obasanjo built an international reputation as a strong promoter of democracy. After he returned to power in the 1999 presidential election, however, whether he governed as an autocrat or democrat depended on his own, often opaque, political calculations.

A Big No to the Big Man

In Cameroon, Eritrea, Ethiopia, Rwanda, Uganda, and Zimbabwe, governments have shut the door on open and competitive democracy. Obasanjo was subtler. In 2005 and 2006, his administration conducted an elaborate constitutional-revision exercise that included amendments meant to allow executives at the state and federal levels to remain in office for more than two consecutive terms. The media challenged this scheme, and soon a coalition of professional and civic groups emerged to stop it. The climax came on 16 May 2006, when the Nigerian National Assembly dealt a strong blow for democracy by defeating the amendment package.

Posner and Young cite this event as evidence of how strong "the rules of the game" have become, and applaud the way in which both the Obasanjo administration and its foes "sought to achieve their goals by working through, not around, formal institutional channels."[19] Yet Posner and Young's account fails to capture the complicated and uncertain interplay that takes place between formal and informal rules, practices, and institutions in Africa's quasi-democracies, including Nigeria.[20] A careful look at each case is required to reveal the dynamics at work and the progress toward, or regress away from, law-based governance.

The crucial National Assembly vote in Nigeria, for instance, required both a huge miscalculation by the administration and a great display of courage by one critically placed individual. Obasanjo and his lieutenants had made a massive investment in the term-extension package, and felt so assured of its success that they permitted AIT, a private media company, to broadcast the expected triumphal vote on national television. Seizing on this mistake, intrepid Senate president Ken Nnamani told his colleagues, "You will stand and vote in your father's name!" Realizing as never before the costs that they might have to pay for backing the administration on what was widely feared would be a sellout of democracy, a decisive number of legislators switched to the "no" side, regardless of whatever informal commitments they might have made to the administration. More than formal rules, therefore, it was a combination of extensive civil society mobilization, "money politics" by administration foes, a timely media intervention, and Senator Nnamani's courage that lay behind Nigeria's big no to the "big man."[21]

The Nigerian people won again a year later, when they resisted the temptation to rise up in mass protest over the mismanaged and fraudulent elections of April 2007. Had they done so, they might have provided the government with a sufficient pretext to push back the opposition in a wave of bloody repression. One of the lessons here is that the struggle for democracy in countries where the door to it has not been systematically barricaded involves a complex collaboration among diverse political, civic, professional, and popular groups, as well as the strategic deployment of institutions of horizontal accountability. With a few exceptions such as Mugabe, African rulers today avoid denying democracy outright, and instead seek to outflank it by expanding their personal powers at the expense of institutions that might constrain them. In such situations, the risk remains that a powerful ruler, if directly threatened by a formal expression of democratic sovereignty at the polls, could drop such tactics in favor of blatant chicanery and physical force, with possibly dire consequences for whatever political and economic progress may have been made.

In the case of Nigeria, not to be overlooked is the judiciary's work in trying to curb electoral malpractice. After the 1999 and 2003 ballotings, election tribunals adjudicated challenges so slowly that dishonest results became *faits accomplis*. During the final months of Obasanjo's tenure, the courts issued rulings meant to block attempts by his camp to derail electoral challengers. Several of the 2007 gubernatorial elections have already been overturned, and even that of President Yar'Adua underwent judicial review before being confirmed in February 2008. This suggests that democracy advocates at home and abroad should make it a priority to strive for the preservation of constitutionally and institutionally protected arenas of political contestation in "frontier Africa."[22]

It is to be expected that there will be advances and setbacks. With regard to few countries can we say that the institutions of law-based democratic governance are firmly consolidated. If prodemocratic forces are adept—as they have shown themselves to be in Ghana, Nigeria, and Zambia—there are many battles that they will be able to win. Yet the continent's entrenched rulers are hardly lonely outliers: They include not only Afwerki of Eritrea, Zenawi of Ethiopia, Kagame of Rwanda, Wade of Senegal, al-Bashir of Sudan, Museveni of Uganda, and Mugabe of Zimbabwe, but also José Eduardo dos Santos of Angola, Paul Biya of Cameroon, Denis Sassou-Nguesso of Congo (Brazzaville), Omar Bongo of Gabon, Yahya Jammeh of the Gambia, and Lansana Conté of Guinea. We should not expect that personal rule will be retired any day soon.

Good Governance and Institution-Building

The most daunting frontier still to be crossed in much of postcolonial Africa is the creation and maintenance of institutions that will uphold transparency and the rule of law. Speaking in Nairobi, Kenya, in August 2006, U.S. senator Barack Obama made this point clearly:

> For all the progress that has been made, neither Kenya nor the African continent has yet fulfilled its potential. Like many nations across this continent, where Kenya is failing is in its ability to create a government that is transparent and accountable, one that serves its people and is free from corruption. We have to admit that here in Kenya it is a crisis. It is a crisis that is robbing honest people of the opportunities they fought for. Corruption erodes the state from the inside out, sickening the justice system until there is no justice to be found, poisoning the police forces until their presence becomes a source of insecurity rather than a source of security. In the end, if the people cannot trust their government to do the job for which it exists, to protect them and to promote their common welfare, all else is lost. This is why the struggle against corruption is one of the great struggles of our time.[23]

Democracy will not flourish in Africa until public institutions perform their most fundamental duties in a reasonably efficient and predictable manner. In the early 1990s, observes Thomas Carothers, democracy promotion in Africa "ran squarely into the sobering reality of devastatingly weak states."[24] Whatever progress may have occurred in state-building since then has been frustratingly sparse. Africans are still overwhelmingly denied basic public goods of health care, education, clean water, electrical power, physical security, a salutary environment, and decent transport infrastructure because the institutions required to provide them are, as Senator Obama complained, constantly being eroded from within. How can the chasm between the people's fundamental aspirations and the enormous institutional debilities that spring from neopatrimonial and personal rule be bridged? Collaboratively, answers must be sought to this fundamental question.

Much of the writing on African politics over the past quarter-century has centered on institution-eroding practices. What will it take to overcome them? How can African countries build institutions that maximize the supplying rather than the pillaging of public goods? In our time we have seen tens of millions uplifted from poverty as a consequence of rapid capitalist growth in Asia, while the expansion of the European Union has improved governance, institutions, and livelihoods in all its member states. Attempts to engender this vital transformation in Africa are now reflected in numerous African and international initiatives.[25]

Some of the boldest efforts to curb the systematic theft of public resources were conducted by the Economic and Financial Crimes Commission (EFCC) of Nigeria under the redoubtable leadership of Nuhu Ribadu. He succeeded in bringing to justice many formerly "untouchable" barons of the Nigerian political system, especially state governors. These advances came to a sudden end on 28 December 2007, however, when the Yar'Adua administration unexpectedly sent Ribadu on "study leave." The official explanation—that this was merely the reassignment of a senior police officer—met with incredulity. Although critics charged the EFCC with partiality during Obasanjo's final years in power, it remains true that never before in the history of corruption-plagued Nigeria had anyone brought so many senior officials to book, or recovered so much stolen public money. Wole Soyinka spoke for many Nigerian activists when he decried this "dismal, contemptuous New Year gift to the nation,"[26] which came just weeks after the EFCC had obtained an indictment for grand theft and money-laundering against James Ibori, the former governor of Delta State.

Two decades ago, I published a study of the deadly embrace of politics and systemic corruption in Nigeria.[27] Some countries have shown that it is possible to build public institutions amid significant theft of national resources—but none so far in Africa. China and India continue to grow at phenomenal rates despite relatively high levels of corruption. When, as in Africa, the proceeds of corruption are siphoned off into nonproductive assets at home and abroad, what is left for domestic development are usually crumbs and crumbling institutions. The democratic awakening in Africa in the 1990s drew strength from the assumption that accountability, transparency, and the rule of law would steadily constrain prebendalist practices. Not even in better-performing emergent democracies such as Ghana, however, has that assumption been borne out. African citizens therefore face two daunting challenges: securing the right to elect those who will govern them in fair and honest elections, and ensuring that elected officials do not continue to treat state treasuries as their personal bank accounts. Aidan Hartley, in a searing commentary on the Kenyan crisis, contends that periodic elections have mainly bestowed "legitimacy on politicians to pillage until the next depressing cycle begins."[28] In Africa, the struggle to prevent the erosion of the state by corruption and the struggle to entrench democracy are deeply interwoven.

As 2007 drew to a close, another striking but precarious democratic advance was made, this time in South Africa. Just a week after Jacob Zuma dethroned President Thabo Mbeki as leader of the ruling African National Congress (ANC) in an assembly of four-thousand party delegates, Zuma faced a formal indictment on corruption charges stemming from a longstanding case involving military procurement. His trial is expected to begin in August 2008. This probably means that South Africa will remain under a cloud of uncertainty, as Mbeki is due to step down from the presidency in 2009 and Zuma, as head of the politically dominant ANC, is his presumptive successor.

The Heavy Burden on Elections

During the long and corrupt reign of Kenya's President Daniel arap Moi (1978–2002), the people were often pushed away from democracy—and they resolutely pushed back. After Moi retired and his successor Mwai Kibaki won election to the presidency in December 2002, the scenario soon enough repeated itself. In December 2007, Kenya seemed on the cusp of a lawful and orderly alternation in power as Raila Odinga surged ahead of Kibaki in the presidential balloting, while many senior government ministers went down to defeat along with more than half the parliamentarians. Yet as has happened on so many other occasions in Africa, a government that the voters had rejected chose to nullify their decision, unleashing state violence and provoking interethnic warfare at the cost of hundreds of lives and a significant setback to economic stability and growth.

Leaving aside small states such as Benin and Cape Verde, and those with single party dominant systems such as Botswana, Namibia, and (mainland) Tanzania, few African countries have established efficient and reliably honest electoral systems. "The only effective check on presidential power" in such countries, argues Nicolas van de Walle, "is through direct elections, if and when they are free and fair."[29] A great onus is therefore placed on competitive elections, in weak and fractious polities, to constrain leaders. So far, few African countries have met this test while staying on a peaceful course of nation-building and development. In this regard, I find particularly pertinent Niall Ferguson's identification of three thresholds that democratizing nations must pass: the nonviolent resolution of political competition, the acceptance of alternation in power, and the supremacy of the rule of law.[30]

Ghana, where the Election Commission has overseen elections of increasing credibility, is a striking demonstration of the observance of these core principles. Even Senegal, which can boast an electoral history going all the way back to the colonial era, and where innovative reforms were introduced from the late 1980s to ensure greater fairness, has backslid under the pseudodemocratic rule of Abdoulaye Wade. In December 2008, Ghana will face a highly contested election in which the two dominant parties, which have traded the presidency back and forth for two terms each since 1992, will compete for power in a nation that is on the cusp of a breakthrough to sustained economic development. Will Ghanaians tumble into the pitfalls that ensnared Nigeria and Kenya in 2007, or will the road to democratic development continue to be widened via free and fair elections, the embrace of nonviolence, and respect for the constitution and rule of law?

Robert Mugabe, the tyrant who has driven Zimbabwe to the bottom of the abyss, is expected to run for a fifth term as president in March 2008. With an inflation rate that has reached more than 66,000 percent at the time of this writing in Feburary 2008, and a quarter of its population huddling as refugees in neighboring countries, the notion of an electoral process in Zimbabwe with Mugabe at the controls can only be described as Orwellian. Angola, following calamitous 1992 elections that triggered an additional decade of civil war, is also expected to hold elections in 2008. Will it register an advance after decades of nondemocratic rule and the corrupt appropriation of the nation's abundant petroleum-export revenues? Or will the risk of losing, or even sharing, power call forth another deplorable electoral exercise by state elites?

Despite the uncertainties and disappointments discussed in this essay, it still cannot be said that democracy in Africa, as in some other areas of the world, is in full retreat. Writing about Vladimir Putin's Russia, Sergei Kovalev laments that "the Byzantine system of power has triumphed for the foreseeable future," and that "democratic mechanisms have been liquidated" so thoroughly that "few of us will live to see the reinstatement of freedom and democracy in Russia."[31] Few students of Africa's politics, I believe, would make such a conclusive statement about the defeat of democracy there. In many countries, "the struggle continues" in a variety of forms, as civil society becomes more robust, the independent media grow more diverse and inventive, human rights and social-justice activists learn new skills, communication technologies get cheaper and more widespread, and the masses of citizens take an ever more jaundiced view of attempts at political deception and manipulation.

Richard L. Sklar once praised African nations as "workshops" of democracy that are contributing to the "aggregate of democratic knowledge and practice."[32] Political and civic activists, helped by international agencies, continue to forge fresh instruments to weaken the barriers to the rise of stable, constitutional, and development-friendly democracies. Africans may not have found definitive answers to the many challenges discussed in this essay, and in some countries their voices may have been temporarily silenced by the brutal exercise of state power. Nevertheless, there is no sign that the search for answers has slackened. While victory flags cannot yet be raised, neither should those of surrender be unfurled.

NOTES

1. I borrow this expression from Joseph J. Ellis, *American Creation: Triumphs and Tragedies at the Founding of the Republic* (New York: Alfred A. Knopf, 2007), 56.

2. Richard Joseph, "Africa, 1990–1997: From *Abertura* to Closure," *Journal of Democracy* 9 (April 1998): 3–17. The central argument of this essay still holds true a decade later.

3. Richard Joseph, "The Reconfiguration of Power in Late Twentieth-Century Africa," in Richard Joseph, ed., *State, Conflict, and Democracy in Africa* (Boulder, Colo.: Lynne Rienner, 1999).

4. Thomas Carothers makes an impressive case for the "recalibration" of democracy promotion in the post-9/11 era. See his "U.S. Democracy Promotion During and After Bush," available at *www.carnegieendowment.org/files/democracy_promotion_after_bush_final.pdf*.

5. The adjective "civilian" needs qualification too, since in Nigeria a military caste that includes many retired officers made rich by oil continues to wield considerable power both inside and outside the formal institutions of government.

6. See also Rotimi Suberu, "Nigeria's Muddled Elections," *Journal of Democracy* 18 (October 2007): 95–110.

7. Lincoln's 4 July 1861 message to Congress is available at *www.millercenter.virginia.edu/scripps/digitalarchive/speeches*.

8. Christopher Clapham, *Africa and the International System: The Politics of State Survival* (New York: Cambridge University Press, 1996).

9. Richard Joseph, "Africa: States in Crisis," *Journal of Democracy* 14 (July 2003): 159–70.

10. Still relevant for understanding African political dynamics are Peter Ekeh's notion of the "two publics" and Richard L. Sklar's of "dual majesty." See Ekeh, "Colonialism and the Two Publics in Africa: A Theoretical Statement," *Comparative Studies in Society and History* 17 (January 1975): 91–112; and Sklar, "The African Frontier for Political

Science," in Robert H. Bates, V.Y. Mudimbe, and Jean O'Barr, eds., *Africa and the Disciplines: The Contributions of Research in Africa to the Social Sciences and Humanities* (Chicago: University of Chicago Press, 1993), 83–110.

11. Also relevant to this discussion is Jeffery Herbst's pathbreaking study, *States and Power in Africa: Comparative Lessons in Authority and Control* (Princeton: Princeton University Press, 2000).

12. Soyinka's comment appears in a report entitled "Nigeria 2007: Political, Social and Economic Transitions," which is available at *www.northwestern.edu/african-studies/ Nigeria2007-ConferenceReport.pdf*.

13. Robert A. Dahl, *A Preface to Democratic Theory* (Chicago: University of Chicago Press, 1956), 3.

14. Larry Diamond, *The Spirit of Democracy: The Struggle to Build Free Societies Throughout the World* (New York: Times Books, 2008).

15. Daniel N. Posner and Daniel J. Young, "The Institutionalization of Political Power in Africa," *Journal of Democracy* 18 (July 2007): 126–40.

16. Andrew M. Mwenda, "Personalizing Power in Uganda," *Journal of Democracy* 18 (July 2007): 23–37.

17. See Steven A. Cook, *Ruling But Not Governing: The Military and Political Development in Egypt, Algeria, and Turkey* (Baltimore: Johns Hopkins University Press, 2007).

18. Posner and Young, "Institutionalization of Political Power in Africa," 126.

19. Posner and Young, "Institutionalization of Political Power in Africa," 127.

20. Michael Bratton presents this duality more clearly in "The Democracy Barometers: Formal versus Informal Institutions in Africa," *Journal of Democracy* 18 (July 2007): 96–110.

21. In keeping with his ambivalent behavior and pronouncements, President Obasanjo described this decision as a victory for democracy, even though his administration had expended much time and national treasure trying to make it go the other way.

22. A fascinating aspect of this struggle in Africa is the need to compel election officers to count ballots correctly and to announce the actual tallies honestly. Often, activists and citizens must form human walls around quantities of completed ballots in order to prevent tampering. After declaring Mwai Kibaki the victor of the 2007 presidential election and plunging Kenya into chaos and violence, Kenya's Electoral Commission head Samuel Kivuitu conceded that he did not really know who had won.

23. Barack Obama, "An Honest Government, A Hopeful Future," address delivered at the University of Nairobi, Kenya, 28 August 2006.

24. Thomas Carothers, "The End of the Transition Paradigm," *Journal of Democracy* 13 (January 2002): 16.

25. These include the African Peer Review Mechanism and the New Partnership for African Development; training programs of the Governance Institute of the World Bank and the UN Economic Commission for Africa; the African networks Publish What You Pay and the Extractive Industries Transparency Initiative; the U.S. Millennium Development Challenge Corporation; and the World Bank's Poverty Reduction Strategic Papers; as well as many national anticorruption agencies.

26. "Soyinka, Reps, Others Condemn Ribadu's Removal," *Vanguard* (Lagos), 20 December 2007.

27. Richard Joseph, *Democracy and Prebendal Politics in Nigeria: The Rise and Fall of the Second Republic* (Cambridge: Cambridge University Press, 1987).

28. Aidan Hartley, "Democracy by Other Means," *New York Times,* 11 January 2008.

29. Nicolas van de Walle, *Overcoming Stagnation in Aid-Dependent Countries* (Washington, D.C.: Center for Global Development, 2005), 14.

30. Niall Ferguson, "Is Political Freedom in Retreat?" *Financial Times,* 26–27 January 2008.

31. Sergei Kovalev, "Why Putin Wins," *New York Review of Books,* 22 November 2007, 66.

32. Richard L. Sklar, "Democracy in Africa," in Toyin Falola, ed., *African Politics in Postimperial Times: The Essays of Richard L. Sklar* (Trenton, N.J.; Africa World Press, 2002), 16. This seminal essay was first published in *African Studies Review* 25 (September–December 1983).

2

PRESIDENTS UNTAMED

H. Kwasi Prempeh

H. Kwasi Prempeh teaches constitutional law and comparative constitutionalism at Seton Hall University School of Law in New Jersey. Previously, he served as director of legal policy and governance at the Ghana Center for Democratic Development. He coedits the Center's quarterly, Democracy Watch. *This essay originally appeared in the April 2008 issue of the* Journal of Democracy.

The revival of democratic politics in Africa over the last two decades is helping to remake the region's old image as a safe haven for rapacious and politically unaccountable autocrats. Single-party political systems, which once dominated the African political landscape, have all but disappeared. Legislative and presidential elections, once episodic and farcical, are now routinely and vigorously contested. "African presidents today," two political scientists have recently noted, "are more than twice as likely to lose power if they subject themselves to contested elections than they were before 1990."[1]

The growing prospect of defeat through competitive elections is only one of many new realities that Africa's presidents now face. Constitutional changes in several African states have brought important new players onto the political scene. Notably, traditional legislative and oversight functions have been restored to Africa's now-representative and multiparty parliaments, and the courts, once passive instruments of legitimation for Africa's "big men," are now empowered to adjudicate constitutional challenges to executive and other governmental acts. Africa's political elites also must now contend with critical reporting and commentary from a newly emboldened private media. A growing number of nongovernmental organizations are similarly revitalizing African civil societies and opening new avenues for the mobilization and expression of civic activism.

By far the most profound change has been the growing popular insistence on presidential term limits. In sharp contrast to the period before 1990, when African presidents could typically hold office as long as they wanted and worried mainly about coups d'état, constitutionally enshrined rules now set definite limits to presidential tenure in a growing number of African states. By the end of 2005, thirty-three African constitutions contained presidential term-limit provisions. Term limits have ended the tenure of fourteen presidents in Africa since 1990. In Malawi, Nigeria, and Zambia, attempts by term-limited presidents to extend their respective tenures met with vigorous resistance and ultimate defeat. Even where presidents have managed to stay on past their original terms, as in Burkina Faso and Uganda, the term extensions came after hard-fought constitutional battles rather than through unconstitutional means. As Daniel Posner and Daniel Young have explained, the combination of term limits and regular elections has displaced the coup d'état as the primary mode of regime change and leadership succession in contemporary Africa.[2]

Despite these precedent-setting changes to Africa's political and constitutional landscape, a notable feature of the *ancien régime* survives. This is the phenomenon of the imperial presidency.[3] Africa's current presidents may be term-limited, but by all accounts they have not yet been tamed. In fact, the modal African presidency has emerged from the recent round of democratic reforms with its extant powers substantially intact. In general, presidential rule in "postauthoritarian" Africa has become less repressive, and the climate for personal liberty and rival political activity has improved appreciably in Africa's democratizing states. Still, power in the African state, and with it control of resources and patronage, continues to rest with the president, making the capture and control of the presidency the singular ambition of Africa's politicians.

Presidents in contemporary Africa routinely pronounce "laws" and announce major policy decisions without recourse to parliamentary legislation. Frederick Chiluba, who became Zambia's first posttransition president after beating longtime incumbent Kenneth Kaunda in a 1996 election, went so far as to declare his country officially a "Christian nation," without prior consultation with his cabinet, his party, or the national legislature. The presidential directive—"government by press release"—remains a common mode of governing. Likewise, African presidents continue to control slush funds that are not subject to legislative oversight. As one commentator describing the state of constitutional politics in postmilitary Nigeria has observed, the contemporary president still "wears a dictatorial toga."[4]

The persistence of the hegemonic presidency in postauthoritarian Africa is puzzling, not least because Africa's postcolonial experience with this mode of rule has been an unmitigated disaster. Defended by its early postcolonial architects as necessary to achieve desperately

needed development and national integration in what were then newly independent states, presidential supremacy in Africa, along with its
standard trappings of one-party legislatures and statist economic policies, ultimately failed to deliver. Instead of a supposed "authoritarian
advantage," presidential hegemony in Africa brought with it a form of
rule—neopatrimonialism—in which unfettered presidential discretion
and informal access to the president became more important than compliance with formal rules. The distribution of national resources and patronage followed such access, fueling corruption, nepotism, and ruinous
economic decision making. Personalistic presidential rule in Africa became, in effect, "a substitute for institutionalization."[5] Institutions outside the presidency—the legislature, the courts, the civil service, local
government—withered as just about every public decision of any import
found its way to the president's "in box." Africa found itself beset by
the strange paradox of strong presidents sitting atop weak states—states
that routinely lacked the requisite institutional capacities and resources
to fulfill even their most basic functions.

The social, political, and economic costs associated with presidential
supremacy supplied one of the main grievances of the protest movements
that propelled recent democratic transitions in Africa. Since weakening
or at least containing the executive was among the anticipated outcomes
of the redemocratization of politics after 1990, the survival of presidential supremacy raises questions about the breadth and depth of recent
democratic and constitutional reforms.

Transition Priorities: Pluralism, Not Constitutionalism

The democratization of national politics in Africa, not the transformation of government as such, was the primary and immediate object,
and thus the effect, of much of the awakening that began almost two
decades ago with the sovereign national conference in Benin and the
faltering of apartheid in South Africa. Galvanized by mass disenchantment with decades of presidential misrule and monopoly of power, the
typical African opposition—a group often top-heavy with sidelined old-
guard politicians eager to regain power and its spoils—rallied popular
sentiment around the cause of electoral reform with a view to voting the
incumbents out. Consequently, the transition agenda in Africa has been
dominated by "access" issues, notably the right of opposition parties and
candidates to contest elections; the free and fair conduct of elections; an
end to government monopoly and censorship of the media; and new limits on presidential tenure. The unifying theme is a concern with opening up a closed political process to allow pluralistic representation and
participation in national government. In terms of constitutional reform,
these limited ends have entailed little more than a few amendments to
existing constitutions, primarily to remove clauses that had hitherto pre-

cluded open contestation for political office. A comprehensive overhaul or redesign of the constitutional order, beyond the restoration of democratic politics, has generally been kept off the agenda by besieged incumbents and regime opponents alike.

The limited ambition behind contemporary constitutional reform in Africa reflects, in large measure, the narrow, self-interested agendas of rival political elites. Besieged incumbents, weakened by a loss of popular legitimacy because of their perennial failure to make good on promises of development and social improvement, have generally found little incentive to initiate reform beyond those limited rule changes deemed necessary to restore democratic accountability and placate external financiers. In fact, in those instances where the authoritarian regime remained strong enough politically at the time of transition to retain control of the transition agenda and timetable, as was the case in Ghana, Tanzania, and Uganda, the ensuing constitutional changes were made with regime continuity—and for that matter, presidential dominance—in mind. Thus apart from removing existing constitutional obstacles to multiparty politics, the "structure of the national presidency of Tanzania has not changed substantially since 1985 when [President Julius] Nyerere left office."[6] In Ghana, the Jerry Rawlings–led military junta rejected a proposal by a commission of experts for the bifurcation of executive power between a nationally elected president and a legislature-backed prime minister in the country's postmilitary (current) constitution. The junta feared that the proposal carried the risk of "personality conflicts" between the president and the prime minister—a fear that was predicated, no doubt, on the assumption (which subsequent events proved to be well founded) that Rawlings would continue as civilian president under the new constitution.

For their part, opposition activists pushing for political change in Africa have been motivated not so much by a desire to *reform* government as by the near-term prospect of *forming* the government themselves. The struggle for control over the extant "political kingdom" has dominated transition politics so far. Although oppositionists commonly promise far-reaching constitutional reforms, including limits on presidential power, enthusiasm for such transformative change tends to wane once yesterday's electoral insurgents become today's officeholders. Thus in Zambia, Chiluba's Movement for Multiparty Democracy (MMD) called for the removal of certain "dictatorial" clauses from the constitution when Kaunda was in power. But once it had defeated Kaunda, the MMD decided that the constitution was "adequate" after all, and defended "presidential democracy" as "the best system of government."[7] In Ghana, the New Patriotic Party (NPP), during its time in opposition (1993–2001), strongly opposed the president's authority to appoint mayors and called for them to be chosen by local popular vote instead. Yet as the governing party since 2001, the NPP has not only zealously guarded the president's power to make appointments to mayoralties, but has even backed the creation of more such offices—which of course can now be filled by NPP loyalists. Similar retreats from vows to push counterauthoritarian constitutional reforms have been seen in Kenya, Malawi, and Nigeria.

In keeping with this lack of enthusiasm among elites, publics at large in Africa have also not brought much pressure to bear on behalf of limits to presidential power. Rather, presidential supremacy continues to benefit politically from a widespread and persistent belief among influential sections of the polity that what Africa sorely needs is strong, no-nonsense presidential leadership. The famous assertion by Nigerian novelist and essayist Chinua Achebe that "the trouble with Nigeria is simply and squarely a failure of leadership,"[8] sums up the opinion of many contemporary Africans about the underlying cause of their perennial national crises of bad governance and underdevelopment.

Tolerance for presidential misrule and indefinite presidential tenure may have worn thin in Africa's democratizing polities, but with voters still caring most about beating the twin scourges of underdevelopment and economic marginalization, belief in the beneficent uses of preponderant executive power continues to run strong. Indeed, in many African polities a resurgent nostalgia—the effect perhaps of popular disenchantment with successive governments of uninspiring politicians—celebrates one or the other erstwhile dictator as exemplifying the kind of strong leadership that the African state is said to need. Even among Africa's influential middle classes, Lee Kuan Yew's "Singapore story" of authoritarian modernization appears to have revived an "autocrat envy" of sorts. In short, problematizing the crisis of African governance or development in a personalistic or leader-centered fashion helps to legitimize presidential dominance, despite the current popular and intellectual repudiation of the old "belly-full" thesis that for so long told Africans the lie that they could have *either* constitutional democracy *or* economic development, but not both.

Due to the failure of rivalrous political classes and publics to prioritize constitutionalism (in the form of credible constitutional limits on executive power), Africa's post-1990 transitions have at best injected a few (but nontrivial) democratizing reforms into an old order that remains in key respects unreconstructed. Progress in democratization thus coexists uneasily with the entrenchment of many of the "original sins" of Africa's founding generation, upon which the tradition of the imperial presidency was built in the early independence years almost a half-century ago.

The highly centralized unitary state—a key pillar of the postcolonial authoritarian project in Africa—remains firmly in place, providing a solid foundation for persistent presidential hegemony. Constitutional reforms have as yet done nothing meaningful to change the territorial distribution of power, so that political power and control over resources continue to reside in capital cities.

Despite the resilience of subnational ethnoregional identities and the enduring strength of "local patriotism," African elites remain firm in their support for the highly centralized unitary state. While support for decentralization, or the idea of local self-government within a unitary-state model, has been gaining ground, recent constitutional changes have done little to empower local government. Local *administration,* not local *government,* still best describes the role played by local councils and officials in contemporary Africa.

As a consequence, the typical African government is framed as one of general, not limited, powers—able to act and legislate regarding all matters unless the national constitution says otherwise. Such a constitutional order naturally lacks the kind of "vertical" countervailing power that might otherwise restrain or check an overbearing central executive. Not surprisingly, the scope of presidential power in such a constitutional regime depends largely on the way in which centralized national power is allocated "horizontally" between the executive and the other branches of government. But here, too, Africa's current constitutions break no new ground.

A Want of Checks and Balances

Despite the restoration of multiparty politics, Africa's legislatures have yet to emerge from the shadows of executive hegemony to which decades of military or presidentialist one-party rule have consigned them. A combination of path dependency, legislative abdication, and constitutional design accounts for this state of affairs.

Unlike the executive branch, which can count on a history of institutional continuity, most of Africa's legislatures have suffered substantial gaps in their institutional lives since independence. Those that do have a record of continuous existence have operated largely under single-party regimes and therefore have little experience with autonomy. The absence of a tradition of legislative autonomy means that most of Africa's current law-making bodies lack a clear conception of their institutional prerogatives. Because the executive branch in Africa has for too long been accustomed to governing without a credible counterbalance, and the legislature is not used to checking or disciplining the executive, this familiar pattern of executive dominance is likely to persist absent explicit constitutional limits on presidential power. Preexisting patterns of presidential behavior, along with conventional understandings of presidential prerogative held over from the *ancien régime,* continue to command wide acceptance.

The force of "old habits" alone, however, does not render a complete account of why Africa's legislatures remain weak. As Joel Barkan has noted, legislators have themselves often conspired in marginalizing their own branch.[9] Notably, opportunities for robust legislative oversight of the executive, in the form of hearings and investigations by legislative committees, have generally gone unused in all but a few African legislatures. Legislation also still routinely gives the African executive wide leeway ("as he thinks fit," "as he may prescribe") in the everyday exercise of authority granted by statute. Examples abound of African legislatures surrendering their legislative prerogatives to the executive.

In Ghana, for example, the National Assembly in 2001 reenacted a 1960s-era law that gives the president authority—without the need for legislative approval—to establish or abolish government ministries or departments. In effect, Ghana's parliament has handed its president the power unilaterally to expand his own branch *ad infinitum*. Even the selection of the speaker of parliament, which is everywhere the common prerogative of legislators, is in many instances ceded to presidents in Africa, enabling them to interfere with the day-to-day business of the legislature.

Constitutional design has helped to ensure presidential dominance over the legislature, typically by doing little to rebalance power between the two political branches. Presidents in Africa continue to be vested with vast powers of appointment, extending to nearly all nonlegislative constitutional and statutory offices. In addition, the power to originate legislation, including the all-important national budget, is the exclusive prerogative of the executive in nearly all African constitutions; the legislature's role is typically limited to approving or rejecting (but not amending) the executive's budget and legislative proposals. This presidential monopoly on legislative and budgetary initiative has had the effect of marginalizing Africa's legislatures in the policy-making process.

Even where the legislature shares with the president the power to initiate or modify legislation, other aspects of contemporary constitutional design and politics in Africa work to skew the balance of power in favor of the executive. Most contemporary African constitutions, though commonly described as presidential in form, in fact follow a "hybrid" presidential model, blending features of parliamentarism (selecting the president's ministers from among members of the legislature, for example) with aspects of U.S.-style presidentialism (such as an executive not subject to removal by parliamentary censure or a vote of no confidence).

In Francophone and Lusophone Africa, constitutional hybridization has been accomplished primarily through the nominal restoration of the position of prime minister (appointed by an executive president), which merely returns those countries to their original postindependence constitutions inspired by the 1958 Gaullist constitution of France's Fifth Republic. In the Anglophone states that have adopted the hybrid form, such as Ghana, Kenya, Uganda, and Zambia, a nationally elected president governs with a team of ministers chosen from serving members of the legislature who continue to hold their legislative seats.

Rather than striking a balance between legislative and presidential power, the hybrid form tends to enhance presidential power. In particular, hybrid presidentialism has enabled African presidents to use the offer or prospect of a ministerial appointment to coopt influential legislators. In Zambia, for example, President Chiluba appointed nearly half the total number of legislators to ministerial positions within his administration. Ghana's posttransition presidents have similarly offered ministerial positions to numerous legislators, including some from minor opposition parties. As Barkan points out, in such hybrid regimes most legislators and legislative candidates care more about winning appointment to executive posts than about building careers as lawmakers.

In those few African countries (including Nigeria, the continent's largest) where the constitutional system features a formal separation of powers or a juridical balance in the allocation of powers between the president and the legislature, presidents still possess ample extraconstitutional (political) resources with which to bend the legislature's will. A critical source of presidential leverage in this regard arises from the nature of the African political economy. African governments get most of their money from external "rents" in the form of commodities or natural-resources exports or foreign-donor support.

Apart from undermining prospects for a meaningful "fiscal social contract" between government and the citizenry, the African state's excessive dependence on foreign rents rather than domestic taxes makes the legislature a marginal player in the realm of public finance. Indeed, throughout Africa, the president's finance minister, not the legislature, has remained the main channel through which external donors and multilateral financiers provide fiscal support to African governments. Even the legislature itself must depend by and large on the good graces of the executive for adequate resources. Moreover, as helping constituents to pay for things such as medical and funeral expenses has become politically obligatory for legislators, Africa's cash-poor lawmakers have, in turn, become ever more vulnerable to the lure of executive patronage and capture.

The Burkean conception of political parties as providing "a sort of extraconstitutional check on the executive or would-be executive"[10]—by committing presidential candidates to policy-oriented party programs—does not describe African parties. Idealistic or programmatic parties are hard to find in Africa's multiparty parliaments. In fact, beyond the platitudes of party manifestos, there is little programmatic difference among rival parties in most African political systems. All offer vague campaign promises of better governance and better times to come while prophesying a dismal future should the people make the "mistake" of choosing the other party. Party candidates almost never commit to or discuss specific policies; in fact, most African parties lack the internal organization or capacity even to generate or evaluate policy recommendations.

What unites—and occasionally divides—president and party in Africa, then, is not commitment to a common programmatic agenda, but the desire to gain and maintain control of state resources. Because the president remains the patron *par excellence* in Africa, the desire to capture—or, for small parties, to form a coalition with—the presidency is the motive force behind the formation and behavior of many of Africa's parties. The zero-sum nature of African political systems, in which electoral defeat for the party often threatens individual livelihoods, works to unite president and party in defense of the president's customary prerogatives.

Moreover, the parties' unstable finances draw them toward near-exclusive dependence on a few influential benefactors to fund their operations and election campaigns. Majority parties typically regard the president as their most important benefactor. As long as the president is willing to use the prerogatives and resources of office to advance party leaders' interests, the party's support for the president is all but guaranteed. But when a president shies away from keeping his end of the deal, his own party may turn against him, as happened when Malawian president Bingu wa Mutharika refused to back down on investigating cases of corruption alleged to have occurred during his predecessor's tenure.

The absence of internal democracy in Africa's political parties also facilitates presidential dominance. Political parties in Africa operate much like private clubs, with no effective public regulation of their internal governance and actions. Loyalty to one's party and its leadership is deemed obligatory and usually trumps all other considerations. Summary expulsion or suspension of dissenters is fairly routine, and parties exert tight top-down control, especially over their legislators. In the case of majority parties, this hierarchical and oligarchic control is usually exercised for the president's benefit, if not at his behest. "Conscience voting" and open displays of independence by a majority-party legislator are strongly frowned on and harshly punished. In 2001, for example, Zambia's ruling MMD expelled 22 of its legislators for their opposition to President Chiluba's ultimately failed bid for a third term.

In some cases, the "iron hand" of the party oligarchy draws strength from the national constitution itself. In Malawi, for instance, one reading of the constitution would make cross-party voting by a legislator, in opposition to his or her party's wishes, grounds for forfeiture of that member's seat. The Sierra Leonean constitution is more explicit: A legislator must vacate his seat "if by his conduct in Parliament by sitting and voting with members of a different party, the Speaker is satisfied after consultation with the Leader of the Member's party that the Member is no longer a member of the political party under whose

symbol he was elected to Parliament."[11] Such undemocratic and oligarchic party control over legislators invariably inures to the benefit
of presidential power.

Given the lack of legislative checks on the executive, the task of restraining presidential power in Africa is left largely to the courts. Bills
of rights and courts with constitutional-review authority are thus *de ri-
gueur* in posttransition Africa, and a number of new constitutions have
liberalized standing requirements in order to encourage the public to
challenge offending governmental actions. In some respects, Africa's
judiciaries have responded positively to this new challenge. Since the
beginning of the 1990s, courts in many African countries have ruled
against obstinate presidents in important cases. Yet despite these early
indications of constitutionalism-friendly judicial activism in contemporary Africa, Africa's courts are still institutionally too enfeebled and
doctrinally too executive-minded to rein in presidential excesses with
much consistency.

Judiciaries across Africa suffer from many of the same handicaps
that undermine legislative effectiveness. The finance ministry's control
of the treasury, which in many African countries has been reinforced by
"cash-budget" laws, places the judiciary at the financial mercy of the
executive. Due to the gross underfunding of the courts, chief justices
often explore informal means of building the court's influence with the
executive in order to obtain the resources necessary to keep the courts
functioning. Turning top jurists into politicians' supplicants carries with
it an obvious risk to judicial independence.

But even if judicial independence were secure, reliance on the judiciary to restrain presidential power has other pitfalls. Often what might
appear as a problem of "bad judges" (or "timorous souls," in Lord Den-
ning's famous words) turns out, in fact, to be a problem of "bad jurisprudence." In the African context, this takes the form of a "jurisprudence
of executive supremacy"—jurisprudence that is habitually deferential
to presidential power and skeptical of "novel" claims rooted in modern
conceptions of constitutionalism. Notably, courts in common-law Africa have continued to rely on archaic common-law doctrines and abstruse
interpretations of constitutional texts to uphold, for example, the current
use of antipress and anti–free-speech statutes enacted during the period
of one-party rule.

The problem is made worse by the number of repressive laws, enacted in the early postcolonial period and by successive authoritarian
regimes, that are still on the books. While these laws are arguably at
odds with the spirit, if not the letter, of contemporary bills of rights in
Africa, they will remain enforceable until they are legislatively repealed
or judicially invalidated. Low levels of legal literacy among Africa's
vulnerable populations, coupled with the absence of *pro bono* representation, have meanwhile kept bills of rights and other constitutional

guarantees underenforced. Africa's presidents and legislatures have not made the repeal of inherited repressive laws a legislative priority. On the contrary, postauthoritarian governments have not been shy about enforcing many of these laws. In Malawi, for example, the Protected Emblems and Names Act, in force since 1967, has been used more than fifteen times since 1994 to arrest or prosecute journalists for "insulting" the president. Similarly, Zambia's Public Order Act, which dates back to the colonial period, has been repeatedly employed in the post-Kaunda era to frustrate the associational freedom of opposition parties.

In short, constitutional litigation and judicial countervailance have not proved as effective an avenue for restraining executive power in Africa as the literal texts of bills of rights and other constitutional guarantees might lead one to expect. Without political momentum for change and a reconfiguration of the existing power map to constrain executive power, the counterauthoritarian judicial rulings handed down during the incipient stages of democratization in a number of countries may well represent a transitory phenomenon.

Divided Government

In some African constitutional systems, a second round of balloting is required to select a president when the first round has failed to produce a winner with an absolute majority. In others, such as Angola's, the presidential term of office does not coincide with the legislative term. Either scenario could give rise to divided government, in which control of the presidency and the legislature is divided between rival political parties.

The possibility is not just theoretical. There have been instances of divided government in posttransition Africa. In Benin, Congo (Brazzaville), Madagascar, and Niger, the president has at one time or another failed to secure an absolute or working majority in the national legislature. While this state of affairs enabled the legislatures in question to "check" presidential dominance, the outcomes demonstrate the undesirability of divided government as an antidote to presidential hegemony.

In the United States, where the tradition of divided government is well established, it has little chance of producing administrative paralysis. The United States operates under a federal system, where most of the everyday concerns of citizens (such as public safety, mass transportation, and sanitation) fall within the jurisdiction of state and local governments with independent revenue-raising powers. Thus in the United States, partisan gridlock at the federal level will not ordinarily create a nationwide governance crisis. The same cannot be said of divided government in Africa.

A postcolonial history of one-party regimes and military juntas has effectively precluded the emergence in Africa of a tradition of workable divided government. The crude zero-sum partisanship of contemporary African politics does not help matters. Above all, the persistence of highly centralized unitary states means that all public administration, even regional and local, must rely on the central government for operational resources and direction. Under these circumstances, divided government is a recipe for nationwide governmental paralysis. This has indeed been the lesson of Africa's recent experiences.

In both Congo (Brazzaville) and Niger, the governmental paralysis generated by divided government eventually gave military adventurers an excuse to intervene, bringing an end to young democratic projects. In Benin, divided government "paralysed reform for many months and compromised the government's capacity to undertake further policy reform."[12] And of late in Malawi, where President Mutharika and his former party (which has a working majority in the legislature) parted ways over the party's objections to Mutharika's stance on corruption, the National Assembly's refusal to bring the president's budget to a vote threatened a constitutional and political crisis.

Because divided government in the African context tends to cripple the orderly administration of the state, relying on this means of checking presidential hegemony is poorly advised. Restrained presidential power, important though it is, must not be purchased at the cost of paralyzing day-to-day governance. Other, less destabilizing avenues must be explored.

Taming Presidential Dominance in Africa

The success of term limits in reversing the tradition of perpetual presidential tenure in Africa suggests that constitutional rules are beginning to matter there as never before. The effectiveness of constitutional term-limit provisions in ending the "president-for-life" syndrome also carries an important lesson: Flat prohibitions and bright-line rules, not open-ended or discretion-based provisions, hold far better prospects for checking runaway presidential power. In their current form, however, African constitutions generally adopt a "neutral" approach to the problem of presidential dominance; they simply allocate formal power between the president and the legislature and then leave it to "normal politics" to "check and balance" presidential supremacy. In so doing, however, contemporary constitutional policy not only ignores the persistence of structural rigidities from the past, but also fails to take into account the realities of "normal politics" in Africa, especially the vastly superior political resources of the president vis-à-vis the legislature.

African constitutions must confront the problem of presidential dominance with the same textual specificity that they have used to tackle the problem of perpetual presidential tenure. The black letter of the constitutional text—and not some politics-driven future negotiation between the executive and the legislature—must be the vehicle for scribing out the desired scope and limits of presidential power. In order to rein in the presidential appetite for excessive ministerial appointments, for instance, constitutions might put numerical caps on the size of the president's ministerial contingent, since relying on the legislature to use its approval power to check the president in this regard has generally proved a lost cause. Presidential patronage opportunities outside the executive branch should be similarly limited—for example, by specifying clear merit-based criteria for appointments to key statutory and constitutional offices and expanding the role of the legislature and relevant professional associations in the nomination and appointment process.

In order to prevent the filling of independent constitutional offices (such as those of chief justice, auditor-general, anticorruption czar, and electoral commissioner) with partisans or politically malleable figures, those presidential appointments must be further constrained by an express constitutional requirement that such nominations obtain the approval of a supermajority of votes in the legislature. Other undesirable but conventional presidential prerogatives, such as unilateral creation of ministries, appointment of legislators to paid directorships on boards of public corporations, and de facto monopoly control over prosecutorial decisions (through control of the office of attorney-general), should be similarly addressed through direct proscription or regulation in the constitution.

If an effective balance of power is ever to be restored in legislative-executive relations, moreover, Africa's political parties are going to have to become more internally democratic. Encouragingly, certain African constitutions, notably Ghana's and Uganda's, contain provisions addressing the issue of intraparty democracy. These provisions are vague and mostly toothless, however. Constitutional rules can help to address the problem of internal party democracy by imposing specific obligations and restraints on political parties, and then granting aggrieved party members or independent election commissions recourse to judicial or administrative action. For example, bright-line constitutional rules regulating party operations—the process of candidate selection, the financing of political campaigns, and the scope and limits of parties' disciplinary powers and procedures—stand a better chance of success in helping to promote internal party democracy than do foggily worded provisions such as those found in the Ghanaian and Ugandan constitutions, which require parties to "conform to democratic principles." In particular, African constitutions must deny parties the power to expel a member or legislator who dissents from the party line.

Judicial countervailance can also be enhanced through constitutional innovation. For example, a constitutional corrective to the problem of preexisting illiberal statutes could take the form of the repeal *ex ante*—that is, by express constitutional provision—of those pieces of repressive legislation (particularly sedition and criminal-libel laws) upon which past authoritarian regimes relied for control. This approach has the advantage of settling once and for all the unconstitutionality of these laws, thereby eliminating the risk of a future court permitting their continued enforcement by the state. Incorporating appropriate "interpretive instructions" along with bills of rights, as the South African constitution does, is yet another effective way to guide judicial review and jurisprudence in a constitutionalism-friendly direction.

African polities must move beyond the fixation with "strong" leadership and focus instead on building credible and effective institutions at both the national and local levels. As the horrifying recent events in Kenya demonstrate, centralizing power in the presidency, and thus making control of that one office the only prize in a zero-sum political game, not only attracts rivalrous political entrepreneurs and exacerbates conflicts, but also carries potentially tragic consequences for Africa's fragile democracies. Hoping for a Lee Kuan Yew may be understandable, considering Africa's longstanding leadership deficit. Yet as Africa's own painful experiences with messianic ideologies and self-proclaimed reformers amply demonstrate, trusting in heroic leadership—and thus concentrating power in the hands of a single individual in the name of "development"—is not only shortsighted, it often disappoints.[13] If anything, an imperial presidency magnifies the costs of having an incompetent or bad leader at the helm.

NOTES

1. Daniel N. Posner and Daniel J. Young, "The Institutionalization of Political Power in Africa," *Journal of Democracy* 18 (July 2007): 131.

2. Posner and Young, "The Institutionalization of Political Power in Africa."

3. The term was coined by Arthur M. Schlesinger, Jr., to describe "the shift in the constitutional balance" in the United States in favor of "presidential supremacy," which has come about through "the appropriation by the Presidency, and especially by the contemporary Presidency, of powers reserved by the Constitution and by long historical practice to Congress." Schlesinger, *The Imperial Presidency* (Boston: Houghton Mifflin, 1973), viii. Its extension to the African context was popularized by H.W.O. Okoth-Ogendo. See Okoth-Ogendo, "Constitutions Without Constitutionalism: Reflections on an African Political Paradox," in Douglas Greenberg et al., eds., *Constitutionalism and Democracy: Transitions in the Contemporary World* (New York: Oxford University Press, 1993), 74.

4. Ochereome Nnanna, "Is Presidentialism a Given?" *Vanguard* (Lagos), 28 February 2005.

5. Naomi Chazan et al., eds., *Politics and Society in Contemporary Africa,* (Boulder, Colo.: Lynne Rienner, 1992), 163.

6. Stephen N. Ndegwa and Ryan E. Letourneau, "Constitutional Reform," in Paul J. Kaiser and F. Wafula Okumu, eds., *Democratic Transitions in East Africa* (Burlington, Vt.: Ashgate, 2004), 84–100.

7. John C. Momba, "Evolution of Parliament-Executive Relations in Zambia," in M.A. Mohammed Salih, ed., *African Parliaments: Between Governance and Government* (New York: Palgrave Macmillan, 2005), 111.

8. Chinua Achebe, *The Trouble with Nigeria* (Enugu, Nigeria: Fourth Dimension, 1983), 1.

9. My discussion here of African legislatures draws extensively on Joel Barkan's essay, "Progress and Retreat in Africa: Legislatures on the Rise?" *Journal of Democracy* 19 (April 2008):124–37.

10. Carnes Lord, *The Modern Prince: What Leaders Need to Know Now* (New Haven: Yale University Press, 2003), 83.

11. The Constitution of Sierra Leone, 1991, Article 77. Available at *www.sierra-leone. org/Laws/constitution1991.pdf.*

12. Nicolas van de Walle, "The Impact of Multi-Party Politics in Sub-Saharan Africa," *Forum for Development Studies* 1 (June 2001): 30.

13. See Thomas Carothers, "How Democracies Emerge: The 'Sequencing' Fallacy," *Journal of Democracy* 18 (January 2007): 15. Carothers notes that "for every Lee Kuan Yew . . . there have been dozens or even hundreds of rapacious, repressive autocrats posing as reformers."

3

LEGISLATURES ON THE RISE?

Joel D. Barkan

Joel D. Barkan *is professor emeritus of political science at the University of Iowa and senior associate at the Center for Strategic and International Studies in Washington, D.C. His most recent book is* Legislative Power in Emerging African Democracies *(2009). This essay originally appeared in the April 2008 issue of the* Journal of Democracy.

Despite the voluminous literature on democratization, there is a puzzling paucity of work on the development of legislatures in emerging democracies. Few scholars have delved into the questions of when and why legislatures evolve into significant political institutions in nascent democracies, or why this happens in some countries but not in others. There are virtually no systematic cross-national explorations of the relationship between legislative development and "third-wave" democratization.[1]

Nearly two decades after Terry Karl called attention to the electoral fallacy, noting that "elections alone do not a democracy make,"[2] little systematic attention has been given to this key institution and potential check on executive power. The judiciary, elections and electoral systems, and civil society have all captured the interest of democracy specialists, yet the legislature has not. Indeed, apart from an essay by M. Steven Fish in the *Journal of Democracy,* neither that journal nor *Democratization* has published a single article on the relationship between legislative development and democratization.

Legislative analysts have likewise failed to examine thoroughly this relationship. The bulk of the legislative-studies literature has instead focused on the U.S. or European experiences—on the legislative process in the context of consolidated democracies in advanced industrial societies rather than of emerging democracies in poor, agrarian, and often culturally divided societies.[3] Although there has been some recent research on legislative development in Latin America and Asia, the work on Africa has been limited to a mere handful of case studies, none of which is comparative in scope. As a result, our theoretical understanding of legislative development in the context of emerging democracies, and of Africa in particular, is still at an early stage.

This essay seeks to fill that gap in scholarship and augment what we currently know about the relationship between the legislature and democratic consolidation by examining the legislatures of six African states. This comparative analysis of legislative development in Benin, Ghana, Kenya, Senegal, South Africa, and Uganda asks how and why some legislatures have evolved into effective and politically significant institutions while others have not. Although all these countries are electoral democracies, the quality of legislative performance and the extent to which it limits the power of the executive branch vary greatly across the six. One principal finding, however, is that if legislatures evolve into significant institutions of countervailing power—thereby contributing to democratization—it is for many reasons *other than* recurring "free and fair" elections.

Legislatures in democracies perform four core and unique functions that distinguish them from other political institutions and explain why they are an essential component in any democracy. First, legislatures are the institutional mechanism through which societies make representative governance real on a day-to-day basis. The first function of individual legislators—no matter what electoral system enabled them to win their seats—and the body to which they belong is to represent the varied and conflicting interests in society as a whole. The legislature is the institutional arena in which competing interests articulate and seek to advance their various objectives in the policy-making process. While the president in a democratic presidential system is also expected to "represent the people," he or she is not expected to act on behalf of particular constituencies' specific interests on a daily basis. Rather, presidents are expected to synthesize, balance, and aggregate interests, and to implement public policy.

Second, legislatures legislate—but at two levels. At a minimum they pass laws, in some cases merely rubber-stamping legislation handed down by the executive. In other cases, however, legislatures shape public policy by crafting legislation—in partnership with or independent of the executive branch—and then passing that legislation into law. It is important to remember that legislating in this broader sense is a process of collective action involving all members of the legislature, although clearly those in leadership positions play more prominent roles. This process often requires intense bargaining and complex compromises between rival interests.

The third core function of legislatures is to exercise oversight of the executive branch, thereby ensuring that policies agreed upon and passed into law are in fact implemented by the state. Oversight is essential to any democracy because it ensures both the vertical accountability of rulers to the ruled as well as the horizontal accountability of all other government agencies to the one branch—the legislature—whose primary function is to represent the citizens. Such scrutiny requires a measure of transparency in governmental operations.

Constituency service is the fourth and final among the legislature's principal tasks—or more accurately, the *legislators'* principal tasks. Unlike the first three, this function requires members to act as individuals rather than as part of a corporate organization that engages in collective decision making. In countries where legislators are elected from single-member districts (SMDs) or multimember districts (MMDs), and especially in Africa where most countries are still predominantly agrarian despite continual migration to towns, constituency service takes two forms: 1) lawmakers regularly visit their home districts to meet constituents and offer them assistance for individual needs; and 2) they support small- to medium-scale development projects that provide district residents with public goods such as roads, water-supply systems, schools, health clinics, and meeting halls. In countries where legislators are elected by proportional representation (PR), constituency service is a lesser priority, because members do not represent citizens on the basis of a shared place of residence.[4]

It is important to note that these core functions exist in tension with one another and that this tension is itself a defining and inherent feature of the legislature as an institution.[5] Representation requires members to advocate the particular concerns of their respective constituencies, while legislating requires bargaining and compromise across these and other interests, and therein lies a huge challenge. Similarly, there is tension between legislating and constituency service: The former seeks to arrive at decisions that serve the entire nation, whereas the latter by definition serves a smaller subsector of society. Oversight duties only sometimes come into conflict with the other core functions, depending on whose interests are at stake.

How individual legislators—and by extension, the legislature as a whole—choose to allocate their time across these four primary responsibilities may bring the intrinsic tensions into sharp relief. Deputies elected from SMDs and MMDs, especially in agrarian societies where political interests are often defined in local geographic terms, are under constant pressure from their constituents to attend to the needs of their districts. Legislative elections are largely referenda on the incumbents' ability to meet this expectation. This in turn leads legislators to spend far more time on constituent services than on legislating or oversight, the two functions that they perform on a collective basis. But there are consequences when members neglect their shared duties to focus mainly on constituent services: The legislature will exist in name only—a conglomeration of elected officials from separate constituencies who rarely act as a whole.

Changing the Incentives

Given these realities, a fundamental challenge to the development of effective legislatures in emerging African democracies is to find a way to restructure legislative incentives so that lawmakers can devote more time and effort to drafting and passing laws, as well as to oversight, without compromising their reputations for constituency service. This means changing the way in which African legislatures do business. As it stands, most still operate according to practices established during the period of one-party rule.

Prior to the reintroduction of multiparty politics in the early 1990s, the legislature had ceased to exist in countries under military rule, and it was merely an appendage of the executive where civilian rule continued. As such, African legislatures legislated only in the narrow sense—passing into law proposals prescribed by the executive, but not meaningfully participating in the creation of these proposals. Nor did lawmakers engage in oversight of the executive branch. Some countries, such as Kenya and Tanzania, maintained under the one-party format a system of semicompetitive elections in which two or more ruling-party candidates competed for office, much as they do in party primary elections in the United States. To the extent that deputies in such countries were elected to represent diverse constituencies, they fulfilled that responsibility, albeit weakly. The result was an asymmetrical allocation of effort to constituency service—the only function of the modern legislature that regimes of the period permitted assembly members to perform.

The scenario was nearly identical across Africa. More than a third of all deputies were appointed to an ever-expanding number of positions as ministers or assistant ministers in bloated administrations consisting of two- to three-dozen cabinet-level departments. Others were appointed to the boards of state-owned enterprises. As a result, few pursued a legislative career with an eye on policy making for the good of the nation. Rather, becoming a member of the legislature was viewed as an avenue to lucrative patronage jobs, a ministerial appointment being the most alluring among them. Those who won the coveted appointments were well compensated. Equally important, they gained access to an array of state resources that could be steered to their constituencies back home. Deputies paid for these positions with their allegiance. Their high-level appointments—and thus their ability to service their constituencies—hinged on their loyalty to the regime and its leader. Rarely, therefore, did they challenge the system or propose shifting more responsibility to the legislature of which they were still nominally members.

By contrast, those who remained on the back bench were barely able to meet their basic financial obligations, or even to pay for regular travel back to their constituencies. They were often dependent on cash handouts from the regime to maintain their local political base and to have any hope of winning reelection. Backbenchers also aspired to executive appointments. Either way, there was no reward for expanding their involvement in legislating or oversight.

The restoration of multiparty politics at the beginning of the 1990s changed the "rules of the game" in two respects. First, the legalization and legitimation of an opposition meant that there now existed a cadre of legislators whose interests and power were served by expanding the role of the legislature. Since members of the opposition do not shape public policy from within government, their only opportunity was to enhance the legislature's capacity both to legislate in the broad sense and to engage in effective oversight of the executive branch. Second, backbenchers now had motivation to support change for the same reason that members of the opposition did—they were poorly compensated and had little or no power vis-à-vis the executive. But by entering into informal coalitions with the opposition, they could expand both their terms of service and their power.

Building legislative capacity, however, was contingent on changes to the formal rules that structure legislative-executive relations as well as the provision of adequate resources both to the legislature as an institution and to its individual members. Indeed, without additional resources, deputies would be unable to take advantage of any rule change or to devote more time to legislation and oversight. Not surprisingly, ruling-party leaders, including presidents and most ministers, were averse to such changes and opposed the provision of more resources to the legislature.

The result in some countries—most notably in Kenya, but also in Uganda and to a much lesser extent in Ghana and South Africa—has been the emergence of "coalitions for change" within the legislature. These are informal groupings of deputies who want to alter the formal balance of power between the executive and the legislature and to increase the flow of resources to their institution and its members. Both are critical if members of parliament (MPs) are to devote more time to crafting legislation and oversight of the executive.

Changing the formal rules that specify the nature of executive-legislative relations requires either a constitutional amendment, the passage of specific legislation, or some combination of the two. Such rules determine the balance of power between the two branches of government by delineating the following: 1) whether the constitution defines the legislature as a fully separate and independent branch of government; 2) whether the executive can dissolve the legislature and call for new elections, or whether members of the legislature are elected for a fixed term; 3) whether the executive can suspend the sitting of the legislature; 4) whether the legislature can pass legislation without the assent of the president, and whether it can override a presidential veto; 5) whether the legislature can require senior members of the executive branch to testify before it about executive actions, and whether the legislature can subpoena official documents from the executive branch; 6) whether the legislature can set its own budget, including salaries for members and professional staff; 7) whether the legislature can recruit and maintain it own staff or must rely on secondments from the public service; 8) whether the legislature can negotiate the preparation of the national budget with the finance ministry and amend the final budget, or is restricted merely to approving or rejecting the budget; 9) whether there is a constituency development fund (CDF) to facilitate the provision of basic services on a constituency-by-constituency basis; and 10) whether members of the legislature are elected from SMDs or MMDs, PR, or some combination of the two.

The cumulative effect of these regulations is to tip the balance of power in favor of either the legislative or executive branch. Of these, the budgetary functions are arguably the most important in terms of blocking the emergence of an omnipotent executive. Where the legislature has a free hand in setting its own budget, it is obviously in a position to raise salaries for its members and staff. Moreover, it can make other expenditures necessary to cultivate an effective legislature. And where the legislature can amend the national budget, it becomes a full partner in the governing process.

Increasing Resources

In order to perform all four core functions effectively, legislatures require resources—financial, human, and physical. To keep their monopoly on power, however, African executives historically have starved their countries' legislatures of cash. In addition to revising the formal rules governing the scope of legislative action, legislatures must therefore also secure adequate funding. This has become a highly controversial area of reform, because even as some African legislatures are becoming meaningful actors in the policy-making process and a counterweight to the executive branch, there are hints of abuse.

Deputies in some countries—most notably Kenya, Uganda, and South Africa—have raised their salaries and granted themselves other perks such as health insurance, pensions, and allowances for travel to and from their constituencies. In Kenya, where members' salaries now exceed US$65,000 annually (the highest in Africa), criticism from the press has been severe. Public-opinion polls indicate that Kenyans have a negative perception of their National Assembly. Consequently, more than two-thirds of the members of the outgoing Ninth Parliament failed to retain their seats in the December 2007 elections. Yet since 1999, Kenya's parliament has implemented a broad series of constitutional and internal reforms, including the strengthening of its committee system, the revision of the Standing Orders (the Assembly's internal rules), and most recently, the establishment of a parliamentary budget office, known as the Office for Fiscal Analysis and Management. In the process, the Ninth Parliament arguably became one of the most effective legislatures on the continent.

In addition to monetary resources, African legislatures face a shortage of human resources, and the two go hand-in-hand. Most African legislatures, with the exception of South Africa's National Assembly, do not have the personnel needed to support a modern legislature. The number of professional staff (those with administrative, parliamentary, and/or policy experience) is small—often no more than one or two dozen individuals—compared to the many secretaries, messengers, drivers, janitors, and other nonprofessional support staff who often number in the hundreds. In this, most African legislatures resemble the bureaucracies prior to civil-service reform—bloated and often manned by individuals who obtained their posts through patronage rather than merit.

Restructuring and professionalizing the staff of the legislature, however, requires not only a will to reform but also sufficient money for adequate compensation. Before any change can occur, members of the legislature must first decide that such restructuring is essential to their institution if they are to carry out their core tasks. Second, they must assume authority over existing staff, which can be done by creating a separate parliamentary service (as in South Africa and Kenya), thereby separating legislative staff from the government civil service. In order to be effective mechanisms for legislation and oversight, committees, which are the heart of the modern legislature, must have expert support. This expansion of the legislature should be guided by a capable and competent managerial staff, recruited at the level of chief clerk and senior-deputy clerk. Finally, to the extent that resources permit, the parliamentarians themselves should maintain a professional staff, both at the capital and in their home districts. In some countries, this is already beginning to happen.

In addition to the dearth of adequate legislative staff, most African legislatures—again with the notable exceptions of Kenya, Uganda, and South Africa—have a woeful shortage of office and meeting space. In Ghana, for example, the National Assembly does not have enough rooms for the legislative committees to meet regularly. Most African legislatures cannot even provide offices for rank-and-file members. Likewise, district offices are almost nonexistent, yet are crucial if deputies are to maintain sustained direct or indirect contact with their constituents.

The transformation of the legislature also requires attention to the issue of campaign finance. African legislators are under intense pressure to provide constituency service, and their reelection depends on it. They are therefore on a neverending quest for funds to support visits back to their home districts and to provide assistance to their local communities in the form of public goods. The pursuit of cash is time-consuming and cuts into hours that could otherwise be devoted to legislation and oversight. Moreover, it renders legislators vulnerable to the enticements of executive patronage, which in turn hinders lawmakers' legislative independence. It is therefore not surprising that in some countries deputies have begun to devise new mechanisms intended to make them less dependent on well-funded patrons.

Most significant among these measures is the establishment of CDFs, which are direct transfers of budgeted funds from the central government to parliamentary districts for financing local development. They were first established in 2003 in Kenya, where they have proved immensely popular among both the public and legislators. A constituency committee, often chaired by the district's representative in parliament, allocates the funds to various projects within the constituency, according to guidelines published by the central government. Kenya's CDFs are now mandated to allocate 2.5 percent of the annual national budget. In 2006 and 2007, this disbursement amounted to roughly US$656,000 per constituency—enough to construct classrooms, health clinics, water systems, and other infrastructure needed in rural communities. Not surprisingly, Kenyan MPs want more. Lawmakers in Tanzania and Zambia established their own CDFs in 2007. A variation of this funding mechanism has also been established in Ghana, where 5 percent of the Regional Development Fund is set aside for reallocation to each parliamentary constituency within the region in question. Most legislators regard this as terribly inadequate.

All this requires the rapid expansion of the legislature's budget, which the executive invariably resists for the obvious reason that such capacity-building and financial support comes at the expense of executive power. For now, only South Africa provides both adequate staff and physical infrastructure for its legislature. This is partly a reflection of the country's relative wealth and government resources and partly a continuation of the level of support provided to parliamentarians during the apartheid era. It also stems from the South African leadership's commitment to democracy. Despite President Thabo Mbeki's reputation as a "centralizer," his government has lavishly funded the South African National Assembly and regularly sings its praises as "one of the cornerstones of our democracy." Without a significant financial boost, building modern legislatures in Africa will be difficult. Fortunately, a small number of countries are demonstrating that funding the legislature is fiscally feasible—and brings results. Yet financing alone does *not* a legislature make.

The Emergence of "Coalitions for Change"

The size, composition, and strength of the "coalitions for change" that have formed in many African legislatures vary greatly from one country to the next, but the following characteristics stand out. First, the number of committed activists involved in these coalitions remains small—no more than thirty to fifty in the legislatures considered in this essay, and sometimes as few as a dozen. Given that the size of these legislatures ranges from a low of 222 seats in Kenya to 400 in South Africa, this means that no more than a fifth to a quarter of all members, and often far fewer, join such coalitions.[6] Despite their low numbers, however, their impact can be profound. Second, the demand for change is articulated most forcefully by members of the opposition in alliance with a portion of ruling-party backbenchers. Third, and perhaps most important, these coalitions include both *reformers* and *opportunists*. That is to say, they are led by deputies who wish to enhance the institutional capacity of the legislature so that it can perform its core functions and advance the process of democratization generally; but they are joined by other members whose main motive is personal gain.

The issue of members' salaries nicely illustrates this distinction. Reformers recognize that better pay is an imperative step in professionalizing the legislature. Well-paid legislators are more likely to be impervious to the allure of executive patronage and more able to perform their entire portfolio of duties. Higher salaries also attract better-qualified candidates who desire to strengthen the institution. Opportunists, by contrast, simply want more money and the possibility of fulfilling their constituents' expectations. While opportunists are not particularly interested in bolstering the legislature as an institution, they do not oppose this goal either. Thus opportunists may have reasons of their own for joining the reformers, but often provide the votes that the reformers need to make the changes they seek. Whereas reformers are never more than an activist minority within the legislature, opportunists often include most members of the opposition and a significant number of ruling-party backbenchers. Without the presence and support of opportunists, reformers could never achieve their objectives.

What conditions or variables determine the size and power of these "coalitions for change," and what determines the size of its core component of "reformers"? The answer is hard to quantify; however, four groups of variables are clearly important. First, the composition of the legislature is key. Who are the reformers? African parliamentarians have historically enjoyed higher levels of income and education than the majority of the population; in other words, they are members of the elite. This is as true of the reformers as it is of the opportunists and opponents of reform. What sets apart the reformers from their peers is not status but ideas and values—the combination of genuine commitment to democratization and a familiarity with and sensitivity to political and economic global norms.

These are outward-looking personalities who analyze society and its institutions from a comparative, global perspective. For example, nearly all reformers are computer-literate and use the Internet, unlike most of their counterparts from the previous political generation who sustained the clientelist foundation of the one-party state. Many are also entrepreneurs in the private sector. They place a greater emphasis on performance than on loyalty cemented by patronage.

The reformers also constitute a "new political generation" of African legislators. They are not necessarily younger in terms of chronological age, although many are. Rather, it is their innovative outlook and approach that differentiate them. Notwithstanding these characteristics, they face the historic challenge of incumbent lawmakers across Africa: Half or more will likely be defeated when seeking reelection, and their prospects depend on their ability to provide constituency service rather than their ability to legislate or engage in executive oversight. The reformist cohort is not immune to this fate and is therefore marked by high turnover, which has eaten away at the core bloc of renegades, making their numbers ever smaller over time.

Finally, the number of reformers varies greatly from country to country, and seems to reflect the relative size and strength of civil society in each. The more urbanized and developed countries tend to have more robust civil societies and are more likely to have legislatures populated by reformers who seek to expand the powers of their institution. This may explain why Kenya's National Assembly has given rise to a viable and continuing coalition for change while the legislatures in Uganda, Benin, and Ghana have not. It may also explain why in Kenya civil society has begun to lobby the legislature through relevant committees to a greater degree than in the other countries included in this study.

A second major factor is the number of seats controlled by the ruling and opposition parties. Reform coalitions are more likely to emerge where there is near parity in the legislature. The reason should be obvious. When the ruling party and opposition parties hold nearly equal numbers of seats, a majority coalition can be formed by the opposition in alliance with a modest number of the ruling party's backbenchers. This is especially true where party identity and discipline are weak. Thus in Kenya during the Eighth Parliament (1997–2002) and in Ghana during the Third Parliament (2001–2004), reformers were able to organize effectively and commence the process of change, whereas this was not possible before parity. Conversely, where the ruling party commands an overwhelming majority, as in South Africa and Senegal, the prospects for expanding the powers of the legislature are limited.

The roles of legislative leadership positions and the character of those who assume them are also key variables. During the period of one-party rule, the roles of the presiding officer (the speaker) and the chief administrative officer (the clerk) conformed to the patronage-based systems of the era. Regime leaders handpicked loyalists for these positions. Their mandate was to keep the legislature compliant and to contain any mavericks seeking to broaden their powers, whether informally or de jure. Rather than being genuinely elected by their colleagues, these speakers were imposed. Rather than seeking to expand the array of services provided to lawmakers, clerks and their staffs were kept on a short leash and provided with few resources.

Even after the return to multiparty politics, the executive often expected that the speaker and clerk would continue to run the legislature as before. This created friction in some legislatures, including Kenya's and Tanzania's, where reformers sought to expand the capacity of the legislature but were repeatedly frustrated by the speaker. In Tanzania, the incumbent speaker retained his position for three terms before eventually retiring after the 2005 elections. His Kenyan counterpart likewise held the position for three terms until he was defeated in his bid for a fourth at the beginning of the Tenth Parliament in 2008. In both cases, the speaker had sought to transform his role from a watchdog for an executive opposed to change to a spokesperson for reform, albeit on his (that is, the government's) timetable.

In South Africa, Frene Ginwala, the first speaker of the National Assembly in the postapartheid era, had to tread a more tortuous path. She was expected to serve the leadership of the ruling African National Congress (ANC) and the executive first, and the legislature second.[7] Following the 1994 election that brought the first nonwhite government to power, Ginwala was faced with the challenge of organizing and presiding over a new legislature with four-hundred members, less than a fifth of whom had ever served before. In this role she was extremely supportive of the deputies, particularly the younger and less-educated members of the ruling party. Ginwala also had the delicate task of presiding over a highly competent holdover staff from the apartheid era. To her credit, she managed this aspect of the transition well. In addition, Ginwala was expected to ensure that ANC members toed the party line as laid down by the leadership. Many legislators, including several committee chairs (all of whom were members of the ANC), chafed under her control.

Finally, the type of electoral system—that is, how votes translate into seats—plays a huge role in determining the propensity or lack thereof for the formation of coalitions for change, especially among backbenchers of the ruling party. Where PR based on party-nominated candidate lists is used, as in South Africa and Namibia, the likelihood of rank-and-file parliamentarians joining a reform movement to challenge the executive is considerably less than in countries with single-member or small multimember districts.

Party discipline within the legislature is generally much stronger where closed-list PR is used, because PR gives the party leadership leverage against MPs who challenge the executive: Rebellious lawmakers can be punished with removal or demotion on the party list in the next election. In South Africa, where the ruling ANC periodically "redeploys" its members to different positions in the government, renegade members have been removed from the National Assembly in the middle of their terms. In 2000, the ANC chair of the Standing Committee on Public Accounts was removed and ultimately forced to resign from the National Assembly after his committee aggressively investigated alleged corruption in the granting of Ministry of Defense procurement contracts.

Contrary to conventional wisdom, cohesive and highly disciplined political parties do not always strengthen the legislature or ensure that it performs the core legislative functions effectively. Nelson Kasfir has noted this in the case of Uganda. Before the February 2006 parliamentary elections, when Uganda operated under the "movement" system and all MPs were members of the National Resistance Movement, the lines between government and opposition were blurred. During this period, a coalition for change emerged in the National Assembly and adopted several significant reforms, including a sizeable increase in deputies' salaries and the passage of legislation providing for their involvement in the budgetary process. The committee system was also strengthened, especially the Public Accounts Committee, the principal mechanism through which the National Assembly scrutinizes executive performance. President Yoweri Museveni and his government, though not enthusiastic about these developments, went along with this expansion of legislative power. However, after the restoration of "multipartism" in 2005, several parliamentarians who had been prominent in the coalition for change joined the opposition, thus drawing the president's ire and fortifying his determination to tame the legislature.

Measuring Performance

It is by no means an easy task to measure the performance and efficacy of legislatures, and space does not permit more than a cursory discussion here. It is nonetheless essential to develop at least some rudimentary measures of legislative performance lest there be no standard to gauge their development over time or to compare and explain why some have developed and others have not. To date, five methods have been used to measure legislative power or performance. The first is a relatively straightforward assessment of the formal powers of the legislature and its independence from the executive branch. This is the approach taken by M. Steven Fish and Michael Kroenig in their construction of the Parliamentary Powers Index (PPI).[8] Fish and Kroenig identify 32 such measures and survey a panel of at least five experts per country. They then tally the "yes" responses for each country. The more positive responses there are, the stronger the legislature.

Although the PPI also explains variations in Freedom House scores and demonstrates a clear relationship between the level of legislative power and the level of democracy, the index does not directly explore the extent to which the legislatures perform any of their four core functions. This type of functional assessment, however, could be carried out using the same panel approach developed by Fish and Kroenig and would reveal more about actual legislative performance than the PPI because of the tensions and tradeoffs arising from the performance of the four duties. In other words, one would expect that any given legislature might score high for one or two functions—say, constituency service and representation—but not for the others.

Yet another approach, and one preferred by this writer, would be to assess the quality of key components and actors in the legislative process. For example, a number of measures can and are being developed to assess the capacity and practice of the committee system. This area of inquiry is surprisingly absent in Fish and Kroenig's study. But most observers agree that a strong committee system is a key to whether or not a legislature is both powerful and effective—that is, how well it performs the core legislative responsibilities, including oversight. Other components of the process, such as the legislature's participation in making the budget, could also be evaluated. According to these standards, Kenya's National Assembly is one of the most powerful legislatures in Africa, whereas Fish and Kroenig—wrongly in the opinion of this writer—rank it among the least powerful.

A fourth approach, one that is often employed by students of the U.S. Congress, is to focus on the number and content of bills passed into law. While this approach attempts to measure directly the productivity of the legislature, it becomes mired in a host of methodological questions, including exactly what weight to assign to individual pieces of legislation. Not all bills that pass into law stand alone; some are "omnibus" laws that must be disaggregated to be properly assessed. Many of the disaggregated measures, however, are not of equal import. Moreover, how does one judge the relative significance or ultimate impact of individual pieces of legislation? This approach is fraught with difficulties yet is perhaps still worthwhile in that the crafting and passage of legislation constitute a defining legislative function.

Fifth and finally, there is what could be called the reputational approach—expert or citizen assessments of how well the legislature is performing its functions. Such measures, however, are subjective at best and may indeed tell us more about those giving their opinions than about the performance of the legislature itself.

Although legislative performance is uneven across the African continent, the legislature is emerging as a "player" in some countries. It has begun to initiate and modify laws to a degree never seen during the era of neopatrimonial rule or even in the early years after the return of multiparty politics. It checks the executive branch. It sometimes exerts meaningful oversight of the executive. And in some countries (Kenya, Malawi, and Nigeria), though not in others (Namibia and Uganda), it has blocked presidents from changing the constitution to repeal limits on presidential terms. Civil society and, increasingly, the business community have begun to lobby the legislature in some countries. In short, legislatures in Africa are beginning to matter. That said, there is no uniformity across Africa and we are only beginning to understand and explain the variations. Yet if the legislature is a defining institution of liberal democracy, then clearly more attention must be given to explaining its development and nurturing its growth.

NOTES

The comparative study on which this essay is based is fully reported in the author's edited volume, *Emerging Legislatures in Emerging African Democracies* (2009).

1. The two notable exceptions are: M. Steven Fish, "Stronger Legislatures, Stronger Democracies," *Journal of Democracy* 17 (January 2006): 5–20; and M. Steven Fish and Matthew Kroenig, *The Handbook of National Legislatures: A Global Survey* (New York: Cambridge University Press, 2009).

2. Terry Karl, "Imposing Consent: Electoralism versus Democratization in El Salvador," in Paul W. Drake and Eduardo Silva, eds., *Elections and Democratization in Latin America, 1980–1985* (San Diego: Center for Iberian and Latin American Studies, University of California Press, 1986), 9–36.

3. Gerald Gamm and John Huber, "Legislatures as Political Institutions: Beyond the Contemporary Congress," in Ira Katznelson and Helen V. Milner, eds., *Political Science: The State of the Discipline,* 3rd ed. (New York: Norton, 2002), 313–41.

4. It is therefore noteworthy that in South Africa, a country which employs PR, the ruling party found it necessary to establish a "shadow" system of single-member districts to which it assigns its MPs for the purpose of maintaining contact with the grassroots.

5. I am indebted to Shaheen Mozaffar for this insight.

6. The National Assembly of Benin, which is included in our study, has only 87 members. Regrettably, no identifiable group of reformers or "coalition for change" has emerged, and Benin has therefore been excluded from these estimates of the percentage of reformer-legislators. We also found no such coalition in Senegal.

7. She was also an ANC loyalist who aspired to a cabinet post.

8. Smith and Kroenig, *Handbook of National Legislatures.*

4

THE RULE OF LAW VERSUS THE BIG MAN

Larry Diamond

Larry Diamond *is senior fellow at the Hoover Institution and coeditor of the* Journal of Democracy. *This essay draws in part from his new book, This essay, which originally appeared in the April 2008 issue of the* Journal of Democracy, *draws in part from his book* The Spirit of Democracy: The Struggle to Build Free Societies Throughout the World *(2008).*

As the first three chapters in this book make clear, governance in Africa is in a state of transition, or some would say, suspension. Two powerful trends vie for dominance. One is the longstanding organization of African politics and states around autocratic personal rulers; highly centralized and overpowering presidencies; and steeply hierarchical, informal networks of patron-client relations that draw their symbolic and emotional glue from ethnic bonds. The other is the surge since 1990 of democratic impulses, principles, and institutions. Of course, the formal institutions of democracy—including free, fair, and competitive elections—can coexist with the informal practices of clientelism, corruption, ethnic mobilization, and personal rule by largely unchecked presidents. Indeed, much of the story of African politics over the last two decades has been the contest between these two approaches to power—even in countries that are formally democratic. But slowly, democracy, with its norms of freedom, participation, accountability, and transparency, is giving rise to new and more vigorous horizontal forms of organization, in both the state and civil society.

According to Freedom House, fully half the 48 states of sub-Saharan Africa (hereafter "Africa") are democracies today, but analysts will inevitably differ on whether the glass is half-full or half-empty. I am more worried than Richard Joseph that democratization is starting to lose momentum in Africa. Certainly Kenya's calamitous December 2007 election, which triggered horrific violence and ethnic cleansing that few analysts fully anticipated, shows that nothing can be taken for granted. As

Joseph and Kwasi Prempeh note, even the high-profile democracies in South Africa and Ghana are showing worrisome trends. Moreover, it is possible to argue that a number of the African countries Freedom House classifies as electoral democracies are really better scored as "competitive authoritarian states."[1]

Nevertheless, even if some of Africa's "democracies" hover in a gray zone between democracy and pseudodemocracy, the larger picture still represents historic progress. In the half-century since decolonization began, there have never been so many democracies and so much public pressure on democracy's behalf. Civil society has never been stronger, mass publics have never been so questioning and vigilant, and the natural impulse toward the reassertion of predatory personal rule has never faced so many constraints. Prempeh is right that these constraints remain weak relative to their counterparts in Europe and now parts of Asia and Latin America that are much more economically developed and better educated. Yet if we take Africa's history of abusive government as our measure, significant progress is evident.

Part of this progress is taking place at the level of specific democratic institutions. As Joel Barkan notes in his comparative analysis of six African legislatures, under certain circumstances, we see (even in Uganda's nondemocracy) the emergence of legislative coalitions for reform. These comprise legislators who (for varying motives) want to enhance their own branch's power relative to that of the executive. Doing so, he writes, entails institutional (and even constitutional) changes to give African legislatures significantly more resources, and more financial independence. The same is true for African judiciaries and other institutions of horizontal accountability, such as ombudsmen and anticorruption commissions. When these bodies have serious leaders, significant resources, and independent legal authority, they can begin to cut away at seemingly impregnable dynamics of predatory corruption and abuse of power. With leadership, resources, and authority, Joseph notes, the Economic and Financial Crimes Commission of Nigeria made unprecedented progress in prosecuting venal governors and other prominent public officials—until the country's new president reassigned the commission's chairman in late 2007.

When Africa's "second liberation" began in 1990, the continent was home to just three countries that could be called democracies (Botswana, Mauritius, and the Gambia) with a total population of only about three million. Between that year and 2008, more than twenty African countries made transitions to democracy or something near it.[2] Today, of the 24 African countries that Freedom House rates as democracies, eight are relatively "liberal," meaning that they score no worse than a 2 on FH's scales of political rights and civil liberties (where 1 is the most free and 7 the most repressive).

Between 2001 and 2007, twenty-two African countries experienced net improvements in their freedom scores (though some were by a small margins from very authoritarian starting points), while only nine countries suffered declines. In 2007 itself, however, eight African countries declined in freedom while only four gained. The most recent trend is moving slightly downward, then, but over the last six years African countries have continued improving in their levels of freedom and democracy, more than a decade after the onset of this democratic wave.

The picture looks worse, however, if we focus on Africa's biggest countries, the seven with populations above thirty million. South Africa is still a liberal democracy. None of the other six—Congo (Kinshasa), Ethiopia, Kenya, Nigeria, Sudan, and Tanzania—can be said to be a democracy at all.

Still, the general transformation of African politics has been extraordinary. Many of the electoral democracies that emerged after 1990—such as those in Benin, Mali, and South Africa—have persisted for more than a decade. Following two decades of rule under coupmaker Jerry Rawlings, Ghana has emerged as one of Africa's most liberal and vibrant democracies, reclaiming a leading position like that of its early postindependence years.

The positive trend is all the more remarkable when one looks at the many unlikely democratizers. They include four of the six poorest countries on the Human Development Index (Mali, Mozambique, Niger, and Sierra Leone) and several others in the bottom twenty (such as Benin, Burundi, Malawi, and Zambia), as well as four countries (Burundi, Liberia, Mozambique, and Sierra Leone) where democratization followed murderous civil conflicts, including the one in Burundi that left 200,000 dead.

Across Africa, the formal constitutional rules governing how leaders acquire and leave power are coming to matter more than ever before. As Daniel Posner and Daniel Young have shown, Africa's politics have grown less violent and more institutionalized since 1990.[3] Between that year and 2005, six presidents, including Uganda's Yoweri Museveni, succeeded in eviscerating term limits. But these cases were the minority. Powerful presidents such as Ghana's Rawlings and Kenya's Daniel arap Moi, joined eventually by ten others, ran into term-limit provisions that forced them to step down. After more than two decades in power, Rawlings and Moi were tempted to hang on, but yielded to domestic and international pressure. Three African leaders—including President Olusegun Obasanjo in Nigeria—tried hard and failed to extend their presidencies. Further, from the 1960s through the 1980s, more than two-thirds of African leaders left power violently—usually, as a result of a coup or assassination. During the 1990s, Posner and Young find, peaceful exits—principally as a result of electoral defeat or voluntary resignation—became the norm. Between 2000 and 2005, roughly four out of five African leaders were replaced this way.

Even more decisive than the rise of democracy has been the end of the one-party state. Since the 1990s, African elections have become increasingly regular and frequent, and almost all of them have been contested. As has been the case in Nigeria—and in Ethiopia, the Gambia, Kenya, Uganda, and Zimbabwe, among others—many of these elections have been brutally fought and outrageously rigged. But the sight of a ruling party or a "big man" losing is no longer quite so odd. Whereas only one African president was defeated at the polls between 1960 and 1990, incumbent presidents lost one out of every seven tries at reelection between 1990 and 2005.[4] Moreover, electoral alternation has significant positive effects on public support for and confidence in democracy.[5]

Why do African presidents feel more constrained now? Posner and Young advance two intriguing explanations. One is greater sensitivity to international pressure. The median level of foreign aid (relative to the overall economy) in countries where presidents did not attempt to secure third terms was almost twice as high as in those countries where the presidents did (and often succeeded). The other explanation points to public opinion. The nine African presidents who declined to seek a third term had narrower electoral mandates than the nine who did, suggesting a greater sensitivity to public opinion.

Building from the Bottom Up

This points to another positive trend in Africa, with potentially lasting consequences: the growth of civil society.[6] As wide varieties of associations independent of ruling parties have begun to engage in political dialogue and advocacy, demands for increased political accountability gain force, challenging and at times even preempting presidents inclined to flirt with the idea of staying in power. Some of these organizations—including many student associations, trade unions, religious bodies, and interest groups based on commercial, professional, and ethnic solidarities—date back to colonial days or the era just after independence. Yet active as well is a new generation of groups devoted explicitly to promoting democracy and good governance: think tanks, bar associations, human rights organizations, women's and civic-education groups, election-monitoring networks, and local as well as national-level development organizations.

More than ever, the building of democracy in Africa is a bottom-up affair. Nongovernmental organizations are teaching people their rights and duties as citizens, giving them the skills and confidence to demand answers from their rulers, to expose and challenge corruption, to resolve conflicts peacefully, to promote accommodation among ethnic and religious groups, to monitor government budgets and spending, to promote community development, and to recruit and train new political leaders. Civic groups and think tanks are also working at the national level to monitor elections, government budgets, and parliamentary deliberations; to expose waste, fraud, and abuses of power; and to lobby for legal reforms and institutional innovations to control corruption and improve the quality and transparency of governance.

These organizations draw strength not only from the funding and advice that international foundations and donors give them, but more importantly from their increasingly dense interactions with one another. The African Democracy Forum now links dozens of organizations from thirty countries on the basis of a common desire to advance the related causes of democracy and good governance.[7] Some African civil society organizations, most notably the Institute for Democracy in South Africa (IDASA), have reached a point of institutional maturity where they are now assisting democratic development elsewhere on the continent.

Also significant has been the growth of independent media and new information and communication technologies in Africa. The long tradition of independent daily newspapers has been enriched by a proliferation of news weeklies and community and cross-border radio stations. Many of the community stations focus on local-development and health issues, from agriculture to HIV/AIDS, but they also address political issues and compensate for their low-wattage signals with high-voltage independence. And some broadcast from exile as the last sources of credible information about the deplorable conditions in their own home countries. One of the best is SW Radio Africa. Accurately self-billed as the "Independent Voice of Zimbabwe," it left the air when the Mugabe regime succeeded in suppressing its signal with Chinese-provided jamming gear. Undaunted, the station then turned to live streaming and posting on the Internet.

Perhaps most revolutionary are the ways that digital technology is being used in Africa, even where few computers (not to mention broadband Internet access) can be found. One nonprofit organization, kiwanja. net, is making available free software—FrontlineSMS—that can be used by charities and NGOs to facilitate text-messaging via short-message service (SMS) on everything from crop, weather, and road conditions to health news and politics. "Originally developed for conservationists to keep in touch with communities in National Parks in South Africa, the system allows mass-messaging to mobile phones and crucially the ability [for recipients] to reply to a central computer."[8]

Then there is the mobile phone, whose beauty is its versatility and astonishingly rapid empowerment of even poor individuals. Today, more than 30 million Nigerians (nearly one in every four) own a mobile phone. In Africa as a whole, the number of mobile users is believed to be approaching 300 million.[9] This rapid spread has enabled quantum leaps forward in election monitoring. In Nigeria in April 2007, millions of ordinary citizens instantly became election monitors by reporting what they saw (much of it bad, unfortunately) at the polls. The profusion of evidence did not stop massive rigging, but it may be helping to provide the legal basis for court challenges to overturn some of the cheating's effects.

The abovementioned FrontlineSMS technology is the brainchild of intrepid British anthropologist and programmer Ken Banks. Now being revised with support from the MacArthur Foundation, FrontlineSMS has also served to facilitate feedback to community radio programs in South Africa, to monitor voting in the Philippines, to send "security alerts to fieldworkers in Afghanistan [and] market prices to smallholder farmers in Aceh, and to circumvent government restrictions in countries including Zimbabwe and Pakistan."[10] Increasingly in Africa, and around the world, text-messaging will give citizens, NGOs, and community radio stations a powerful tool not only to extend their reach and connect people in ways that enhance development, but to monitor what governments do, document human rights abuses as they happen, and facilitate civic organization and demonstrations.

As text-messaging gains momentum in Africa, it will probably encounter a technological challenge from its biggest global nemesis, the communist regime in China. The rulers of the People's Republic are continually and desperately looking for ways to contain and disrupt any uncontrolled citizen activity that takes on a political edge. African dictatorships can be expected to call on Beijing for help in fighting this new tool for promoting democratic mobilization. African civil societies, meanwhile, can be expected to look for ways around the control mechanisms—one hopes with plenty of technical support from sympathetic actors in international civil society.

Coinciding with the flowering of civil society has been a visible public demand for and appreciation of democracy. When surveyed by the Afrobarometer in 2005 and 2006, an average of 62 percent of the public in eighteen countries said that "democracy is preferable to any other kind of government."[11] Levels of support for democracy ran as high as 75 percent in Ghana, Kenya, and Senegal, and reached 65 percent or higher in ten of the countries surveyed. In fact, in only a few African countries can one find much of an avowed appetite for any specific form of authoritarian rule, and never does it rise above a fifth of the population. Moreover, this is not just an abstract commitment to democracy in general. Four out of five Africans surveyed believe that "regular, open, and honest elections" are the only way to choose their country's leaders, and two-thirds agree that elected assemblies (not the president) should make the laws in the country, even if the president disagrees with them.[12] Only about one in six Africans, on average, expresses a positive preference for an authoritarian option such as military or one-party rule. And a slight majority (52 percent) actively rejects all three authoritarian options offered.

Africans' support for democracy seems to flow from something other than a naïve sense that democracy must spell quick economic progress. When asked to define what democracy means to them, "a majority of Africans interviewed (54 percent) regard it in procedural terms by referring to the protection of civil liberties, participation in decision making, voting in elections, and governance reforms."[13] And when asked whether they felt that their system of electoral democracy "should be given more time to deal with inherited problems" or instead, if it "cannot produce results soon, we should try another form of government," 56 percent of Africans in 2005–2006 chose to give democracy more time. This represents a significant increase in patience with democracy since 2000.

Michael Bratton notes that while the demand for democracy is proving fairly resilient in Africa, the perceived supply is more questionable. For example, while 81 percent of Africans want free and fair elections that can remove incumbents, only 47 percent think they are getting this in their countries. Two-thirds of Africans want their president to be subject to the rule of law, but barely a third (36 percent) thinks that he is.[14] Clearly, Africans value and demand democracy—but African parties and politicians are not meeting citizens' aspirations.

Consequently, disillusionment is rising. Between 2000 and 2005, satisfaction with the way democracy works declined an average of 13 percentage points (from 58 to 45 percent) across the countries surveyed While satisfaction rose in a few relatively well-functioning democracies such as Ghana and South Africa, it declined in eight of the twelve countries surveyed both times. Nevertheless, even on the supply side there are cautious grounds for optimism. The perception that one's own country is a democracy has held constant at around 50 percent, and 54 percent think it is likely that their country will remain a democracy.[15] Nor are the problematic numbers set in stone. On the contrary, there is evidence that actually delivering democracy can dramatically improve citizen attitudes and perceptions. Analyzing the 2005 data, Bratton found that respondents' perception of the most recent national election as free and fair was the most powerful predictor of their readiness to agree that their countries were democracies. In other words, the ruler's performance is no longer enough to satisfy the public—formal institutions are starting to matter more than informal ones.[16]

The Deadening Hand of Personal Rule

These trends, hopeful as they are, nonetheless tell only part of the story. Countries such as Cameroon, Eritrea, Ethiopia, Gabon, Sudan, and Togo remained trapped in longstanding patterns of authoritarian rule. Nigeria, Uganda under the increasingly corrupt Museveni, and now Kenya have been slipping backwards. And in Zimbabwe, deepening repression is morphing into a psychosis of authoritarian misrule under an aging dictator, Robert Mugabe, who seems increasingly detached from reality as his country's economy collapses amid hyperinflation that his policies have bred.

No less worrisome are the poor governance, persistent corruption, and stubborn personalism that so often continue to beset Africa's democracies. Of the six measures that the World Bank Institute uses to gauge the quality of governance in a country, the one known as "voice and accountability" (which includes freedom of expression and citizen participation in selecting the government) is a rough and partial surrogate for democracy. The others measure political stability and the absence of violence; the effectiveness of public services and administration; whether or not public regulations "permit and promote private sector development"; the rule of law (including the quality of policing and the courts); and control of corruption.

Africa does poorly on all these measures. On average, it ranks in the thirtieth percentile—a little better on the political measures of accountability and stability, but slightly worse on the measures of rule of law, corruption control, regulatory quality, and governmental effectiveness. On these latter four measures, which I collect together as a gauge of "state quality," Africa's mean percentile ranking, twenty-eighth, trails well behind Eastern Europe (fifty-ninth), Latin America and East Asia (forty-seventh), the Middle East (forty-second), and even South Asia (thirty-sixth).

Save for South Africa, the other six largest countries in Africa rank very low in their quality of governance. Five of the six have worse governance than the continent as a whole, and three of them dismally so. Across all six measures, Nigeria ranks in the thirteenth percentile. On rule of law plus control of corruption and political stability plus control of violence, only 5 percent of countries score worse. Ethiopia ranks in the eighteenth percentile, Sudan in the fifth, Congo (Kinshasa) in the third. Kenya and Tanzania do better, at the twenty-sixth and thirty-sixth percentiles, respectively, but Kenya still scores below the African average.

Underlying these painful figures is the continuing neopatrimonial character of politics in Africa. Experts call postcolonial African states *neo*patrimonial because they combine the forms of a modern bureaucratic state—constrained in theory by laws, constitutions, and other impersonal rules and standards—with the informal reality of personalized, unaccountable power and pervasive patron-client ties. These ties radiate out and down from the biggest "big man"—the autocratic president—to his lieutenants and allies, who in turn serve as patrons to lower-level power brokers, and down to the fragmented mass of ordinary citizens, who are trapped by their dependence on local political patrons.

In such systems, the informal always trumps the formal. Subordinates owe loyalty to their personal patrons, not to laws and institutions. Presidents and their minions use state resources as a personal slush fund to maintain political dominance, giving their clients state offices, jobs, licenses, contracts, vehicles, bribes, and other access to illicit rents, while getting unconditional support in return.[17] State offices at every level become permits to loot, either for an individual or a somewhat wider network of family members, ethnic kin, political clients, and business cronies.[18] Corruption, clientelism, and personal rule thus seep into the culture, making the system even more resilient. In Africa, contending patron-client networks organize along ethnic or subethnic lines, and the president sees his ethnic kin as the most reliable loyalists in the struggle for power. This makes the system particularly unstable, as conflicts over pelf, power, and identity mix in a volatile, even explosive brew.[19] The typical African pattern of concentrating extreme power in the presidency makes politics even more of a tense, zero-sum game. This helps to explain how a single rigged election can ignite the paroxysms of violence and ethnic cleansing that a horrified world has been watching lately in Kenya, where ethnic groups that have been shut out of the presidency ever since independence nurse deep anger.

The fundamental purpose of neopatrimonial governments is not to produce *public* goods—roads, bridges, markets, irrigation, education, health care, public sanitation, clean drinking water, effective legal systems—that increase productivity, improve human capital, stimulate investment, and generate development. The point of neopatrimonialism, rather, is to produce *private* goods for those with access to power. Contracts are granted not on the basis of who can deliver the best service for the lowest price, but rather on who will pay the biggest bribe. Budgets are steered to projects that can readily generate bribes. Government funds disappear into the overseas accounts of officeholders. Public payrolls are swollen with the ranks of phantom workers and soldiers whose pay goes into the pockets of higher-ups.

One thing that can arrest the decay and refresh the system is a change in leadership. But a key feature of the neopatrimonial system is the way the "king of the hill" hangs on and on. In 2005, Uganda's President Museveni, whose original claim to his office was being the top general of the strongest private army in his conflict-wracked homeland, "openly bribed members of parliament, blackmailed and intimidated others to amend the constitution and remove term limits on the presidency so that he can run again, and again, and again."[20] In the run-up to the February 2006 election, he stepped up his harassment of the independent media and those elements of civil society that he had not already coopted. Then he jailed the main opposition presidential candidate, before finally claiming a highly suspect first-round victory through apparent manipulation of the vote count.[21]

Museveni's two decades in power hardly make him Africa's longest-serving president, however. Omar Bongo of small but oil-rich Gabon in West Africa has ruled for nearly four decades. Robert Mugabe's merciless reign in Zimbabwe has stretched past a quarter-century. In Angola, Cameroon, and Guinea, presidents have also ruled for well over twenty years, and in Burkina Faso for nearly that. Sudan's Hassan al-Bashir has held power for eighteen years, and Meles Zenawi in Ethiopia and Yahya Jammeh in the Gambia for more than a decade each. None of them shows any sign of surrendering office. Of course, such prolonged personal reigns are hardly new in Africa—witness the late Mobutu Sese Seko's 32 years in power in Zaire, now Congo (Kinshasa)—but they have always been associated with national decline, if not disaster.

If Africa is now suspended between democracy and personal rule, what can tip it toward democracy? The deciding factor will not be economic development. For probably decades to come, much of Africa will remain well below the high level of development that seems to assure democratic survival. Steady economic growth can help to give people more confidence in democracy, building up its long-term legitimacy. But sustainable development has been stymied by the same factor that has undermined democracy itself: bad governance. If both democracy and development are to have a future in Africa, the core priority must be to improve the quality of governance.

Social scientists often lament their lack of adequate understanding of the policy challenges of our time, calling for more research. We do need to understand better how winning coalitions can be generated and sustained for the kinds of institutional reforms that will gain traction on Africa's core problem of bad, corrupt, abusive governance. But broadly, we know where the answers lie. Countervailing institutions of power—the judiciary, the legislature, and the whole apparatus of countercorruption, audit, human rights, and other oversight bodies that are sometimes called a "fourth branch of government"—must be greatly strengthened in their political autonomy, statutory authority, and financial and human resources. Power and resources must be decentralized down to elected lower levels of government, ideally (in any large country) through a federal system (the one saving grace that has held Nigeria together). Political parties must themselves be democratized internally and made more effective as organizations, independent of ethnicity or personal ties. Elections must be truly free and fair, and thus electoral administrations must be made up of career civil-service professionals who, as in India, have the training, resources, autonomy, and *esprit de corps* to resist partisan pressures. State economic ownership and control must be diminished, but the state must be strengthened in its capacity to deliver its essential mission of managing the economy and generating the public goods (such as schools, roads, courts, markets, and other infrastructure) needed for development. And citizens must have the freedom to monitor and report on what government does, and to organize to challenge it and pursue their interests.

It is not difficult to find, in African civil societies and in the state itself, numerous actors ready to rise to the challenge. The problem is that African leaders are not generally to be found among these coalitions for reform, because they calculate that their own interests lie not in reform, but in building or reinforcing monopolies of power and wealth. Of course, in the absence of democracy, it is always the monopolists who triumph. But democracy in itself is no guarantee against the resurgence of many bad practices.

For much of the last half-century (and well before that of course, under colonial rule), the missing link has been the international community, which has been only too happy to embrace any African despot in the quest for resources and strategic advantage. Idealists, by contrast, have thought that the answer lies in "foreign aid," which is supposed to make up for the vast shortages of financial resources needed to deliver health, education, and roads. About US$600 billion later, we know (or at least we *should* know) that pouring more aid unconditionally on bad governments is like pouring gasoline on a fire. In the circumstances of predatory rule in Africa, aid functions like the revenue that gushes in from oil exports—it is just another source of external rents that enables rulers to float on a cushion above their societies, controlling the state without having to answer to their own people.

Certainly Richard Joseph is correct that the entry of China into the "great game" of aid, investment, and resources in Africa creates a new context, in some ways akin to the superpower competition of the Cold War. And the "new cold war" against international terrorism has not helped. Both developments have given African authoritarian regimes new alternatives and new forms of leverage against Western pressure for democratic reform. But this is not the 1960s or 1970s. African societies are informed and autonomously organized as never before. Africans are aware of their political rights and demanding of democracy as never before. And together, Europe and the United States still provide the vast bulk of aid and investment in Africa.

Most of all, principled pressure is needed from international actors, tying substantial flows of development assistance to concrete institutional improvements in governance. Donors can also provide generous financial and technical assistance to the institutions of governance— African legislatures, judiciaries, countercorruption commissions, and other agencies of horizontal accountability—that must work well if the balance is to tip from autocracy to democracy. It is the very fluidity of things on the continent today—so powerfully evoked by Joseph's concept of "frontier Africa"—that makes so much possible. From the experience of a small but growing number of better-functioning African democracies, we know that the continent is not condemned to perpetual misrule. The challenge now is for the international donors to join with Africans in demanding that their governments be truly accountable.

NOTES

1. Steven Levitsky and Lucan Way, *Competitive Authoritarianism: International Linkage, Organizational Power, and the Fate of Hybrid Regimes* (Cambridge University Press, forthcoming). They classify countries on the basis of their respective regimes during the period 1990–95, and then track their evolution. On this basis, they classify Benin, Malawi, Mozambique, and Zambia all as competitive authoritarian regimes, whereas other analyses (including that of Freedom House) often have considered them democracies. I exclude the Central African Republic because of its very poor freedom score, average 5 on the two seven-point scales of Freedom House.

2. The Gambia, whose politics had been dominated for almost thirty years by one leader

and his party, slipped entirely from democratic ranks after a military coup in 1994. Retrospectively, some analysts have questioned just how democratic the Gambia was at that point.

3. Daniel N. Posner and Daniel J. Young, "The Institutionalization of Political Power in Africa," *Journal of Democracy* 18 (July 2007): 126–40.

4. Posner and Young, "Institutionalization of Political Power in Africa," 131.

5. Michael Bratton, "The 'Alternation Effect' in Africa," *Journal of Democracy* 15 (October 2004): 147–58.

6. The evidence and arguments here are developed at greater length in Larry Diamond, *Developing Democracy: Toward Consolidation* (Baltimore: Johns Hopkins University Press, 1999), ch. 6.

7. See *www.africandemocracyforum.org*.

8. "Texts Monitor Nigerian Elections," BBC News, 20 April 2007. Available at *http:// news.bbc.co.uk/2/hi/technology/6570919.stm*.

9. This would probably represent something like 30 percent of the roughly 750 million people in sub-Saharan Africa, even allowing for some people owning multiple devices.

10. From *http://frontlinesms.kiwanja.net*.

11. Most of the data presented here from the Afrobarometer is available in the publications of the project, at *www.afrobarometer.org/publications.html*. See in particular, "The Status of Democracy, 2005–2006: Findings from Afrobarometer Round 3 for 18 Countries," Afrobarometer Briefing Paper No. 40, June 2006.

12. Michael Bratton, "The Democracy Barometers: Formal versus Informal Institutions in Africa," *Journal of Democracy* 18 (July 2007): 96–110.

13. Michael Bratton, Robert Mattes, and E. Gyimah-Boadi, *Public Opinion, Democracy, and Market Reform in Africa* (Cambridge: Cambridge University Press, 2005), 69–70.

14. Bratton, "Democracy Barometers: Formal versus Informal," Figure 2, 106.

15. Bratton, "Democracy Barometers: Formal versus Informal," 102.

16. Bratton, "Democracy Barometers: Formal versus Informal," Table 2, 107.

17. Michael Bratton and Nicolas van de Walle, *Democratic Experiments in Africa: Regime Transitions in Comparative Perspective* (Cambridge: Cambridge University Press, 1997), 61–68; Robert H. Jackson and Carl G. Rosberg, *Personal Rule in Black Africa: Prince, Autocrat, Prophet, Tyrant* (Berkeley: University of California Press, 1982), 38–42.

18. Drawing on Max Weber, Joseph has called such systems "prebendal." Richard A. Joseph, *Democracy and Prebendal Politics in Nigeria: The Rise and Fall of the Second Republic* (Cambridge: Cambridge University Press, 1987), 6; see also 55–68 for elaboration of the concept and its relationship to clientelism.

19. Joseph, *Democracy and Prebendal Politics in Nigeria,* 8. This work develops these themes at length.

20. Andew Mwenda, "Please Stop Helping Us," paper presented to the Novartis Foundation, 12 August 2006, 3.

21. Andrew Mwenda, "Personalizing Power in Uganda," *Journal of Democracy* 18 (July 2007): 23–37.

5

THE INSTITUTIONALIZATION OF POLITICAL POWER IN AFRICA

Daniel N. Posner and Daniel J. Young

Daniel N. Posner *is associate professor of political science at the University of California–Los Angeles (UCLA) and author of* Institutions and Ethnic Politics in Africa *(2005) and coauthor of* Coethnicity *(2009).* **Daniel J. Young** *is assistant professor of political science at Georgia State University. This essay originally appeared in the July 2007 issue of the* Journal of Democracy.

On 16 May 2006, after months of intense and divisive national debate, the Senate of Nigeria rejected a bill which would have changed that country's constitution to permit President Olusegun Obasanjo a third term in office. By asserting the supremacy of the constitution (with its two-term limit) over the desires of President Obasanjo's supporters that the popular leader be permitted to run for a third term, the Senate's vote marked a watershed in Nigeria's political history. As important as the outcome was the way in which the conflict was resolved—by the votes of duly elected legislators rather than through force or the threat of same. Given that Nigeria's First and Second Republics (1963–66 and 1979–83) were overthrown by military coups, the settlement of this political struggle via the Senate chamber rather than the gun barrel represents a major shift in the way that decisions over executive tenure in Nigeria have been made.[1]

Both the outcome of Obasanjo's third-term campaign and the process through which it was reached signal a growing trend in sub-Saharan Africa: The formal rules of the game are beginning to matter in ways that they previously have not. Scholarly and popular writers alike have traditionally depicted Africa as a place where formal institutional rules are largely irrelevant. Although every African country has a constitution as well as a body of laws and administrative procedures that place formal limits on executive power, the long-held consensus among observers has been that these rules play little role in actually constraining leaders' behavior. This view is reflected in the "personal rule" or "Big Man" paradigm that has dominated the study of African politics for the past

FIGURE 1—HOW AFRICAN LEADERS HAVE LEFT POWER, BY DECADE

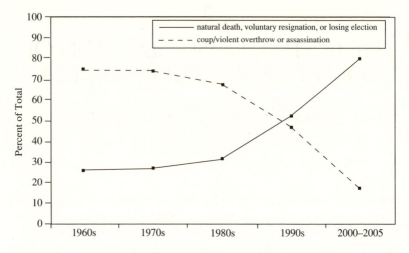

thirty years. This paradigm's foundational idea is that personal relation-ships are more important than formal rules and that a leader's decisions will always take precedence over the laws that those decisions might contradict. The field's conventional wisdom has been that rules do not shape leaders' behavior; leaders' behavior trumps rules.

The significance of the Nigerian Senate's actions must be seen against the backdrop of this entrenched view. Contrary to depictions of African politics as "not beholden to formal procedures but to personal decisions," President Obasanjo was forced by the rules of the game (the constitution) to accept something other than his preferred outcome.[2] Also, contrary to portrayals of political conduct in Africa as "governed by the awareness that constitutional rules or administrative regulations can, and probably ought, to be evaded,"[3] both supporters and opponents of the president's bid for a third term sought to achieve their goals by working through, not around, formal institutional channels. Although these efforts did involve attempts to bribe and otherwise influence the governors and senators who would vote on the third-term issue, what is more important is that the actors whose support was being sought were politicians—people whose influence stems from their position within the formal political system—rather than soldiers or other elements operating outside of it.

Across sub-Saharan Africa, formal institutional rules are coming to matter much more than they used to, and have displaced violence as the primary source of constraints on executive behavior. From de-colonization in the early 1960s through the 1980s, most African rulers left office through a coup, assassination, or some other form of violent overthrow. Since 1990, however, the majority have left through insti-tutionalized means—chiefly through voluntary resignation at the end of a constitutionally defined term or by losing an election. Elections

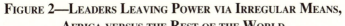

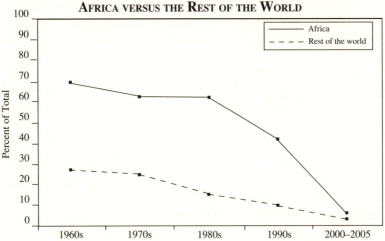

FIGURE 2—LEADERS LEAVING POWER VIA IRREGULAR MEANS, AFRICA VERSUS THE REST OF THE WORLD

are also becoming more important as a mechanism for selecting leaders in Africa, as reflected in the large increase in both their number and their competitiveness. The fact that incumbents still almost always win, however, underscores that the major challenge connected with the task of limiting presidential power in Africa today is not so much promoting elections as making certain that leaders adhere to constitutional limits on their continued eligibility to contest them.

Some African leaders have managed to circumvent restrictions on seeking more than two terms in office, yet have done so through formal institutional channels rather than extraconstitutional means. Thus, while institutional rules may not yet always determine outcomes in Africa today, such rules are consistently and dependably affecting the strategies through which those outcomes are reached. This represents a major change in how power is exercised, and it challenges us to ask again whether the Big Man still bestrides the world of African politics with as much ease as he once did.

How Leaders Exit Power

During its first decade after independence in 1960, the small West African country of Benin had no fewer than twelve heads of state, every one of whom was overthrown in a coup d'état. This striking record of serial leadership change by force stands in complete contrast to Benin's record since 1990. From that date to 2006, Mathieu Kérékou and Nicéphore Soglo alternated as president following wins and losses in national elections. Moreover, both men have refrained from running for terms beyond those allowed by constitutional limits.[4] While Benin provides perhaps the most dramatic example of the change that has taken place in how leaders leave power in Africa, it is nonetheless indicative of a broader trend.

To document this trend, we have collected data on how every African head of state exited power between independence and the end of 2005. Our sample includes some 227 leaders from 46 sub-Saharan African countries.[5] We coded each leader's means of exit from office into one of five categories: coup or violent overthrow (including civil war); assassination; natural death; voluntary resignation; and losing an election. We further grouped these categories into two broader classes of cases: those in which leaders left power through regular means (which include natural death, voluntary resignation, or losing an election) and those in which leaders were removed by irregular means (coup or violent overthrow, or assassination). Figure 1 presents the decade-by-decade averages.

As Figure 1 makes clear, nearly three-quarters of the African leaders who left power in the 1960s and 1970s did so through a coup, violent overthrow, or assassination (depicted by the dashed line). In the 1980s, this dropped to just below 70 percent, and by the 1990s it was surpassed by the share of those who left power through natural death, voluntary resignation, or electoral defeat (depicted by the solid line). Between 2000 and 2005, the share of leaders leaving power through irregular means dropped to just 19 percent. Whereas the modal means by which heads of state in Africa left office used to be coup or assassination, it is now voluntary resignation, in most cases triggered by constitutional term limits (9 of the 17 cases between 2000 and 2005).

Another way of looking at this transformation is to compare Africa with the rest of the world. To do this, we use data from the Archigos project, which codes the way that heads of state in every independent country in the world entered and exited power between 1875 and 2004.[6] This comparison, seen in Figure 2, reveals a remarkable degree of convergence. With respect to how leaders leave power, Africa (depicted by the solid line) used to be truly a place unto itself—a place befitting its own theories about politics and power.[7] Yet by the first years of the current century, Africa had joined the rest of the world. Whereas African leaders were two to three times more likely than leaders elsewhere in the world to leave power by violent means in the 1960s, 1970s, and 1980s, they are equally likely—or to be more precise, equally *unlikely*— to leave power under violent circumstances today.[8]

These trends point to the increasing institutionalization of political power in Africa. Whereas political power used to change hands principally through violence—at a time and in a manner chosen by coup plotters—it now changes hands principally in accord with institutional rules. Of course, the manner in which executives leave office is only one indicator of how beholden they are to formal constraints in their exercise of power more generally. It says nothing, for example, about the extent to which they adhere to objective procedures when they allocate jobs, award contracts, enforce regulations, or exercise other powers of office. Nonetheless, whether a leader departs office via regular as opposed to irregular means is critical. A regular departure means that there is an understood set of basic limits on how long a head of state may stay in power, as well as on how his opponents may seek to replace him. It therefore marks the most important step toward restraining executive power and institutionalizing political authority more broadly.

One of the clearest manifestations of the increasing institutionaliza-tion of executive power in Africa is the increasing importance of elec-tions. Elections have been held in Africa since the independence era, albeit sometimes only intermittently and with varying degrees of contes-tation. Even so, both the total number of elections held per decade and the share of elections that are meaningfully contested have risen over time, particularly since the early 1990s.

In the 1960s and 1970s, sub-Sarahan Africa saw an average of 28 elections per decade. That number climbed slightly to 36 in the 1980s, and then shot up to 65 in the 1990s, a decade that began auspiciously with the national-conference movement in Benin and the beginning of the end of apartheid in South Africa. From 2000 through the end of 2005, 41 elections had already been held in Africa, and thus this up-ward trend appears to be continuing. This pattern is largely a product of two developments. First, countries such as Malawi that did not hold elections in the immediate postindependence period have begun to hold them. Second, countries such as Togo that once held sporadic elections have begun to regularize their electoral processes.[9]

Elections are also becoming more intensely contested.[10] In only two of the 26 presidential elections held in Africa in the 1960s did the in-cumbent actually face an opponent. The vast majority of presidential elections during this period were little more than plebiscites or grass-roots-mobilization exercises in which the head of state stood no risk of losing power. By the 1990s, however, more than 90 percent of presiden-tial elections were contested, and by the 2000–2005 period, this share had risen to 98 percent. This dramatic change reflects the growing rec-ognition by African leaders that, to maintain their legitimacy in the eyes of both their own citizens and the international community, they must subject themselves to elections in which opponents have at least a theo-retical possibility of winning.

Permitting a challenger to run, however, is not the same thing as put-ting oneself at real risk of losing power. In many cases, African leaders who bowed to popular or international pressure to hold contested elec-tions found ways of rigging them so that the contests never brought a meaningful risk that the incumbent would be unseated. Nonetheless, our data suggest that such rigging is becoming harder to accomplish. When we compare across decades the reelection rates of presidents who per-mitted challengers to run against them, we find that elections in Africa are not only becoming more often contested but also more robustly com-petitive. During the entire period between 1960 and 1990, only one Afri-

FIGURE 3—PRESIDENTIAL-TERM LIMITS IN AFRICA, 1990–2005

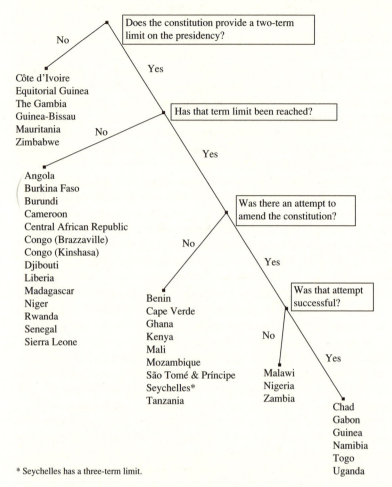

* Seychelles has a three-term limit.

can president lost an election—Aden Abdullah Osman of Somalia, who was defeated by challenger Abdirashid Ali Shermarke in 1967.[11] Since 1990, the loss rate of incumbents has risen to a modest but nonetheless meaningful 14 percent (incumbents lost 14 times in 100 opportunities). African presidents today are thus more than twice as likely to lose power if they subject themselves to contested elections than they were before 1990, when the loss rate was just over 6 percent (just a single electoral defeat in 16 contested elections).

Despite this trend of increasing competitiveness, however, the more important point to underscore is that African leaders who want to stay in power are usually able to do so, even if they allow competitive elections. Incumbent presidents in Africa today still win reelection more than 85 percent of the time. The advantages of incumbency in Africa are so great that elections alone—even free and fair elections—are not enough to put meaningful limits on presidential power. The institutionalization of political power thus depends less on whether sitting presidents are willing to permit challengers to run against them than on whether incumbents will stand down (thereby forgoing likely reelection) when they have completed as many terms as their respective countries' constitutional laws allow.[12]

Third-Term Experiences

Since 1990, more than three dozen African countries have adopted new constitutions, the vast majority of which have included prohibitions against a president serving more than two terms. Figure 3 sorts the region's countries into five categories depending on four factors: 1) whether or not their post-1990 constitution puts a two-term limit on the presidency; 2) whether at any point between 1990 and 2005 that term limit had been reached; 3) whether, if reached, an attempt was made to amend the constitution to overturn the limit; and 4) whether that attempt succeeded.[13]

As Figure 3 shows, eighteen African presidents during this period found themselves in the position of having completed two terms and being constitutionally barred from seeking a third.[14] These incumbents had three options: 1) abide by the constitutional term limit and stand down; 2) attempt to change the constitution to permit a third term; or 3) scrap the constitution altogether and prolong their tenure through extraconstitutional means. No African leader has thus far taken this third course, which indicates just how much has changed in the region. In the 1960s and 1970s, it was commonplace for leaders who wanted to perpetuate their rule to have themselves declared "president for life"—as did the Central African Republic's Jean-Bédel Bokassa (who later promoted himself to "emperor"), Equatorial Guinea's Francisco Macías Nguema, Ghana's Kwame Nkrumah, Malawi's Hastings Kamuzu Banda, Togo's Gnassingbé Eyadéma, Uganda's Idi Amin, and Zaire's Mobutu Sese Seko. Today that option would appear to be closed.

All eighteen directly elected presidents who faced term limits heard strong calls from their supporters to find a way to stay in power. Nine of these chief executives—Kérékou of Benin, António Monteiro of Cape Verde, Jerry Rawlings of Ghana, Daniel arap Moi of Kenya, Alpha Konaré of Mali, Joaquim Chissano of Mozambique, Miguel Trovoada of São Tomé and Príncipe, France Albert René of Seychelles, and Benjamin Mkapa of Tanzania—resisted these appeals and announced that they would abide by their countries' constitutions and refrain from seeking a third term. It is unclear whether this was because these leaders feared that they lacked the votes needed to change the constitution, were wary of the concerted opposition that they would face, worried that they might lose a third election, or simply believed that abiding by the constitution was the right thing to do. The answer almost certainly lies in a combination of these considerations and varies from case to case.

Whatever the rationale may have been, the point to emphasize is that stepping down was not necessarily these presidents' most preferred outcome. They agreed to relinquish power because the constitutional prohibition on extending their rule raised the cost of staying in power beyond a level that they were willing to bear. Indeed, several leaders (Moi, Chissano, and Mkapa) made initial moves in the direction of seeking a third term only to change course when it became clear that powerful coalitions were ready to oppose them. Such voluntary relinquishment of power in the face of formal rules telling them that their time was up directly challenges the caricature of Africa as a place where "abstract constitutions and formal institutions exist on paper, but they do not shape the conduct of individual actors, especially those in power."[15]

Still, the nine leaders who agreed to step down represent just half the universe of sitting presidents who faced term limits. The other nine tried to change their respective constitutions to make a third term possible. Presidents Frederick Chiluba of Zambia, Bakili Muluzi of Malawi, and Obasanjo of Nigeria were rebuffed in their efforts. Chiluba's attempt to secure a third term was undermined by a groundswell of public opposition from civil society groups and a deep split within his own party. Fifteen senior members of the National Executive Committee of the ruling Movement for Multiparty Democracy (MMD) publicly opposed his bid to amend the constitution, and 59 MMD lawmakers, including several cabinet ministers and his own vice-president, signed a document in which they pledged to block any effort to allow him to run for a third term. In the face of such solid opposition, Chiluba backed down. Muluzi also faced strong public opposition to his bid for a third term. Even so, he very nearly succeeded: An amendment that would have abolished term limits fell just three votes short of the necessary two-thirds majority in the legislature.[16] As discussed earlier, Obasanjo's bid for a third term failed in the Nigerian Senate.

In six other cases, leaders facing term limits were able to change the constitutional provisions that prevented them from running for reelection and continuing their rule. Presidents Idriss Déby of Chad, Omar Bongo of Gabon, Lansana Conté of Guinea, Samuel Nujoma of Namibia, Gnassingbé Eyadéma of Togo, and Yoweri Museveni of Uganda all succeeded in changing their constitutions to allow themselves the ability to compete for third terms, and all six won their ensuing elections handily. In Gabon, Namibia, Togo, and Uganda, the constitution was amended by an act of parliament. In Guinea, the amendment came through a national referendum (which third-term supporters won with 98 percent of the vote). In Chad, the change was achieved through both mechanisms: A two-thirds parliamentary vote in favor of amending the constitution triggered a national referendum on the question, which was carried by a two-to-one margin.

These cases remind us that many African leaders still possess the power to shape outcomes to suit their preferences, even when those preferences conflict with formal limitations on what they are legally permitted to do. Presidents Déby, Bongo, Nujoma, and Eyadéma were able to change their countries' constitutions because their respective parties controlled more than two-thirds of the seats in parliament. President Museveni lacked the supermajority required to change the constitution, but was able to use his control of state resources to buy the parliamentary votes he needed to pass the third-term amendment—just as Nigeria's Obasanjo tried to do, unsuccessfully. In contrast to the cases described earlier, these examples would appear to vindicate the view of Africa as a place where leaders monopolize political and economic power so completely that their preferences do in fact take precedence over the formal rules of the game.

Yet this conclusion ignores these rulers' decision to use their considerable powers to work *within,* rather than around, institutionalized channels. Each of these leaders was probably strong enough to have voided his country's constitution and declared himself president for life, as many previous African leaders once did. Yet each of these more recent presidents felt the need to spend considerable political and financial capital trying to secure the votes to change the constitution—a feeling that in itself shows how heavily the formal rules have come to weigh. Even in the six cases where the rules and their boundaries were circumvented, the very presence of the rules shaped the strategies that the leaders pursued to achieve their favored outcomes.

It is true that earlier leaders also sought to legitimate their seizure of power through institutional means: The declaration of a one-party state in Ghana (and effectively, a life presidency for Nkrumah) was achieved through a 1964 national referendum, and Banda was named Malawi's life president in 1970 by a legislative act. Yet these earlier leaders were only superficially working through the system. It would have been unthinkable for them to fail to win their referendum or necessary legislative supermajority. This differs from the cases since 1990, in which leaders have not enjoyed such undisputed power. Indeed, it was precisely the anticipation of rebuke that prevented leaders such as Chiluba and Muluzi from pushing the third-term issue further, and that led Obasanjo to respond to the Senate's vote by declaring that he would respect its verdict. The roles that referenda and legislatures played in sanctifying life presidencies in the 1960s and 1970s were little more than formalizations of the facts on the ground rather than, as has been the case since the 1990s, a means of establishing new facts.

Explaining Third-Term Outcomes

The institutionalization of executive power in sub-Saharan Africa depends heavily on third-term issues. Thus an important question to ask is why certain term-limited executives decide either to step down or to attempt to amend the constitution in order to extend their tenure. One potential factor is public opinion. Popular leaders who believe that they will win reelection presumably have a greater incentive to try to change the constitution than those who have reason to doubt their electoral prospects. The contrasting examples of Kenya's Moi and Namibia's Nujoma illustrate this logic. Moi was elected to his second term in 1997 with only 40 percent of the vote and decided not to try to change the rules to allow himself a third term in 2002, while Nujoma, who began his second term in 1994 with 76 percent of the popular vote, decided to push for an amendment that would allow him to run for a third term in 1999. Among the eighteen African presidents who faced term limits between 1990 and 2005, the median margin of victory in the previous election among the nine presidents who decided to try to seek third terms was 41.5 percent. Among the nine who did not, it was only 17.8 percent.

A second potentially relevant factor is a leader's expected benefits of staying in power. It seems a fair assumption that younger leaders—who can expect to spend more years benefiting from office and also more years when they might be out of power and worried about prosecution—will have a stronger urge than older rulers to hang on to power. Our data appear to bear this out: At the time that their second terms expired, the nine presidents who faced term limits between 1990 and 2005 and who attempted to secure a third term had a median age of 60, whereas the median age of the nine who chose to stand down was 66.

A third factor focuses not on the value of staying in power but on the cost of trying to change the constitution. Given the strong emphasis that Western donors have put on the rule of law since the end of the Cold War, the ability of donors to impose their will in a given country should affect whether or not that country's president will try to alter the rules to permit a third term. To the extent that a country's reliance on foreign aid indicates its susceptibility to donor pressure, we should expect presidents in countries that receive high levels of aid relative to GDP to be less likely to seek third terms than presidents in countries that receive low levels of aid relative to GDP. Indeed, the median level of aid in the nine countries in which presidents attempted to secure third terms was 7.3 percent of GDP, whereas it was 12.1 percent of GDP in the nine countries where presidents did not. In keeping with this pattern, the presidents of the only two significant oil exporters in the sample, Nigeria and Gabon, were among the group that attempted to change the constitution to remove third-term limits.

With just eighteen cases to explore, this analysis can only be suggestive—indeed, none of the differences we have highlighted are statistically significant in a two-tailed t-test. Nonetheless, in addition to providing potential explanations for what has happened in the past, these factors also provide a set of expectations about what may happen in countries with formal term limits that have yet to be reached (see the list in Figure 3). If a leader's popularity matters, for example, then we would expect Rwanda's Paul Kagame—who was elected to his second term in 2003 by a margin of 91 percent—to be more likely to push for a third-term amendment than Liberia's Ellen Johnson-Sirleaf, who will not face a third-term limit until 2018 but who finished second in the first round of the election that brought her to power in 2006.

Similarly, if a leader's age is important, then we would expect Cameroon's Paul Biya and Senegal's Abdoulaye Wade to be more likely to step down when their second terms expire (they will be 81 and 88 years old, respectively) than Burkina Faso's Blaise Compaoré or Madagascar's Marc Ravalomanana, who will be in their early sixties when their second terms end. Finally, if donor leverage matters, then we would expect Johnson-Sirleaf and Sierra Leone's Ahmad Tejan Kabbah, whose countries are heavily dependent on foreign aid, to be much less likely to try to surmount constitutional term limits than Paul Biya or, when his second term ends in 2016, Congo-Brazzaville's Denis Sassou-Nguesso, since both their countries are major oil producers that receive little foreign assistance. Tracing what happens in these countries when the third-term issue eventually presents itself will put us in a better position to assess the causal weight of each of these factors.

The suggestion that donor pressure may be at least partly responsible for the decisions of African leaders who face third-term limits raises the critical question of whether the changes that we have documented with respect to the more general institutionalization of political power may be epiphenomenal—a product of outside forces rather than internal change. Yet even if donor pressure (or the broader international norm that leaders who come to power by means other than elections will not be viewed as legitimate) has contributed to making the rules matter, it remains true that the rules *do* matter much more than they have in the past. This realization directly contradicts some of the central assumptions so often heard about African politics.

A Case for Cautious Optimism

In 1982, Robert Jackson and Carl Rosberg wrote that "the inquiring student of African politics may be better advised to read Machiavelli or Hobbes than the 'constitutions,' official plans, or party programs of most African governments if he wishes to understand their central characteristics and dynamics." They saw "little sign that the drama of personal rule will soon give way to more settled institutional forms of conducting the affairs of states."[17] Nearly twenty-five years later, Goran Hyden maintained the same position when he wrote that, in Africa, "the notion that constitutional norms and principles are binding on political leaders is still very much in doubt."[18] Yet recent evidence suggests that the personal-rule paradigm that has been used to understand African politics for the past thirty years needs to be rethought.

By highlighting the growing importance of formal rules and their constraining effect, we would like to suggest a shift in emphasis in African political studies from its current preoccupation with classifying regimes to a focus on the factors that constrain executive power. An astute reader may have noticed that the word "democracy" has not appeared in this essay. The omission has been deliberate. In the past twenty years, there has been much debate about whether various African regimes should properly be viewed as "pseudodemocracies," "façade democracies," "hybrid democracies," or in terms of some other label that connotes democratic imperfection. Such efforts, we believe, risk diverting attention from the more basic issue of whether or not the behavior of political actors is constrained and, if so, whether by rules or by violence or the threat of violence. A focus on the degree to which formal rules matter (or the degree to which formal rules have displaced informal ones—a topic treated by Michael Bratton elsewhere in this volume[19]), will lead to research and typologies that better capture the salient characteristics of African politics today.

We are making broad claims, and should offer a few cautions and clarifications. First, we are not saying that African leaders today have any less desire to stay in power than their predecessors did; our claim is simply that leaders today are more constrained by formal rules in trying to achieve their most preferred outcomes. They accept electoral defeats when they might prefer to stay in office. Many of them (roughly half) stand down in the face of two-term limits when they would prefer to run for a third term. Or they change the rules so that their preferred outcome no longer violates those rules (in which case the impact of the rules is felt not in the outcome that is reached but in the way it is achieved).

As a final caution, we remind the reader that there are important exceptions to these general trends. There have been recent coups in the Central African Republic, Mauritania, and São Tomé and Príncipe, as well as reversals in the institutionalization of political power in the Gambia, Zimbabwe, and Uganda (as Andrew M. Mwenda shows elsewhere in this volume[20]). Leaders who have ruled for decades remain in power in Equatorial Guinea and Gabon. Furthermore, one could make a compelling case that reversals are not out of the question in several of the countries that fit the trends we have described—including Nigeria, the country with which we began our discussion. It is therefore important to temper whatever optimism might arise from the arguments and evidence we have presented with the recognition that, despite these general trends, not every African country is moving in a direction of greater institutionalization of political power, and that reversals remain possible in some of the countries that currently appear to be heading toward greater institutionalization.

Nonetheless, in the past fifteen years there has been a substantial change in African politics. It is entirely possible that the power of formal constraints over some African rulers may decline, or that the frequency of coups d'état may again rise, but the lines in Figure 1 are extremely unlikely to recross. In order to grasp this new reality, we need to adjust our theories. African politics needs to be viewed through a lens that recognizes the formal constraints on executives and rejects the assumption that African leaders simply get what they want.

NOTES

The authors thank Michael Bratton, Danga Mughogho, and members of the Working Group in African Political Economy for their comments on an earlier version of this paper.

1. For a detailed discussion, see Richard L. Sklar, Ebere Onwudiwe, and Darren Kew, "Nigeria: Completing Obasanjo's Legacy," *Journal of Democracy* 17 (July 2006): 100–15; and Jibrin Ibrahim, "Nigeria's 2007 Elections: The Fitful Path to Democratic Citizenship," USIP Special Report No. 182, January 2007.

2. Although Obasanjo never publicly declared his desire for a third term, the effort to extend his tenure was widely understood to have his strong endorsement. The quoted phrase is from David K. Leonard and Scott Straus, *Africa's Stalled Development: International Causes and Cures* (Boulder, Colo.: Lynne Rienner, 2003), 3.

3. Robert H. Jackson and Carl G. Rosberg, "Personal Rule: Theory and Practice in Africa," *Comparative Politics* 16 (July 1984): 425.

4. Kérékou first took power following a coup in 1972. After nearly twenty years in power, he agreed to hold an election in 1991, which was won by Soglo. Soglo then permitted elections to take place five years later, as prescribed by the constitution, and stepped down when Kérékou won. In 2001, Kérékou easily won reelection in a runoff after Soglo and Parliament speaker Adrien Houngbédji decided to boycott the second round, citing irregularities. In 2006, Kérékou stepped down after agreeing not to attempt to change the constitution, which prohibited him from running both because of a two-term limit for the presidency and a maximum-age limit of 70 years (Kérékou was 72). Soglo, who was 71 at the time, also announced that he would abide by the constitutional age constraint and not run, and the presidential election was won by Yayi Boni.

5. For a similar recent data collection effort, see Arthur A. Goldsmith, "Predatory versus Developmental Rule in Africa," *Democratization* 11 (June 2004): 88–110. We exclude Swaziland because it is a kingdom in which all leadership appointments are made by royal succession.

6. Hein Goemans et al., *Archigos: A Database on Political Leaders,* version 1.4, University of Rochester and University of California–San Diego, November 2004.

7. If we restrict the non-African sample to developing nations, the pattern remains the same: Through the 1990s, African leaders were nearly twice as likely to leave power by irregular means as leaders in other non-OECD countries.

8. There is a difference in the share of leaders leaving power through irregular means in the 2000–2005 period in the Archigos data set (5 percent) and our own (19 percent), which we attribute to differences in the coding rules applied. But since the key comparison in Figure 2 is between Africa and the rest of the world (and uses only Archigos data), this difference across data sets is less important than consistency in coding across regions within the Archigos data set, which we assume to be high.

9. A third development has been the increase in the number of independent countries in Africa, which rose from 36 in the 1960s to 44 in the 1970s, 45 in the 1980s, and 47 in the 1990s. Yet even if every newly independent country held elections at the same rate as those countries already in existence, these changes would not account for the increase we observe in the number of elections over time.

10. We define a contested election as one in which an opposition candidate is permitted to run against the incumbent.

11. Seewoosagur Ramgoolam lost power in Mauritius following an election in 1982. Mauritius has a parliamentary system of government, however, and Ramgoolam lost his post of prime minister when his party lost its majority in parliament rather than through a direct election, so we do not count this as another case.

12. For an analysis of the importance of term limits on a global basis, see Gideon Maltz, "The Case for Presidential Term Limits," *Journal of Democracy* 18 (January 2007): 128–42.

13. In Figure 3, we exclude Africa's five parliamentary countries—Botswana, Ethiopia, Lesotho, Mauritius, and South Africa—because they do not directly elect their presidents. We also exclude Comoros (because of its rotating presidency), Somalia (because it has lacked a clear executive during the period under study), Swaziland (because it is a kingdom), Eritrea (because it has never held national elections), and Sudan (because of ambiguity about which constitution should apply). We code Zimbabwe as not having a constitution that provides a two-term limit because the clause that provided for such a limit was changed before 1990, the starting point of our analysis. Similarly, President Mugabe's efforts to extend his current term through 2010 are taking place after the end point of our analysis.

14. President Compaoré of Burkina Faso could be argued to represent a nineteenth case. His opponents called for him to be barred from running in 2005 on the grounds that he would, by that time, already have served two elected terms in office. The Constitutional Council, however, ruled that the two-term limit, which had been suspended in 1997 but was reinstated in 2000, did not apply retroactively and that Compaoré's term of office should be counted from the time of the most recent amendment. Consequently, we code this as a case where a term limit has not been reached.

15. Goran Hyden, summarizing the personal-rule paradigm, in *African Politics in Comparative Perspective* (New York: Cambridge University Press, 2006), 98.

16. Muluzi actually pushed for two separate amendments—first, for an "open term" (abolishing term limits altogether), and then for an amendment allowing the incumbent president to stand for a third term. It was the vote for the former bill that very nearly passed. With declining support for Muluzi's bid, the latter was withdrawn before being put to a vote. It is also worth noting that Malawi's constitution specifies the limit only as two *consecutive* terms, and at the moment Muluzi's party, the United Democratic Front, looks poised to nominate him to run in the 2009 presidential election.

17. Robert H. Jackson and Carl G. Rosberg, *Personal Rule in Black Africa: Prince, Autocrat, Prophet, Tyrant* (Berkeley: University of California Press, 1982), 266.

18. Hyden, *African Politics in Comparative Perspective*, 111.

19. Michael Bratton, "The Democracy Barometers: Formal versus Informal Institutions in Africa," *Journal of Democracy* 18 (July 2007): 96–110.

20. Andrew M. Mwenda, "Personalizing Power in Uganda," *Journal of Democracy* 18 (July 2007): 23–37.

6

THE DECLINE OF THE AFRICAN MILITARY COUP

John F. Clark

John F. Clark, *professor in the Department of Politics and International Relations at Florida International University, is author of* The Failure of Democracy in the Republic of Congo *(2008). This essay originally appeared in the July 2007 issue of the* Journal of Democracy.

From the 1960s through the 1980s, military forces intervened against many civilian regimes in Africa. Elected regimes were overthrown in Benin, Ghana, Nigeria, Togo, and Uganda, among other states. The coupmakers often justified their actions by pointing to the corruption, inefficacy, or growing authoritarianism of the elected regimes, though in most cases the military rulers turned out to be at least as corrupt and authoritarian as the civilians whom they replaced.

In the early 1990s, a wave of political reform began to sweep the continent, robbing military rule of its legitimacy in most African states. During that decade many military rulers were overthrown, either by civilian-organized "revolutions," as was the case in most of these states, or by other military officers who promised rapid political liberalization, as in Mali. Only in a few nonreforming states such as Sudan have military rulers remained in power with no promise of competitive elections.

These political reforms, if sustained, could lead to a demilitarization of African politics—yet the postcolonial experience of military intervention and rule in many African states has created a culture in which military officers may still feel that interventions are legitimate.[1] Civilian populations, for their part, may feel so resigned to such behavior that they will tolerate military rule; in the past, they have even applauded military interventions against ineffective civilian regimes.

There are countless incentives for military officers, and sometimes ordinary soldiers, to seize power in African states. Successful coupmakers stand to gain the psychological satisfaction, status, and material riches that accrue to African rulers without having to take on the drawn-out and often frustrating task of building a political constituency. In virtually every African army, a charismatic military figure must at some time ponder the prospect of seizing power.[2] Also, many African societies are so inured to military intervention as not to regard it as aberrant. Even states long run by civilian rulers and with an apparent resistance to military rule, such as Côte d'Ivoire and the Gambia, have fallen victim to the ambitions of uniformed power-seekers.

So perhaps the question for Africa-watchers is not why military coups happen there, but why they do not. According to Samuel Decalo, there are three main "modalities" of civil-military stability that tend to avert military thrusts against African civilian governments: the external-guarantor modality, the tradeoff modality, and the legitimized modality. In the first of these, an outside power with massive local clout guarantees the civilian regime against military intervention. This was often the case in such former French colonies as Cameroon, Côte d'Ivoire, Gabon, and Senegal, where Paris backed civilian rule and that was that. Under the tradeoff modality, which is arguably found in Kenya and Zambia, the state's civilian rulers buy off key military officers with material benefits that keep the soldiers in their barracks. Commenting on the legitimized modality, Decalo identifies "a few polities that have been able to develop a measure of systemic legitimacy that in and of itself can serve to discourage praetorian assaults from armed forces." His examples include Botswana, the Gambia, and Mauritius (each of which had a democratic government dating to before 1990), as well as Malawi, Swaziland, and Tanzania.[3]

Reflection on these three modalities of civilian control reveals a fundamental distinction: The first two depend upon "negative controls" against military intervention, while the third depends on a change of political consciousness. The first two methods assume that military officers will always want to take power, but that incentives, threats, or some mixture of the two can prevent them from acting upon their impulses. The third modality involves a strategy to transform the consciousness of officers and soldiers so that they internalize the *legitimacy* of civilian rule and eventually stop contemplating even the possibility of military intervention—which surely makes this the most reliable long-term strategy for stable civilian rule.

Thus the wave of political reforms that began in the early 1990s raises many important questions: Has political liberalization in Africa delegitimized military intervention in politics?[4] Can states that start along a path of political liberalization expect to avoid military intervention in the future? If not, at what points in a state's political trajectory, or at which key moments, is military intervention most likely?

Legitimacy Through Democracy

Political legitimacy is a highly contested phenomenon. Those on the socialist left often equate political legitimacy with a fair allocation or reallocation of economic goods within society. Realist social analysts, from Hobbes onward, have connected legitimacy with the provision of basic order. In contemporary Africa, as in Hobbes's strife-ridden seventeenth-century England, this provision is not to be taken for granted. Yet the liberals have made the concept central to their political thinking, consistently connecting legitimacy with popular rule. While there is a wide range between the "continental" liberalism of Rousseau and the Anglo-American liberalism of Locke and Jefferson, political legitimacy remains a central idea. It is the liberal conception of legitimacy that we will test, by asking whether liberalizing government leads to a withdrawal of the military from politics. Before expanding on this idea, however, we need to consider several interrelated aspects of legitimacy that the nature of African politics makes undeniable.

First, legitimacy is a psychological phenomenon, not a legal one. Political legitimacy must be earned by those who govern, mainly by their being responsive to citizens' needs. Since not all societies regard procedural democracy as an important value, regimes can earn legitimacy (in the sense of popular acceptance) by responding to people's illiberal aspirations—which may include demands for international aggrandizement, the reinforcement of traditional or patriarchal social norms, and so on. Thus the interplay of public demands and state response does not necessarily lead to a more liberal society.

Second, political legitimacy depends heavily on context. As Hobbes astutely recognized, when societies are in utter chaos, populations prioritize basic order; this is as true for contemporary Somalia or Sierra Leone as it was for Hobbes's England. Political legitimacy can flow to rulers who restore basic order to a failed, collapsed, or warring state—such as it did to Uganda's Yoweri Museveni after he gained power at the head of an armed faction in 1986—though such order is almost always restored through force. Likewise, when the people are impoverished or starving, they are unlikely to prize procedural democracy above all else. Yet this kind of legitimacy may be a wasting asset, for the more time that passes after the period of chaos, the more the population may hold the regime accountable.

Third, a regime will never enjoy absolutely complete political legitimacy in the eyes of the whole populace. Even if a society is free of active rebellions, it will still have philosophical anarchists or other individuals who will deny legitimacy to regimes that may otherwise be widely accepted. A regime's degree of legitimacy rises and falls not only with its own performance, but also with the public's expectations. The public may gradually take for granted a regime's past successes (successes in terms of having met public demands) and begin to make even greater demands.

Before 1990, political legitimacy accrued to African regimes on a variety of different bases. As Decalo writes, Malawi's longtime president Hastings Kamuzu Banda enjoyed legitimacy based on the leader's traditional authority and personal standing in society. Decalo also writes of the political legitimacy enjoyed by Tanzania's rulers during the one-party era (which lasted from independence in 1961 until multiparty elections were held in the mid-1990s). During that time, legitimacy in Tanzania was based on claims that the rulers bolstered the alleged traditional African value of intracommunity support and formalized a putative African social-support network at the village and community level. From the early 1960s on, many regimes staked their claims to legitimacy on having led the struggle against European colonialism. Others claimed legitimacy on the basis of their ability to bring about revolutionary social change or to hasten the end of apartheid in southern Africa. By the early 1990s, however, with apartheid ending and three decades having passed since colonialism had begun winding down, the one-party model was losing legitimacy across sub-Saharan Africa.

Unlike Decalo, we are interested in not just any form of regime legitimacy but in legitimacy achieved through liberalization, as this will help us to understand the relationship between liberalization and military intervention in politics. While looking into these topics, however, we must remember that having a formal multiparty system does not translate instantly into legitimacy. One election, however free and fair it may be, is insufficient to imbue a regime with popular legitimacy. Elected governments must continue to provide public order at least as well as their authoritarian predecessors did; must deliver some level of economic growth (or at least offer plausible reasons why they have not); and generally must be responsive to the public.

History shows that popular elections often fail to produce such regimes. Yet when they do, friends of liberal democracy expect that such regimes will enjoy at least a modicum of political legitimacy, and that this should have an impact on African militaries: Soldiers, in other words, should become ever warier of stepping in against a regime that enjoys such legitimacy. Since the 1990s, African regimes have enjoyed deep legitimacy only if they have 1) sprung from free elections and 2) governed with a degree of effectiveness. Do events in Africa since 1990 reveal any patterns in the relationship between a trajectory of liberalization and military interventions? Is there anything else that the idea of political legitimacy can tell us about this relationship?

Identifying Cases

Examining the relationship between political liberalization and military interventions is hard since most analysts thus far have sought simply to understand why military coups occur. The strategy is to identify all cases of military coups (and sometimes also attempted coups) in Africa, to frame hypotheses about what causes them, and then to isolate those causes as much as possible.[5] Here, however, we limit our review to those African countries that have known a period of political liberalization, and to the years since 1990, when legitimacy has been most closely linked to democratic participation. According to the careful operational definition that Michael Bratton and Nicolas van de Walle offer, sixteen African states experienced clear democratic transitions between 1990 and 1994.[6] In their study, the key element in a democratic transition is a free and fair multiparty election that led to a change of the top executive leader or party.

While such transitions clearly signal that states have started along a democratic path, they are not the only sign of a democratic trajectory: The Freedom House (FH) scores are also instructive. This organization ranks countries annually on a 1-to-7 scale in two categories, Political Rights (PR) and Civil Liberties (CL),[7] with lower scores indicating more freedom and higher scores indicating less. Since both PR and CL are important to liberalization, it makes sense simply to add them in order to arrive at a rough but not unreasonable measure of liberalization.

To identify other states with a liberalization trajectory, we have examined the FH scores for all African states from 1990 through 2002. One way to measure liberalization would be to look for cases where the scores moved significantly in a positive direction and stayed there for some time. Thus we began by looking for an improvement of at least three points in a state's combined FH score (the best-possible score being 2 and the worst 14), and then checked to see if that improvement lasted for at least three years. This exercise identified fifteen of the sixteen states that Bratton and van de Walle believed had undergone a transition—which was their entire set except Madagascar, though we still included Madagascar for the purpose of comparative analysis. We also uncovered eight additional states that met these criteria. Of these eight, Senegal meets the criteria only if we extend the time period to 2004; although Senegal's liberalization period began somewhat later, it is appropriate to include it in this survey.

A final exercise was to exclude states whose combined FH scores failed to improve to a combined score of 8 or below, and to remain at or below that level for at least three years. The states thus excluded were Djibouti, Ethiopia, and Sierra Leone. The former two only experienced superficial liberalization, beginning from a level of extreme authoritarianism, while Sierra Leone was politically volatile until 2002.

Table 1 reveals a variety of different patterns and liberalization trajectories. The states that experienced democratic transitions and the sudden advent of new regimes in the early 1990s (a list that includes Benin, Cape Verde, Mozambique, and South Africa) showed quick improvements in their combined PR and CL scores, often followed by several years in which no further liberalization took place. Still other transitional regimes were subsequently overturned or saw their democratic experi-

TABLE 1—COMBINED FREEDOM HOUSE SCORES FOR SELECTED AFRICAN REGIMES, 1990–2002

STATE	1990	1991	1992	1993	1994	1995	1996	1997	1998	1999	2000	2001	2002
Benin	10	5	5	5	5	4	4	4	4	5	4	5	4
Cape Verde	10	5	3	3	3	3	3	3	3	3	3	3	3
Central African Republic	11	11	11	7	7	7	8	8	7	7	7	10	10
Congo (Brazzaville)	12	10	6	8	8	8	8	12	12	11	10	9	10
The Gambia	4	4	3	4	13	13	13	13	12	12	12	10	8
Ghana	11	12	10	9	9	8	7	6	6	6	5	5	5
Guinea-Bissau	11	11	11	11	7	7	7	7	8	8	9	9	9
Lesotho	11	10	10	7	8	8	8	8	8	8	8	8	5
Madagascar	8	8	8	6	6	6	6	6	6	6	6	6	7
Malawi	13	13	13	11	5	5	5	5	5	6	6	7	8
Mali	11	10	5	5	6	5	4	6	6	6	5	5	5
Mozambique	12	10	10	11	8	7	7	7	7	7	7	7	7
Niger	11	11	9	7	8	8	12	12	12	10	8	8	8
Nigeria	10	9	9	12	13	14	13	13	10	7	8	9	9
São Tomé and Príncipe	10	5	5	3	3	3	3	3	3	3	3	3	3
Senegal	7	7	7	9	9	9	8	8	8	8	7	7	5
Seychelles	12	12	10	7	7	6	6	6	6	6	6	6	6
South Africa	9	9	9	9	5	3	3	3	3	3	3	3	3
Tanzania	11	11	11	11	12	10	10	10	9	8	8	8	7
Uganda	11	12	11	11	10	9	8	8	8	10	11	11	10
Zambia	11	5	5	7	7	7	9	9	9	9	9	9	8

ments fail, in which case their scores quickly got worse, which is what happened in Niger in 1996 and Congo (Brazzaville) a year later. Still other countries, including Zambia and Malawi, had more ambiguous experiments with democracy and experienced gradual authoritarian drift rather than dramatic democratic collapse. The Central African Republic (CAR) experienced first an authoritarian drift, and then a total democratic collapse in 2001. Several states that had undergone no transition as of the early 1990s—Ghana, Senegal, and Tanzania—experienced a more gradual and sustained liberalization.

A second task is to define "military intervention" and to identify cases of it among the states listed in Table 1. Military intervention is a more useful concept than "coup d'état" for our purposes, because staging a coup is far from the only way in which military units or individuals can intervene in politics. One tactic seen in Africa is to start a rebellion as a way of toppling a regime whose top officials seem too well protected by praetorian guards to be easy targets for a putsch. Such a rebellion is not exactly a coup, yet it certainly demonstrates that a significant portion of a state's military has deemed its regime a legitimate target for overthrow. Certain interventions are not included, such as military rebellions or mutinies that are clearly aimed at gaining higher pay for soldiers and not at regime overthrow; rebellions that seek regional autonomy, such as the one that is currently going on in Casamance (Senegal); and coup plots, which are impossible to verify or catalogue, may take place without coming to public notice, and may be fabricated as *agent provocateur* operations by regimes that seek a pretext for harsh measures designed to bring the military or political opposition groups under control.[8] Table 2 records military interventions that have taken place in the selected set of states.

Because each of these states has a unique political trajectory, the incidence of military intervention is better examined in a general comparative fashion than by a statistical method. Experts can discern patterns among various categories of states more easily and reliably by looking systematically for patterns of military intervention or nonintervention, and by considering the timing of the intervention in specific states.

In thirteen of the twenty-one cases listed in Table 1, there was no incidence of military intervention *after the onset of a period of liberalization,* whether that onset was gradual or abrupt. Of the sixteen countries that experienced an abrupt improvement in their combined PR and CL scores after a clear democratic transition, eight experienced no subsequent military intervention (Cape Verde, Lesotho, Mali, Malawi, Mozambique, Nigeria, Seychelles, and South Africa).

The 1991 military intervention in Mali may rate special mention for having been the catalyst which began that country's ongoing experiment with multiparty political rule.[9] Executed to overthrow a dictator and make way for democracy, the intervention in Mali could even be

TABLE 2—MILITARY INTERVENTIONS IN LIBERALIZING
AFRICAN STATES, 1990–2003

	SUCCESSFUL COUP	FAILED COUP	NEW ARMED REBELLION
Benin	—	1992	—
Central African Republic	—	1996,1997, 2001	1996, 1997, 2001
Congo (Brazzaville)	—	—	1993, 1997, 1998, 2001
The Gambia	1994	1994	—
Guinea-Bissau	—	1993,1998	1998
Madagascar	—	—	2002
Mali	1991	—	—
Niger	1996,1999	—	—
Nigeria	1993	1990	—
São Tomé and Príncipe	—	1995,2003	—
Uganda	—	—	*
Zambia	—	1990,1997	—

* Lord's Resistance Army rebellion, ongoing
Note: Data on coups and coup attempts for 1990–2001 is taken from Patrick McGowan, "African Military Coups d'Etat, 1956–2001: Frequency, Trends and Distribution," Appendix A, 363–64. See note 5.

taken to suggest—problematic as this may seem—that African militaries sometimes may intervene to promote democracy.

In another group of states in which liberalization occurred at a more gradual pace, there was no case of military intervention after the start of liberalization. In this group, Ghana, Senegal, and Tanzania appear to be following a similar pattern and can usefully be considered together. All three countries have held three successive elections, with the quality of each an improvement over the last. In both Ghana and Senegal the third multiparty elections (both held in 2000) ushered in a new head of state from a different political party, which constitutes a democratic transition as defined by Bratton and van de Walle. In Tanzania, the Chama cha Mapinduzi—the old party from the country's de jure single-party days—continues to win every contest, though elections have been deemed substantially free and fair by international standards.[10] Senegal and Tanzania had no histories of military intervention even before liberalization, but in Ghana there were frequent coups and coup attempts before the 1990s. In any case, the sad case of Côte d'Ivoire, struck by a coup in 1999 and the eruption of civil war in 2002, suggests that a history of freedom from military intervention does not guarantee that pattern forever.

Uganda is a unique case. It first experienced significant liberalization beginning in 1991, culminating during the period from 1997 to 1999, and then suffered a reversal of course not involving military intervention. Since the country's highly contested referendum on the "no-party" constitution in 2000, President Museveni has revealed that he is intent on remaining in power by any means necessary. In 2006, he successfully maneuvered to run for and win another term as president. Still, his regime did compile a record of liberalization during the 1990s, and there was no military intervention.

Thus we have identified three categories of states that have enjoyed liberalizing periods free of military interventions. The first category features clear transitions followed by periods of continued liberalization (8 states); the second is marked by more gradual but ongoing liberalization (3 states); and the third (which contains only Uganda) saw mild liberalization followed by increasing authoritarianism. These dozen cases conform to the idea that liberalizing states which enjoy relatively high levels of public legitimacy do not experience military interventions. Nine other cases (some 43 percent of the 21 states listed), however, did experience some form of military intervention following a formal transition to multiparty political competition and liberalization.

Military Intervention After Liberalization

The nine cases in which military interventions did follow a moment or period of liberalization can be divided into two groups. The experiences of the first group—which includes Benin, the CAR, Congo (Brazzaville), Guinea-Bissau, and Zambia—show that military intervention may actually support liberalization or come as a reaction to increasing authoritarianism. The four cases in the second group—Niger, the Gambia, and the island republics of Madagascar and São Tomé and Príncipe—are ambiguous or troubling with respect to their implications for the notion that liberalization and democratic legitimacy deter intervention. These cases suggest that African states can retain a stubborn culture of military interventionism that the wave of political reform which began in the early 1990s has not sufficed to wash away.

Among the military interventions in the first group of cases, the 1992 apparent coup attempt in Benin is distinctive. It is unclear whether this was a military intervention at all, but since Patrick McGowan includes this case in his "attempted coups" category, it should be discussed. The military action in question was a shooting outside the presidential palace that was not at first thought to be a coup. According to Chris Allen, "This relatively minor event was *soon* [that is, not originally] being described as an attempted coup, or coup plot."[11] An officer whom Benin's recently elected president Nicéphore Soglo distrusted, Captain Pascal Tawes, was arrested soon after, along with several other northern-born officers who were thought to be loyal to former president Mathieu Kérékou. The "coup," which the army quickly suppressed, could have been orchestrated or fabricated by Soglo to create a pretext for Tawes's arrest. If the coup attempt was genuine, it happened early in Benin's democratic experiment, and there have since been no military interventions in the country of any kind. Benin has had two further changes of leadership through elections, first in 1996 and then again in 2006 (there was an election in 2001 as well, which the incumbent won).

The four other cases in the first group share commonalities that may not be entirely apparent from the FH scores, though specialists would likely agree on them. Military interventions in the CAR, Congo (Brazzaville), Guinea-Bissau, and Zambia all occurred after significant "democratic backsliding" had taken place. In all four cases, the winner in the founding multiparty elections, even if those ballotings were considered relatively free and fair, subsequently exhibited distinctly undemocratic behavior. This is less than surprising given that Africa had virtually no culture of democratic rule before 1990. In each of these four countries, the period leading up to the military's intervention was a time when the elected leader's legitimacy was flagging, in no small part because of the undemocratic and illiberal streak that he was showing.[12] Sadly, the new rulers of Congo (Brazzaville) and Guinea-Bissau behaved in this way and lost power in military rebellions led by their political opponents. Zambia's "democratic decline" under Frederick Chiluba, the country's first multiparty president, is better reflected in the FH data, as Chiluba had already taken a nondemocratic tack before he sought to amend the constitution in 2001 to allow himself to remain in office.[13]

The nature, intent, and outcome of the military interventions in these four "democratic backsliders" were varied. In the CAR there were repeated rebellions by forces in the regular army, which first aimed at better conditions of service (notably, receiving back pay) and later took on political goals. While several earlier rebellions failed, a more serious rebellion led by an exiled officer and backed by Chad succeeded in 2002. In Congo (Brazzaville), private militias controlled by political figures rebelled in 1993 after the president illegally dissolved parliament and staged new elections that were perceived to be flawed. A private militia protected Denis Sassou-Nguesso from arrest on the eve of elections in 1997, helping to return the former president to office.[14]

In Guinea-Bissau, an army faction turned on the president after he went authoritarian in 1998. The coup attempt in Zambia was a relatively minor affair that was suppressed without much difficulty. In Congo (Brazzaville) and Guinea-Bissau, the timing of the rebellions suggests that the resort to violence was a direct response to illegal or nondemocratic steps taken by elected officials. In the cases of the CAR and Zambia, the shape of events is less clear, but simple military opportunism in the face of declining legitimacy may have been a strong motive. Still, in all cases intervention occurred when democratic legitimacy was on the decline.

The second group of cases poses much more serious challenges to the idea that liberalization deters military intervention. In Madagascar, it is highly unclear whether or not the events surrounding the brief civil

war of 2002 suggest military support for democracy. The fighting followed the disputed December 2001 presidential election. In first-round
vote-counting, the government-controlled national election commission
reported that challenger Marc Ravalomanana had won 46.6 percent to
incumbent president Didier Ratsiraka's 40.4 percent—a situation that
would have made necessary a second-round runoff. Meanwhile, an independent consortium of civil society groups claimed that Ravalomanana
had actually won 50.5 percent to Ratsiraka's 37.7 percent, implying that
no runoff should be needed. The candidates began to mobilize armed
supporters, who in Ravalomanana's case included the significant portion of the military that had defected to his camp. In the midst of this
gathering storm, the Supreme Court weighed in with a decision in favor
of Ravalomanana—but it was too late. The standoff was ended by military force rather than peaceful constitutional methods. Yet the apparent
winner of the election that touched off the trouble—a figure who did *not*
officially command the army at the time—was installed because of that
very military force.

Niger's two military interventions of 1996 and 1999, considered together, also point to no clear conclusion about the restraining power
that democratic legitimacy may or may not exert. The January 1996
intervention was provoked by a standoff between President Mahamane
Ousmane and the opposition coalition that controlled the national legislature. Niger had adopted a semipresidential system, and thus the opposition elected one of its own as prime minister to share executive power
with Ousmane. This awkward "cohabitation" threw the country into a
months-long political crisis, and the new institutions installed only a
few years earlier began to lose their fragile hold on legitimacy.

Colonel Ibrahim Mainassara Baré took power and indicated immediately that he would organize a constitutional revision and new elections;
thus one might initially have viewed this coup as being supportive of
legitimate civilian institutions. Unfortunately, Baré himself stood in the
subsequent August 1996 elections, and then stopped the vote-counting
when it became clear that he would lose. At that point, it was apparent that a military figure had used the political standoff as a pretext to
cloak his true aim of seizing power for himself. But Niger's military
redeemed itself, from the standpoint of democratic legitimacy, in April
1999. Members of Baré's presidential guard assassinated the dictator
and organized new elections, thus restoring power to civilian authorities. This second intervention, like the Malian intervention of 1991, was
clearly aimed at restoring legitimate civilian authority.

The July 1994 coup in the Gambia is yet another ambiguous case.
The military intervention there disturbed a long experiment in multipartism that had won the Gambia considerable renown as one of Africa's
few democracies. But even this case may not be as troubling as it seems.
The Gambia's democracy was not consolidated, as there had been no

peaceful handover of power since the winning of independence from Britain in 1965.[15] At the time of the coup, President Dawda Jawara had remained in power for twenty-nine consecutive years, mostly by keeping the opposition divided and off-balance and by building a cult of personality in the rural areas of this tiny West African riverbank state. Jawara's ouster even provoked "euphoria" among a large number of Gambians.[16] Nonetheless, Lieutenant Yahya Jammeh's coup demonstrated the ability of a military leader to seize power successfully from an elected civilian leader, and without a plausible democratic rationale. Jammeh subsequently won manipulated elections in 1996 and somewhat less manipulated (and less contested) elections in 2001. Although Jammeh has put the Gambia on a path of gradual liberalization, his reelection in the flawed September 2006 elections, with 67 percent of the vote, suggests that he seized power with the intention of holding on to it. The coup of 1994 thus clearly interrupted one of Africa's longest democratic experiments, unconsolidated though the experiment certainly was.

The São Tomé and Príncipe case appears to be the most troubling in the survey. This pair of islands near the Equator in the Gulf of Guinea experienced two coup attempts, in 1995 and 2003, even as democracy seemed to have been consolidating since the democratic experiment began in 1991. There were two important contexts for the first intervention.[17] First, as in Niger, there was serious conflict between President Miguel Trovoada and the parliament following the legislative elections of October 1994. These elections put Trovoada's most powerful political rival, Carlos de Graça, in the premiership. Also, the International Monetary Fund's demands for structural adjustment put intense political pressure on the government, which led to strikes and demonstrations against proposed government cutbacks. A major cause of the military intervention was the government's failure to meet its salary obligations to army troops. The army only restored the civilian officials once they had attained assurances of amnesty and promises of more reliable salary payments.

The officers who attempted the July 2003 coup had even less of a legitimate pretext for their intervention, and thus this coup attempt is even more troubling. In 2001, Fradique de Menezes came to power in a presidential election that the international community judged to be free and fair. Before de Menezes's rise to power, however, the government of São Tomé and the international community at large had become aware of the possibly significant petroleum resources within the country's territorial waters. These discoveries led to intense negotiations between São Tomé and nearby Nigeria over the demarcation of maritime boundaries, and to other intense negotiations between the São Tomé government and several international oil companies. With the stakes of controlling the country rising as rapidly as estimates of its petroleum-income potential, several outside players, including Nigeria and Angola, may have been behind the 2003 coup attempt. It is most likely, however, that the would-be coupmakers were motivated by their own homegrown greed for power and money.[18] As is the case in hydrocarbon-endowed Congo (Brazzaville), the democratic experiment in São Tomé seems to be vulnerable to military intervention due to the high stakes created by oil wealth.

Lessons Learned

Despite the experiences of this last group of states, the bulk of evidence suggests that democratic legitimacy makes African states much less vulnerable to military intervention than they otherwise would be. To establish this with more certainty, one would have to undertake a statistical study comparing the experiences of military regimes and other authoritarian states with those of liberalizing regimes. In such a study, those states that experienced a steady and long-term trajectory of liberalization would almost certainly appear to be the least vulnerable to military intervention (particularly Ghana, Senegal, and Tanzania). Military intervention appears to be a bigger threat at the beginning of a democratic experiment, when the legitimacy of a new government has not yet been firmly established.[19] The coup attempt in Benin—if it was one—came very early in the course of its democratic experiment. It is notable that military intervention becomes less likely as duly elected regimes gain legitimacy over time.

Nonetheless, the experiences of African states such as São Tomé and the Gambia show that democratic legitimacy does not entirely insulate African states from military intervention. São Tomé serves to remind us that keeping the military out of politics can be a challenge even after legitimizing elections, especially if there is a crisis of institutions or a sudden change in a country's economic fortunes. The case of the Gambia shows that frustrations can build up in "uncompetitive" democracies, giving military officers a pretext for intervention.

Other cases seem to show that military interventions are most likely in states that start down a path of liberalization but then give way to "democratic backsliding." Countries with a long history of military rule, and thus a culture of military interventionism—such as the CAR, Congo (Brazzaville), and Guinea-Bissau—were prone to renewed military interventions in politics under these circumstances. Arguably, the most recent coup attempt in São Tomé can also be understood in this way. If these cases represent a pattern, then Uganda may be growing more vulnerable to military intervention as Museveni shows himself to be increasingly authoritarian. Democratic backsliding even provided the pretext for a coup attempt in Zambia, where there was no history of military intervention. It is also worth noting that liberalization had not gone as deep in most of these states as it had in Benin, Cape Verde, or

Ghana. The case of Benin shows that even a long history of military rule does not preclude "control" of the military through the establishment of a legitimate civilian government.

A remaining question is whether the power of democratic legitimacy or a liberalizing trajectory to prevent military intervention has run its course. International norms in favor of democratization suddenly waxed powerful in the early 1990s, but have since faded. Meanwhile, economic progress and public order are as important to state legitimacy as are democratic credentials, and woe betide the government—no matter how democratic—that cannot provide the former two. If Africa's liberalizing states are not also able to provide these public goods, the threat of military intervention will likely grow. Yet if liberalizing states do prove capable of providing these goods—or at least show serious advances in that direction—then one might expect the still-weak culture of political restraint to become stronger in the ranks of African militaries during the years to come.

NOTES

1. Several scholars continue to view military intervention as one of the greatest threats to continuing democratization in Africa. See Chuka Onwumechili, *African Democratization and Military Coups* (Westport, Conn.: Praeger, 1998), esp. ch. 4; George Klay Kieh and Pita Ogaba Agbese, eds., *The Military and Politics in Africa: From Engagement to Democratic and Constitutional Control* (Burlington, Vt.: Ashgate, 2005), esp. ch. 8.

2. On the motivations of officers in considering coups, see the classic studies by Donald L. Horowitz, *Coup Theories and Officers' Motives: Sri Lanka in Comparative Perspective* (Princeton: Princeton University Press, 1980), esp. chs. 1, 4, and 5; and Robin Luckham, *The Nigerian Military: A Sociological Analysis of Authority and Revolt, 1960–1967* (Cambridge: Cambridge University Press, 1971).

3. See Samuel Decalo, *The Stable Minority: Civilian Rule in Africa* (Gainesville: Florida Academic Press, 1998), 39. Also, those familiar with Malawi under the dictatorial Kamuzu Banda may find it odd to see the state described as "legitimate." Decalo uses the term here somewhat as Pierre Englebert does in his study, *State Legitimacy and Development in Africa* (Boulder, Colo.: Lynne Rienner, 2000), 4. According to Englebert, "a state is *legitimate* when its structures have evolved endogenously to its own society and there is some level of historical continuity to its institutions" (italics in original). He goes on to stress that, "As used here, the concept of legitimacy does not imply a normative judgment about the moral righteousness of states."

4. In this study, "political liberalization" refers to improvements in civil liberties and political rights that may fall short of actual democratic transition or consolidation.

5. One of the ablest practitioners of this approach is Patrick McGowan. See his study, "African Military Coups d'Etat, 1956–2001: Frequency, Trends and Distribution," *Journal of Modern African Studies* 41 (September 2003): 339–70.

6. Michael Bratton and Nicolas van de Walle, *Democratic Experiments in Africa: Regime Transitions in Comparative Perspective* (Cambridge: Cambridge University Press, 1997): 116–22.

7. For exact definitions of PR and CL, see *www.freedomhouse.org*.

8. For instance, this was apparently the case with an alleged coup plot in Malawi in 2001. See "Malawi: Brown Bounces Back," *Africa Confidential,* 6 April 2001.

9. On Mali, see Zeric Kay Smith, "Mali's Decade of Democracy," *Journal of Democracy* 12 (July 2001): 73–79.

10. See the 2005 U.S. State Department Human Rights Report findings on the Tanzanian elections at *www.state.gov.* This was true except in Zanzibar—an autonomous island province that has sought greater autonomy or independence—where the elections of both 2000 and 2005 were seriously flawed.

11. Chris Allen, "Republic of Benin: President Soglo Begins to Lose His Grip on Power," *Africa Contemporary Record, 1992–1994,* vol. 24 (New York: Africana Publishing, 2000): B6. Emphasis added.

12. See, for example, Andreas Mehler, "The Shaky Foundations, Adverse Circumstances, and Limited Achievements of Democratic Transition in the Central African Republic," in Leonardo A. Villalón and Peter VonDoepp, eds., *The Fate of Africa's Democratic Experiments: Elites and Institutions* (Bloomington: University of Indiana Press, 2005), 133.

13. On Congo (Brazzaville), see John F. Clark, "The Collapse of the Democratic Experiment in the Republic of Congo: A Thick Description"; on Guinea-Bissau, see Joshua B. Forrest, "Democratization in a Divided Urban Political Culture: Guinea-Bissau; and on Zambia, see David J. Simon, "Democracy Unrealized: Zambia's Third Republic under Frederick Chiluba." All are found in Villalón and VonDoepp, eds., *The Fate of Africa's Democratic Experiments.*

14. This episode is probably not called a "coup" since it was the government forces that first went into action against Sassou's militia. The resistance of Sassou's fighters is more properly described as an armed rebellion aimed at overthrow of the state; see Table 2.

15. Since President Dawda Jawara and his ruling party had won five consecutive elections beginning in 1970, however, there was reason to doubt the competitiveness of Gambian democracy, despite its impressive FH scores in the years leading up to the coup. Adam Przeworski and his coauthors argue that electoral regimes that have not experienced alternation of individuals or parties in the chief executive's office should be considered "unconsolidated" democracies. See "What Makes Democracies Endure?" in Larry Diamond et al., eds., *Consolidating the Third Wave Democracies* (Baltimore: Johns Hopkins University Press, 1997), 295–311.

16. Peter da Costa, "Out with the Old," *Africa Report,* January–February 1995, 48.

17. See Malyn D.D. Newitt, "São Tomé and Príncipe: Democracy Survives Continued Political Instability," *Africa Contemporary Record, 1994–1996,* vol. 25 (New York: Africana Publishing, 2002), B264–66.

18. See "Desperados," *Africa Confidential,* 25 July 2003.

19. Among others who have noted this tendency is Juan J. Linz in *The Breakdown of Democratic Regimes: Crisis, Breakdown and Reequilibration* (Baltimore: Johns Hopkins University Press, 1978), 8–9.

7

GROWTH WITHOUT PROSPERITY IN AFRICA

Peter Lewis

Peter Lewis *is director of the African Studies Program at the Johns Hopkins School of Advanced International Studies in Washington, D.C. His most recent book is* Growing Apart: Oil, Politics, and Economic Change in Indonesia and Nigeria *(2007). This essay originally appeared in the October 2008 issue of the* Journal of Democracy.

There is a generally recognized link between governance, economic performance, and popular welfare in Africa.[1] Many analysts trace the continent's protracted economic crisis and lagging recovery to the nature of its political regimes. Authoritarian governments have misused public resources, impeded the development of markets, and refrained from providing crucial public goods needed for economic expansion. Analysts of economic failure in the region have emphasized the role of dictatorial leaders and political systems grounded in patronage relations. The depredations of predatory rulers in the Central African Republic, Congo (Kinshasa), Kenya, Liberia, Nigeria, Sierra Leone, and Uganda are well documented. Economic mismanagement and authoritarianism have also been evident in Ethiopia, Ghana, Guinea, Tanzania, Togo, Zambia, and Zimbabwe. A few observers of other regions, notably Asia and Latin America, have proffered the possibility of an "authoritarian advantage" in economic development. In Africa, however, it is difficult to escape the association between nondemocratic rule and economic failure.

Historically, most African regimes have had little accountability to their people, as rulers have maintained political control largely through authoritarian institutions and patron-client networks. In these clientelist systems, leaders enjoy broad latitude in the use of public resources, procuring political support through ad hoc redistribution rather than by furnishing collective goods such as the rule of law, infrastructure, or social services. Authoritarian rulers commonly divert state revenues in order to maintain the support bases of their regimes, and governments serve as gatekeepers for access to resources, jobs, and market opportunities.

The result has been economic stagnation, recurring fiscal crises, and deepening poverty in many countries. Under such regimes, the political incentives of elites and the nature of governing institutions undermine the requisites of growth and popular welfare.

The trend toward democratization that swept the African continent in the early 1990s kindled hopes that political reform could lead to economic regeneration. If governments become more accountable, transparent, and rule-driven, it has long been held, they will be inclined to perform better and work toward broad economic improvement as a basis for support. The presumed link between democratic rule and economic growth has several foundations. At the most general level, there is an "elective affinity" between democracy and markets.[2] Both systems rely on open information, freedom of choice, and decentralized decision making. Authoritarian regimes struggle to manage the flow of information and to make the pragmatic decisions needed for a dynamic market economy. Conversely, market systems give rise to demands for information and to assertive social groups that impel governments to relax control. That all the world's mature democracies are also market systems affirms this connection.

Democratic systems also rest on accountability to voters and civic constituencies, thereby reinforcing pressures on leaders to improve the economy and better popular welfare. In a system characterized by regular elections, political competition, civic activism, and independent media, politicians will find stronger incentives to furnish public goods, expand the economy, and enhance citizens' well-being and livelihoods. As Amartya Sen has argued, even in circumstances where government accountability is limited, a relatively open public sphere allowing for the free flow of information and popular discourse makes it difficult for leaders to disregard public welfare entirely or to commit flagrant violations of rights.[3] Public access to information and institutions of accountability drive officials toward better performance in order to ensure their political survival.

A further reason to anticipate improvements in economic management and distribution arises from the sources of democratic transition in Africa.[4] Economic grievances were prominent among the catalysts of popular protest in the late 1980s and early 1990s, as charges of corruption and malfeasance by rulers were levied by virtually all the opposition movements in the region during this period of political ferment.[5] A similar animus was evident during later transitions in Nigeria and Kenya. Although civic activists and political challengers were not wholly focused on economic concerns, the narrative of deprivation informed movements for change, and prominent partners in opposition coalitions were expected to press for better oversight of the economy.

In particular, democratic reforms afforded space for the establishment of business associations that could lobby for conditions favorable to business and for greater access to markets. During the 1990s, advocates of improved governance also mobilized around such issues as corruption, legal reform, and budgetary transparency. Political change emboldened labor unions and other popular groupings who demanded social services, enhanced incomes, and efforts to bring about greater socioeconomic parity. A renascent civil society, as seen in Ghana, Kenya, Nigeria, South Africa, Zambia, and elsewhere, was thus a potential vehicle for economic change.

The Democracy-Development Disconnect

Over the last decade, however, the record of economic change in Africa has not borne out these expectations. On the positive side of the ledger, many African countries have consolidated macroeconomic reforms, and in the past few years regional growth has accelerated. Improved policies have helped to create a foundation for better performance, though much of this buoyancy can be attributed to rising commodity prices and new sources of investment from Asia and southern Africa. In most countries, however, economic expansion has not been accompanied by rising incomes or popular welfare. In Ghana, Kenya, Nigeria, South Africa, and Tanzania, indicators of public well-being lag far behind strong overall economic performance. Officials and average citizens alike often note the "disconnect" between macroeconomic indicators and microeconomic performance. In addition to this anecdotal evidence, data on poverty and human development are showing few significant improvements, and citizens report discouragement when surveyed about attitudes and economic conditions.

Indeed, a crucial paradox—that of growth without prosperity—besets Africa's new democracies. There is sound evidence that political liberalization bolsters economic-policy reform and enhances some of the institutional requisites for economic performance. Yet there are few signs that these improvements foster significant reductions in poverty or inequality, even when local regimes and external donors appear concerned with achieving such change. This paradox presents a basic challenge for Africa's new democracies. However desirable democracy may be in its own right, political liberalization does not ensure economic regeneration or improved popular welfare. Both the relationship between political and economic reform and the politics of poverty reduction remain problematic for researchers, practitioners, and African citizens. Some observers suggest that if democratic rule cannot deliver improvements in the lives of average citizens, these regimes will lose support and legitimacy, leading to more contentious and violent politics or even regime breakdown.[6] Alternatively, citizens in new democracies may evaluate political and economic "goods" separately, thus maintaining their commitment to democracy while pressing for improvements in welfare.[7]

While the tension between democracy and welfare is evident, the effects of democratic performance and consolidation (or lack thereof) on economic development are less clear. A brief review of economic performance among African regimes helps to frame the issue. Early observations suggested that Africa's new democracies did not economically outperform their authoritarian counterparts. One late-1990s assessment of key economic indicators in 36 sub-Saharan African states found that many democratic regimes in the region had undistinguished economic records.[8] At that time, African democracies averaged slightly lower growth rates, higher inflation, and greater budget deficits than nondemocracies. These patterns suggested that "political business cycles"—set in motion when ruling politicians, in order to secure reelection, manipulate policy to produce short-term economic gains and thus political support—and concomitant high spending may impede growth in democracies.[9]

More recently, however, a number of studies have concluded that democracies do register advantages in economic performance when compared to authoritarian states. Brian Levy has conducted a study of 21 African states from 1975 to 2000 which finds that countries pursuing superior economic-policy regimes performed better.[10] Furthermore, when these countries are categorized according to the quality of their policy-adjustment initiatives, the better-adjusting countries are those that were democracies and transitional states; the late adjusters were predominantly nondemocratic; and the nonadjusting ("polarized") states were all authoritarian during the period of the study.[11] A larger multicountry study produced by the African Economic Research Consortium strongly affirms the relationship between regime characteristics, governance, and policy approaches to the economy, with corresponding differences in economic performance.[12] Recent work by David Stasavage augments this view, demonstrating comparatively higher expenditures on education in African democracies.[13]

Some basic indicators can offer perspective. Figure 1 provides a simple illustrative comparison of 36 African states, showing comparative economic growth during 1986–2006.[14] For this assessment, countries were classified according to their regime type and then tracked separately to compare economic growth over time. There are clear differences in relative growth, as democracies generally perform better than nondemocratic regimes. During the late 1980s, the economies of the small group of African democracies grew substantially faster than did those of their authoritarian neighbors. During the early 1990s, the number of democracies increased, as numerous countries experienced turbulent reforms. Political transitions were often disruptive and frequently coincided with economic distress. This is reflected in the dramatic reduction in growth among democracies, from about 6 percent in the initial period down to a little over 3 percent in the 1992–96 period. Thereafter, growth increases among democratic countries, remaining above 4 percent during the next decade.

By contrast, African countries under authoritarian rule averaged only lackluster growth—about 3 percent for fifteen years, increasing only modestly in the last few years as commodity prices rose. Even with more favorable external conditions, growth has accelerated less quickly among nondemocratic countries than among democracies.

FIGURE 1—REGIMES AND ECONOMIC GROWTH IN AFRICA, 1986–2006

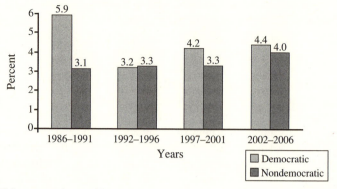

This comparison affirms the conclusion reached by other studies: Over the longer term, regime type does appear to influence economic performance. During the last fifteen years, countries undertaking liberalizing political reforms have generally seen increased economic growth, while the economies of those countries abjuring political change have lagged.

A more discriminating measure of welfare is the Human Development Index (HDI), which provides a composite measure of average income, life expectancy, and literacy within countries. As a group, Africa's democracies attain better Human Development scores than the region's nondemocratic countries. Among 177 countries assessed by the HDI in 2005, only two of Africa's authoritarian regimes ranked above 135 (Gabon at 119, and Equatorial Guinea at 127), compared with nine democracies (Seychelles, Mauritius, Cape Verde, South Africa, São Tomé and Príncipe, Botswana, Namibia, Comoros, and Ghana). With the highest-possible composite score being 1.0, the average among twenty electoral democracies was 0.56, compared with 0.48 for nineteen nondemocracies.[15] Regime type thus appears to be associated with better outcomes in popular welfare.

Yet this comparison is qualified when we assess progress over time. Tables 1 and 2 (see pp. 100 and 102) show the available HDI for 25 countries tracked over a fifteen-year period. Table 1 shows the HDI composite scores of thirteen countries that have been democracies for a decade or more, while Table 2 shows the scores of a dozen countries that have not had a political transition (or have had one only very recently). Between 1990 (the eve of the transition period in Africa) and 2005, there is scarcely any difference in the overall trend among democratic and authoritarian regimes. On average, the sample of democracies advanced by a small increment of 0.03, while nondemocratic regimes increased their average HDI by just 0.02.

Nonetheless, there are some differences among the samples. As we might expect, countries with high HIV/AIDS infection rates (Botswana, Lesotho, Namibia, South Africa, Swaziland, Zambia, and Zimbabwe) all

TABLE 1—HUMAN DEVELOPMENT INDEX (HDI)
IN SELECTED AFRICAN DEMOCRACIES, 1990–2005

COUNTRY	1990	1995	2000	2005	CHANGE (1990–2005)
Benin	0.37	0.40	0.42	0.44	0.06
Botswana	0.67	0.66	0.63	0.65	-0.02
Cape Verde	0.63	0.68	0.71	0.74	0.11
Ghana*	0.52	0.54	0.57	0.55	0.01
Lesotho	0.61	0.62	0.58	0.55	-0.06
Madagascar	0.45	0.46	0.49	0.53	0.08
Mali	0.30	0.32	0.35	0.38	0.08
Mauritius	0.73	0.75	0.78	0.80	0.08
Mozambique	0.32	0.34	0.38	0.38	0.07
Namibia*	..	0.70	0.66	0.65	-0.05
Senegal	0.43	0.45	0.47	0.50	0.07
South Africa	0.73	0.75	0.71	0.67	-0.06
Zambia	0.48	0.44	0.42	0.43	-0.04
AVERAGE					0.03

Trends in HDI for selected countries that were continuous electoral democracies from 1995 to 2005.

*Later transition or missing data: measurement from 1995–2005.

Source: United Nations Development Programme (UNDP), available at *http://hdrstats.undp. org/buildtables.*

show declines in HDI. All but two of these countries—Swaziland and Zimbabwe—are democracies, which lowers the overall scores in that regime category. In Zimbabwe, which is ruled by an authoritarian regime, the substantial drop in the Human Development score is compounded by economic failure and the collapse of public services. Zimbabwe has also seen the greatest decline in HDI, while Cape Verde, a democracy, registers the greatest gain. Furthermore, during this period, seven of thirteen democracies increased their HDI by 0.06 or greater; authoritarian regimes tended to show lower gains.

While it is possible to infer from these data a small democratic advantage in popular welfare, the comparison underscores the limited progress in popular welfare among all African countries, regardless of regime type. Keeping these qualifications in mind, we can conclude that democracies in Africa perform at least as well as nondemocratic regimes in the economic domain, and that in some areas their performance is measurably better.

Another way of assessing economic performance is to consider the subjective experience of average citizens. Survey data from African democracies reflect a restrained assessment of economic conditions and prospects. The Afrobarometer network completed three rounds of surveys in twelve countries (mostly democracies) between 1999 and 2006, asking Africans to assess their country's economic condition, their own personal circumstances, and whether or not they have experienced periodic or chronic shortages of food (an indicator of poverty).[16]

These measures suggest that difficult economic conditions have not changed significantly in recent years. Citizens express low assessments of the general economy and of their personal circumstances, with scant movement over time. In fact, in 2000 and in 2005, only 29 percent of respondents believed their country's current economic condition to be "fairly good" or "very good." Their perceptions of their own situations were worse still, with those reporting their personal economic conditions to be "fairly good" or "very good" dropping from 31 percent in 2000 to only 27 percent in 2005. Respondents also confirmed a slight increase in food shortages, with more than half stating that they had gone without food at some point during the previous year.[17] Africans in new democracies do not perceive substantial improvements in their economies, and they note few advances in living conditions. While broad measures of macroeconomic performance and welfare show that democracies perform comparatively well, citizens' perceptions in these countries reflect a more somber reality.

Explanations of Performance

Although democracy appears to yield economic benefits over time, the transition to democracy has not fostered dynamic economies or substantial improvements in welfare in most of Africa. Certain domestic and international factors have contributed to these failings. Political reform in Africa has produced important changes in actors and institutions, yet well-entrenched and resilient political patterns limit the depth and extent of change. African politics have long been characterized by strong presidential regimes, the dominance of a single party or elite cohort, the maintenance of control through extended patron-client networks, and the dispensation of patronage in exchange for political support.

The concept of neopatrimonialism, which captures the tensions between institutional rule and the clientelist management shaping most African political systems, neatly sums up the nature of politics in Africa. Neopatrimonialism is largely incompatible with democracy and economic growth.[18] As discussed above, clientelist politics tend to reinforce inequality, undermine accountability, and hamper the provision of public goods. Moreover, weak formal institutions, unregulated elite discretion over resources, and a propensity for consumption instead of investment all erode the possibilities for capital formation.

Neopatrimonialism in authoritarian regimes has been closely associated with personal rule, oligarchic control, and pervasive corruption. The transition to electoral democracy, however, does not necessarily eclipse neopatrimonial structures and practices. In many African countries undergoing political reform, neopatrimonialism has been reconfigured rather than displaced by the new democratic structures.[19] Presidents continue to exercise broad discretionary powers, even if they must now contend with constitutional restraints and countervailing institutions.

The relative weakness of opposition groups and civil society often creates latitude for executive control, prompting leaders to extend their

TABLE 2—HUMAN DEVELOPMENT INDEX (HDI)
IN SELECTED AFRICAN NONDEMOCRACIES, 1990–2005

COUNTRY	1990	1995	2000	2005	CHANGE (1990–2005)
Burkina Faso	0.32	0.34	0.35	0.37	0.05
Cameroon	0.53	0.51	0.53	0.53	0.00
Chad	0.36	0.38	0.40	0.39	0.02
Congo (Rep.)	0.56	0.55	0.52	0.55	-0.01
Eritrea*	..	0.44	0.46	0.48	0.05
Ethiopia	0.33	0.35	0.38	0.41	0.06
Gambia*	..	0.44	0.47	0.50	0.07
Mauritania	0.46	0.49	0.51	0.55	0.10
Swaziland	0.63	0.64	0.59	0.55	-0.09
Togo	0.50	0.51	0.52	0.51	0.02
Uganda	0.43	0.43	0.48	0.51	0.07
Zimbabwe	0.65	0.61	0.54	0.51	-0.14
AVERAGE					0.02

Trends in HDI for selected countries that were continuously ruled by authoritarian regimes from 1995 to 2007.
*Missing data: measurement from 1995 to 2005.
Source: UNDP, available at http://hdrstats.undp.org/buildtables.

power through both formal and informal means. Many elected presidents have adapted to patronage structures, cultivating crony relationships with key notables and marginalizing political rivals or opponents.[20] Leaders often attempt to manipulate or alter democratic institutions to bolster their control. The effort to extend presidential term limits, as seen for instance in Namibia and (unsuccessfully) in Nigeria, is a further reflection of executive ambition. In weak institutional settings without an effective legislature or judiciary to provide checks and balances, presidential control tends to foster many of the same problems that characterized earlier systems of personal rule, including a lack of government accountability and transparency.

The dominance of a single, strong party in countries across Africa reinforces the strength of political clientelism. In Mozambique, Namibia, Nigeria, South Africa, Tanzania, and Zambia, for example, ruling parties have held substantial majorities through several elections, consequently marginalizing the opposition. Parties from the old regime govern in Mozambique and Tanzania, while new parties that took power during the political transition have become entrenched in Nigeria and Zambia. The dominance of ruling parties is mirrored by the resilience of political elites, who often manage to reconstitute networks of control even as political structures and institutions change.

Elite groups in transitional democracies often sustain traditional networks or, where the old regime has been eclipsed, form new ones. In Tanzania, incumbent-party cohorts still govern, while in Zambia and Senegal the posttransition ruling parties comprise veteran leaders from the trade-union movement or the traditional opposition. In Nigeria, retired military officers permeate the political parties. Executives from the predemocratic era may also return to power, as did Mathieu Kérékou in Benin and Didier Ratsiraka in Madagascar. Adaptable, enduring elites tend to reproduce clientelist systems and outlets for patronage. These inherently limit competition—and thus accountability—in the political domain. Clientelism also fosters crony networks linking politicians to the private sector. Elite rivalries within these networks, combined with the volatility of electoral politics, may shorten officeholders' time horizons. All these patterns encourage corruption, weak oversight, and politically driven fiscal cycles.

The lack of a developed and vibrant civil society in many of these countries also hinders accountability and improved government performance. Political reform has undoubtedly opened new outlets for civic expression in much of the region, which is reflected in the proliferation of independent associations and media and in a wider public sphere. Few countries, however, have seen the growth of an autonomous domain of civil society that can effectively press politicians for better policies or economic performance. In countries such as Benin, Ghana, Mali, Malawi, Mozambique, Senegal, and even Nigeria, we commonly find that many associations are small, urban-based, reliant on donor funding, or fragmented regionally and ethnically. Most African democracies have yet to develop habits of effective advocacy and critical citizenship. Even in South Africa, which has the strongest tradition of dissent and civic mobilization in Africa, the hegemony of the ruling party, the African National Congress, limits the efficacy of popular protest.

In consequence, in most of Africa's new democracies, there are few coherent lobbies for public goods or coalitions for reform. With limited countervailing pressures from below, politicians find little inducement to focus their efforts on general improvements for constituents. Instead, elected leaders seek to preserve their standing among ruling networks while dispensing piecemeal benefits to supporters. This generally reinforces distribution through clientelist links rather than programmatic or policy-driven agendas.

A related problem stems from the longstanding institutional deficiencies of Africa's weak states. Democratic rule cannot easily escape the legacy of state degeneration found in most countries in the region. Elected leaders must contend with feeble bureaucracies, cumbersome government enterprises, sparse public services, deteriorating infrastructure, and (in more than a few cases) depleted treasuries. Regime change offers few curatives for the resource constraints and institutional weaknesses that have accumulated over decades. Countries such as Botswana, Mauritius, Namibia, and South Africa are exceptions to this generalization, but most new democracies in Africa operate under severe limitations in both resources and capacity. In addition, weak financial, regulatory, information, and legal systems hinder investment and undermine the credibility of the incentives offered by policy reform.

These political legacies have implications for the extent of reform and the distributional effects of policy change. Politicians in new democracies are reluctant to forgo patronage resources by relinquishing influence over the economy. The slow pace of change in institutions and market structures hampers investment in such key sectors as manufacturing, commercial agriculture, and value-added services that could generate employment and disperse wealth. Moreover, political elites often capture rents from privatization, financial liberalization, the removal of subsidies, and trade reform. As a result, the wider economic benefits never filter down to the masses.

The International Dimension

Disappointing economic outcomes in new democracies are the consequence of more than just domestic political dynamics, however. Several aspects of the international environment also influence the possibilities for redistribution and poverty reduction. First, policy choices for African regimes remain limited. The overarching influence of external donors, led by the multilateral financial institutions (the International Monetary Fund [IMF] and the World Bank), has reinforced policy orthodoxy across the region. This framework emphasizes balanced budgets, low inflation, reduced subsidies, trade liberalization, smaller government, and less-intrusive state economic activities. African governments, under continuing fiscal pressure, are subject to donor leverage and find it difficult to break from orthodox prescriptions. Policies of redistribution are effectively omitted from policy choice. Nor have African democrats been drawn to the type of resurgent populism that has recently spread across Latin America. They cannot afford it, and they gain little electoral advantage from adopting a populist stance.

More by circumstance than by design, orthodox adjustment policies have had adverse distributional effects in many African countries. In theory, structural adjustment calls for both reductions in government spending and a shift of resources away from less efficient uses (such as subsidies or loss-making government companies) toward more-productive sectors and social services. In practice, governments have come to realize that compliance with core macroeconomic indicators—notably fiscal balance, low inflation, and market-determined exchange rates—is often sufficient to maintain a flow of needed resources from the donors. Fiscal balance is often achieved by limiting expenditures and levying user fees on public goods such as health and education.[21]

For African leaders, penalizing rural groups or the urban poor with such fees is less hazardous politically than cutting the military budget or divesting state enterprises, both of which could create large job losses among urban constituencies. While donors do not encourage the contraction of social provisions, they strongly emphasize budgetary discipline as a condition for assistance. Governments economize in the areas that are least risky, though this often creates hardship among politically vulnerable groups. Redistributive or populist policies are largely precluded by the need to maintain fiscal and monetary restraint in order to obtain foreign assistance.

Some external donors, however, have launched programs aimed at directly addressing poverty and redistribution. Such donor-sponsored efforts have yielded only modest results. The Heavily-Indebted Poor Country (HIPC) initiative, launched by the World Bank and the IMF in 1996, is an effort to reduce substantially debt loads for countries that follow prudent economic policies, with the intention of freeing up resources for investment and social provision. The poverty-alleviation goals of HIPC have been accentuated through the requirement for debtor countries to submit Poverty Reduction Strategy Papers (PRSPs). The PRSP process calls for plans to channel the resources earned from debt cancellation toward services and programs for deprived segments of society. Another initiative, the U.S.-sponsored Millennium Challenge Account (MCA), a bilateral fund run by the Millennium Challenge Corporation, provides significant amounts of supplementary aid to countries that meet benchmarks of economic responsibility and good governance.

These policies appear to support desirable priorities on the part of benign governments, but the results have not been unambiguously positive. Many of these programs are excessively bureaucratic and cumbersome, resulting in the slow delivery of resources and indefinite outcomes for target groups. Moreover, the PRSP and MCA processes are often criticized for absorbing energies and resources from weak African bureaucracies that are already overextended, thereby straining rather than building institutional capacity. While some of the region's new democracies have reaped benefits from debt relief and aid premiums, it is not clear that these resources have significantly reduced poverty or improved welfare in recipient countries.

Finally, it should be noted that African countries, regardless of regime type, continue to face hindrances in trade and investment that limit their potential for growth. Democratizing states in the region have few advantages over their authoritarian counterparts in gaining access to overseas markets, offsetting the effects of agricultural subsidies in industrialized countries, buffering the consequences of rising energy and food costs, or soliciting investment in crucial productive sectors. The U.S. African Growth and Opportunity Act (AGOA) has opened export windows for several African countries, many of which are democratizing states undergoing economic reform. Yet the intractability of subsidy issues in the World Trade Organization's Doha Round of trade negotiations shows that African exporters of agricultural commodities still face substantial obstacles to improving their performance. Soaring fuel and grain prices afflict African countries without regard to political regime. Beyond the observable barriers to expansion, the handicaps of poor reputation and weak credibility in global markets can be seen in lagging investment responses, even in such stable democracies as Ghana, Benin, Mali, Mozambique, and Namibia.

Prospects for Change?

In this overview, I suggest that Africa's new democracies have achieved limited progress in revitalizing their economies and alleviating poverty. This should not be taken to mean that regimes are irrelevant to economic outcomes, or that the region's economic problems are intractable. Democratic governance clearly provides stronger protection against predatory rule, blatant neglect of public welfare, and purely self-aggrandizing behavior by leaders. Democracy fosters institutions that rein in the arbitrary power of the executive. More stable and transparent legal settings, even if flawed, strengthen the potential for investment and exchange. Moreover, political liberalization affords space for civic mobilization, public-interest lobbying, and independent media outlets that can disseminate information and hold leaders to account. Electoral democracy may not be sufficient to transform African economies, but it seems to be necessary for economic advancement. A growing body of data and analysis affirms a democratic advantage, however modest, in economic performance throughout the region.

In order for African democracies to move toward the next stage of reform, however, several factors must come into play.[22] The first involves the selection and orientation of leadership. In a number of African democracies, including Benin, Ghana, Kenya, Mozambique, Nigeria, and South Africa, a newer generation of technocratic, reform-minded leaders has made its mark on the political scene. Institutionalized electoral systems and a more active opposition help to shift incentives for political aspirants, while creating opportunities for the entry of newcomers into the political sphere. Some of these elements can help to drive change beyond the limits of current political and institutional arrangements.

Forward-looking politicians need allies among constituencies and civic groups. This points to a second important factor: the formation of broader coalitions for change in democratizing states. In much of Africa, reform elements in the civic sphere currently lack cohesion and focus. Yet the possibilities for more capable and better-coordinated movements for change can be glimpsed in several countries. In South Africa, civic organizations are demanding better public services and welfare provision. In Ghana, business groups lobby for improved economic policies. Nigerian activists successfully resisted efforts by the president in 2006 to extend term limits. Zambians have protested government corruption and pushed for greater transparency. These initiatives do not constitute coherent movements for economic reform, but they do represent new demands and pressures on incumbent elites.

A third factor is the continued need for institutional development in democratizing states. This is an incremental and uneven process, but there is evidence from many countries that governments are making

TABLE 3—ATTITUDES TOWARD DEMOCRACY AND THE ECONOMY

SURVEY CATEGORIES AND QUESTIONS	CA. 2000	CA. 2005	CHANGE
SATISFACTION WITH DEMOCRACY % fairly/very satisfied	58	45	-13
SUPPORT FOR DEMOCRACY % agree: "Democracy is preferable to any other kind of government."	69	61	-8
PATIENCE WITH DEMOCRACY % agree: "Our present system of elected government should be given more time to deal with inherited problems."	46	56	+10
ECONOMIC PATIENCE % agree/agree very strongly: "In order for the economy to get better in the future, it is necessary for us to accept some hardships now."	46	57	+11

Source: "The Afrobarometer Network, Where Is Africa Going? Views from Below," Working Paper No. 60, May 2006, available at *www.afrobarometer.org*.

Samples: ca. 2000, n=21,531; ca. 2005, n=17,917. Countries included: Botswana, Ghana, Lesotho, Malawi, Mali, Namibia, Nigeria, South Africa, Tanzania, Uganda, Zambia, and Zimbabwe.

headway in stemming corruption, improving the legal environment, building workable financial systems, and regulating such key sectors as banking and telecommunications. Institutional development in democratizing states is a crucial requisite for achieving sustainable economic expansion and any prospect of poverty reduction.

Now is the time to revisit the question raised earlier regarding democratic legitimacy and citizen support. If Africans are discouraged by their economic circumstances, does this create political disillusionment and possibly even attraction to nondemocratic alternatives? Table 3 above, again based on survey data from the twelve-country Afrobarometer sample, shows Africans' assessments of democratic performance, as well as their overall commitment to democracy, their patience with democracy, and their patience with the economy. African citizens are clearly disappointed by the performance of democracy, yet their general commitment to democracy as a political regime remains relatively strong. While average satisfaction with democracy has declined markedly, support for democracy has subsided only modestly. Without more sophisticated regression analysis, it is difficult to say how much of this declining confidence arises from economic concerns, and how much from other factors such as corruption, insecurity, opposition grievances, and the like. Yet this measure does not show a regional crisis of democratic legitimacy, notwithstanding widespread dissatisfaction with economic conditions.

The resilience of support for democracy looks all the stronger when we consider citizens' patience with current conditions. Increasing numbers of Africans are inclined to wait for democracy to deliver better results, and to accept present economic difficulties in the hope of future improvements. In African democracies, about six in ten citizens support the democratic system over all others, and nearly the same proportion is prepared to show forbearance with regard to current problems. The short-comings of economic performance in democratizing Africa do not yet appear to pose a critical challenge to the sustainability of democracy.

Still, it must be acknowledged that, fifteen years after the wave of de-mocratization crested in Africa, political reform has not fostered a regenera-tion of the region's economies. While democratization can offer intrinsic benefits with regard to rights, liberties, and accountability, it furnishes no panacea for the prevailing economic malaise, nor any blanket prescription for accelerating economic growth and reducing poverty. Many of Africa's new democracies have significantly improved their growth rates, but they have not achieved broad-based prosperity. The resulting disjunction be-tween popular expectations and political realities creates an impediment to the consolidation of democracy. Poor economic performance restricts gov-ernment resources, fosters social conflict, and undermines the legitimacy of electoral regimes. Despite these challenges, there is evidence that most citizens in Africa's fledgling democracies are willing to allow time for eco-nomic improvements. At the same time, there are political trends—includ-ing generational changes in leadership, increasingly assertive civic engage-ment, and incremental improvements in institutions—that appear promising for longer-term reform. Africa's quest for democratic development still has a long way to go. Fortunately, Africans appear to be patient, recognizing that effective democratic institutions and practices must take root before the benefits of democracy begin accruing to the average person.

NOTES

1. A compelling argument about the link between governance and economic perfor-mance in Africa is presented by Benno J. Ndulu et al., eds., *The Political Economy of Economic Growth in Africa, 1960–2000* (Cambridge: Cambridge University Press, 2007). This linkage is not universally emphasized. For instance, Jeffrey Sachs discounts the im-portance of governance as a determinant of economic performance, stressing instead the region's unfavorable geography, capital shortages, and limited access to global markets.

2. Charles E. Lindblom, *Politics and Markets: The World's Political-Economic Systems* (New York: Basic Books, 1977), 164–65.

3. Amartya Sen, *Development as Freedom* (New York: Anchor, 1999).

4. Claude Ake, *Democracy and Development in Africa* (Washington, D.C.: Brookings Institution Press, 1996).

5. Michael Bratton and Nicolas van de Walle, *Democratic Experiments in Africa: Regime Transitions in Comparative Perspective* (Cambridge: Cambridge University Press, 1997).

6. Adam Przeworski, *Democracy and the Market: Political and Economic Reforms in Eastern Europe and Latin America* (Cambridge: Cambridge University Press, 1991), 188.

7. Larry Diamond, *Developing Democracy: Toward Consolidation* (Baltimore: Johns Hopkins University Press, 1999); see also Michael Bratton and Peter Lewis, "The Dura-

bility of Political Goods: Evidence from Nigeria's New Democracy," *Commonwealth and Comparative Politics* 45 (March 2007): 1–33.

8. Nicolas van de Walle, *African Economies and the Politics of Permanent Crisis, 1979–1999* (Cambridge: Cambridge University Press, 2001).

9. Democracies also registered substantially higher investment spending than nondemocracies, which over time could compensate for the growth-hampering effects of inflation and fiscal deficits; see van de Walle, *African Economies and the Politics of Permanent Crisis*, 255.

10. Brian Levy, "Are Africa's Economic Reforms Sustainable? Bringing Governance Back In," in Muna Ndulo, ed., *Democratic Reform in Africa: Its Impact on Governance and Poverty Alleviation* (Athens, Ohio: Ohio University Press, 2006).

11. In Levy's classification, "strong adjustors" include Benin, Burkina Faso, Ghana, Malawi, Mali, Mozambique, Uganda, and Zambia; all but two were electoral democracies by 2000; "later adjustors" include Cameroon, Chad, Guinea, Madagascar, Mauritania, Niger, Senegal and Tanzania, three of which were democratic by 2000; the "polarized governance" countries include Côte d'Ivoire, Kenya, Nigeria, Togo, and Zimbabwe, all of which were essentially authoritarian regimes during the 1990s.

12. Ndulu et al., *Political Economy of Economic Growth in Africa.*

13. David Stasavage, "Democracy and Education Spending in Africa," *American Journal of Political Science* 49 (April 2005): 343–58.

14. Thirty-six (of 48) sub-Saharan African countries were included in the comparison. Countries with sustained internal conflict (Angola, Burundi, Côte d'Ivoire, Democratic Republic of the Congo [Kinshasa], Liberia, Rwanda, Sierra Leone, Somalia, and Sudan) were excluded. Data were missing for some countries. Countries were classified by regime type for each year during the twenty-year period. Average growth rates among regime categories were calculated for five-year periods.

15. The actual scores among 177 countries range from a low of 0.33 to a high of 0.98. All African countries with available data were included.

16. Afrobarometer Network, "Where Is Africa Going? Views from Below," Working Paper No. 50, May 2006; available at *www.afrobarometer.org.* Samples: ca. 2000, n=21,531; ca. 2005, n=17,917. Countries included: Botswana, Ghana, Lesotho, Malawi, Mali, Namibia, Nigeria, South Africa, Tanzania, Uganda, Zambia, and Zimbabwe.

17. Although the situation in Zimbabwe is especially acute, reported food shortages have also become significantly more common in Malawi and Nigeria, with more modest increases in Tanzania and Uganda. The "food shortage" measure is not driven by a single case.

18. Van de Walle, *African Economies and the Politics of Permanent Crisis*; see also Peter Lewis, "Economic Reform and Political Transition in Africa: The Quest for a Politics of Development," *World Politics* 49 (October 1996): 92–129.

19. Ake, *Democracy and Development in Africa,* 139.

20. Nicolas van de Walle, "Presidentialism and Clientelism in Africa's Emerging Party Systems," *Journal of Modern African Studies* 41 (June 2003): 297–321.

21. Surveys suggest that many Africans are willing to accept user fees if the quality of service improves. Unfortunately, user fees often limit access to services while education and health remain underprovided.

22. Peter Lewis, "A Virtuous Circle? Democratization and Economic Reform in Africa," in Calvin Jillson and James Hollifield, eds., *Pathways to Democracy* (London: Routledge, 2000); see also Henry Bienen and Jeffrey Herbst, "The Relationship between Political and Economic Reform in Africa," *Comparative Politics* 29 (October 1996): 23–42.

8

FORMAL VERSUS INFORMAL INSTITUTIONS IN AFRICA

Michael Bratton

Michael Bratton is University Distinguished Professor of Political Science and African Studies at Michigan State University. He is also a founder and former director of the Afrobarometer, a collaborative international survey-research project that measures public opinion regarding democracy, markets, and civil society in eighteen African countries. This essay originally appeared in the July 2007 issue of the Journal of Democracy.

Few political scientists would dispute that political institutions help to shape the attitudes and behavior of citizens. Indeed, one of the leading paradigms in the study of political life today is known as the "new institutionalism."[1] This body of theory assumes that ordinary people—when they think and act politically—take their cues from the structure of rules, procedures, and customs prevailing in the polity in which they live. As such, political institutions provide a revealing aperture through which to view—and to explain—regularities in public opinion and mass participation.

But a lively debate persists about the relative importance of formal and informal institutions. What is the operative framework for studying the politics of new democracies? Is it a sovereign constitution, along with the rule-governed agencies and legal procedures with which a constitution is associated? Or is real-world politics driven by more contextual dynamics, in which "actual existing" social and power relations—not words on paper—determine who gets what, when, and how? Put differently, do citizens respond primarily to the inscribed regulations of formal institutions or to the unwritten codes embedded in everyday social practice?

According to Douglass C. North's classic formulation, political institutions can be "any form of constraint that human beings devise to shape human interaction," and can work through "both formal constraints—such as rules that human beings devise—and informal constraints—such as conventions and codes of behavior."[2]

Most practitioners of the new institutionalism disregard North's qualification and focus only on formal institutions, thereby underrating the impact of the informal realm. This bias may be reasonable for established democracies, where the rule of law guides political actors and a widespread ethic of "constitutionalism" reinforces written constitutions. But these conditions rarely hold in emergent democracies, where legal limits on state power are usually novel and untested.[3] Even if the rule of law is not completely absent in such societies, it is often weakly developed or sometimes ignored with impunity, usually in deference to personal or communal ties. Under these conditions, the influence of formal institutions may be sharply attenuated as political actors align themselves with more familiar relationships and routines.

Such considerations bear on the study of how ordinary Africans arrive at assessments of democracy. When they judge the new political regime, are they thinking of its formal institutions, such as elections, multiple parties, and control of executive power by independent legislatures and courts? Or do African publics still view politics in their countries mainly through the lens of such informal institutions as clientelism, corruption, and trust in (or fear of) "Big Men"? If, as expected, public opinion is mediated by both formal and informal institutions, which are the more salient? And assuming that informal institutions remain important, do they on balance help or harm democracy?

As exemplified by North's broad usage, the term "institution" is one of the loosest in the social-science lexicon. It has been used variously to refer to the rules of the political game, to organizations that link individuals to the political system, or even to "stable, valued and recurring patterns of (political) behavior."[4] In this article, I mean by *formal institutions* the organized routines of political democracy, such as regular elections for top officeholders and legal constraints on the political executive. By *informal institutions* I mean the patterns of patron-client relations by which power is also exercised. Sadly, neither of these two types of political institutions, nor their interactions, are well understood as they exist in and touch on Africa.

One group of Africa scholars—whom we may characterize as "formalists"—contends that the nature of official state institutions decisively shapes citizens' stances toward democracy. Relevant institutions include the constitution (whether it is unitary or federal, presidential or parliamentary); the electoral system (whether it is majoritarian, plurality-based, or proportional); and the party system (whether it is fragmented or one party dominates it). Donald Horowitz, for example, has argued that a federal constitution helps to ease political conflict in deeply divided societies.[5] Andrew Reynolds recommends proportional representation as an electoral formula to protect minority rights.[6] And Daniel N. Posner discovers that the competitiveness of the party system affects whether ethnic groups mobilize along language or tribal lines.[7]

Other scholars—whom we might dub "informalists"—remind us that official state institutions are usually weak in Africa, where unwritten rules hold far more sway. Indeed, Goran Hyden asserts that "Africa is the best starting point for exploring the role of informal institutions" and that these derive from a social logic he calls "the economy of affection."[8] As examples of informal institutions, he includes charisma (an authority relationship based on personal trust); clientelism (the expression of political loyalty to providers of patronage); pooling (horizontal exchanges within small groups); and collective self-defense (for example, the development of shared norms of sovereignty and noninterference).

Within this rich social matrix, three informal institutions seem especially pertinent to struggles for democracy in Africa: clientelism, corruption, and "Big Man" presidentialism. René Lemarchand has argued that, by distributing material rewards to clients, political patrons help to integrate a diversity of cultural groups into a national political community.[9] By contrast, Sahr Kpundeh argues that corruption—defined as the misuse of public office for private gain—"adversely impedes development . . . and participatory governance."[10]

And Nicolas van de Walle draws attention to presidentialism, especially in its informal guises:

> Regardless of constitutional arrangements . . . power is intensely personalized around the figure of the president . . . He is literally above the law, controls in many cases a large proportion of state finance without accountability, and delegates remarkably little of his authority on important matters . . . Only the apex of the executive really matters.[11]

Corruption, clientelism, and "Big Man" presidentialism—all dimensions of neopatrimonial rule—tend to go together as a package. They are "stable, valued and recurring patterns of behavior" to which all political actors are acutely attuned. Indeed, these practices are so ingrained in African political life as to constitute veritable political institutions.

Before turning to empirical analysis, a few final points of conceptual clarification are in order. First, I distinguish formal and informal institutions for analytical purposes only; in reality, these structures thoroughly interpenetrate one another. Indeed, hybrid regimes such as the neopatrimonial variety so common in Africa arise precisely when informal practices of presidential dominance, official corruption, and patron-client ties seep into the formal operations of the state. Second, the assumption that both types of institutions affect the development of democracy is only a first step. The more critical question is which matters *more*: formality or informality? Guillermo O'Donnell argues that in Latin America "the actual rules being followed" often trump mere "parchment" institutions.[12] As a working hypothesis, one would expect this balance to prevail in African countries as well.

Finally, in an important insight, Gretchen Helmke and Steven Levitsky show that informal institutions are a double-edged sword with regard to democracy.[13] Illicit procedures (such as corruption) usually undermine the fair and equal treatment of citizens. Yet in situations where formal institutions remain weak, personal connections (ties of personal loyalty to an incumbent president, for example) can help to secure legitimacy for a fragile democratic regime.

Data and Measurement

Data from the Afrobarometer (AB), a comparative series of public attitude surveys on democracy, governance, markets, and civil society, will help us to analyze the manner and extent of political institutions' effects on popular attitudes toward democracy in Africa.[14] Because the AB uses a standard questionnaire with identical or functionally equivalent items, it affords unique opportunities to compare results across countries and over time. Still, caution should be used in extrapolating findings to the continent as a whole: Survey work can go forward only in Africa's more open and stable societies, so the most authoritarian and conflict-ridden countries have to be left out. The trends reported here are based on three rounds of AB surveys. Round 1 took place in a dozen countries between 1999 and 2001 ("circa 2000"); Round 2 covered sixteen countries from 2002 to 2003 ("circa 2002"); and Round 3 was carried out in eighteen countries in 2005 and 2006 ("circa 2005").[15]

Let us look first at the "demand side" of public opinion. Do Africans *want* democracy and, if so, has popular support been rising or falling? Moreover, as the collective memory of democratic transition fades, are Africans more or less nostalgic for previous systems of authoritarian rule? The analysis then moves to the "supply side" by asking whether Africans think that they are *getting* the political regimes they desire. Now that they have experienced democracy in practice, are Africans satisfied with the quality of rule delivered by their leaders? And, over time, how much democracy do they think their respective countries have achieved?

The analysis finally turns to possible institutional explanations for democratic attitudes. Unlike in conventional macro-level studies, here political institutions are measured from a micro-level perspective. For example, do Africans prefer multiparty elections to other sets of rules for choosing leaders? Do they think that elections are adequate mechanisms for ejecting nonperforming politicians? Do they think the president ought to obey the constitution? Do they conclude that he actually does so?

Regardless of methodology, informal institutions are harder to observe than formal ones. Survey-based indicators are admittedly approximate and fail to capture the full dimensions of complex informal phenomena. But the following indicators represent a sustained effort to capture empirically some key, but slippery, concepts.

Clientelism is measured by an average construct of two related survey questions that ask respondents to "choose either A or B": first, either "A) As citizens, we should be more active in questioning our leaders," or "B) In our country these days, there is not enough respect for authority"; and second, either "A) Since leaders represent everyone, they should not favor their own family or group," or "B) Once in office, leaders are obliged to help their home community." I classify as clients those individuals expressing loyalty toward hometown patrons (in both cases option B).

The indicator of *corruption* is more straightforward: "How many national assembly representatives/local government councilors do you think are involved in corruption?" Regardless of actual levels of graft, those saying "most" or "all" perceive widespread official corruption.

In closing, *presidentialism*—ties of personal loyalty to a presidential "Big Man"—is probed with a question asking: "How much do you trust the President?" Those saying "a lot" or "completely" are taken to be complicit in the informal aspects of presidentialism because, even if the ruler oversteps his constitutional role, these individuals are likely to give him the benefit of the doubt.

Trends in Attitudes Toward Democracy

In 2005, a decade and a half after regime transitions began in earnest in Africa, a clear majority (62 percent) of citizens interviewed prefer democracy to any other kind of government. But is the term "democracy" broadly understood? Almost three-quarters (73 percent) of the more than 25,000 respondents to AB Round 3 could attach a meaning to the "d-word." And, among this better-informed group, 75 percent prefer a democratic regime.

People have the most confidence in democracy in Ghana, Kenya, and Senegal, all countries in which recent elections have brought about an alternation of ruling groups. But support for democracy is a minority sentiment in Madagascar, where leadership alternation was violently resisted by the last loser; and Tanzania, where many residents of the island of Zanzibar were unhappy with the outcome of the previous election. Low levels of support for democracy, however, should not be mistaken for support for a nondemocratic alternative, as large numbers say they "don't know" enough about regime alternatives (Tanzania) or have no regime preference (Madagascar).

To probe the depth of expressed democratic commitments, the survey asks people whether they harbor nostalgia for any of the autocratic forms of government previously common in Africa. Fully 73 percent of all Africans polled, for example, now reject military rule. Compared to the 62 percent who support democracy, this result suggests that feelings of hostility toward authoritarianism are more common than feelings of support for democracy. More people can specify the type of regime that they *do not* want than the kind of regime that they *do* desire. They may be attached to the general *idea* of democracy, but have limited knowledge of or commitment to its specific component *institutions*.

There is little relation between popular rejection of military rule and a country's experience. In those countries where no military coup has ever succeeded (Zambia, Kenya, and Zimbabwe), as well as in those where successful coups have led to long periods of praetorians in power (Ghana and Lesotho), more than four out of five people reject this regime. It is troubling to discover, however, that a majority of Namibians—a population with memories of strong-arm rule from apartheid-era South Africa but no other history of military intervention in politics—say that they would be unconcerned if "the army came in to govern the country."

Similarly, there is little connection between a legacy of single-party rule and its rejection today. With few exceptions, Africans everywhere now seem to prefer a plural polity: On average, 71 percent reject one-party rule. Citizens of Zimbabwe and Zambia have experienced de facto or de jure one-party monopolies, while people in Nigeria and Botswana have never experienced either. Yet at least four out of five respondents in all these countries reject one-party rule. Tanzanians remain more sympathetic to single-party rule than all other Africans, perhaps because the ruling Chama Cha Mapinduzi has always held power in Tanzania, bridging the one-party and multiparty eras. And the liberation-movement heritage in Mozambique, Namibia, and Uganda—and even in South Africa—leads significant minorities still to find appeal in the idea of a vanguard party.

Democracy's trajectory in Africa is reflected in trends in the levels of popular demand for various types of political regime. Are prodemocratic attitudes rising or falling? In the twelve countries for which we have three observations, mass support for democracy has fallen slightly over the past six years, from 69 to 61 percent (see Table 1).[16]

The proportion of people who reject military rule has also dipped (from 82 to 73 percent). Because people continue to reject one-party and one-man rule—the latter at very high levels—the greatest threat to popular support for democracy appears to come from people who are beginning to feel nostalgia for military rule.

But these changes are evident only at the margins. As of our most recent observation in 2005, clear majorities were still dismissing military rule and backing democracy. Moreover, a half or more of all respondents have always rejected *all three* authoritarian alternatives. Finally, to the extent that people learn to be politically consistent—that is, by *simultaneously* rejecting all forms of autocracy *and* embracing democracy—*demand for democracy* is basically holding steady.

Lest we mistakenly take Africa-wide averages to be more representative than they really are, let us examine the cases of extreme change

TABLE 1—TRENDS IN ATTITUDES TO DEMOCRACY, 12 AFRICAN COUNTRIES, 2000–2005 (IN PERCENTAGES)

	CIRCA 2000	CIRCA 2002	CIRCA 2005
DEMAND			
Support democracy	69	62	61
Reject military rule	82	78	73
Reject one-party rule	69	66	70
Reject one-man rule	80	78	78
Reject all 3 authoritarian alternatives	59	50	52
Express demand for democracy*	44	37	46
Display political patience	46	56	56
SUPPLY			
Satisfied with democracy	58	52	46
Perceive extensive democracy	50	49	48
Perceive supply of democracy†	54	51	47
Expect democratic future	—	—	54

* reject all three authoritarian alternatives and also support democracy
† average of satisfaction with, and extent of, democracy

within countries. Popular support for democracy is down most sharply in Tanzania, perhaps because people are becoming confused about whether a one-party–dominant system is truly a democracy. But popular support is up by 10 percentage points in Lesotho, mainly because of the introduction between 1999 and 2002 of a more proportional electoral system. Because this institutional reform was the only major change between elections, herein lies *prima facie* case evidence that formal institutions are beginning to matter in building democratic attachments.[17]

Finally, the most promising sign for democracy's prospects concerns popular political patience. The survey question asked: "Choose either A or B: A) Our present system of elected government should be given more time to deal with inherited problems; or B) If our present system cannot produce results soon, we should try another form of government." The proportion selecting A—the patient option—actually rose and then sta-bilized (at 56 percent), suggesting that, even as some democratic com-mitments weaken with time, Africans are nonetheless willing to accept democracy, "warts and all."

Turning to the supply of democracy, many citizens are beginning to perceive that democracy has distinct shortcomings—"warts" if you will—that include defamatory political discourse, a poor record of ser-vice delivery, and new opportunities for corruption. These concerns are reflected in the sharply declining proportion of Africans interviewed who say that they are "satisfied with the way democracy works in [my country]." Down an average 13 percentage points (from 58 percent circa 2000 to 45 percent circa 2005), the direction of this trend applies to eight of the twelve countries for which three observations are available.

Satisfaction with democracy has risen only in Ghana, Lesotho, Namibia, and South Africa. The continental average is pulled sharply downward by Nigeria, where satisfaction with democracy has collapsed by 58 percentage points in just six years—a steep decline that parallels popular approval of President Olusegun Obasanjo's job performance. Standing in sharp contrast to Nigeria is its smaller West African neighbor Ghana, where democracy's approval rating is up 16 percentage points. This again draws attention to formal political institutions such as Ghana's impressive and steadily improving national Electoral Commission, which has clearly helped democracy to consolidate in that country.

In 2005, for the first time, mass satisfaction with democracy dipped below 50 percent.[18] This means that in nine of the eighteen countries surveyed, fewer than half of all citizens were satisfied. In Madagascar, Malawi, Nigeria, and Zambia, those who approved of democracy's performance amounted to barely a quarter of the population. Judging by this yardstick, these were the Afrobarometer countries in which democracy was at greatest risk. And just 14 percent of Zimbabweans were satisfied with democracy's condition—a sign of just how far, under Robert Mugabe, that country has fallen from the ranks of Africa's open societies.

Several hopeful signs offset this bad news. First, as an alternate measure of democracy's health, the survey asked: "In your opinion, how much of a democracy is [your country] today?" This indicator—which we call the "extent of democracy"—has remained stable over the three rounds of surveys, with about half those interviewed continuing to say that they live in a reasonably high-quality democracy. An apparent slight decline is not statistically significant.

Second, our respondents expressed hope about the future stability of democracy. When asked for the first time in 2005, "In your opinion, how likely is it that [your country] will remain a democracy?" some 54 percent replied that they thought democracy was more likely than not to endure. Taken together with the positive finding about popular patience, these results suggest that Africans have not yet given up on democracy. Indeed, they seem to have emerged from the elated honeymoon of regime transition with the sober view that democracy is imperfect, but still better than the alternatives and thus worth keeping.

To conclude the description of recent trends, I want to make a passing comment about the reliability of the Afrobarometer data. If public opinion constitutes an accurate portrayal of real levels of and trends regarding democracy, then aggregate survey results should correlate with standard measures based on expert opinion. As a test, I compare AB assessments of the "extent of democracy" with the familiar Freedom House (FH) index. Figure 1 confirms that the different research methods tend to validate each other: The AB and FH country-level results correlate very closely (Pearson's r greater than 0.8); accordingly, most observations hug the same regression line. The few exceptions are mi-

FIGURE 1—FREEDOM HOUSE SCORES BY
PERCEIVED EXTENT OF DEMOCRACY, 2005

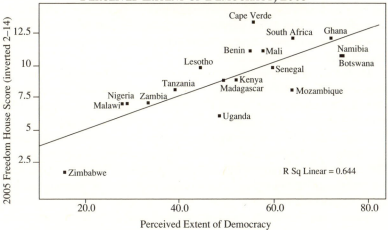

nor: Zimbabweans tend to see a little more democracy than do scholars, while the experts are slightly more sanguine about democracy in Cape Verde than that country's citizens. For the most part, however, ordinary Africans and specialists arrive at almost identical assessments.

Explaining Democratic Attitudes

If survey research says basically the same thing as expert opinion, why bother with the time and expense that surveys require? The reason is that survey data give us a fuller, more fine-grained picture. They permit us to peer below the country level to portray results by different social, economic, regional, and cultural groups. Survey data can also reveal *how* individuals arrive at their opinions, including via routes that run through formal as well as informal institutions.

For example: *Who* among the electorate *wants* democracy? When sociodemographic influences are regressed on *demand for democracy,* the results are revealing. Being a woman or living in a rural area suppresses demand. And aging raises it. Predictably, education is the most important social factor shaping demand for democracy, with an impact three times larger than age or habitat. Perhaps surprisingly, however, Muslims are *more* likely to demand democracy than adherents of other religions, though this result may reflect the inclusion in the Afrobarometer of Mali and Senegal, where democratic procedures readily coexist with moderate forms of Islam.

Take an even more interesting question: *On what basis* do Africans conclude that they are *getting* democracy? What institutional points of reference, if any, do they use? With the popularly perceived *extent of democracy* as the object to be explained, we can postulate that people will base this opinion on their assessments of the quality of political institutions, both formal and informal. Previous analysis has shown that the two most powerful attitudinal predictors of the extent of democracy concern a formal political institution (whether citizens see the last election as "free and fair") and an informal personal tie (whether citizens trust the incumbent national president).[19]

Do the qualities of these institutions continue to predict the supply of democracy circa 2005? And which is the more important: the formal or the informal institution? Model 1 in Table 2 shows the powerful impacts of *both* formal elections *and* informal trust. In a regression analysis, the qualities of these two institutions together predict a third of the variance in popular estimates of the extent of democracy (see adjusted R square). This compares favorably with the 8 percent of variance that is explained by a respondent's education, which is usually held to be a strong predictor of democratic attitudes.[20]

Indeed, the quality of national elections seems to be the principal standard by which ordinary Africans judge their country's degree of democracy. But people also look for excellence in leadership. They must trust the incumbent president before they will judge that democracy is taking root.

Strikingly, the formal institution seems to matter more than the informal one. Here we have additional, cross-national evidence that the rules of democracy (that is, high-quality elections) are formative for popular regime assessments. This finding casts doubt on Staffan Lindberg's assertion that *any* kind of election, regardless of quality, will strengthen the regime.[21] But since this finding also contradicts conventional wisdom about the weakness of institutions in Africa, it must be explored and tested further. To that end, we note that when the impact of the same two predictors is tracked over time, we find citizens' judgment that elections have been "free and fair" accounting for a larger proportion of the explained variance in "extent of democracy" in 2005 (64 percent) than was the case in 2002 (59 percent). Because the explanatory power of the official institution increased significantly from 2002 to 2005, we can tentatively infer that formal rules are gradually displacing informal ones in the public mind.

As a set of formal institutions, however, democracy consists of more than elections alone. Do Africans also endorse the full array of democracy's component institutions? Here we consider four formal institutions, including elections.

First, the Africans we interviewed overwhelmingly prefer to "choose leaders through regular, open and honest *elections*" rather than "adopt other methods." Over time, this preference has held steady among four out of five respondents, and is especially strong in Ghana and Benin. In my opinion, popular support for open elections is now an institutionalized norm of African politics.

Second, competitive elections imply support for another formal institu-

FIGURE 2—FORMAL INSTITUTIONS: POPULAR DEMAND VERSUS PERCEIVED SUPPLY, 18 AFRICAN COUNTRIES, 2005 (IN PERCENTAGES)

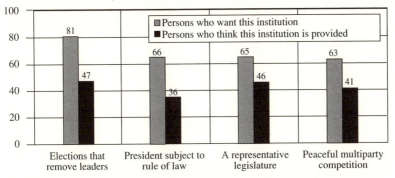

tion of democracy: *multiple political parties*. People say that they prefer "many political parties . . . to make sure [they] have real choices in who governs them" versus finding multiparty competition "unnecessary . . . [because] parties create division and confusion." Abandoning earlier reservations, publics approved of multiple parties at a rate that shot up by an average of 12 percentage points over the three short years from 2002 to 2005, with even greater increases appearing in Lesotho and Zimbabwe.

Third, Africans want their executive presidents held accountable, at least to *parliament*. A gradually rising proportion of citizens—two-thirds by 2005—require that "the members of parliament (rather than the president) make laws." This sentiment is most widespread in Senegal and Mozambique.

Finally, the only formal democratic institution that may be losing support is the rule of law. The proportion that wants the president to "obey the laws and the courts, even if he thinks they are wrong," has recently fallen from three-quarters to two-thirds of all respondents. But this anomalous result may simply be an artifact of a change in the wording of a question that earlier had made explicit reference to constitutional term limits on presidents.

On balance, therefore, growing numbers of Africans seem to support several key political institutions that constitute the formal foundation of a democratic regime. But is this progress on the demand side (the institutions that people *want*) matched by equal satisfaction on the supply side (the institutions that people *get*)?

Figure 2 suggests that Africans are not getting the institutions they want. While 81 percent call for open elections, just 47 percent think that elections actually "enable voters to remove leaders from office." Whereas 66 percent wish to subject the president to the rule of law, a mere 36 percent acknowledge that, in practice, the president "never ignores the constitution." While a similar two-thirds demand a representative legislature, fewer than half think they have actually elected a parliament that "reflect(s) the views of voters." Finally, while a clear majority (63 per-

TABLE 2—EXPLAINING THE PERCEIVED EXTENT OF DEMOCRACY: FORMAL AND INFORMAL INSTITUTIONS

	MODEL 1	MODEL 2
Constant	1.314*	2.615*
FORMAL INSTITUTIONS		
Free and fair elections	.427*	
Elections that remove leaders		.033†
Peaceful multiparty competition		.045*
A representative legislature		.121*
President subject to rule of law		.097*
INFORMAL INSTITUTIONS		
Clientelism		.033*
Corruption		-.121*
Trust in the president	.242*	.255*
Adjusted R square	.330	.187

Unless otherwise indicated in row heading, cell entries are standardized regression coefficients (beta).
* p<.001, † p<.01

cent) yearns for peaceful multiparty competition, a large minority (41 percent) still fears that, in reality, "competition between political parties leads to violent conflict."

Because the performance of all formal institutions systematically falls short of popular expectations, we postulate that people will seek to make up for perceived institutional deficiencies by counting on the informal ties characteristic of clientelism, corruption, and presidentialism—each of which represents a dimension of neopatrimonial rule. Some 28 percent of Africans interviewed exhibited clientelist tendencies when they agreed that they should "respect [the] authority" of leaders who "help their home communities." Twenty-six percent of respondents thought "all" or "most" MPs and local councilors to be "involved in corruption." And, as before, the 64 percent of adults who say that they trust the incumbent president "somewhat" or "a lot" give us a sense of the personal ties that underlie presidentialism.

To weigh the relative importance of specific institutions in shaping the perceived extent of democracy, I enter all four formal institutions and all three informal institutions into a more comprehensive regression analysis (see Model 2 in Table 2). Based on the size and the signs of the regression coefficients, we arrive at several interesting conclusions.

First, once a full range of institutions is considered, an informal linkage stands out. People are most likely to judge the extent of democracy in terms of their trust in the incumbent president. The evidence therefore suggests that African politics has not yet moved fully from the realm of personalities and factions to the realm of policies and formal institutions.

Second, other informal institutions perform as expected: Clientelism (in the form of loyalty to hometown patrons) has a positive effect on perceived extent of democracy; but the perception that elected leaders are corrupt has an effect that is strongly negative. Our data therefore confirm theoretical claims that informal institutions can have either positive or negative effects as regards democracy. In this light, clientelism and corruption are best viewed as two sides of the same coin of distributive politics: Citizens defer to authority when they benefit materially, but question and condemn their leaders when benefits accrue to others, especially political elites.[22]

Third, all formal institutions are statistically significant, reaffirming that—if effectively applied—written rules can help to form popular attachments to democracy. Among the four formal institutions that we have considered, however, a representative legislature seems to have the most effect on ordinary people's judgments of democratic progress. We conclude, therefore, that Africans demand *more* than clean elections. They also require that their leaders spend the time between elections being responsive to popular needs and accepting accountability for their performance in office.

The Institutionalization of Democracy in Africa

Is democracy becoming institutionalized in Africa? It is, if only in part. A decade and a half after the first African regime transitions and despite growing popular disillusionment with democracy in practice, the general *idea* of "rule by the people" remains an attractive prospect for solid majorities of citizens. But popular attachment to the specific *institutions* of a democratic regime—and how willing citizens feel to apply formal criteria of institutional development to the evaluation of regime performance—is a much more varied and tentative matter.

Survey research suggests that regular, open elections are now an institutionalized feature of African politics. Ordinary people use the quality of elections—are they "free and fair"?—as the main gauge of democracy's development in their countries. Moreover, the reform of electoral institutions—for example, the introduction of a proportional electoral system in Lesotho and the creation of an effective electoral commission in Ghana—can have additional positive effects.

Yet even as elections take root, people still question the competitiveness of formal institutions. Many harbor doubts that elections can bring about alternations of incumbent presidents and ruling parties, while others are realizing that an "electoral" democracy alone does not ensure the presence of a responsive and accountable leadership between elections.

Public support for such other formal institutions of democracy as multiple parties, independent courts, and assertive legislatures lags behind support for elections. In addition, the supply of all formal institutions fails to meet popular demands. People continue to think that presidents ignore constitutions, that legislatures fail to represent popular desires, and that multiparty competition all too easily spills over into political violence. As such, Africans estimate that the key elements in a well-functioning democracy—notably institutions that check the executive—are performing below par.

Because formal rules mandating public accountability are persistently weak, people turn to other standards for judging the extent of democratic growth. Informal values and patterns of behavior continue to shape Africans' orientations toward their respective polities. When asked to appraise the quality of democracy in their own countries, citizens still fall back on personal ties of trust—especially trust in the "Big Man" president who continues to personify the government and the regime. As long as loyal clients are rewarded by the distribution of material benefits, informal ties can help to generate legitimacy for a democratic regime. But if political elites monopolize available resources, then citizens tend to see corruption, an informal institution that is clearly corrosive to democracy.

NOTES

1. James March and Johan Olsen, "The New Institutionalism: Organizational Factors in Political Life," *American Political Science Review* 78 (September 1984): 734–49. See also their "Elaborating the 'New Institutionalism,'" in R.A.W. Rhodes, Sarah Binder, and Bert Rockman, eds., *The Oxford Handbook of Political Institutions* (Oxford: Oxford University Press, 2006).

2. Douglass C. North, *Institutions, Institutional Change and Economic Performance* (New York: Cambridge University Press, 1990), 4.

3. H.W.O. Okoth-Ogendo, "Constitutions Without Constitutionalism: Reflections on an African Political Paradox," in Issa Shivji, ed., *The State and Constitutionalism: An African Debate on Democracy* (Harare: SAPES Trust, 1991), 3–25.

4. Samuel P. Huntington, *Political Order in Changing Societies* (New Haven: Yale University Press, 1968), 12.

5. Donald L. Horowitz, *A Democratic South Africa? Constitutional Engineering in a Divided Society* (Berkeley: University of California Press, 1991).

6. Andrew Reynolds, *Electoral Systems and Democratization in Southern Africa* (Oxford: Oxford University Press, 1999).

7. Daniel N. Posner, *Institutions and Ethnic Politics in Africa* (New York: Cambridge University Press, 2005).

8. Goran Hyden, *African Politics in Comparative Perspective* (New York: Cambridge University Press, 2006), 7 and 78.

9. René Lemarchand, "Political Clientelism and Ethnicity in Tropical Africa: Competing Solidarities in Nation-Building," *American Political Science Review* 66 (February 1972): 91–112.

10. Sahr J. Kpundeh, "Corruption and Corruption Control," in E. Gyimah-Boadi, ed.,

Democratic Reform in Africa: The Quality of Progress (Boulder, Colo.: Lynne Rienner, 2004), 121.

11. Nicolas van de Walle, "Presidentialism and Clientelism in Africa's Emerging Party Systems," *Journal of Modern African Studies* 41 (June 2003): 310.

12. Guillermo O'Donnell, "Another Institutionalization: Latin America and Elsewhere," *Kellogg Institute Working Paper No. 222* (Indiana: University of Notre Dame, 1996).

13. Gretchen Helmke and Steven Levitsky, *Informal Institutions and Democracy: Lessons from Latin America* (Baltimore: Johns Hopkins University Press, 2006).

14. Afrobarometer surveys are based on randomly selected national probability samples ranging in size from 1,200 to 2,400 respondents per country and representing a cross-section of citizens in each country aged 18 years or older. Samples are selected from the best available census frames and yield a margin of sampling error of no more than plus or minus three percentage points at a 95 percent confidence level. All interviews are conducted face-to-face by trained fieldworkers in the language of the respondent's choice. Response rates average above 80 percent.

15. Benin, Botswana, Cape Verde, Ghana, Kenya, Lesotho, Madagascar, Malawi, Mali, Mozambique, Namibia, Nigeria, Senegal, South Africa, Tanzania, Uganda, Zambia, and Zimbabwe. Zimbabwe is included since, at the time of the first survey in 1999, it was still a relatively open society. Uganda is also covered because, even in the country's conflict-wracked northern zones, survey research has proven possible.

16. The figure of 61 percent diverges from the previously reported average of 62 percent because it refers to only 12 countries. AB does not yet have three observations for all 18 countries.

17. For in-depth analysis, see Wonbin Cho and Michael Bratton, "Electoral Institutions, Partisan Status, and Political Support in Lesotho," *Electoral Studies* 25 (December 2006): 731–50.

18. Although only 46 percent expressed high levels of satisfaction ("fairly" plus "very" satisfied), even fewer (36 percent) expressed low levels ("not very" and "not at all").

19. Calculated from AB Round 1 data. See also Michael Bratton, Robert Mattes, and E. Gyimah Boadi, *Public Opinion, Democracy and Market Reform in Africa* (New York: Cambridge University Press, 2005), 278.

20. Because educated people have developed their critical faculties, education is negative for the perceived extent of democracy, whereas the institutional indicators are positive.

21. Staffan Lindberg, *Democracy and Elections in Africa* (Baltimore: Johns Hopkins University Press, 2006).

22. I am indebted to E. Gyimah-Boadi for helping me think through this puzzle. Other useful comments from Wonbin Cho, Adrienne LeBas, and Daniel Posner were received gratefully.

II

West Africa

9

NIGERIA'S MUDDLED ELECTIONS

Rotimi T. Suberu

Rotimi T. Suberu, *professor of politics at Bennington College, Ver-*
mont, was Senior Fellow at the United States Institute of Peace in
2006–2007. This essay originally appeared in the October 2007 issue
of the Journal of Democracy.

The Nigerian general elections of 14 and 21 April 2007 marked the
first time in the nearly half-century-long postindependence history of
this most populous African country that one civilian government would
hand over power to another. Yet what should have been a milestone for
democracy threatens instead to become a millstone, as an electoral process riddled with corruption and malfeasance raises doubts about prospects for democratic stability and consolidation.

In the voting's most high-profile result, Umaru Yar'Adua of the ruling People's Democratic Party (PDP) emerged as the official winner of
the presidential race with a reported 70 percent of the vote. The PDP
also won 28 of the 36 state governorships and more than two-thirds of
the seats in both houses of the National Assembly. Yet the sordid manipulation and outrageous maladministration that foreign and domestic
observers documented made a travesty of the voting. Foreshadowed by
a depressingly long history of corrupt and chaotic elections as well as
by more immediate preelection shenanigans, the failure of the 2007 balloting to meet basic standards of fairness, efficiency, and transparency
has thrown Nigeria once more into a frustrating impasse. This comes at
a moment when the country should be looking forward to greater progress toward democratic stability, national unity, development-friendly
governance, and continental leadership.

The tragedy is that the 2007 elections presented such a promising opportunity for Nigeria to break with a legacy of violent political instability, including multiple bloody military coups and the collapse or abor-
tion of three democratic republics. Launched in 1999, Nigeria's Fourth
Democratic Republic has seen the longest period of civilian rule since

independence from Britain in 1960. April 2007, following the elections of 1999 and 2003, should have sounded a favorable note to preface the historic intercivilian transition that took place with the presidential inauguration at the end of May. Yar'Adua did take office as scheduled, but it was amid the sour aftermath of a corrupted process that further entrenched PDP hegemony.

On a positive note, the April elections were happily well-insulated from Nigeria's combustible internal divisions—no small thing in a federation long troubled by ethnoregional and religious splits, including a bitter secessionist war from 1967 to 1970. The containment of divisiveness was the result of an informal power-sharing bargain among elites from each of the federation's six quasi-official geopolitical zones, three each in the north and south.

In an echo of the 1999 election—when the two contenders for the presidency had both been Christian Yorubas from the southwest—the three leading candidates in 2007 were Muslim Hausa-Fulanis from the north. Yet even this creative attempt at accommodation has been overshadowed by the 2007 electoral process's sheer fraudulence, which makes the federation less able to manage challenges to its stability. Although the country is not about to disintegrate, it is well to remember that intercommunal clashes have killed at least ten thousand Nigerians since 1999. Electoral corruption could wind up exacting a price in blood if it aggravates or impedes the solution of existing regional conflicts that include a spiraling insurgency among the Ijaw of the oil-rich Niger Delta, Islamist pressures in the Muslim north, and autonomist agitations among the Igbo and the Yoruba in the southeast and southwest, respectively.

The manipulated balloting of 2007 underlines the disheartening degree to which dishonest elites have systematically mismanaged this oil-rich but governance-poor country. Nigeria has earned around US$500 billion in oil revenues since the 1970s, yet remains mired in poverty, unemployment, a burgeoning domestic debt, infrastructural squalor, insecurity of lives and property, abysmal health and educational services, and attendant social frustration and unrest.

The eight-year administration of former military ruler Olusegun Obasanjo (he was uniformed head of state from 1976 to 1979 and served as elected president from 1999 to 2007) was not without achievements to its credit. These included macroeconomic reforms that enhanced economic growth, reduced external debt, expanded external reserves, promoted the saving of windfall oil revenues, improved budgetary transparency, and spawned an unprecedented anticorruption campaign. And yet, these successes have so far yielded little in terms of enhanced socioeconomic opportunities for ordinary Nigerians. Furthermore, Obasanjo's legacy is heavily tainted not only by his role in the 2007 electoral mess, but also by his 2006 scheme—stymied by the Senate in May of that year—to set up a third-term run for himself by changing the constitution.[1] Critics even insinuate that Yar'Adua is a "puppet-President" through whom Obasanjo has won a "third term in disguise."[2] At the same time, while he is explicitly committed to continuing Obasanjo's macroeconomic reforms, Yar'Adua's mild manner, background in civilian politics (he was governor of Katsina state), and progressive ideological outlook distinguish him from his forceful, military-trained, and politically conservative predecessor.

Electoral Brigandage

If the 2003 general elections were "hardly credible," the 2007 balloting was blatantly fraudulent.[3] Most independent observers described it as the ugliest that they had ever witnessed anywhere, in Africa or beyond. Some called for canceling the results and rerunning the vote. At the heart of the problem was President Obasanjo's and the PDP's interference with the Independent National Electoral Commission (INEC). Wole Soyinka, the Nobel Prize–winning novelist and courageous social critic, claims that the charade was "premeditated" by what he calls "the Gang of Four," namely, Nigeria Police Force (NPF) inspector-general Sunday Ehindero, INEC chief Maurice Iwu, PDP national chairman Ahmadu Ali, and "the principal of the Gang . . . Obasanjo."[4]

While Obasanjo had avoided playing a directly visible role in the politically disruptive and fraud- and bribery-riddled third-term effort, he was at the forefront of his party's violent and corrupt 2007 election campaign. Obasanjo's tools were the vast resources of the Nigerian presidency. These include control over federal oil-based patronage, as well as personnel and operational authority over the NPF, the armed forces, the security services, the Economic and Financial Crimes Commission (EFCC), and the INEC.

When the third-term agenda failed, Obasanjo set out to pick the next president. The first step was to stop Obasanjo's bitter rival, Vice-President Abubakar Atiku, from gaining the PDP nomination. Obasanjo installed his loyalists in place of Atiku's supporters in the PDP hierarchy, while Atiku found himself suspended from membership due to alleged antiparty activities. The vice-president would end up running on the ticket of a new party called the Action Congress (AC) and coming in a distant third with 7 percent of the vote.

Obasanjo's endorsement of the reluctant and frail Yar'Adua for the PDP's nomination sidelined other aspirants, including several prominent governors. Thus, the PDP's December 2006 presidential primary, not unlike the undemocratic primaries held by several of the country's remaining 49 parties, became a "coronation" for Yar'Adua rather than a democratic contestation.

President Obasanjo then set a thuggish tone for the electoral campaign by infamously describing the 2007 elections as a "do-or-die" affair for the PDP. This added tension to an already-fraught atmosphere that would be marred by about seventy election-related deaths, including political assassinations, in the five months preceding the voting. More important, Obasanjo's inflammatory words bespoke the federal government's determination to tilt the board in the PDP's favor and cripple the opposition, especially the AC and the All Nigerian Peoples Party (ANPP). The police would brazenly intimidate or detain opposition supporters and candidates, ransack the offices and campaign headquarters of opposition parties, and deny permits for major opposition rallies and meetings. Even independent organizations, including private media and civic organizations, suspected of opposition sympathies would become targets of police and security-service harassment and intimidation. Nor would police misconduct be the end of it. The EFCC, INEC, and an ad hoc panel of presidential appointees—sometimes acting in defiance of court rulings—began issuing politically motivated corruption indictments in order to disqualify targeted candidates. Although several PDP figures were affected, the main casualties were key opposition candidates and opponents of the president, including Vice-President Atiku.

To their credit, Nigeria's judges were ready to hear appeals for remedy, but presidential maneuvering impeded them. The ploys included a malevolent declaration of public holidays that prevented the Supreme Court from sitting during the run-up to the April 14 gubernatorial elections, thereby foiling the Court's subsequent April 16 ruling denying INEC's authority to disqualify political aspirants, including the AC or ANPP gubernatorial candidates in Adamawa, Anambra, Delta, and Kogi states. At the same time, INEC ignored (or selectively enforced) court rulings undoing its decertifications of opposition candidates. The Commission typically claimed that the order in question clashed with INEC's constitutional mandate, would pose logistical problems, or else came from a court without proper jurisdiction.

Such partisan abuse of a nominally "independent" body was possible because of its parallel existence as a subordinate presidential or "federal executive" body. The naming of INEC's chairman and twelve national commissioners is effectively in the hands of the president (subject to Senate confirmation). INEC's resident electoral commissioners (there is one in each of the 36 states and the Federal Capital Territory [FCT] of Abuja) are direct presidential appointees. Despite efforts in the National Assembly to guarantee INEC's budgetary autonomy, INEC still depends directly on funds from the federal executive.

Under Maurice Iwu, a professor of pharmacy whom Obasanjo had nominated for the chairman's post in 2005, INEC not only helped the president and hampered his foes, but also turned a hostile eye on foreign election observers and domestic monitors alike. Spuriously claiming that "election observation is different from election monitoring," INEC officials insisted that "it is only INEC that is constitutionally permitted to monitor the elections in Nigeria."[5]

Some domestic monitors and opposition figures alleged that INEC was aiming beyond pro-PDP rigging toward a level of deliberate incompetence or "programmed failure" so abysmal that Obasanjo would have a pretext for ignoring the elections and staying in power.[6] The Commission's mismanagement of the voter-registration process did nothing to undermine such charges. Innovative biometric Direct Data Capture (DDC) machines were not made available by the Commission in a functional, sufficient, transparent, or timely manner. Instead, several of the devices were "directly captured" by so-called godfathers (political patrons who sponsor and manipulate candidates into political offices in return for government patronage) associated with the PDP rigging operation.

The mishandling of the DDC machines caused many prospective voters to be left off the rolls while underage voters were often included; delayed the conclusion of the voter-registration process beyond the deadline set by the 2006 Electoral Act; impeded the display, verification, and revision of the rolls; prevented the issuing of permanent voter ID cards (as distinct from temporary voting slips); and generally littered the voter lists with errors. Close observers were accordingly skeptical when INEC proudly but implausibly announced that it had successfully registered 61 million voters out of an estimated voting-age population of 70 million.

Aside from this bungling (or bungling-with-intent) regarding the voter rolls, INEC was unable or unwilling to fulfill its statutory responsibility to regulate campaign financing, failed to conduct voter education (or to make sample ballot papers available for such education), and also failed transparently to recruit and adequately to train the half-million temporary staffers needed to run the elections. These lapses presaged the administrative chaos that would engulf the April 14 subfederal elections as well as the federal balloting a week later.

Both rounds were marred by grave administrative shortcomings. These included poor matching of the voter lists to Nigeria's 120,000 polling stations; the delayed arrival or nonarrival of polling officials or materials; serious printing errors (including omissions of candidates or parties) on ballot papers; lack of ballot secrecy due to the nonprovision of polling booths; uneven or lopsided distribution of ballot papers to polling stations; absence of adequate security at polling stations; the seemingly deliberate undersupply or nonsupply of crucial voting materials (such as ballot papers, results sheets, ink pads, and rechargeable lanterns) to polling stations in opposition strongholds; and, most crucially, the absence of a transparent process for collating, tabulating, recording, transmitting, announcing, and publishing the voting results.

These failures set the stage for numerous abuses and irregularities. Registered voters found themselves disenfranchised or intimidated by armed party thugs; votes were bought or cast *en bloc* by bosses rather than by individuals; ballot boxes were diverted, stolen, or stuffed; opposition politicians and voters virtually boycotted the process in many areas; and results were doctored or fabricated. In several locales the process collapsed so utterly that INEC found itself on 28 April 2007 forced to rerun a pair of governor's races (in Imo and Enugu states, respectively) and more than a hundred national and state legislative contests across 27 states.

Across the federation (and notably in Anambra, Delta, Jigawa, Katsina, Nasarawa, Ondo, and Osun states) violence surrounding the voting's conduct or outcome took an estimated two-hundred lives, including those of 39 police officers. Arsonists struck INEC offices, police stations, and the houses of local PDP leaders.

As in 1999 and 2003, some of the worst cases of electoral chicanery took place in the volatile, oil-endowed, and arms-infested Niger Delta. Here there were credible reports of "PDP gunmen beating up opponents, intimidating voters, snatching ballot papers, and stuffing them with pre-marked ballots," the sad signs of an electoral travesty in which "winning candidates piled up huge victories on high turnouts in places where the ballot papers had never arrived."[7] The 2007 elections had represented a chance for Nigeria to take at least a step toward easing the crisis (fueled by environmental degradation, socioeconomic deprivation, and political corruption and marginalization) that grips the troubled oil region. The area desperately needs legitimate and accountable governments, and competitive politics offers the only path that can lead to them. Thanks to the electoral abuses, however, even this glimmer of hope has been dimmed if not snuffed out altogether.

Missed Opportunities

Having recently seen their country take a major part in efforts to promote democratization or conflict resolution in Liberia, Sudan, and Sierra Leone, Nigerians could look forward to the 2007 races as a chance not only to mitigate internal conflicts but also to take on a leading role in Africa as a whole. But again, these hopes turned to ashes. The conduct of the April elections fell abysmally short of the markers laid down by recent ballotings in Liberia and the Democratic Republic of Congo— each of which is less endowed and more conflicted than Nigeria. Friends of Nigerian democracy both at home and abroad have been left to worry whether Nigeria is not only setting a bad example for the rest of Africa, but also courting an internal crisis that could spawn violence and instability across the already-fragile region.

After eight years of uninterrupted civilian rule—the longest such period in Nigerian history—and with Obasanjo and most of the governors ineligible for reelection, the 2007 races also offered the possibility of a break with Nigeria's history of corrupt, civilian-run elections. Instead, the elections saw abuses worse than those that had debilitated previous civilian regimes and precipitated military coups. Although few Nigerians want to see a return to the days of arbitrary military rule, the failure of the elections casts doubts on Nigeria's capacity to evolve a stable system of civilian succession that can permanently insulate the polity from the political ambitions of those in uniform.

The elections were a missed opportunity for party political development. Without the competitive discipline of a credible electoral system that rewards partisan coalitions with offices on the basis of the voters' verdict, Nigeria's parties will continue to be weak, faction-ridden, personality-driven institutions lacking internal democracy, viable organizations, coherent policy platforms, robust social bases, genuine cross-regional appeal, or effective representation for women and other marginalized social groups. Even the PDP—which proclaims itself to be Africa's largest party and is in fact impressively multiregional—remains a fractious and ideologically inarticulate congeries of politicians whose great common enterprise is the doling out of patronage along ethnogeographical lines.

To continue the litany of chances not seized, the misconducted elections formed a huge setback in Nigeria's quest for participatory, legitimate, and stable governance. The Obasanjo years saw popular approval of the performance of Nigeria's fledging democratic institutions drop sharply owing to the perceived absence of a "democracy dividend" in the form of improved living standards for the impoverished majority. Nevertheless, Nigerians' preference for democracy over authoritarian alternatives wavered relatively little, suggesting that a credible electoral process in 2007 could have bolstered confidence in and patience with key institutions.[8] April's electoral debacle, however, left the Nigerian citizenry further alienated by the "willful destruction of democratic culture and institutions, the . . . tyranny of a few, the relentless assault on the people . . . [and] the corruption of the system," as a coalition of Nigeria's labor and civil society organizations put it in a statement published in the Lagos newspaper *This Day* on 24 May 2007.

Finally, the elections were a missed opportunity for the consolidation of Nigeria's federalism. A promise of constitutional decentralization in Nigeria is that the existence of multiple state governments, with significant policy autonomy and access to resources, can "spread the stakes" of political competition, making struggles for control over the center less intense and helping political pluralism and policy innovations to gain footholds in different states governed by various parties. In a sign of how well voters grasp this, the campaign period found them showing more interest in gubernatorial races than they did in the presidential contest.[9] But the malign hand of electoral manipulation suppressed the federalist genius, producing an artificial condition of near-monolithic PDP dominion over both the federal and subfederal levels of government. The only bright spots were the opposition wins in key states such

as Lagos and Kano (the country's two most populous). These hold out
hope that federalism, despite the ruling party's efforts to undermine it,
might have a future after all.

Muddling Through a Historic Transition

The failure of the 2007 elections has been partly mitigated by a few
pockets of electoral rectitude across the federation, by the hope of judicial review of electoral malfeasance, and by the sheer stabilizing inge-
nuity of ethnoregional power-sharing, all of which have enabled Nigeria
to muddle through its first-ever transition from one civilian government
to another.

Given INEC's deliberately shoddy logistical performance and the
cloud of uncertainty that veiled Obasanjo's intentions, perhaps the most
remarkable things about the 2007 elections are that they took place at
all, and that Obasanjo stepped down and let a civilian successor take office on the date set by law, 29 May 2007. Neither of these outcomes was
guaranteed, and Nigeria's civil society and political opposition, including factions within the PDP itself, deserve credit for their resolute collective stand against any extension of Obasanjo's eight years in power.

A balanced assessment of the elections would also acknowledge the
relative credibility of some of the processes and outcomes. Testifying before the Africa subcommittee of the U.S. House of Representatives Foreign Affairs Committee in June 2007, Wole Soyinka conceded that the
results in the states of Abia, Bauchi, Kano, Lagos, and Zamfara "reflected,
fairly accurately, the electoral will of the people."[10] Similarly, observers
from the Washington-based National Democratic Institute described having seen on April 21 "a relatively smooth electoral process in some parts
of the FCT, Niger, Plateau and Lagos states. In these places . . . polling officials and party agents generally performed professionally and operated
to produce a credible voting process on elections day."[11]

Candidly if more controversially, it should also be admitted that even
in a free and fair election Yar'Adua would probably still have won.
It is true that Yar'Adua's official landslide victory diverged from pre-
election opinion surveys showing a close race, with the PDP standard-
bearer as only a "marginal favorite" possibly facing a runoff against the
ANPP's Mohammed Buhari.[12] In retrospect, however, the reasons for
Yar'Adua's victory are easy to see: the PDP's enormous patronage and
incumbency powers, the divided opposition, and the negative personal
qualities of major opponents such as Buhari (a former military dictator
with a reputation for ethnoreligious chauvinism) and the AC's Atiku
(arguably one of the more corrupt politicians in a country not noticeably
short of them).

Friends of democracy can take some solace from the opposition's
ability to hold its own at the state level. While the PDP had gone from

controlling 21 state governments in 1999 to running 28 in 2003, the 2007 election process actually saw one state governorship (Anambra) slip from PDP to All-Progressive Grand Alliance control as a result of a courageous June 2007 Supreme Court ruling.[13] In addition, opposition parties triumphed in the states of Bauchi, Borno, Kano, Yobe, and Zamfara (under ANPP); Abia and Imo (PPA); and Lagos (AC).

The opposition campaigned strongly and was probably robbed of victory in several other states, including Adamawa, Edo, Ekiti and Osun (all of which are places where the AC is strong), Ondo (Labor Party), and Oyo (ANPP). A credible electoral-adjudication process could displace the PDP from a number of these states, potentially culminating in opposition control of no less than a third of the Nigerian states, thereby enhancing the vitality of the country's federal democracy. Although the prospect of such judicial intervention on behalf of the opposition is a real and ongoing one, the PDP's virtual stranglehold on the country's political institutions and resources makes the prognosis quite precarious.

In some states (Lagos, Abia, Borno, Kano, Yobe, Zamfara), the opposition won because it was already in office and had ample patronage to use for keeping itself there. In Bauchi state, it had by far the most appealing gubernatorial candidate. In Bauchi, as well as in Kano and Lagos, it was able to mobilize the electorate behind a campaign of "mandate protection" against election riggers. In a few states (Abia, Bauchi, Imo), the PDP had split. And in Anambra, as we have seen, the judges stepped in to enforce the law and deny the PDP an ill-gotten gain.

Indeed, the real prospect of electoral justice via the judiciary or elections tribunals has been a crucial mitigating element in Nigeria's muddled elections and transition. This has undoubtedly contributed to the containment of postelection turmoil, as aggrieved opposition candidates have mainly sought redress through the elections tribunals rather than violent street protests or the incitement of military intervention. The recourse to the judiciary derives from the exemplary independence and integrity that the courts, especially the Supreme Court, have exhibited since 1999. Such independence is, in turn, the result of the substantial political insulation enjoyed by the judiciary under the 1999 Constitution.

Unlike INEC, which is a virtual appendage of the presidency, the topmost federal judges are first "nominated" by the professional Federal Judicial Service Commission, then "recommended" by the National Judicial Council (NJC), formally appointed by the president, and finally confirmed by the Senate. The NJC, chaired by the chief justice of the Supreme Court and incorporating senior serving and retired jurists as well as representatives from the legal and other professions, has earned broad praise for its contribution to the nonpartisan staffing and oversight of the judiciary.

No one should think, however, that the electoral-adjudication process is free from severe constraints. For starters, INEC has been hiding, destroying, and altering documents.[14] Then there are the frustrating delays that can beset a judicial process ungoverned by statutory time limits. Major petitions arising from the 2003 elections took an average of three years to conclude. These included the APGA's ultimately successful challenge in Anambra as well as Buhari's failed effort to overturn Obasanjo's reelection. What makes these delays especially problematic is the practice of letting cases drag on while also inaugurating the "official" (even if challenged) winners before petitions are resolved. In several states, a governor-elect under challenge has, upon taking the oath of office, immediately begun using state resources to back his legal defense, coopt parts of the opposition, and generally corrupt or impede the course of electoral justice.

Sadly, that course has all too often proved all too corruptible. Although the Supreme Court has stood firm as a beacon of independence and integrity, the lower tiers of the judicial system have been vulnerable to manipulation. After the 2003 voting, for instance, four members of the Akwa Ibom Governorship Election Tribunal, two justices of the Court of Appeal, and a judge of the Federal High Court were dismissed on the NJC's recommendation for taking bribes designed to influence their adjudication of election petitions.[15] Indeed, an official survey of the Lagos state judiciary (the largest in the federation) showed that 99 percent of lawyers who frequently used the judiciary agreed that there was corruption in the courts, with 53 percent saying that they "would not report judicial corruption through fear of being victimized."[16]

A final problem has been the sheer number of petitions arising from the 2007 balloting. About 1,250 separate legal challenges have been filed at all levels. This total is sure to overburden and overpoliticize the judiciary, leading not only to temporary delays but also perhaps to permanent diminution of the courts' reputation. This difficult situation underlines the truth that judicial review of elections—even if carried out by honest and efficient courts—cannot take the place of credible and competent electoral administration.[17] That is a lesson for the future, however. For the present, Nigerian democracy will have to rely on the court system to do the best job it can of acting as a key redeeming institution.

If the judiciary (or at least its upper ranks) has been a silver lining in the electoral cloud, so has been the polity's remarkable ability to contain sectionalism by developing a broad national consensus behind the election of a northern Muslim to succeed to the federal presidency after eight years of leadership by a southern Christian chief executive. This process of ethnoregional and sectarian power-sharing has been reinforced by the emergence of Goodluck Jonathan (an Ijaw from Bayelsa in the restive Niger Delta) as Yar'Adua's running mate and vice-president; David Mark (from Benue in the north-central region) as Senate president; Olubunmi Ette (from Osun in the southwest) as speaker of the House of Representatives; and Gana Kingibe (from Borno in the northeast) as secretary to the Government of the Federation. Yar'Adua's July 2007 appointments of figures from the southeastern Igbo elites to the leadership of strategic ministries such as external affairs, education, and commerce and industry, could cement this power-sharing ethic.

Although such elite-level accommodations are helpful, they are not nearly enough. Having a few top people agree on how to divide up offices and their spoils cannot take the place of principled reforms designed to address grassroots socioeconomic grievances, and might even alienate mass constituencies enough to rouse ethnoregional back-lashes that separately or together would undercut the very stability that elite pacts are meant to secure. Along with the task of containing the crisis of legitimacy that their flawed elections have left behind, Yar'Adua and the governors now must tackle the crucial task of saving Nigeria's faltering federal democracy from possible implosion or stagnation.

Implosion, Stagnation, or Reform?

In his inaugural address, President Yar'Adua acknowledged the "shortcomings" of the 2007 balloting and pledged to "set up a panel to examine the entire electoral process with a view to ensuring that we raise the quality and standard of our general elections, and thereby deepen our democracy." He also promised to give "urgent attention" to the Niger Delta crisis, physical infrastructure (especially power generation, transmission, and distribution), security of life and private investments, corruption control, and poverty eradication.

Despite these brave words, many fear that governance under Yar'Adua will be stymied by his tainted legitimacy, the multiple legal challenges (by Buhari and Atiku, among others) to his election, and the corrupting influence of the PDP rigging machine that brought him to power. An early concern has been his administration's failure vigorously to pursue corruption charges against most of the former governors, who no longer enjoy constitutional immunity from prosecution. Of the approximately thirty former governors that the EFCC has indicted for corruption, only six (the erstwhile chief executives of Abia, Bayelsa, Enugu, Jigawa, Plateau, and Taraba states) have been arraigned, convicted, or sentenced. This is because most of the former PDP governors actively supported Yar'Adua's presidential campaign, while former ANPP governors have been supportive of Yar'Adua's inclusion of a faction of that party in a government of national unity as a means of dampening political grievances and legal challenges over the misconduct of the elections. Thus, despite the new president's symbolic and nationally unprecedented act of transparency in publicly declaring his financial assets, there are fears that the Yar'Adua government may sacrifice Obasanjo's anticorruption legacy on the altar of political expediency.

Without any significant progress on corruption control and on the president's other declared policy priorities, including electoral reform and the Niger Delta, the administration could collapse (or at least be rendered irrelevant) amid a legitimacy crisis, electoral lawsuits, governmental paralysis, popular frustration, social conflict, and military adventurism. The soldiers are in the barracks, but they are watching. As the chief of the Defence Staff, General Martin Luther Agwai, remarked ominously in June 2007: "If the politicians . . . start burning . . . this country, what do you want the military to do? To fold their arms and keep quiet?"[18]

Implosion is less likely than simple stagnation, for several reasons. First, the public mood, even among the disenfranchised electorate and the shortchanged opposition, is against the return of the military, whose record in power has never been anything but catastrophic. Second, the military has become more professionalized since 1999 and is clearly less inclined than before to meddle in politics. Third, contemporary Nigerian politics is a form of de facto civilian-military diarchy in which the corporate interests of the military are substantially preserved through the continuing prominence of former military officers in the PDP government and party machinery. For example, Obasanjo heads the PDP's board of trustees, while Ahmadu Ali is party chairman, David Mark is Senate president, Godwin Abbe is interior minister, and Murtala Nyako, Jonah Jang, and Olagunsoye Oyinlola are state governors. All are retired officers.

What is more, Yar'Adua's shrewd response to some of the initial challenges to his administration, including a nationwide strike over hikes in value-added taxes and fuel prices that Obasanjo decreed during his eleventh hour in office, has underscored the new president's ability to sustain civilian rule amid potential turbulence. What is in doubt is whether he can go beyond token tinkering with Obasanjo's conflicted legacy to implement the reforms that must happen if Nigeria is to shake off its political and socioeconomic malaise.

To be sure, hopes for structural reform face unfavorable odds. The country is a classic rentier state in which politics revolves around personal and factional competition for control over the precious oil resource, rather than a contestation among political coalitions with alternative policy programs or reform agendas.

A syndrome of this neopatrimonial political culture in Nigeria is the entrenchment of a form of "gray-zone" politics in which democratic attributes (civil society activism, an independent judiciary, and even some genuine political competition and alternation at the subfederal level) coexist with serious democratic deficits. The latter include corrupt patronage politics that is far removed from the aspirations of the citizenry, the unrestrained use of state resources to buttress PDP dominance, elections that offer little prospect of prying the ruling party away from the patronage font, the readiness of elites to use force and fraud to stifle competition, and a progressive tendency toward the emasculation and collapse of state authority.[19]

At the same time, these antidemocratic tendencies are coming under greater challenge than ever from several sources. Among these are a pluralistic and irrepressible civil society and citizenry at large, the continuing influence of the federalist idea with its longstanding insistence on the virtues of dispersing power, and an evolving commitment to the rule of law as evidenced by the growing assertiveness of the independent judiciary. Upon these forces—beleaguered but by no means beaten or bowed—rest hopes for democratic reform and development in Nigeria.

An Agenda for Reform

There is a growing recognition of the need for reform of the electoral process—above all, for some method of insulating INEC from partisan politics. Proposals now under discussion range from the use of interim administrations to replace the regular party-based government during election periods, to giving parties formal representation within INEC, to putting INEC seats under the control of civil society organizations.

Nigeria's one experience with an interim administration—handpicked by the military in 1993—was not a happy one, and no one today seems to have any feasible notion of how such a government can be democratically constituted, constitutionally legitimated, or made truly nonpartisan and independent. An explicitly multipartisan INEC is also an idea that could backfire, given the welter of factions—some bitter opponents of the ruling party, but others its clients—that vie with one another today in a climate of mutual distrust and untransparency.

One of the more compelling proposals envisions letting a council of independent groups from civil society appoint and supervise members of key regulatory institutions, including the electoral commission.[20] Perhaps more practical is the suggestion to place INEC, along with other vital agencies such as the police force and the anticorruption commission, under the stewardship of the independent judiciary. The NJC, acting on the basis of nominations submitted by nonpartisan civil society groups, would take the lead in filling the top posts in these governance bodies. Like candidates for federal judicial posts, those recommended for INEC seats would have to be formally appointed by the president and then confirmed by the Senate. The current 36 state-level independent electoral commissions would be similarly appointed and confirmed by governors and state legislatures on the recommendations of the NJC; better still, these commissions could be merged into a politically insulated INEC in order to avoid duplication and better harness scarce technical and financial resources.

In addition to walling off (as much as possible) electoral-oversight bodies from partisan politics, two other widely talked about and complementary ideas hold promise. One is to stagger the schedule of elections, and the other is to streamline the process for resolving disputes over their outcomes. Currently, federal as well as state legislative and executive elections are all held during more or less the same two- to three-week period every four years, which puts too much strain on the electoral commission, to say nothing of the entire political system.[21] To remedy this, former INEC chairman Abel Guobadia suggests a "constitutional arrangement" that would allow elections "to be held . . . a year or two years apart."[22] Guobadia also proposes a constitutional amendment that would require every valid election appeal to be resolved before anyone can be sworn into the affected office. Among other things, this will probably mean extending (possibly by several months) the constitutionally specified interim (usually thirty or sixty days) that comes between balloting for an office and the seating of the election winner.

As the frustrating history of the constitutional-reform movement since 1999 suggests, changes to Nigeria's basic law will be hard to achieve. Standing in the way are not only the concurrent federal and state legislative supermajorities that amendments must attract and the sheer number of such proposed changes (currently it is more than a hundred), but also the existence of clashing ethnopolitical perspectives on the direction that reform should take. An underlying fault line divides the decentralizing aspirations of the relatively economically endowed south from the more procentralization north, which worries that more devolution could threaten the existing system for sharing oil revenue among the regions. The best hope of surmounting this difficulty lies in taking on the least divisive proposals first—the reform of electoral administration would be a good place to start—while deferring debate on flashpoint amendments such as those that would abolish or trim back presidentialism or radically decentralize the federation.

Fortunately, there is much that can be done to curb electoral brigandage without having to change the constitution. First, as is underscored by the Supreme Court's June 2007 decision that a fresh vote for the Anambra governorship is not due until 2010, careful handling of electoral appeals can create a de facto staggering of at least some elections. Second, a revised electoral act can explicitly prohibit the use of state resources in political campaigning. Third, in line with President Yar'Adua's commitment to inclusive governance and improved elections, an interparty deal on naming new, more credible, and more independent-minded commissioners to INEC seems reachable. Finally, as the 50,000-strong Domestic Election Observation Group proposes, an official, but independent, inquiry can be launched into the misconduct of the 2007 elections.[23] Along with ongoing judicial review of the elections, such an independent administrative inquiry could strike a blow against the culture of official impunity that made possible the brazen theft and mismanagement of the 2007 elections.

NOTES

The author gratefully acknowledges the support of the U.S. Institute of Peace (USIP) and the research assistance of Alison Wittcoff.

1. See Daniel N. Posner and Daniel J. Young, "The Institutionalization of Political Power in Africa," *Journal of Democracy* 18 (July 2007): 126.

2. See the editorial "Yar'Adua: The Challenges Ahead," in *The Guardian* (Lagos), 4 June 2007; and "Yar'Adua's Election is Third Term in Disguise, Says AC," *The Guardian,* 26 April 2007.

3. Darren Kew, "The 2003 Elections: Hardly Credible, but Acceptable," in Robert I. Rotberg, ed., *Crafting the New Nigeria: Confronting the Challenges* (Boulder, Colo.: Lynne Rienner, 2004); International Crisis Group, *Nigeria: Failed Elections, Failing State?* Africa Report No. 126, 30 May 2007.

4. Wole Soyinka, "2007 Elections and the Gang of Four," at *www.nigerianmuse.com/opessays.*

5. Independent National Electoral Commission (INEC), *2007 General Elections: Guidelines for Election Monitoring and Observations* (Abuja: INEC, 2007), 2, 11.

6. See Usman Bugaje, "Polls—Neither Free, Fair nor Credible," *Daily Trust* (Abuja), 17 May 2007; Jibrin Ibrahim, "Nigeria's 2007 Elections: The Fitful Path to Democratic Citizenship," U.S. Institute of Peace Special Report 182, January 2007, 3–4.

7. "Nigeria's Elections: Big Men, Big Fraud and Big Trouble," *Economist,* 26 April 2007.

8. Peter Lewis and Etannibi Alemika, *Seeking the Democratic Dividend: Public Attitudes and Attempted Reform in Nigeria,* Afrobarometer Working Paper No. 52, October 2005.

9. See "Expectations for the 2007 Nigerian Elections," Afrobarometer Press Release No. 2, 12 April 2007.

10. Testimony of Wole Soyinka Before the U.S. House Foreign Affairs Subcommittee on Africa, Hearing on "Nigeria at a Crossroads: Elections, Legitimacy and a Way Forward," Washington, D.C., 7 June 2007.

11. Statement of the National Democratic Institute (NDI) International Observation Delegation to Nigeria's April 21 Presidential and National Assembly Elections, Abuja, 23 April 2007, 3.

12. See, for instance, "Country Briefings: Nigeria," Economist Intelligence Unit, 23 January 2007; "This Day Nationwide Opinion Poll," *This Day* (Lagos), 21 April 2007. A survey by the International Foundation for Elections System (IFES) actually reported Buhari, and not Yar'Adua, to be the marginal frontrunner in the presidential race. See IFES, "What Nigerians Think: Nigerian Public Opinion in the Pre-Election Environment," April 2007.

13. Peter Obi of APGA had been robbed of victory by the PDP in the 2003 Anambra gubernatorial elections. After protracted litigation, he finally replaced the PDP's Chris Nigige as the state governor in March 2006. In April 2007, INEC ignored Obi's protests

that he had yet to serve out his constitutional term and held a fresh gubernatorial election in Anambra. This led to another controversial victory for a different PDP candidate, Andy Uba, who assumed the governorship in May 2007. On 14 June 2007, however, the Supreme Court voided Uba's election, restored Obi to power, and affirmed that a new gubernatorial election in Anambra must be timed to coincide with the end of Obi's four-year tenure in 2010.

14. See, for instance, Niyi Bello, "Questions over INEC's Documentation in Ondo," *The Guardian,* 12 June 2007; John Ameh, "INEC Frustrates Ngige's Bid to Inspect Electoral Materials," *Punch* (Lagos) 12 June 2007; Sheriff Balogun, "INEC Wants to Thwart the Process at the Tribunal-Fayemi," *This Day,* 26 June 2007; and Phillip Ogunmade, "Politics of Election Tribunal Sittings," *This Day,* 29 May 2007.

15. Gani Fawehinmi, "The Role of the Election Tribunals," *The Guardian* (Lagos), 2 May 2007.

16. Oluyemi Osinbajo, "Sub-national Reform Efforts: The Lagos State Experience," in Transparency International, *Global Corruption Report 2007* (Cambridge: Cambridge University Press, 2007): 147–48.

17. Donald L. Horowitz, "Constitutional Courts: A Primer for Decision Makers," *Journal of Democracy* 17 (October 2006): 125–37.

18. See *The Guardian* (Lagos), 5 June 2007.

19. Thomas Carothers, "The End of the Transition Paradigm," *Journal of Democracy* 13 (January 2002): 5–21.

20. Larry Diamond, "Issues in the Constitutional Design of a Third Nigerian Republic," *African Affairs* 86 (April 1987): 209–26.

21. Diamond, "Issues in the Constitutional Design," 221–22.

22. Abel Guobadia, "How to Improve Nigeria's Electoral System," Memorandum Prepared for the National Political Reform Conference, Abuja, 26 April 2005.

23. See Innocent Chukwuma, "'An Election Programmed to Fail': Preliminary Report of the Domestic Election Observation Group on the Presidential and National Assembly Elections Held on Saturday, April 21, 2007," at *www.tmgnigeria.org.*

10

ANOTHER STEP FORWARD FOR GHANA

E. Gyimah-Boadi

E. Gyimah-Boadi, *professor of political science at the University of Ghana, Legon, is executive director of the Ghana Center for Democratic Development (CDD-Ghana) in Accra and executive director of the Afrobarometer. This essay originally appeared in the April 2009 issue of the* Journal of Democracy.

On 7 January 2009, President John Kufuor of the New Patriotic Party (NPP) handed over power to John Evans Atta Mills of the National Democratic Congress (NDC) after the NPP narrowly lost the 28 December 2008 runoff election with 49.9 percent of the vote. Mills's inauguration signified Ghana's second peaceful transition of power from incumbent party to opposition.[1] In parliamentary elections held concurrently with the first-round presidential contest on December 7, the NDC won 114 of the 230 seats to the NPP's 107. These exceptional events have confirmed Ghana's place as a beacon of hope for democracy in Africa.

Still politically stable after four successful presidential and parliamentary elections in 1992, 1996, 2000, and 2004, Ghana is rare among new African democracies. The country has enjoyed vast improvements in the quality of each successive election under its Fourth Republic.[2] Despite persistent challenges, the independence and administrative capacity of Ghana's Electoral Commission (EC) improved with each election, while levels of public interest in national elections remained high (evidenced by voter turnouts consistently above 70 percent). In addition, the country's key democratic institutions—the judiciary, the Commission on Human Rights and Administrative Justice (CHRAJ), and, arguably, Parliament—continued to develop and solidify, and media freedoms and human rights expanded from one election to the next.[3]

Yet the stakes in Ghana's fifth scheduled presidential and parliamentary polls were high. The recent trend of botched elections on the continent, with stalemated outcomes in Kenya and Zimbabwe, and ongoing electoral challenges in Côte d'Ivoire, Nigeria, and Senegal, had cast a pall over

Africa's democratic progress. Thus the polls in Ghana tested the prospects of sustaining multiparty democracy at precisely the moment when its success on the continent appeared most tenuous.

The 2008 balloting was, moreover, a test of whether Ghana could maintain, or even improve, its own record of relatively peaceful and transparent elections with reasonably credible outcomes that would be accepted by the main contestants. Success would help to instill much-needed confidence in the democratic process among Ghanaians and all Africans. Also in question was whether the governing center-right NPP was becoming the permanent dominant party in Ghana or whether the NDC, once the ruling party (1993–2000) and now the main opposition, was resilient enough to regain a leading political role. Furthermore, the 2008 elections would clarify the chances that the party of Ghanaian independence, the Convention People's Party (CPP), could reemerge as a third force in Ghanaian politics. Ultimately, the successful December polling confirmed the strength of multiparty democracy in Ghana while at the same time exposing certain weaknesses in the country's democratic structures.

The elections were mainly a two-horse race between the NPP and the NDC, though there were five other contesting parties—the CPP, the Democratic Freedom Party, the Democratic People's Party, the People's National Convention, and the Reformed Patriotic Democrats—and one independent presidential candidate. Going into the elections, the ruling NPP enjoyed significant advantages. Two terms in office had given it an unprecedented opportunity to consolidate its grip on political power. The party also enjoyed the vast advantages of incumbency, growing international prestige (which had helped to bring external assistance under the World Bank and IMF's Heavily Indebted Poor Countries Initiative and the U.S. Millennium Challenge Account), and an energetic and resourceful presidential candidate in Nana Addo Dankwa Akufo-Addo. A distinguished lawyer and veteran campaigner for human rights, democracy, and civilian rule who had served as attorney general and foreign minister during Kufuor's administration, Akufo-Addo also happened to be the son of a former president.

In addition, the NPP stood to benefit from its positive record on human rights—most notably with regard to civil liberties and media openness—and its record of good governance, which were confirmed in Ghana's African Peer Review Mechanism (APRM) report and in the Ibrahim Index of African Governance.[4] Finally, though the NPP government's reputation had been tarnished by high fuel prices and the rising cost of living (largely beyond the government's control due to the global financial crisis that emerged in the fall of 2008), Akufo-Addo could nonetheless boast of his party's prudent economic management, reflected in macroeconomic stability, annually rising economic-growth rates, infrastructure development, significant progress in poverty reduction, and well-received social-welfare programs such as the National Health In-

MAP—GHANA

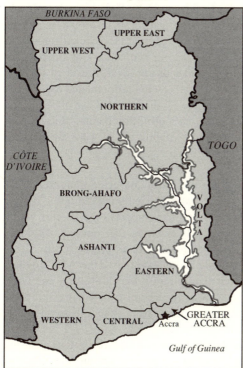

surance Scheme (NHIS), the School Feeding Programme, and the National Youth Employment Program.

At the same time, however, the NPP also carried some significant liabilities into the election. Anxiety related to the rising cost of living and fuel prices was mounting, and persistent deficits in social-service delivery left some segments of society frustrated. High unemployment rates, which raised some doubts over whether the NPP's economic-management strategy was sustainable, were a further source of trouble for the incumbent party.

The perception of corruption also dogged the Kufuor government. Reports of extravagant expenditures abounded, including the president's son's purchase of a multimillion-dollar hotel that adjoined his father's private residence and excessive spending during the NPP's December 2007 presidential primaries, in which as many as seventeen aspirants—eight of whom were cabinet members—vied for the nomination. The government's reputation was also tainted by allegations of narcotics trafficking, highlighted by the 2007 conviction and imprisonment in the United States of ruling-party parliamentarian Eric Amoateng and the botched investigation into cocaine scandals involving senior police officers. Finally, the governing party had to overcome issues related to its internal democracy, reflected not only in its highly acrimonious presidential and parliamentary primaries but also in constituency-level disputes over candidate selection that drove some candidates to go independent.

Worst of all, the NPP appeared more and more to be disregarding the public and taking the electorate for granted. During the election year, the government purchased presidential airplanes, dismissed the concerns of local fishermen about poaching by foreign trawlers, and stubbornly refused to reduce the price of petroleum despite the fall in the world-market price of crude oil in the latter part of the year. In addition, the administration increasingly displayed an arrogance of power and sense of official impunity. It cavalierly presented Parliament with bills and loan proposals backed by insufficient or inaccurate information. After a year and a half, the administration had still failed to account for spending on the lavish celebration of the fiftieth anniversary of Ghana's independence. Moreover, despite popular disapproval, President Kufour, citing a Supreme Court ruling based on a technicality related to jurisdiction, reinstated a minister who had been indicted for abuse of office and contempt of Parliament by Ghana's anticorruption commission (part of CHRAJ). Furthermore, land and other public assets were allocated to party and government officials through a process that was opaque at best.

In addition, the president controversially conferred gold medals on himself and many of his associates, and hurriedly moved into a luxurious though unfinished presidential office complex, the cost of which had reportedly ballooned to more than twice the amount originally approved by Parliament. Already saddled with a perceived pro–Akan-Ashanti bias and insufficient ethnic inclusiveness, the NPP government was deemed by some to be complicit in the chieftaincy and communal crises in Dagbon and Bawku in the north of Ghana and Anlo in the east, suggesting a neglect or disregard of voters in some ethnic groups and regions.[5]

The NDC faced its share of handicaps as well, however, thus ensuring that the race would be close. First, it had to contend with the negative implications of choosing a twice-defeated candidate—Mills had been the NDC's presidential standard-bearer in 2000 and 2004. Mills himself was dogged by well-publicized health problems and the widespread perception that he was little more than a lackey of former president Jerry John Rawlings (1993–2001), who was also the strongman of the last military administration in the 1980s. The party also suffered disadvantages associated with being in opposition, including a lack of campaign funds, and endured negative publicity stemming from its ties to the earlier Rawlings military regimes.

At the same time, the NDC ticket possessed some strong attributes. Having solved its problems with disaffected factions and splinter groups (the National Reform Party and the Democratic Freedom Party, for example), the NDC had unified and increased its organizational capacity since the 2004 elections. By selecting its standard-bearer in December 2006, nearly two years prior to the 2008 polls, the NDC allowed itself time to mend internal wounds and to focus exclusively on the campaign. Moreover, Mills was already well known, having been not only a former presidential candidate but also vice-president from 1997 to 2001. His own solid elite credentials as a graduate of the prestigious Achimota secondary school, a star athlete at university, and a former law professor were complemented by those of his running mate, John Dramani Mahama, an affable former minister and three-term parliamentarian. Finally, the NDC could of course count on the electoral pull, especially among its grassroots supporters, of its leading personality, Jerry Rawlings. (It must be noted, however, that Rawlings likewise repelled certain sections of the middle class.) On the whole, the NDC's confidence in its ability to capture power from the NPP continued to grow as the polling date drew near, especially as the public's disenchantment with economic conditions rose in the second half of the year.

The 2008 Campaign

The 2008 campaigns followed familiar patterns. The candidates depicted themselves as "God-fearing" and dedicated to the material uplift of Ghanaians. The NPP, for its part, focused on its achievements during its two terms in office. Its campaign slogan, "We are moving forward," suggested a sparkling future for Ghana as a modern industrialized and technologically advanced middle-income country. The NDC and other opposition parties, on the other hand, fastened on the incumbent party's perceived corruption, abuse of power, failure to distribute national goods equitably, and lack of ethnic inclusiveness, and emphasized the need for a change in leadership and direction.

The leading parties campaigned in all regions of the country but tended to concentrate on their respective strongholds, indirectly courting ethnic votes. The NPP pinned its hopes on generating votes from the regions dominated by the Akan group—especially the Ashanti, Brong-Ahafo, and Eastern regions—while the NDC systematically mobilized votes in its traditional centers of support, the Volta Region and the three northern regions, as well as in non-Akan communities in the other areas.

What differed in the 2008 cycle was the environment in which the campaigning was conducted. The electoral playing field was generally level, and the parties pursued their campaign objectives with little hindrance. Most parties had developed and publicized their manifestos, helping to make the elections relatively issue-based. There were, however, some unexpected challenges. The Electoral Commission's management of the 2008 elections betrayed troubling weaknesses and gaps, as it was not sufficiently attentive to emerging concerns until almost too late in the election cycle. For example, the Commission presented the nation with a crowded and somewhat compressed electoral timetable, leaving too little time to resolve irregularities, such as a voters register that was most likely bloated. The NDC forcefully made known its lack of confidence in the EC and, to some extent, the entire electoral process. In addition, unexpectedly tense local disputes led to episodes of sporadic violence in the north of the country. Nevertheless, in the context of a hotly contested election, the major parties enjoyed relatively equal opportunities to pursue votes.

On December 7, the day of the first-round elections, voting was orderly and peaceful, and the results were generally credible. Akufo-Addo won 49.1 percent of the vote and Mills won 47.8 percent, while Paa Kwesi Nduom of the CPP won 1.3 percent. By contrast, the December 28 presidential runoff—mandated by the constitution since no candidate had won a majority of the vote—proved far more contentious. Having won a plurality of parliamentary seats and having finished a close second in the first round, the NDC ticket possessed clear momentum heading into the second round. The Akufo-Addo campaign, for its part, blamed its failure to secure a victory in the first round on low voter turnout due to its supporters' certainty of a win,[6] on the popular outgoing president's inadequate involvement in the campaign, and on weakly substantiated claims of NDC poll rigging.

The two contestants considerably revised their campaign strategies for the second round of voting. The massive rallies that were prevalent in the run-up to the first round gave way to more personal outreach, including door-to-door canvassing as well as television and radio pitches. The incumbent party also seemed to abandon caution, engaging in cheap tactics in a bid to secure votes. Immediately after the first round of voting, the NPP government reduced the price of fuel, ordered the release of drivers who had been jailed under an unpopular traffic law, and deployed military personnel to patrol the coast for illegal poaching by foreign fishing trawlers.

More disturbingly, both the NDC and the NPP resorted to negative and non–issue-based campaigning. NPP propaganda insisted that a future Mills administration would put an end to the NHIS and other popular Kufuor-era social-welfare programs. Worse yet, NPP agents, in an obvious attempt to link the Mills campaign with the human rights atrocities of the earlier Rawlings military administrations, circulated a bogus "hit list" of prominent Ghanaians supposedly targeted for assassination.

The NDC, meanwhile, tried to marshal non-Akan voters by stoking their hatred of the NPP and depicting it as the party of Ashantis and the affluent. Both parties shamelessly attempted to mobilize ethnic votes, virtually declaring their respective strongholds—the Ashanti Region for the NPP and the Volta Region for the NDC—as "no-go" zones for their opponents.

The menace of violence and intimidation had surfaced during the first round of voting, as members of "keep fit clubs" acted in essence as vigilantes for their preferred parties and candidates and sparked violent pre-election clashes in Bawku and Accra. During the run-up to the second round, such threats escalated. Former president Rawlings spearheaded the NDC's "popular-resistance" movement: His campaign messages actually exhorted supporters to take up arms, and flanked by retired military commanders, he led emotionally charged rallies that climaxed with the militaristic hymn "Onward, Christian Soldiers."

In the end, the runoff election itself was orderly and peaceful overall, but there were more instances of intimidation and violence than in the first round, especially in the Volta and Ashanti regions. Both parties' polling agents were harassed and prevented from observing the voting in opposition strongholds. Moreover, local vigilantes mounted illegal roadblocks to prevent "outsiders" from observing the polls in parts of the Volta Region.[7]

Two days passed between the balloting and the announcement of the outcome, and the wait only exacerbated an already charged situation. A group of NDC supporters, incited by a local pro-NDC radio station, marched on the Electoral Commission as it was in the process of certifying the votes and camped there overnight to demand that Mills be declared the victor. NPP supporters, meanwhile, besieged another local radio station to protest its reporting of the NDC's lead in the vote tally.

After two days, the EC announced an electoral deadlock: Neither candidate had yet obtained the requisite number of votes to ensure his victory, necessitating a wait for the votes from a single constituency (Tain, in Brong-Ahafo Region) that had been unable to participate in the runoff for logistical reasons. In the meantime, NPP operatives presented polling figures of doubtful provenance from Kumasi that supposedly favored Akufo-Addo, and both parties petitioned the Electoral Commission to investigate allegations of irregularities and to exclude votes from the strongholds of their opponents. The NPP followed up with a last-minute lawsuit seeking to place an injunction on the Tain election and to prevent the EC from declaring the final results until allegations of irregularities in the Volta Region had been fully investigated. It eventually boycotted the Tain polls. Nearly 24 hours passed before Akufo-Addo conceded defeat to Mills, who had managed to edge out his opponent by the narrowest of margins—40,586 votes out of 9,001,478 or 0.46 percent of the valid votes cast.

Addressing Gaps and Consolidating Gains

Despite difficulties with the electoral process, democracy in Ghana survived the balloting intact. The impasse over the results was broken after only a few days and, most important, postelection tensions did not devolve into anything like what happened in Kenya in early 2008 or the continuing nightmare in Zimbabwe. John Atta Mills was sworn in as president on 7 January 2009, and an NDC-led Parliament was inaugurated on the same day. It is fair to say that the key democratic institutions held up well: The EC withstood furious attacks from the contestants, demonstrating professionalism, independence, and neutrality; the security agencies (notably, the Election Security Task Force) proved sufficiently professional, even if at times overwhelmed; and the judiciary proved reasonably capable and neutral, establishing credible mechanisms for expeditiously adjudicating election disputes.

Although the leaderships of the two main parties resorted to negative tactics, alarmism, and brinkmanship, they eventually restrained themselves. Outgoing president Kufuor refused to declare a state of emergency in the face of looming violence in NDC strongholds, and he urged the presidential candidates not to take to the streets but rather to accept the authenticated results of the elections and to rely on the courts to redress outstanding grievances. Akufo-Addo therefore conceded defeat despite considerable resistance from hawks within his party. Thus while votes were mobilized feverishly during the elections, weapons thankfully were not.

Ghana's civil society—including religious, secular, and professional organizations, as well as think tanks and civic-advocacy bodies—acting individually and in groups, was strong and savvy enough to monitor the entire electoral process from beginning to end, thereby enhancing its transparency. Civil society's interventions, along with media vigilance, helped to keep the campaign issue-based and peaceful. For example, the Institute of Economic Affairs (IEA) held live televised presidential and vice-presidential debates; the Association of Ghanaian Industries hosted meetings with all the presidential candidates to discuss economic and business policies; and the Coalition of Domestic Election Observers (CODEO), in collaboration with the Ghana Center for Democratic Development (CDD-Ghana), provided forums for parliamentary candidates to interact with their constituents. In addition, the IEA, CODEO/CDD-Ghana, the Civic Forum, and religious organizations actively monitored the pre-election landscape, with special emphasis on promoting peaceful balloting. The media helped to keep the electorate well-informed about the parties and their programs and, for the most part, acted responsibly.

Domestic election-observation activities also contributed to the peaceful and transparent outcome. CODEO trained and deployed throughout the country more than four-thousand observers drawn from 34 secular and religious organizations, for both rounds of elections. It also undertook for the first time a parallel vote-tabulation project to provide independent verification of the official election results. Television and radio stations sent reporters all over the country to cover the voting process and provided constant updates on the vote tally, taking full advantage of instant-communication technology. Mobile-phone text messaging and calls to radio stations had the most notable impact on the election. These independent monitoring and verification efforts boosted confidence in the EC's official tally, and thus helped to discourage the losing parties and candidates from challenging the results.

These efforts by Ghanaian civil society were bolstered by support from the international community. Ghana-based diplomats and visiting delegations, especially from OECD countries, met with the presidential candidates, party leaders, EC officials, civic leaders, and other key actors, offering counsel and material assistance. For example, the United

Nations Development Programme, along with other external donors, sponsored the National Peace Council, a consortium of religious and civic bodies and leaders that actively monitored and helped to resolve electoral conflicts. Western bilateral donors funded domestic election-observation projects, and NGOs provided technical support for the parallel vote tabulation. Finally, the visible presence of a large number of international election-observer groups (from the African Union, the Carter Center, the Commonwealth, the Electoral Institute of Southern Africa, the European Union, the Economic Community of West African States, and the Pan-African Parliament) as well as foreign media increased transparency and public confidence in the process.

Lingering Challenges

The successful 2008 elections and the peaceful handover of power have provided Ghana with yet another opportunity to deepen its democratic processes and institutions. To be sure, the recent election debacles in Kenya and Zimbabwe, and before that Nigeria, had heightened public anxiety over the December 2008 polls. The increasing parity in the electoral strength of the NPP and NDC—a reflection of the level playing field and the competitiveness of Ghana's multiparty system—had added to the tension. The two main parties each believed that they could triumph by subtly manipulating the process and intensifying mobilization efforts. At the same time, the CPP, with even a modest showing, seemed likely to prevent either the NPP or the NDC from scoring a first-round victory—a scenario borne out in the actual results. With less than 2 percent of the first-round votes, however, the CPP clearly fell short of reestablishing itself as a major player, and competition between the two main parties for CPP support in the second round began even before the first round had come to a close.

Such tensions underscored gaps in Ghana's efforts to build a democratic culture in the Fourth Republic, as reflected in persistent polarization and the mutual loathing of the two main parties.[8] The NDC and its supporters lacked trust in the independence of key electoral institutions and viewed the criminal prosecution and jailing of leading NDC figures (such as former Ghana National Petroleum Corporation boss Tsatsu Tsikata, former finance minister Kwame Preprah, and Preprah's deputy, Victor Selormey) during the Kufuor administration as witch-hunting. The NPP and its supporters, for their part, remained adamant in their belief that the NDC was promoting electoral violence and hatching other plans to disrupt the election.

Above all, the December 2008 polls brought into sharp relief some unresolved weaknesses in the country's constitutional and legal practices. The failure to reform an excessively powerful presidency (rooted particularly in the Office of the Chief of Staff) has created a situation in which control of the executive branch is the overwhelmingly dominant objective of multiparty political competition in Ghana. The allure of "state capture" via the presidency has now been enhanced by the recent discovery of oil reserves off Ghana's western shores.[9] Without thoroughly independent institutions to cope with this change, an opportunistic executive branch could undermine any potential gains for the people.

While Ghana may have successfully made the transition from quasi-military authoritarian rule to pluralistic democracy under the Fourth Republic, it is still struggling to make a clean break with neopatrimonialism.[10] Power remains overly concentrated in the hands of the executive branch, which has undermined institutional checks and balances and interbranch accountability. For instance, through the use of discretionary authority to make temporary appointments, presidents are able to evade parliamentary scrutiny of their favored appointees and also to undermine the security of tenure of those responsible for policing the executive (such as the staffs of the Serious Fraud Office and the Auditor General) by keeping them perpetually in "acting" positions. By virtue of the same constitutional laxness, presidents are free to appoint an outrageously large number of ministers (nearly ninety in the Kufuor administration) and other executive-branch staff, which comes, of course, at the expense of the professional public service. Finally, excessive executive power has placed in the hands of the president the ability unilaterally to create and to restructure ministries, departments, and agencies.[11]

A hegemonic presidency presents other perils as well. It tends to encourage reliance on political patronage and corruption. The president and the ruling party can abuse incumbency for personal as well as partisan electoral gain. This explains the lack of transparency in the management of public assets such as forests, mines, and state enterprises, as well as the official tolerance of nonperforming boards of state and parastatal organizations. Indeed, executive dominance has made it possible for successive administrations to resist the introduction of transparency-promoting instruments such as access to information about legislation and public-officeholder asset-disclosure laws.[12] The direct negative consequences for Ghanaian democracy include unregulated campaign spending and an active rumor mill that keeps alive unsubstantiated scandals involving political figures.

The executive branch's grip on power and control of patronage have also stalled the constitutionally mandated devolution of administrative power to district assemblies and their substructures. Presidential appointments of district chief executives and a third of the members of the district assemblies often are made on the basis of loyalty and kickbacks rather than merit. This has impeded any meaningful decentralization and has led to a lack of responsiveness and accountability to the citizenry on the part of these agencies and their officials. Local development also suffers from the awarding of service-delivery contracts to party chair-men and their cronies.

Still, popular support for democracy in Ghana is high and continues to grow. The 2008 Afrobarometer survey found that 79 percent of adult Ghanaians prefer democracy to other forms of government. This is a 4 percent increase from 2005 and the highest rating since 1999.[13] Yet severe deficits in the political culture remain. Voting patterns indicate persistent ethnic and regional chauvinism: The NDC captured parlia-mentary seats in 21 of the 22 constituencies in the Volta Region, while the NPP secured 36 of the 39 seats in the Ashanti Region. The presiden-tial results likewise show nearly total ethnic-bloc voting in Volta and Ashanti.

Due in part to insufficient civic education, popular understanding of the political process is underdeveloped, and passive rather than active forms of political and civic participation predominate. According to data from the 2008 Afrobarometer report, only a minority engages in active forms of secular community and civic activities: 43 percent report never having attended a community meeting; 46 percent have never come to-gether with others to raise an issue; and fewer than one in ten Ghanaians have ever attended a demonstration or protest march. Popular attitudes also betray an extremely weak sense of civic responsibility and, by im-plication, weak demand for political accountability.[14] For example, the same survey found that only a quarter of the population believes that voters have a responsibility to ensure that MPs do their jobs; and only 28 percent think it is the responsibility of citizens to ensure that the president performs his duties.

Ghana's economy presents another set of challenges. With annual per capita income at only US$450, the country is far below middle-income status, and unemployment remains high. Levels of inequality across the regions and between the sexes are also high, despite impressive growth rates that have averaged over 5 percent since 2001 and poverty rates that have dropped from more than 50 percent of the population in the early 1990s to 28.5 percent in 2006. (Ghana now ranks eleventh out of 45 sub-Saharan African countries on the Human Development Index.) Nonetheless, the still-high poverty rates and lingering inequality mean that there is no shortage of class and ethnic resentments to be exploited for political gain.

These socioeconomic woes are exacerbated by shortcomings in do-mestic-revenue mobilization, the failure to collect taxes from the self-em-ployed, an overreliance on export duties on primary commodities, and the tendency to underprice and misuse government-controlled resources and commodities (timber or real estate, for example). As a result, the country relies on external donors for roughly 40 percent of its annual budget. De-layed public-sector reforms and persistent distortions in the structure of public wages also hinder the government's popular legitimacy.[15]

Multiparty democracy in Ghana has thrived despite an inauspicious beginning in the early 1990s. The country has made tremendous progress in institutionalizing democracy under the 1992 Constitution and has not only upheld but even extended civil liberties. Moreover, a robust civil society and vibrant media have emerged. It is particularly significant that the constitution has become the normative point of reference for popular expectations of democratic governance. In addition, many of the institutions and processes established under that constitution continue to enjoy widespread public support and legitimacy.

The future of liberal democracy nevertheless remains precarious due to a number of flaws in constitutional design: The constitution grants vast appointment powers to the president, resulting in excessive patronage; the system of checks and balances is weak, which limits the effectiveness of oversight institutions such as Parliament and leads to deficits in transparency and accountability; formal democratic institutions and processes fail to give adequate voice to the poor and other marginalized groups; and power is poorly devolved to the local level. So while Ghana's democracy survived the pressures and conflicts of the country's December 2008 elections, and praise for both the transparency of the outcome and the peacefulness of the turnover is merited, the polling also exposed critical problems with the country's legal-constitutional practices that threaten democratic development and ongoing good governance.

Looking Forward

Of course, it may be unrealistic to expect that all of Ghana's democratic and governance deficiencies can be overcome during one administration's tenure, but small steps, at least, are possible. To begin with, the new Mills administration faces the urgent task of healing the wounds opened during the bitterly fought election. To govern successfully, it must find a way to contain the ethnoregional and interclass animosities that were roused during the course of the electoral battle. Given Mills's narrow margin of victory in the second-round presidential poll and the fact that the NDC is still two seats shy of a parliamentary majority,[16] the new administration will be forced to seek consensus. Doing so will likely require that the party distinguish its positions from the populist, revolutionary orientation of the Rawlings-led Provisional National Defense Council military regime (1982–93).

Other immediate goals include additional improvements to election administration in order to reduce undue tension in future elections. For example, the chaos and controversies that attended voter registration and screening in past elections could be curbed by introducing open voter registration in lieu of the present system, which reserves only a few days for registering newly qualified voters and those who could not register previously. This would also allow enough time to catch and remove bad names from the register. Campaign-finance regulation would help to check the abuse of incumbency and the growing monetization of democratic politics. Improvements in voter education could help to reduce the high number of spoiled and rejected ballots, which accounted for up to 2.4 percent of total votes cast in the first-round presidential election—perhaps enough to have produced a clear winner in that round.

The Mills government must initiate a comprehensive review of the constitution and promote public discussions to identify crucial deficiencies and bottlenecks. It must also work closely with Parliament to formulate legislation to curb excessive presidential discretion. For instance, the Office of the Attorney General could be separated from the Ministry of Justice, and an Office of the Independent Prosecutor could be established. The new administration could also make fairly quick and decisive improvements by restricting responsibility for the criminal prosecution of politicians to professional civil servants in the attorney general's office (as opposed to the attorney general himself, who is usually a senior minister in the administration) and by placing time limits on how long presidential appointees can serve in "acting" capacities. The new government can and should urgently pursue the passage of legislation to enhance the right to public information and to reform public-officeholder asset-disclosure laws. Finally, all office-holders should be encouraged to adhere to strict ethical standards.

Meaningful reforms must aim at building institutions and structures that will reduce the incentives for state capture and partisan abuse. These should include the development of an oil-sector regulatory and governance framework that provides for maximum transparency, accountability, and equity in the use of the new oil-generated revenues, as well as tax reforms to expand the revenue base and improve compliance. Having more citizens as taxpayers would help to strengthen grassroots demands for accountability. Finally, the Mills administration must aid the National Commission for Civic Education in sharpening its focus on education for democratic citizenship. The abatement of intolerance and the improvement of Ghanaian political culture depend upon it.

NOTES

1. See E. Gyimah-Boadi, "A Peaceful Turnover in Ghana," *Journal of Democracy* 12 (April 2001): 103–17; and Gyimah-Boadi, "Ghana's Encouraging Elections: The Challenges Ahead," *Journal of Democracy* 8 (April 1997): 78–91.

2. Freedom House ranked Ghana as Partly Free beginning in 1994, and has ranked it as Free since 2001.

3. For an overview of Ghana's progress in democracy-building, see E. Gyimah-Boadi, "Politics in Ghana since 1957: The Quest for Freedom, Prosperity and National Unity," *Ghana Studies* (forthcoming); and J.R.A. Ayee, ed., *Ghana at 50: Government, Politics and Development* (Accra: Friedrich Ebert Foundation, 2007). For details on the relaxation of state control over the public broadcast media, which has led to the emergence of more than a hundred independent FM radio and several TV stations since the mid-1990s, see Audrey Gadzekpo, "When the Watchman Slips: Media Accountability and Democratic Reforms in Ghana," *Critical Perspectives*, No. 22, CDD-Ghana, Accra, August 2008.

4. "African Peer Review Mechanism, Republic of Ghana," APRM Secretariat, Midrand, South Africa, June 2005. Available at *www.nepad.org*. Ghana ranked seventh out of 48 nations in the 2008 Ibrahim Index of African Governance. See Robert I. Rotberg and Rachel M. Gisselquist, "Strengthening African Governance: Results and Rankings 2008," Ibrahim Index of African Governance, October 2008, 15. Available at *http://belfercenter. ksg.harvard.edu/publication/18541/strengthening_african_governance.html*.

5. The Akan, who are concentrated in the Ashanti, Brong-Ahafo, Eastern, Western, and Central regions, are the largest ethnic group (49.1 percent), followed by the Mole-Dagbani (16.5 percent) in the Northern Region, the Ewe (12.7 percent) in the Volta Region, and the Ga-Adangbe (8 percent) in the Greater Accra Region. The Ashanti (a subgroup of the Akan) constitute 14.8 percent of the total population. See Ghana Statistical Service, *Population and Housing Census*, Accra, March 2000.

6. There may be some truth to this claim, as voter turnout was down slightly from 74 percent in 2004 to 70 percent in 2008.

7. The physical assault against NPP polling agents in some parts of the Volta Region has been confirmed.

8. Attitudes of tolerance, consensus, and trust among the population, and especially the political elite, are widely regarded as key elements of a democratic political culture. See Robert Putnam, *Making Democracy Work* (Princeton: Princeton University Press, 1993); and Robert Dahl, *On Democracy* (New Haven: Yale University Press, 1998).

9. Based on projections of 120,000 barrels per day by 2010 and 250,000 by 2012, at US$100 per barrel in March 2008, with the government getting a 50 percent cut negotiated by the Ghana National Petroleum Corporation, the discovery was expected to yield about $3 billion of revenue per year within the first term of the new administration.

10. The growing literature on the struggle in Africa's young democracies between personal and neopatrimonial rule on the one hand and constitutionalism on the other includes H. Kwasi Prempeh, "Progress and Retreat in Africa: Presidents Untamed," *Journal of Democracy* 19 (April 2008): 109–23; Daniel N. Posner and Daniel J. Young, "The Institutionalization of Political Power in Africa," *Journal of Democracy* 18 (July 2007): 126–40; and E. Gyimah-Boadi, "Political Parties, Elections and Patronage: Random Thoughts on Neo-Patrimonialism and African Democratization," in Matthias Basedau, Gero Erdmann, and Andreas Mehler, eds., *Votes, Money and Violence: Political Parties and Elections in Sub-Saharan Africa* (Scottsville: University of Kwazulu Press, 2007).

11. For an insightful discussion of the challenges of constitutionalism in Ghana, see H. Kwasi Prempeh, "The Challenge of Constitutionalism," in Baffour Agyeman-Duah, ed., *Ghana: Governance in the Fourth Republic* (Accra: CDD-Ghana, 2008), 97–125.

12. Articles 107 and 108 of the 1992 Constitution give the president this monopoly. Consequently, no private-member bill has to date been introduced in Parliament.

13. See "Popular Attitudes to Democracy in Ghana, 2008," Afrobarometer Briefing Paper No. 51, June 2008. Available at *www.afrobarometer.org/papers/AfrobriefNo51. pdf*.

14. "Popular Attitudes to Democracy in Ghana, 2008," and "Summary of Results," Ghana Afrobarometer Round 4, 2008.

15. See Tony Killick, "What Drives Change in Ghana? A Political-Economy View of Economic Prospects," in Ernest Aryeetey and Ravi Kanbur, eds., *The Economy of Ghana: Analytical Perspectives on Stability, Growth and Poverty* (James Currey Ltd., 2008), 20–35; also David Booth et al., "What are the Drivers of Change in Ghana," CDD/ODI Policy Brief No. 1, November 2005.

16. The outcome of the parliamentary race in the Akwatia in the Eastern Region and Asutifi South in Brong-Ahafo awaits court decisions.

11

SENEGAL: THE RETURN OF PERSONALISM

Penda Mbow

***Penda Mbow** is associate professor of history at Cheikh Anta Diop University in Dakar, where she has published widely on African political and social issues. She is also the president of Mouvement Citoyen and has previously served as Senegal's minister of culture. This essay, translated from the French by Philip Costopoulos, originally appeared in the January 2008 issue of the* Journal of Democracy.

The turnover of power that took place as a result of Senegal's March 2000 presidential election was hailed by democrats throughout the world and especially in Africa. The second-round victory by longtime opposition leader Abdoulaye Wade of the Senegalese Democratic Party (PDS) not only toppled incumbent president Abdou Diouf after twenty years in power, but marked the end of forty years of Socialist Party (PS) rule. Yet from a democratic perspective, the era of President Wade has been a severe disappointment, dashing hopes that the great turnover of 2000 would pave the way for democratic consolidation.

President Wade was reelected to a fresh (now five-year) term on 25 February 2007 with nearly 56 percent of the vote in the first and only round,[1] but the problems gripping the country have done nothing but intensify since his reelection. The signs of trouble include a twelve-party boycott of the 3 June 2007 elections for the 150-seat National Assembly, the lack of dialogue among contending political factions, and the demand by Siggil Senegal (the leading opposition coalition, whose name in Wolof means "give Senegal back its pride") for a national conference. Despite the promise of democracy in 2000, Senegal today has declined to the point of mere electoral authoritarianism.

Why should this be so? What makes Senegal's quest for democracy so difficult? Is the problem one of a weak democratic culture? A rigid society saddled with inert political and social forces? A fragmented civil society and ineffectual women's, youth, and labor organizations? An outmoded leadership class still hanging on to the highest state offices?

The politically motivated use of public resources to bolster the influence of traditional groups such as religious brotherhoods, confessional organizations, and customary associations? Or a greedy oligarchy that has kept a tight grip on resources even as the average Senegalese citizen's standard of living has fallen, and a business community that cares little about the fair distribution of the country's scarce assets?[2] All these factors are probably at work, compounded by a succession crisis that appears to be in the offing as the octogenarian president's son Karim Wade maneuvers to become the next chief executive.

Almost since the day after the 2000 election, the enthusiasm and high hopes roused by Abdoulaye Wade's victory have been ebbing away, first among Senegalese intellectuals and then among foreign analysts. The opposition, civil society, the press, and various observers have regularly decried the Wade administration's turn toward autocracy and patrimonialism, which has given rise to a crisis of legitimacy and a loss of citizens' trust in their own government.[3] The roots of such ills, however, reach back before Wade's time in power and help to explain why there was such a large appetite for change in 2000, when people spoke of how "the glass was cracking."

Before going on, it will be helpful to recall briefly some relevant events in Senegal's recent history. The first that bears mention was the tragic sinking of the government-owned ferry MV *Joola* in a storm off the Gambian coast on the night of 26–27 September 2002. The death toll was more than 1,800, making it one of the worst maritime disasters on record anywhere. High-level official negligence was a factor. There were some firings, but otherwise no one has yet been punished for contributing to this catastrophe. Other notable circumstances include the ongoing crisis of the energy and chemical sectors of the economy, the continuing attempts at illegal immigration by young people (thousands of whom have been lost at sea in desperate efforts to reach the Spanish-owned Canary Islands), the unregulated urbanization exacerbated by building projects that Wade used to help his bid for reelection, as well as a crisis over land ownership. Senegal's situation, in short, has been difficult.

Reigning, Not Governing

Senegal elected its first president, Léopold Sédar Senghor (1906–2001), in 1960, the year of independence. Under Senghor and the Socialist Party (PS), Senegal developed into a virtual single-party state. Still, elections were held regularly, and a limited number of opposition parties were eventually permitted, thus making Senegal more liberal and pluralistic than most African countries at the time. In 1981, Senghor decided to step down, handing the reins to his chosen successor, Abdou Diouf. Diouf and the PS ruled for another twenty years—during which election regulations became ever more restrictive while presidential term limits were abolished—until the landmark 2000 elections that brought Wade to power and the legislative elections the following year that saw the continued triumph of the PDS.

Abdoulaye Wade belongs to the generation that was in its prime a half-century ago, around the time of independence. He bears the stamp of his politically formative years, the 1950s, when nationalism, dirigisme, and the will of the strong leader were exalted (D&F, 13). Convinced of his legitimacy and believing that he carries with him all the hopes of the people, Wade's use of power smacks of authoritarianism, even though he battled for twenty-five years in the name of democracy. Ironically, the opposition now calls him a "divine-right" president who conceives of the state as a "monarchy without limits." Wade does not govern; he reigns. The constitution that was approved by referendum in January 2001 has in fact brought with it a hyperpersonalization of power that is especially evident in the political prominence and influence enjoyed by the president's wife, son, and daughter.

In Senegal, as in France, when the president's party has tight control of the National Assembly, the prime minister serves at the will of the president. Wade has had five prime ministers in the last seven years. Rather than building on the political openings and democratic institutional progress of the late 1990s, the president has reversed course, draining institutions of their substance and stripping the other branches of government of their powers in order to subordinate them to the executive and render them impotent. This has been the case with the Autonomous National Electoral Commission. Most of its members have, since the outset of their terms, faced challenges from the president or the National Council for Audiovisual Regulation, which has come to control the media (meaning mostly private radio stations). Moreover, the opposition has complained of Wade's many changes to the electoral timetable. For example, just two months before the February 2007 presidential election, its exact date remained uncertain.

An observer of the Senegalese state cannot fail to notice its administrative haplessness. There is no shortage of examples. A case in point is the anticorruption commission, a gimmicky body that has struggled under the weight of numerous scandals and the general climate of impunity that besmirched Wade's first term. The revenue and customs services, meanwhile, are virtually helpless against the basic greed of the regime's power players. The Constitutional Council, despite its formal mandate to rule on political questions, often declares itself incompetent to deal with the opposition's many complaints, as in the runup to the June 2007 legislative elections.

This situation encourages the tendency to backslide toward authoritarianism and the dynastic urges that go with it. Rather than an executive who serves as an arbiter, Senegal has a partisan president who wants to rebuild the party-state—with himself, of course, at the head of the ruling party. Along with the drive toward authoritarianism goes a liquidation of autonomous political forces, speeded by party-switching and the distortion of democracy through the creation of parties generated and financed by the ruling powers. These groups—such as the Waar-wi Coalition of Modou Diagne Fada, former environmental minister and Wade loyalist—sprang into being on the eve of the last elections and won a handful of legislators. What came out of the legislative races had more to do with various deputies' whims than with the voters' will. Of the 150 seats in the National Assembly, 131 were won by the president's coalition. The remainder of the seats were won by parties and coalitions funded by Wade. Most of these smaller parties wound up with three seats each, in races boycotted by as many as three-quarters of registered voters.

The broader coalition that had brought Wade to power in 2000 swiftly fell apart (D&F, 17). Its demise began after the January 2001 referendum on the new constitution, which for Wade was a means of outmaneuvering and defeating his onetime allies. The legislative elections of 2001 and and local elections of 2002 sealed matters. The Alliance of Forces for Progress (AFP)—the party of Moustapha Niasse, onetime Wade ally and prime minister from 2000 to 2001—was too obviously a competitor for the coalition to survive the 2001 legislative races, and the disintegration then reached the leftist parties that had played a crucial role in bringing about the change in power in 2000 (D&F, 17). One by one, these parties split off, and today these old allies of Wade are his fiercest opponents.

The problems began immediately after the referendum, as Wade started to exhibit his desire to monopolize power. Other than shortening the presidential term to five years (to take effect only after the end of Wade's first, seven-year term), the new constitution did nothing to soften the regime's highly presidentialist character. The National Assembly remains notoriously weak and dependent. The anticorruption fight, such as it is, remains a tool for waging political conflicts rather than a means of improving governance. Wade is becoming a veritable caricature of Senghorism. He has pressed members of the former socialist regime to join him, dangling over them the Damoclean sword of public audits that would review their stints as directors of the national railway or the lottery or daily newspaper. This has made a mockery of the public-audits process, but has had the effect of convincing many of the targets that the only safe course is to go over to the presidential camp (D&F, 14).

Since coming to power, Wade has sought by all available means to control every political force. He has tried to control labor unions even at the cost of destabilizing them, and has interfered in the election of traditional chiefs such as the Grand Serigne of Dakar's historic Léboue community. Even the women's movement has not escaped Wade's maneuverings: The law on gender parity for electoral lists, proposed by Wade and passed just months before the 2007 legislative elections, was intended to destabilize any coalition that might threaten his parliamentary majority. Due to a pending appeal, however, the law was not in force for the June 2007 elections.

One of Wade's goals is to reproduce the model of Senghor. Beginning in 1962, Senghor built a single-party regime that swallowed up all existing formations and drove the leftist parties underground. This lasted until 1974, when four alternative currents were allowed to emerge—one of which was Wade's own PDS. How could someone with Wade's background have become so politically regressive, boasting that while Senghor and his party may have enjoyed a forty-year run in power, Wade and his group will make it to fifty?

Among the ruling party's weaknesses is the persistent factionalism that flows from the personalization of power. In order to keep their positions, the president's lieutenants must lie low and appear to be mediocre and unthreatening. Wade has fallen out not only with his first prime minister, Moustapha Niasse, but also and more surprisingly with Idrissa Seck, longtime chief of the presidential staff before becoming premier and heir apparent to the presidential sash in 2002 (D&F, 16–17).

Yet the most serious obstacles to a democratic future remain the triumph of the single will of the president and the absence of political cooperation or even dialogue on questions of national interest or the electoral process. What is urgently needed is political discussion not only about laws to guarantee the transparency of the electoral process, but also about the dynamics that are holding Senegal back and preventing it from achieving its democratic potential.

The Key Role of Religious Forces

If Wade has succeeded in essentially controlling all government institutions and putting Senegal's democratic achievements in jeopardy, it is because he knows how to pressure the traditional chiefs and notables, turning the game of alliances in his own favor and further entrenching the system of clientelism. Sociocultural inertia reinforces the terrible confusion of identities that besets so many Senegalese, who are at once Muslim religious disciples *(talibés)* or leaders *(marabouts)* and (to a lesser degree) citizens, in a society where there are no clear boundaries between the religious and civic spheres. Communal logic exacerbates matters, for besides religion there are cleavages based on ethnicity and geography. The ties that bind the nation together are becoming ever looser.

Wade's manipulation of religious affairs is his oldest strategem. He is a keen student of the Senegalese mental universe and knows how to use religious concerns in order to manipulate it. We no longer know whether

Senegal's Muslim brotherhoods are religious or sociopolitical entities. Senegalese democracy has always been supported by an Islam that acts as, among other things, a locus of debate and pluralist clientelism. In kneeling before the caliph of Touba (a city sacred to the Sufi Murid brotherhood) on national television just after his election in 2000, Wade showed that alliances were shifting massively. He snubbed the Tidjan brotherhood, which had been so influential under Abdou Diouf, in favor of the better organized, though fewer in number, Murids. Later, Wade would split the Tidjans—the largest of the brotherhoods—by favoring one regional segment of the confraternity over another, traditionally more politically influential one.[4]

The president found the Murids to be a handy instrument for reshaping the coalition that brought him to power, and then for sending a signal to the international community and Senegal's traditional allies about his own steadfastness. He uses the Murids of Touba in several ways. During the runup to the 2002 local elections, the name of the Murid caliph, Serigne Saliou Mbacké, appeared on the PDS candidate list. It was withdrawn after widespread protests, but the point had been made. Then, just before the 2007 presidential election, the caliph of Touba appeared on national television to assert that Wade, if reelected, would complete the modernization of the city's infrastructure. This endorsement sounded like an order to vote for Wade, which was surprising since in 1993 most Murids strongly disapproved of the call issued by the caliph of the time to vote for President Abdou Diouf.

The display that Wade has made of "belonging" to the Murid brotherhood and the real or supposed favors that he has done for Touba have left other Muslim brotherhoods as well as Senegal's Christian minority (the country is 95 percent Muslim) feeling frustrated and resentful. Anxious to calm the resulting turbulence, the state busies itself with soothing the grievances of various religious authorities rather than seeing to the needs of the poor. Cultivating the Murids allows the administration to keep a sure and steady clientele in its camp, but to the detriment of national cohesion. Such is the patrimonialist version of democracy.

Economic factors are also at play in the relationship between the Wade administration and religious groups. The true motor of Senegal's economy is remittances, which continue to increase dramatically. Migration abroad, which was rooted historically along the Senegal River and later adopted in the old peanut-growing region that is the Murid heartland, now affects the whole country (D&F, 8). For the moment, migration serves as a safety valve that tends to stabilize the economy and give an exit option to many young Senegalese (the country's demographic profile features a large youth bulge) whose opportunities at home are blocked by growing unemployment and a continued degradation of social conditions (D&F, 10). Both this migration and the remittances it produces are organized by religious networks.

These economic trends, together with the breakdown of the quasi-monopoly of the state, confirmed the political pluralization that began to set in around the end of the 1970s as the single-party regime looked for ways to "decompress" what had become a potentially explosive situation. With the dismantling of the state's economic-control structures and the privatization of public enterprises, the state-run spheres of production could no longer be an arena for political accommodation. This weakening of the state's capacity for clientelism played a role in the process of change (D&F, 9–10).

The advent of political alternation was the achievement of citizens who, through a mobilization that brought together civil society groups, the media, and the Senegalese diaspora, became aware of their own strength. But with the presidential election of 2007, this dynamic seems to have been broken. The state has learned to cultivate more sustained ties with the marabouts, granting its clients diplomatic passports, which in principle should be available only to public officials, and similarly making use of the pilgrimage *(hajj)* to Mecca or the question of land ownership by migrants. Privatization and clientelism now affect all of Senegal and partly explain the erosion of the "social contract" under which the state supported the marabouts as a kind of caste (D&F, 10). This erosion in turn has sparked rivalries and jockeyings among the minor religious authorities, who now commonly throw their support to politicians and try to stay close to power.

The manipulation of religion saps the foundations of Senegalese secularism, thereby putting stability and tolerance in jeopardy. In a multiconfessional country with numerous religious brotherhoods, secularism or state neutrality in religious matters is indispensable to the building of democracy. Yet despite a constitutional ban, we now see the rise of parties that are essentially religious in nature. Among these is the Party for Truth of Serigne Modou Kara Mbacké, nephew of the caliph and husband of presidentially appointed senator Sokhna Dieng Mbacké. Worse still, some religious groups, such as the one headed by the Murid marabout Sheik Béthio Thioune, are perpetrators of violence. His followers—mostly jobless young men—attacked a rally of Idrissa Seck's Rewmi party on the last day of the 2007 presidential campaign. Such retrograde forces hold back the deepening of democracy by denying the idea of autonomous citizenship. The disciple who acts in the name of faith places religious identity above the title of citizen.

The Retreat of Individual Liberties

If individual liberties are not secure, democracy is in peril. In its most recent annual report, Amnesty International (AI) rightly cites the continued threat to free expression in Senegal under Wade, noting that journalists and intellectuals have been harassed, intimidated, interrogated, and jailed, and certain books have been banned.[5] The police Criminal Investigation Division (DIC) has become a political force, and relations between the government and the press have become riddled with conflict, in part because the administration has created its own attack-dog press to go after anyone seen as critical of the current powerholders. The new regime's firmness no doubt owes much to the PDS leaders' strong sense of legitimacy born of their struggle, their sacrifices, and the historic nature of their victory—even if it was in fact secured by a much broader coalition than Wade typically admits (D&F, 13).

Examples abound of police and judicial actions against opposition leaders, civil society figures, and journalists. Security forces severely cracked down on the opposition's 27 January 2007 march to demand respect for the electoral calendar. Under a general ban on marches—decreed despite the consitution's guarantee of the right to peaceable assembly—opposition leaders were manhandled and even beaten. This was not the first time that demonstrators had felt the mailed fist of repression. Upon becoming president, Wade cited his own victimization by the Diouf regime and boasted that tear gas would not be used under his rule. But the Wade administration's reaction to the student movement that sprang up in early 2001 amid the post-turnover excitement was a textbook case of police repression followed by a mix of strategic concessions and clientelist cooptations.

Alongside police crackdowns on marchers and DIC roundups of civil society leaders goes a still more pernicious form of repression: the censoring of works addressing political matters, particularly pieces that criticize those in power. Two of Dakar's biggest bookstores refused to carry a pair of books by journalist and professor Abdou Latif Coulibaly because of their political content. Although Coulibaly has run afoul of the regime with his two satirical novels—in one of which an African president declares himself king and reproduces Versailles within his country—he remains protected by vigilant foreign and domestic groups that follow his case closely.

Coulibaly is far from being the only media figure who has suffered persecution. Madiambal Diagne, editor of the newspaper *Le Quotidien,* was jailed on 9 July 2004 for "releasing secret reports and correspondence" and "spreading news for the purpose of causing serious political turmoil." He owes his freedom to a massive international campaign by journalists, lawyers, and civil society groups that aimed not only to free him but also to overturn Article 80 of the penal code, which deals with national security but is often used against the press, as in the case of Diagne.

Another illustration of the troubled relations between the press and the government is the takeover by security forces of the Sud FM radio station. This station, founded in 1994, is Senegal's leading private radio outlet. Interior Minister Ousmane Ngom took it off the air for a day on

17 October 2005 and pulled *Sud quotidien,* the newspaper associated with it, from newsstands after having thirty journalists arrested. His pretext was an interview that a Sud correspondent had conducted with a rebel chieftain. These actions roused a wave of indignation throughout all of Senegal and abroad as well.

Politicians have also become targets for repressive tactics. Jean Paul Dias, a former PDS member and now leader of the Gainde Centrist Bloc, was dragged out of bed and arrested on 9 August 2006. The police beat his wife and damaged his home in the process. His son, Socialist Party activist Bathélémy Dias, was hauled in three days later for speaking up on behalf of his father and raising questions about President Wade's advanced age. The younger Dias was sent to a prison in the east of Senegal—200 kilometers from Dakar to stiffen the punishment—though protests later resulted in his release.

Relations between the president and his former prime minister and protegé, Idrissa Seck, remain the deepest mystery in Senegalese politics. Wade named Seck premier in November 2002 and sacked him in April 2004. There followed a heated debate about Seck's possible misappropriation of public funds. In July 2005, Seck was arrested for threatening the security of the state, but was never tried. In September 2006, he announced the formation of his Rewmi party and said that he would run for president (he did, and received slightly less than 15 percent of the vote). Seck's perennial rival, Interior Minister Ngom, has publicly called Seck a thief. Wade has veered between accusing and exonerating Seck. It is rumored that much of the tension between the two men stems from Wade's suspicion that the former prime minister served as a source for Latif Coulibaly, perhaps with the intention of setting Wade up to be overthrown by a coup.

In retaliation for denouncing government dysfunction, virtually all administration critics have had to brave some combination of insults, anonymous defamatory letters, death threats, harassing phone calls, police interrogations, and stints in jail. The justice minister plays a central role in keeping dissidence under tight control, and the justice system itself remains the least independent of all the institutions that affect individual liberties.

A Democracy in Crisis

Senegal's crisis reveals itself in multiple ways. On the economic level, for instance, the current rulers generally favor cooptation and corruption, which are widespread in all sectors of society. The new regime has methodically appropriated the state and its parastatal fringes. The current powerholders have infiltrated enterprise management and put themselves in charge of a proliferating series of special "agencies," with plainly negative economic effects (D&F, 15). The most prominent exemplar of the problem is Karim Wade, the president's son, who runs the National Agency for the Organization of the Islamic Conference and the Agency for Investments. These two bodies are unaccountable sinkholes that have consumed millions of dollars in lucrative contracts.

Other symptoms of the crisis are the lack of dialogue within Senegal's political class and the abuse of money in politics. There have been various studies of how to clean up the corruption, but their conclusions are never acted upon. The ruling party has a giant campaign chest into which it can dip to buy support not only from the poor but also from midlevel chieftains, minor marabouts, traditional notables, and local officials. Thus is the spirit of democracy utterly perverted. Moreover, as some have ironically noted, the results of the 2007 presidential race correlated with the various candidates' relative wealth. One may well wonder how a system in which Wade could win with almost no money in 2000 has become, just seven years later, a system in which cash appears to have been the decisive factor.

The reversal of alliances and the dislocation of coalitions is impelling those in power to starve genuine opposition parties of funds. This is not hard in a country such as Senegal, where the state is the sole channel by which to access resources. The president, moreover, has a great deal of power over how public money is spent, and usually steers it to the most docile. His dealings with the media, for instance, are thoroughly clientelist. One of Senegalese democracy's greatest weaknesses is the degree to which those in power have in effect confiscated the media and turned them into tools of propaganda. Civil society and the opposition complain, of course, but their cries fall on deaf ears. Those press organs still in private hands have preserved a degree of pluralism, but the regime's use of clientelism, controlled factionalism, and strong personalism naturally create political frustrations that contribute to the strained relations between Wade and the press.

Senegalese democracy's true Achilles' heel, however, is undeniably the justice system. By presiding over the Superior Council of Magistrates, the president essentially controls the careers of judges. Moreover, when questions about money dealings loomed over former prime minister Idrissa Seck, in an attempt to protect himself he threatened to publish a list of all those senior magistrates who were taking political-party money or who had received their posts through favoritism.

The Council of State is typical of nearly all the institutions of the Senegalese Republic in being subject to the influence—indeed manipulation and control—of the executive branch. When President Wade and his cohorts decided that they wanted to hold the presidential and legislative elections on separate days, the Council of State decreed this wish into policy in January 2007, trapping an unprepared, divided, and leaderless opposition into an uneven contest against a very well-prepared PDS. The press, civil society, and the opposition are reduced to fruitless complaining, so what can be done to address the increasingly obvious marginalization of the country's intellectual, economic, and political elites?

The ruling party has no capacity for debating ideas. The president is surrounded by PDS members whose disputes revolve around matters of precedence and the dividing up of privileges and sinecures. Guiding notions of what the nation should strive to become—or of why (beyond the most purely selfish motives) one should want to gain power in the first place—are lacking. Forums for discussion are nowhere to be found. Worse still, Senegal's intellectuals have surrendered to this sad situation. In Wade's orbit, the only path to success is flunkyism.

The rising figure in the regime appears to be Karim Wade, who has gathered into his hands enormous resources connected with major public projects. Under the pretext of preparing to host the next summit of the Organization of the Islamic Conference in March 2008, the president's son has created a network of influence that adds up to a parallel government operating outside public or legal control. He likes to appear in public handing out tickets for pilgrimages to Mecca or giving gifts to mosques. For a young man who spent his formative years in Europe and who speaks none of Senegal's indigenous national languages, these interactions with the pious are a brilliant way of improving his image and raising his national profile. Like his father, he calculates that religion is a tool which he can use to attain his goals.

What is his father's design? No prime minister has been given enough time in office to become a true fixture. When the relationship between the president and Prime Minister Seck soured in 2004, Seck was sacked, charged with embezzlement, ousted from the PDS, and replaced by Macky Sall. Sall rose quickly through the PDS ranks and began to believe in his own destiny, only to have Wade take the premiership away from him without explanation after the June 2007 legislative elections.

Although Senegal's opposition has come in for much fair criticism, it is not lacking in spirit. It is true that the parties which form the opposition Siggil Senegal Front have made some strategic errors, especially by letting themselves appear complicit in the maneuvering over the electoral calendar. Yet the high level of voter abstention from the legislative elections has cast doubt on the February presidential results and discredit on a parliament that has been put in place by a mere 35 percent (if that) of the electorate. The newly reconstituted Senate, meanwhile, is nothing more than a tool in the hands of the president, who names 65 of its 100 members. Moreover, as a result of the boycott, only one senator comes from outside of Wade's coalition. The Senate is now a more powerful body than the National Assembly, and its president would become interim president of Senegal if Wade became unable to serve.

Thinking about how to protect and enhance Senegal's democracy should start with the way that political parties work and should include the renewal of the political class and the ending or at least reduction of the country's excessive political fragmentation (there are more than eighty parties). Parties never turn over their own leaderships, and that needs to change. Most of those who currently run Senegal's parties are incapable of practicing democracy. Broadly speaking, the case of Senegal teaches a lesson about the limits of electoral democracy. Politicians tend to adopt a minimalist perspective centered on respect for procedures, meaning above all free and transparent elections. As we know, without parties there cannot be free elections. But however indispensable to democracy they may be, the parties are beginning to arouse the people's mistrust. Their biggest problem is that they are dominated by a minority of professional politicians to the detriment of the majority of the people.

In Senegal as in many other countries, political parties proliferate and disappear at will in dizzying bouts of fusion and floor-crossing that on the whole make it hard to take the country's party scene seriously. And yet parties must be taken into account by anyone who wishes to see the gains of democracy's "third wave" consolidated and extended. E.R. McMahon[6] thus examines some of the failings for which African parties are often blamed, namely, their tendency to fuel conflicts within fragile nation-states as well as their tendencies to be elitist, corrupt, too heavily urban, and—with no middle class to hold them in check—too ready to give in to antidemocratic temptations.

Larry Diamond and Richard Gunther, for their part, are interested precisely in the functions of political parties as well as the links between the state of parties and the future of the democratization process.[7] Senegal is a classic case. What can be the future of political parties when, for example, religious groups and the crowds who follow them interfere (above all at the behest of those in power) in strictly political decisions? Today, one wonders whether these central institutions of democracy can continue to serve as intermediaries for the recruitment of leaders, the structuring of electoral choices, and the formation of governments. The mobilization of religious groups as well as the persistence of mechanisms for vote-buying, clientelism, and pauperization demand reflection about the future.

In addition, one can only deplore the absence of programmatic debate and the dessication of political thought. The case of the ruling party is illustrative in more than one regard. With the PDS's victories in the presidential, legislative, and local elections in 2000, 2001, and 2002, respectively, the threat of factional strife became so real that, in order to avoid inflaming it, there have been no internal changes in the PDS since 1996 (D&F, 16). Party switchers and new activists have been incorporated on an ad hoc basis, often by means of purpose-built parallel structures or support movements. Despite talk of renewal, there has been no change in this situation.

Facing a multifaceted crisis and a regime that seems to be aiming at a Togo-style succession in which the longtime president's son takes his father's place, the Senegalese opposition has begun a series of meetings with civil society and the so-called *forces vives* of the nation in order to pave the way for the holding of a national conference. Perhaps the much-desired breakthrough will come from that quarter.

In March 2000, Senegal witnessed an orderly transfer of power from Diouf to Wade. Almost eight years later, the country finds itself caught up in the difficulties created by the new ruling group's method of governing, but also by the important question of presidential succession. The time has come to reassess decades of political practice. The social, political, and economic ambitions of Senegal's elites have progressively lost their vigor. Perhaps we can agree with Momar Coumba Diop's conclusion about the mode of governance that effectivly characterized the country from Senghor to Diouf: a president who enjoyed dominance thanks to political and administrative centralization, the cooptation of political figures with an eye to reinforcing presidential leadership, and a permanent concern with raising the president's profile on the international scene (this last motivated in no small part by the regime's dependence on foreign aid, which adds up to nearly half a billion dollars per year or a quarter of the national budget).

The coalition that Wade rode to power has collapsed. Since 2004, the PDS has been in shards, and Wade has been openly at odds with his premiers. The 2007 elections ended up revealing the regime's incapacity to maintain, much less improve, the country's democratic achievements. The turnover of 2000 has led to great disappointment. The functioning of institutions that do not obey clear rules and the ambiguous answers given to the Senegalese people as they try to deal with the problems of their crisis-ridden democracy have sown doubt among even the country's most convinced democrats.

After a long political struggle, Wade realized "his historic mission: to uproot the baobab tree of socialism."[8] Yet the president is now uprooting the fragile flower of democracy that was planted in the historic 2000 election. Wade the longtime oppositionist was and is little accustomed to the task of managing public institutions. And a society that has remained inert in the face of powerful forces of retrogression has left many Senegalese wondering about the future path of their country's still-fragile experiment in democratic self-rule. Is it too much to hope that a national conference can help us to find the strength, the means, and above all the institutions that we need to breathe new life into our gasping democracy?

NOTES

1. See Momar Coumba Diop, "Le Sénégal à la croisée des chemins," *Politique africaine* 104 (December 2006): 103–26.

2. Never has a sitting African president inspired so many authors. Several critical works have appeared in recent years. In addition to the writings of Abdou Latif Coulibaly, the following are notable: Mamadou Seck, *Les scandales politiques sous la présidence d'Abdoulaye Wade* (Paris: l'Harmattan, 2006); Mody Niang, *Qui est cet homme qui dirige le Sénégal?* (Paris: l'Harmattan, 2006); Babacar Sall, *Le stagiaire: Journal d'un Président de la République* (Dakar: Les Sentinelles, 2007); each has been barred from distribution in Senegal.

3. Tarik Dahou and Vincent Foucher, "Le Sénégal, entre changement politique et révolution passive. 'Sopi' or not 'Sopi'?" *Politique africaine* 96 (December 2004): 6. Passages in the remainder of the text that either directly quote or closely parallel this article are followed by a parenthetical notation indicating the source (D&F) and page number.

4. According to the General Census of 1988, nearly 90 percent of Senegalese belong to a Muslim brotherhood: Tidjans, 47.4 percent; Murids, 30.1 percent; Qadrya, 10.9 percent; Layènes, 0.6 percent.

5. Amnesty International Report 2007, 225, available at *http://thereport.amnesty.org/document/15*.

6. E.R. McMahon, "Catching the 'Third Wave' of Democratization? Debating Political Party Effectiveness in Africa Since 1980," *African and Asian Studies* 3, no. 3–4 (2004): 295–320, cited in Mamadou Gazibo, "Pour une réhabilitation de l'analyse des partis en Afrique," *Politique africaine* 104 (December 2006): 11.

7. Larry Diamond and Richard Gunther, eds., *Political Parties and Democracy* (Baltimore: Johns Hopkins University Press, 2001), cited by Gazibo, in "Pour une réhabilitation de l'analyse des partis en Afrique"; see also Larry Diamond, *Developing Democracy: Toward Consolidation* (Baltimore: Johns Hopkins University Press, 1999).

8. M.C. Diop, M. Diouf, and A. Diaw, "Le Baobab a été déraciné: L'alternance au Sénégal," *Politique africaine* 78 (June 2000): 157–79.

12

SIERRA LEONE: A VOTE FOR BETTER GOVERNANCE

Christopher Wyrod

Christopher Wyrod *coordinated democracy assistance to Sierra Leone for the National Endowment for Democracy from 2003 to 2007 as the Program Officer for West Africa. He is currently the country director in Sri Lanka for Internews International. This essay originally appeared in the January 2008 issue of the* Journal of Democracy.

The small West African country of Sierra Leone captured the world's attention in the 1990s with the brutality of its civil war. Infamous for recruitment of child soldiers, mutilation of civilians, and illicit diamond trafficking, Sierra Leone came to typify the worst elements of contemporary civil conflicts and, to some, all that was wrong with Africa. Journalist Robert Kaplan made the country the focus of his widely discussed 1994 *Atlantic Monthly* article "The Coming Anarchy," which foretold a future of global insecurity spawned by failed states.

Although the war ended in 2002, this dystopian depiction has gained fresh currency from the recent box-office success of the film *Blood Diamond* and the best-selling autobiography of former boy soldier Ishmael Beah. Estimates of the conflict's human toll vary widely, but the war's devastating nature is beyond doubt. At least 50,000 people perished, 20,000 were deliberately maimed, and more than two million—or more than one out of every three Sierra Leoneans—suffered displacement.

Although the civil war's legacy continues to weigh heavily, Sierra Leone has a new story to tell. On 11 August and 8 September 2007, five years after the war's end, the country held national elections that stand as the freest and most participatory in its history. The five-year mark is auspicious for postconflict countries such as Sierra Leone, since almost half the countries emerging from war return to violent conflict within five years.[1] The 2007 vote was Sierra Leone's first postconflict transition between civilian governments, which is considered a critical test of a country's democratic development. Fewer than half of Africa's states have succeeded in holding more than two elections in a row without interruption by a coup or renewed fighting. Even more unusual in

Africa was Sierra Leone's peaceful ouster of the ruling party via the ballot box.

Ernest Bai Koroma of the opposition All People's Congress (APC) took the presidential oath on September 17 after having won the September 8 runoff with almost 55 percent of the vote. During the initial round on August 11, he was the plurality victor with just over 44 percent, and his party captured 59 out of 112 seats in Sierra Leone's unicameral Parliament. His chief rival, Solomon Berewa of the ruling Sierra Leone People's Party (SLPP), attended the swearing-in along with outgoing president Ahmed Tejan Kabbah (also of the SLPP). Berewa won 38 percent in the first round, and saw his party's share of Parliament plummet from 83 to 43 seats.

The presidential poll was essentially a contest among Koroma, Berewa, and Charles Margai of the newly formed People's Movement for Democratic Change (PMDC) to replace outgoing president Kabbah, a former UN official who had presided over the end of the war. The addition of the outspoken Margai, a breakaway SLPP figure who won almost 15 percent of the first-round vote, enlivened the race and made it less predictable. Although a two-week delay caused the elections to coincide with the height of the rainy season, more than two-thirds of registered voters turned out.

The handover marked a new high in a trajectory of political progress that began in 1996 when multiparty competition was restored. Although the 2007 races featured many of the same old political figures whose misrule had caused the country's crisis,[2] the high turnout revealed voters' persistent faith in electoral democracy and resolve to enact change constitutionally. Sierra Leone has known the worst kind of violence. Now it is giving hope that it and similar recent postconflict countries can regain their democratic footing. But for Sierra Leone to break with its dark and violent past, its leaders must learn to see their country's recent electoral achievement as a foundation upon which to build rather than as a set of laurels on which to rest. It will take committed, reform-minded leadership to reduce pervasive problems such as corruption and impunity before they undermine the country's progress. Furthermore, Koroma must not misinterpret his success as license to seek revenge against his rivals, since the country remains politically divided and fragile.

Sierra Leone's electoral success contrasts with its elected leaders' persistent failure to govern justly and improve citizens' welfare. Despite consolidating a hard-won peace, Kabbah and his SLPP neglected the underlying problems of corruption, poverty, and marginalization that fueled the conflict. Indeed, if the first postconflict elections in 2002 had been a public endorsement of how the ruling party had brought an end to the war, the 2007 balloting was a popular rejection of how that party had managed the peace.

To a degree, the SLPP may have been the victim of unrealistically high expectations for development that followed the return of peace

and competitive multipartism. Sierra Leone still ranks among the worst
cases in the Failed State Index of the Fund for Peace, and bottoms out
the UN Human Development Index as the poorest country in the world.
Under these dire conditions, Sierra Leone's ability to hold competitive
elections is remarkable. Yet a successful electoral event will not secure
the country's democracy unless Sierra Leone's leaders can foster effective and accountable institutions that promote the general welfare while
protecting fundamental liberties.

From Democracy to Conflict

Sierra Leone has a long but checkered electoral history. Early on, the
country's democratic system set it apart from most of its contemporaries
in Africa. In the first vote after independence from Britain, held in 1962,
the newly formed APC challenged the ruling SLPP in parliamentary
polls that were largely free and fair. Continuing to build its northern
support base, the APC won a majority in the 1967 parliamentary elections, becoming the first opposition party to oust a ruling party by the
ballot box in sub-Saharan Africa. Sadly, there followed a decade of turmoil as a torturous series of coups, countercoups, and rigged or boycotted elections led to the 1978 authorization of a single-party regime under
President Siaka Stevens.

The APC's consolidation of power began the downward spiral that
ended in the phantasmagoric violence of the 1990s. Under single-party
rule, elections became increasingly crooked and violent. State-sponsored
thuggery and suppression of dissent became widespread. Using his familiarity with Sierra Leone's crucial mining sector, Stevens enriched
himself and secured his grip on the presidency by diverting diamond
proceeds to create a "shadow state" controlled by himself and his cronies.[3] Itself wedged like a rough diamond between Liberia and Guinea,
Sierra Leone hemorrhaged its single most valuable asset to illicit neighboring markets and fueled a bloody insurgency in Liberia with devastating cross-border effects.

By the time Stevens retired in 1985, the economy was in ruins. Under
his hand-picked successor, army commander Joseph Momoh, the APC
government continued to neglect national development and ransack the
diamond trade, while most Sierra Leoneans were forced to eke out a
living from subsistence farming. The stage was set for upheaval. Momoh's decision to reintroduce multipartism was too little, too late, as
a March 1991 rebel foray into the southeast from Liberia began Sierra
Leone's decade of bloody internal strife. The warring factions that tore
at Sierra Leone took many forms, but all cited the corruption and tyranny of elected leaders as justification for the use of force. In order to
stop the 1996 elections, the Revolutionary United Front (RUF) rebels
and the National Provisional Ruling Council (NPRC) military regime

stepped up their attacks on civilians. Rebels amputated victims' hands to prevent them from voting,[4] but the first multiparty elections in 23 years went forward in early 1996 as Ahmed Tejan Kabbah of the SLPP won 59 percent in a March presidential runoff that capped a mostly free and fair voting process.

But soldiers staged another coup, and the Armed Forces Revolutionary Council (AFRC) took control, inviting the RUF to join the junta. Sierra Leone's Truth and Reconciliation Commission would later recount "astonishing factional fluidity" and "chameleonic tendencies" among the different armed groups involved in the war, especially with soldiers moonlighting as rebels—so-called sobels.[5] With the multiplication of armed factions, attacks on civilians grew. Those whom the rebels suspected of supporting Kabbah's government were targeted for amputation and told to go ask "Pa Kabbah" for new limbs.[6]

But with increasing foreign diplomatic and military pressure and the disarmament of 72,000 ex-fighters, elections were finally set for 2002. Capitalizing on strong popular support for democracy and building on the 1996 interwar vote, the government and the UN successfully organized the new balloting. In polls that were largely free and fair, Kabbah won by a landslide as the SLPP rode his coattails to a parliamentary majority. In contrast, the rebellion's political wing, the RUFP, failed to win a single seat. Former sobel and AFRC junta leader Johnny Paul Koroma fared only marginally better, garnering just 3 percent of the vote and three legislative seats for his Peace and Liberation Party.

Between 2002 and 2007, Sierra Leone's administration of elections underwent several important reforms. After the 2004 local-council elections (the first since President Stevens's 1972 abolition of local government) suffered rigging widespread and flagrant enough to result in a partial suspension of British aid, a new and more independent National Election Commission (NEC) was set up. The new chairperson was the civil society leader, Catholic nun, and former cabinet minister Christiana Thorpe, who took over in May 2005. She proved sincere and even-handed, lending much-needed credibility to this beleaguered institution. Much of the credit for the 2007 elections' success belongs to her.

While the United Nations had largely run Sierra Leone's 2002 elections under the watchful eyes of what was at that time the world's largest UN peacekeeping force in decades, the last blue-helmeted UN peacekeeping troops went home in December 2005, and the UN downgraded its mission in January 2006. Thus, for the first time since the end of the civil war, the government of Sierra Leone was solely responsible for running its own elections.

The NEC gained public confidence by registering 2.6 million voters—or about 90 percent of the eligible voting population—in just three weeks. Observers from the National Election Watch (NEW) civil society coalition praised the Commission's handling of the exercise as proof of its "credibility as an independent and trustworthy institution."[7] The NEC recruited and trained more than 37,000 polling staff, and blacklisted 1,500 officials implicated in rigging during the 2004 local-government elections. The NEC coordinated voter education and the training of party polling agents, and demonstrated transparency by working openly with all parties and monitoring organizations.

The 2002 Electoral Act mandated important reforms in election administration that the government instituted in the runup to the 2007 poll. It set up a new Election Offenses Court to hear cases on procedural irregularities and an Election Petitions Court to rule on contested results. As mandated under the 2002 Political Parties Act, a Political Parties Registration Commission (PPRC) was established with a Political Party Liaison Committee to monitor parties and buffer the NEC from its previous role in directly overseeing parties. The PPRC developed a code of conduct condemning violence. All registered parties signed the code, and a monitoring committee supervised compliance. For the first time, all parties submitted their statement of assets to the PPRC, as is constitutionally required.

While the 2002 parliamentary elections had used a proportional-representation system based on party lists in multimember districts in order to compensate for population displacements that had occurred during the war, for 2007 the NEC revived the old constituency-based majoritarian system. In a tense environment, the NEC drew boundaries dividing the country's fourteen districts into 112 single-member electoral constituencies (an additional twelve parliamentary seats are filled by traditional chieftains chosen through special elections). In 2002, each district was allotted eight seats in Parliament. For 2007, district representation was weighted by population, changing the allocation of seats. The Western Area Urban District, comprising the capital city of Freetown and its environs, gained the most (9 seats), while the southern Bonthe District lost the most (5 seats). The constituency-based system diluted party control and raised the stakes by giving more weight to individual candidates and traditional chiefs who can deliver votes. This system was thought to increase the chances for violence and decrease women's chances to win. While violence was minimal during the parliamentary elections, women candidates did indeed lose ground under the constituency system.

A last-minute delay till August 11 roused fears (exaggerated, as we have seen) that torrential rains would make roads impassable and discourage voters. The NEC turned the postponement to good use by opening 156 additional polling places in thirteen districts.

Political Parties and Candidates

Nine parties registered for the 2007 elections, down from eleven in 2002. Only seven parties nominated candidates for the presidential and parliamentary races. The political party formed out of the former rebel group, the RUFP, dropped out of the race. Between 1996 and 2007, the number of registered parties has fallen by about half, indicating that successive elections are simplifying Sierra Leone's political landscape.

Every election since independence has been mainly an SLPP-versus-APC face-off, and 2007 was no exception. Both parties have created strong ethnic affiliations and deep-seated patronage networks that benefit their respective elites. The SLPP's base is among the Mende in Southern and Eastern provinces, while the APC draws on the Temne and Limba of Northern Province. Despite their regional and ethnic division of the country, little differentiates the two parties in terms of policy or platform. Both have historically poor track records on corruption, governance, and development, but the APC bears the added onus of having imposed the one-party regime that led to economic collapse and civil war.

Under President Kabbah, the SLPP won a resounding victory in the 2002 elections. The SLPP's dominance began to slip with the 2004 local-council elections, however, when the APC made significant gains, thanks in part to its greater skill at rigging. Rivalries fissured the SLPP in 2005 when Kabbah, preparing to step down after completing two terms in office, anointed his vice president, Solomon Berewa, to lead the party. A Mende, Berewa hails from Bo, the capital of Southern Province. Vice-president since 2002, he is a lawyer by training and served as attorney-general and justice minister following the SLPP's 1996 election victory. Despite holding these offices, he is considered politically untested since he has never won an elected position.

Following his failure to win the SLPP presidential nomination, Charles Margai formed the PMDC. A Mende lawyer like Berewa, Margai comes from the country's oldest political family: His uncle was independent Sierra Leone's first prime minister and his father was the second. A candidate in various races since 1973, Charles Margai has never won elective office. He appealed to disenchanted SLPP members, adopting as the PMDC symbol a broom (to stress his goal of "sweeping out" the ossified SLPP elite). He also claimed support from some former combatants, both rebels and members of civil-defense militias, on the way to his distant third-place finish in the first round.

Given its record of decades of disastrous misrule, the APC's ability to bounce back from its low point in 1996—when it won just 5 out of 68 seats and its presidential candidate came in fifth—has been remarkable. Ernest Bai Koroma, a long-time APC stalwart, won a hard-fought nomination battle in 2002 but went on to carry Northern Province (his party's traditional stronghold) by a narrow margin and lose to Kabbah everywhere else. In 2004 local-council elections, the APC gained ground in the north and Freetown, foreshadowing its 2007 triumph.

An insurance broker and a Temne from Northern Province, Koroma ran as the candidate of change and promised to manage Sierra Leone like an efficient business. Although critics saw him as bland and charmless, Koroma's supporters viewed him as a reformer capable of freeing the APC from its past. The campaign period before the first round was largely calm. Parties generally adhered to the PPRC's code of conduct, and the PPRC staggered party-registration dates to avoid face-offs between supporters of rival parties. However, the political environment in contested areas in Southern and Eastern provinces was tense as the SLPP and PMDC jockeyed for control.

The main presidential contenders all claimed to be victims of plots or attacks orchestrated by their opponents. The APC and the PMDC, both with support from ex-combatants, threatened to mobilize their backers against SLPP provocations and rigging. The few outbreaks of communal violence that disturbed the campaign period revealed tensions that were rising as rural political alliances shifted. Traditional leaders remained political mobilizers for the ruling party, but they met unprecedented resistance (including arson) in SLPP strongholds. The worst clashes came in July in Kono District, Eastern Province, when the army had to step in to quell clashes between APC and SLPP supporters. The PPRC structure proved effective in mediating some of these political conflicts, according to the European Union Observation Mission.[8]

On election eve, each of the three major parties held a rally in Freetown without incident. Despite fears that the rainy season would prevent voters from coming to the polls, turnout was a record 76 percent. Domestic and international monitors found that the first-round elections were almost entirely peaceful and orderly.

Tensions rose with the stakes in the second round. The official declaration of a presidential runoff sparked incidents of intimidation and violence in Freetown and elsewhere. As skirmishes between party supporters grew, President Kabbah threatened to declare a state of emergency. While September 8 was calm, the drawn-out vote count, the invalidation of results from hundreds of polling stations, and charges of cheating leveled by both parties raised tensions again. Despite asking for a last-minute court injunction to stop the NEC from announcing an APC victory, Berewa conceded defeat and attended Koroma's inauguration on September 17. Outbreaks of violence following Koroma's victory were short-lived as national leaders called for calm and the national police restored order.

Presidential and Parliamentary Results

Voters chose from a field of seven presidential contenders as well as 566 parliamentary candidates running in 112 constituencies. Analyzed by region, the results show how Margai's breakaway PMDC cut into the SLPP's support in the south and east (see Table 1). Especially significant was the PMDC's winning of 41 percent of the vote in the SLPP stronghold of Southern Province. In Northern Province, which has the largest voting population, the APC maintained its support and Koroma got almost 77 percent of the vote, the largest share by region for any of the candidates. The APC also received strong support in Western Area.

Comparing the first-round performances of the SLPP and APC presidential candidates in 2002 and 2007 makes clear the SLPP's loss of ground in the south and east. While in 2002 Kabbah won 92 and 95 percent in Eastern and Southern provinces, respectively, five years later Berewa won just 66 and 46 percent. Even if Margai's votes in these two regions are added to Berewa's totals, however, they still fall well short of Kabbah's 2002 tallies. The APC's support in the south and east improved some over its 2002 results, but almost 180,000 fewer people voted in Southern Province in 2007 than did in 2002. By contrast, Western Area grew in voting population by about 140,000. Shifts in voting population plus changes in party preference helped the APC and hurt the SLPP.

In the parliamentary election, the three leading parties similarly divided the vote. In addition to the APC's 59 seats and the SLPP's 43 seats, the PMDC won the remaining 10 seats. The APC secured control of the legislature without needing to enter into a coalition with the PMDC. As with the presidential results, PMDC's seats all came from Southern Province, biting into the SLPP's traditional power base. The SLPP won 26 seats in Eastern Province, only 14 in Southern Province, and 3 in Northern Province. Surprisingly, the SLPP won no seats in the Western Area around Freetown. Those seats were all taken by the APC, which also gained a pair of seats in SLPP territory and 36 in Northern Province. The SLPP controlled 9 seats in Western Area in 2002, but the APC swept all 21 seats there in 2007. The constituency-based weighting of seats also hurt the SLPP. Its southern stronghold lost 7 seats, while Western Area, won by the APC, gained 5 seats.

Even in the presidential runoff, with the PMDC's Margai off the ballot, the vote distribution between the APC and the SLPP showed little change from the first round (see Table 2). Berewa's support held steady in Western Area and he gained in the south and east, but Koroma made gains there as well. In Southern Province, Koroma gained more than 18 percentage points, splitting the first-round PMDC voters with the SLPP. In Northern Province, Berewa lost ground, while Koroma mopped up the PMDC vote as well as some votes that had gone to a minor party in the August first round.

The second round shows that voters made their own choices and paid little attention to the parties that the losing candidates endorsed. Most PMDC voters in Southern Province, for instance, seem to have ignored Charles Margai's endorsement of Koroma in the runoff and voted SLPP. Minor parties in the north, meanwhile, threw their support behind Berewa, yet Koroma's gains in that region suggest that many of those smaller parties' supporters ignored this advice and voted APC in the second round.

The NEC was criticized for the large number of disqualified votes. In

TABLE 1—RESULTS OF 2007 FIRST-ROUND PRESIDENTIAL ELECTION BY REGION

PRESIDENTIAL CANDIDATE (PARTY)	WESTERN AREA	NORTHERN PROVINCE	SOUTHERN PROVINCE	EASTERN PROVINCE	TOTALS
Ernest Bai Koroma	273,172	431,896	36,255	74,200	815,523
(APC)	(61.3%)	(76.8%)	(9.6%)	(16.4%)	(44.3%)
Solomon E. Berewa	139,378	96,506	171,345	296,783	704,012
(SLPP)	(31.3%)	(17.1%)	(45.5%)	(65.5%)	(38.3%)
Charles F. Margai	23,555	9,182	155,844	66,918	255,499
(PMDC)	(5.3%)	(1.6%)	(41.3%)	(14.8%)	(13.9%)

the first presidential round, the NEC reported a 7.3 percent disqualification rate, which dropped to 2.5 percent in the runoff. After ordering a recount, the NEC made a controversial decision to annul second-round results from 477 (out of a total of 5,679) polling stations where more votes had been cast than there were voters on the rolls. Contested areas in the south and east were especially affected, with results from 426 stations eliminated there.

Some cried foul at this move, and two electoral commissioners from the hardest-hit provinces resigned in protest. But votes cast exceeding registered voters (especially in Pujehun and Kailahun districts) has been a recurring problem in national elections since 1996—and one that previous electoral commissions ignored despite overwhelming evidence. Only this time did the electoral commission have the resolve to act. The percentage of votes voided in the first round was in fact high even by regional standards, almost double that of neighboring Liberia's 2005 postconflict vote. With more than 160,000 votes separating the two runoff contenders, however, the invalidated ballots could not have changed the outcome.

Voting on the Management of the Peace

The SLPP's sweeping success in 2002 flowed from the advantages of incumbency and the political capital that Kabbah had accumulated from presiding over the war's end. The APC's victory in 2007, by contrast, came despite the autocratic and rapacious rule of its past leaders. But Kabbah's 2002 landslide victory can also be understood as a rejection of the war rather than as an endorsement of the SLPP's platform or performance.[9] Likewise, Koroma's 2007 victory did not necessarily result from a popular endorsement of the APC, but was rather a protest vote against the SLPP's mismanagement of the peace.

The SLPP losses to the PMDC in Southern and Eastern provinces stem from war grievances. Traditional authority structures remained closely tied to the ruling party, and paramount chiefs tried to deliver votes for the SLPP. Youth marginalized and exploited for their labor by

TABLE 2—RESULTS OF 2007 SECOND-ROUND PRESIDENTIAL
ELECTION BY REGION

PRESIDENTIAL CANDIDATE (PARTY)	WESTERN AREA	NORTHERN PROVINCE	SOUTHERN PROVINCE	EASTERN PROVINCE	TOTALS
Ernest Bai Koroma (APC)	304,388 (68.7%)	462,430 (84.9%)	86,384 (28.0%)	97,205 (21.9%)	950,407 (54.6%)
Solomon E. Berewa (SLPP)	138,613 (31.3%)	82,421 (15.1%)	221,765 (72.0%)	346,852 (78.1%)	789,651 (45.4%)

chiefs proved ready fodder for rebels during the war and for the PMDC's Mende opposition movement during the elections. With an exploitive rural social system still firmly in place and few economic opportunities available for youth, the SLPP failed to address many of the root causes of the war after securing the peace, fatally weakening its support base.

The indictment on war-crimes charges and early 2007 death in custody of the popular civil-defense leader Sam Hinga Norman—deemed a hero by many southerners for his work in protecting their communities during the war—also cost the SLPP dearly in Southern Province. Many former SLPP supporters there blamed President Kabbah for Norman's death and for what they saw as the injustice not only in Norman's trial but also in those of other civil-defense officers charged with war crimes. These disaffected voters readily joined the PMDC in opposing SLPP rule.

As a result of the trial and exploitive local governance, the PMDC made its strongest showing in Southern Province, where it gained 41 percent of the vote and all ten of its parliamentary seats. Championing Norman's cause, Charles Margai had even served as a defense attorney for Norman's fellow leaders before the Special Court. The PMDC's support of Norman created a protest vote, splitting the SLPP's support in what had traditionally been its main stronghold. In the runoff, the SLPP could not recoup its support in the south and east as people voted against the SLPP to the benefit of the APC.

But the SLPP's biggest losses were in the Western Area districts around Freetown. While in 2002 the SLPP won 9 of 16 seats in Western Area parliamentary elections, voters turned away from the SLPP in droves five years later and the party lost all 21 seats in Western Area to the APC. Similarly, in the Western Area presidential ballotings, Kabbah won more than half the vote in 2002, whereas Berewa in 2007 failed to exceed a third in either round. These results suggest that residents in and around Freetown, who represent about a quarter of the country's eligible voters, became dissatisfied with the performance of the government that they observed daily. During a preelection assessment, residents complained to me that the pace of reform was not keeping up with the worsening problems of poverty, decaying infrastructure, insufficient water and electricity, urban migrants, and egregious corruption by government officials. Although residents in Western Area suffered some of the worst brutality of the war, they seemed to disregard the SLPP's campaign message, so successful in 2002, that it had ended the conflict. Instead, these residents voted on the SLPP's peacetime record, and they were not pleased.

The answer to the question of "why the country's oldest palm tree fell," asked by the *Independent* newspaper in reference to the SLPP symbol, can be found in popular dissatisfaction with how the SLPP managed the peace. The justice system, the economy, traditional leadership, and corruption all worked to turn many SLPP supporters against the party. Continued lack of opportunity and basic services in and around the capital, despite ever-increasing population pressure, sapped support for the party in power. Campaigns of arrests and intimidation aimed at journalists inspired little public confidence in the SLPP's respect for intellectual pluralism or human rights. An ineffectual anticorruption strategy proved an expensive public-relations tool while graft remained rampant. The opposition's call for change resounded among voters. The PMDC's split from the SLPP certainly divided its constituents and weakened the party at its roots. However, the loss of confidence by residents around the capital also cut deeply into the SLPP base. Thus both internal party divisions and protest votes against the party's peacetime management precipitated the SLPP's dramatic fall.

Just five years after the end of its civil war, Sierra Leone has achieved a free and lawful transition between elected civilian leaders—something that has eluded so many other fragile states. The country's organization of a successful election resulted from several factors. A genuinely independent system of electoral administration with impartial leadership and strong technical support and planning made the 2007 poll one of the country's best-run to date. Training of poll watchers and election oversight by independent civil society groups and international organizations improved transparency. Participation by informed and interested citizens produced a high turnout and put popular momentum behind the conduct of a credible process. Depoliticizing control over security forces and courts diminished their interference while reinforcing the rule of law. And the failure of wartime factions to gain support in peacetime politics created a more open, democratic environment where impunity and the fear of a return to violent conflict were much reduced.

The Problems Ahead

While the elections are doubtless a milestone, Sierra Leone faces many deep-rooted problems that could impede its continued development. Foremost among them is corruption. Despite pressure from international financial institutions and support from international donors to improve accountability, corruption remains endemic among Sierra Leone's political class. The government's solution, the Anti-Corruption Commission (ACC) established in 2000 by an act of Parliament, has proven ineffectual. The ACC investigated 22 cases in its first six months, setting an impressive precedent. However, it quickly became hamstrung by political manipulation and torpid leadership, and its few convictions targeted low-ranking government officials on minor charges. The Kabbah administration withheld parts of the ACC's budget, hampering its work with a lack of political will and a corresponding lack of public confidence.

In his inaugural address, President Koroma pledged to adopt a "zero-tolerance" policy on corruption and promised to revitalize the ACC with stronger prosecutorial powers. The subsequent flight of the governor of Sierra Leone's central bank, who is alleged to have misappropriated half a million dollars for SLPP supporters, shows that Koroma's vow is being taken seriously. In Sierra Leone, however, the "borbor belly" phenomenon of corrupt officials growing fat off stolen state assets is not limited to a single party. If Koroma uses a stronger ACC only to punish political opponents while ignoring the APC's long legacy of corruption, he risks dangerously exacerbating political tensions and raising the potential for conflict.

Access to justice remains severely restricted in Sierra Leone. The Special Court has been the focus of international attention and funding to the justice sector to prosecute war crimes. The Court took four years to hand down its first judgment. In most cases, the trials have outlasted the indictees, with not only Sam Hinga Norman but also RUF leaders Foday Sankoh and Sam Bockarie dying before sentencing. Another major war criminal, Johnny Paul Koroma, avoided custody and disappeared; the Court officially declared him dead in 2003. With the arrest of Liberian strongman Charles Taylor and his transfer to stand trial at The Hague, the Special Court in Freetown will not try the main instigator of the civil war. Meanwhile, district courts and customary-law bodies controlled by local chiefs remain corrupt and dysfunctional, effectively denying most citizens access to justice. If the government hopes to cool the simmering grievances of political opponents and marginalized young people, it must strengthen the justice sector so that it can become a real forum for fair and impartial dispute resolution. The performance of the two election tribunals will be a critical test of the new administration.

Finally, restrictions on freedom of information and the press continue to limit oversight and criticism of the government to an unhealthy degree. The APC, the SLPP, and the AFRC junta have all used the criminal-libel provisions of the outdated 1965 Public Order Act to intimidate and imprison independent journalists. During Kabbah's first term, the SLPP also pushed the Newspaper Bill and the Media Practitioners Bill through Parliament in order to give the government extraordinary powers to revoke licenses and fire journalists and editors. Protected by their political connections, the killers of newspaper editor Harry Yansaneh continue to enjoy impunity. Whether the new administration will act to repeal outdated and restrictive legislation or will continue to limit critical discourse and information will also reveal much about its character.

As David Keen argues, "in the aftermath of war, it is important to challenge simplistic interpretations of 'reconstruction' that could reconstruct the source of the problem . . . . [I]f we are not simply to reconstruct the political economy that made the war possible in the first place, then the state must not simply be rebuilt but re-formed."[10] With a successful election behind it, Koroma and his party face the formidable task of converting the state from a vehicle for elite patronage to a means of improving citizens' lives through better governance. As underscored in the final report of Sierra Leone's Truth and Reconciliation Commission, failure to reform will be tantamount to inviting the country's tragic history to repeat itself.

NOTES

1. Paul Collier et al., *Breaking the Conflict Trap: Civil War and Development Policy* (Washington, D.C.: World Bank, 2003).

2. One preelection survey found that more than half the eligible voters polled placed little or no trust in national politicians. BBC World Service Trust and Search for Common Ground, "Sierra Leone Elections 2007: A Comprehensive Baseline Study of Knowledge, Priorities and Trust," U.K. Government Department for International Development, June 2007.

3. William Reno, *Corruption and State Politics in Sierra Leone* (Cambridge: Cambridge University Press, 1995).

4. Human Rights Watch, "Sowing Terror: Atrocities against Civilians in Sierra Leone," New York, July 1998, vol. 10, no. 3 (A), *www.hrw.org/reports98/sierra*.

5. TRC Report, "Findings," in *The Final Report of the Truth and Reconciliation Commission of Sierra Leone,* vol. 2 (2004), paras. 95–97, *www.trcsierraleone.org*.

6. Human Rights Watch, "Getting Away with Murder, Mutilation, Rape: New Testimony from Sierra Leone," New York, July 1999, vol. 11, no. 3 (A).

7. National Election Watch, "Report on the Voter Registration Process," March 2007.

8. European Union Observation Mission to Sierra Leone, "Statement of Preliminary Findings and Conclusions," 13 August 2007.

9. Jimmy D. Kandeh, "Sierra Leone's Post-conflict Elections of 2002," *Journal of Modern African Studies* 41 (June 2003): 189–216.

10. David Keen, *Conflict and Collusion in Sierra Leone* (Oxford: James Currey, 2005), 296–97.

13

LIBERIA STARTS OVER

Dave Peterson

Dave Peterson *is senior director for Africa programs at the National Endowment for Democracy. He has published twice before on Liberia in the* Journal of Democracy.

From 1990 to 2003, the small West African country of Liberia was wracked by a vicious civil war that killed a tenth of the populace (then roughly 2.5 million) and forced half the survivors to flee. The capital city of Monrovia was reduced to an anarchic, bullet-pocked shambles, its jobless residents ravaged by hunger and disease while violent militias roamed the countryside, setting up roadblocks where child soldiers shook down travelers for cash and valuables.

Today, Liberia is a relative success at both peace-building and democratization. A presidential election, held with massive UN and other international support in late 2005, brought former finance minister and World Bank official Ellen Johnson-Sirleaf to power as Africa's first elected female head of state. Chinese investment has paid for road repairs, and electric streetlamps light up the Monrovia night for the first time in almost two decades. New construction and the refurbishment of war-damaged buildings proceed apace. Street life bustles; the militias are demobilized and their roadblocks have vanished. The country is mostly conflict-free as commerce and agriculture resume. The new government is performing reasonably well. International assistance has poured in. The legislature is independent, the judiciary is recovering, the press is free, and civil society is robust. Yet there is a danger that all the relief, euphoria, international accolades, and wishful thinking could obscure the many remaining dangers to democracy and peace. Liberia's achievement is genuine, but tenuous—and huge challenges remain.

In order to understand where Liberia may be headed, it is necessary to look at where it has been. In 1822, the first of what would ultimately be some 1,200 freed slaves arrived from the United States and landed at a site that would soon be named for U.S. president James Monroe. Spon-

sored by the American Colonization Society, their mission was to build a
republic in Africa, complete with U.S.-style institutions, to which freed
slaves in the United States could emigrate upon emancipation.

Although Liberia is the only country in West Africa never to have
been colonized by Europeans, the Americo-Liberians—as the handful
of freed-slave settlers came to be known—eventually extended their
dominance over the native inhabitants of the new republic, leaving them
thoroughly sidelined. This marginalization finally began to ease during
the time in office of President William Tolbert, Jr., as greater opportunities for education and political participation opened up. Instead of
continuing to subside slowly, however, Americo-Liberian control came
to an abrupt and violent end when 28-year-old Master Sergeant Samuel
K. Doe overthrew the Tolbert government on 12 April 1980, murdering
the deposed president along with much of his cabinet.

Doe's repressive, inept, and corrupt rule eventually led to Charles
Taylor's rebellion. Taylor was a Doe ally and high official who, after be-
ing fired for embezzlement, fled to the United States, was arrested pending extradition, and then escaped back to West Africa. Taylor and 150
supporters invaded Liberia from Côte d'Ivoire on 24 December 1989.
Within six months, they had overrun most of the country. A renegade
Taylor lieutenant named Prince Johnson slaughtered Doe and frustrated
Taylor's desire to seize the capital. An alphabet soup of armed factions
launched more bloody fighting, which soon coagulated into a stalemate.
Taylor joined an interim national-unity government and in 1997 won
election to the presidency. His government failed to gain much international support, and his repressive actions, including support for a brutal
rebellion in neighboring Sierra Leone, made him a pariah and fueled
an insurgency that by August 2003 had forced him to flee to Nigeria in
search of asylum.[1]

A transitional government led by businessman Gyude Bryant, with
copious international support, was able to hold democratic elections
for the presidency and the bicameral legislature on 11 October 2005.
Amid heavy but peaceful turnout, the populist international football star
George Weah won a plurality of 28 percent of the vote. In the runoff,
however, Johnson-Sirleaf won by 59.4 to 40.6 percent, and in January
2006 took office with much fanfare. At the request of her government,
the Nigerians a few months later returned Taylor to Liberia, which in
turn handed him over to the Special Court for Sierra Leone at The Hague,
where his trial on 650 counts of war crimes and crimes against humanity
is slowly nearing its conclusion.

The elections left Johnson-Sirleaf's Unity Party in a precarious position, with only 8 seats in the 64-member House and 3 in the 30-member
Senate. Weah's Congress for Democratic Change, by contrast, had 15
House and 3 Senate seats, while Charles Taylor's National Patriotic Party had 4 seats in each, with a congeries of other parties and coalitions

rounding out the two chambers. Thus far, the legislature has worked fairly smoothly. The opposition seems to accept its role in a democratic dispensation, the president works constructively with opposition parties, and the occasional controversy notwithstanding, the two chambers function as an independent branch of government. Unlike other African legislatures that have gone along with presidents' moves to extend their terms, Liberia's lawmaking body has moved to cut the presidential term from six to four years, and has taken away the president's power to remove elected chiefs and county officials. Legislators have also sought to strengthen the independence of the Electoral Commission, passed a controversial "Threshold Bill" to redraw electoral districts, and insisted on actively debating and revising the budget.[2]

Controlling Corruption and Growing the Economy

Perhaps the greatest challenge for any nascent democracy rebuilding after conflict is delivering economic benefits to the people. This has become even more difficult in the wake of the global economic crisis. Johnson-Sirleaf inherited a government that was deeply in debt and had a paltry annual budget. In an extraordinary abrogation of national sovereignty, donors imposed a parallel government of international civil servants in key ministries and government agencies to oversee economic policy and limit the corruption that was anticipated. Known as the Governance and Economic Management Assistance Programme (GEMAP), the system is finally winding down and being handed over to Liberians. Although initially criticized, ironically, for its lack of transparency and the vagueness of its accomplishments, GEMAP undoubtedly helped Liberia to get back on its feet. The training of new supervisors and emplacement of financial controls at the airport, port authority, forestry authority, petroleum-refinery corporation, finance department, ministry of lands, and general-services agency have boosted revenue, improved management, and made budgeting and contracts more transparent.[3] Tax receipts have gone up dramatically, from just US$80 million in 2005 to $347 million in 2008. Debt has been slashed from $4.9 billion in 2007—the highest debt-to-GDP ratio ever among developing countries, according to the World Bank—to an anticipated level of between $100 million to $200 million, once Liberia completes its IMF negotiations in 2010.[4] Infrastructure has been repaired, and the civil service is working better.

Corruption remains a grave problem, however. Despite GEMAP and the creation of the Anticorruption Commission, dishonest and abusive officials are still a concern. According to a corruption scorecard developed by Global Integrity, in 2006 Liberia's overall score was 57 out of 100, "very weak."[5] The Heritage Foundation's 2009 Economic Freedom Index gives Liberia a low score of 21 out of 100 for corruption, citing a culture of impunity, financial mismanagement, and low accountability within government agencies.[6] Transparency International ranked Liberia 138th out of 180 countries with an aggregate score of 2.4 out of 10 in its Corruption Perceptions Index for 2008, an improvement over its ranking at 150th in 2007.[7]

The new National Anti-Corruption Strategy has yet to be implemented; the government has failed to act on several audit reports issued by the General Auditing Commission; and the legislature has yet to pass the Code of Conduct for Public Officials, the Freedom of Information Act, or the Whistleblower Protection Act. Only in September 2009 was a senior official, national oil-refinery head Harry Greaves, at least sacked, if not yet prosecuted, for misconduct (in his case, embezzlement).[8]

On the positive side, Liberia has a relatively independent legislature, a free press, and active (even contentious) civil society organizations—all of which can help to fight corruption. At the Center for Transparency and Accountability in Liberia (CENTAL), one can consult hundreds of Liberian press accounts of bureaucratic and legislative corruption. But journalists get no free pass: On the contrary, they often come under criticism for accepting "cado" or transport expenses, essentially payments from individuals interested in receiving favorable coverage. And as CENTAL notes, "[t]here [are] today increased demands emerging from government and other stakeholders for transparency and accountability on the part of CSOs [civil society organizations], in order to legitimize the quest to inculcate similar values into others."[9]

In short, as troubling as corruption may remain, corrective measures and structures are set to mitigate the situation, and a culture of greater transparency seems to be gaining ground. In August 2009, President Johnson-Sirleaf announced that the General Auditing Commission reports would be acted upon and officials would be prosecuted, that government officials would be required to declare their assets, and that Liberia would join the Extractive Industries Transparency Initiative (EITI). "The purge of a long entrenched system is being felt through exposure and condemnation. We thank the institutions of government, civil society and the media for their relentless effort in this regard," she said.[10] But Liberians have heard such promises before.

While some government officials build big new homes and drive around in suspiciously pricey vehicles, at least 80 percent of the population is unemployed, and annual per capita income is just $334, or less than a dollar a day. Economic conditions may not be as bad as statistics suggest, but they are clearly a major preoccupation for most citizens. Liberians are resourceful. The activities of the droves of hawkers in the market, the street stalls, furniture makers, used-clothes vendors, sidewalk restaurants, and the rest of the burgeoning informal sector are largely uncaptured by official statistics. Liberians are returning to their farms, going back to work on the rubber plantations, and finding jobs in the mines, forests, and port. Visually, compared to a few years ago, there can be no doubt that the great majority of the urban population is making do, if not prospering, through its own efforts. Some of this economic activity may depend on the generous international support that Liberia has received, including the brigades of expatriate staffers who patronize the restaurants and hotels, build the new offices, and employ locals as aides. These relatively deep-pocketed foreigners will mostly be leaving within a few years. The Chinese are making long-term investments. In some African countries their presence is bad for democratic prospects, but in Liberia they appear to have no problem with a democratic government (so long, one assumes, as it remains stable).

The benefits of six years of peace are clearly taking hold: The World Bank recorded Liberia's economic-growth rate as 9.4 percent for 2007. Yet that was at the peak of a worldwide boom for commodities such as Liberia's rubber and timber. Even in July 2008, before the global financial crisis and downturn struck, more than 50 percent of Liberians polled by the International Republican Institute were naming hunger as the number-one problem facing the country, with unemployment second. This was in contrast to high job approval ratings (63 to 75 percent) for President Johnson-Sirleaf found in the same poll.[11]

One clear sign that economic justice and democratic culture are making progress has been the victory of the Firestone Agricultural Workers Union of Liberia (FAWUL). In July 2007, five-thousand workers at Firestone, one of the world's largest rubber plantations, suspended their union leaders and elected new and reform-minded representatives. The plantation managers refused to recognize the new leaders and took the case to the Supreme Court, where delays ensued. Frustrated, the workers went on strike. Government and civil society organizations mediated the dispute, and in late December the Supreme Court finally acknowledged the new leadership's legitimacy. In July 2008, union members ratified a collective-bargaining agreement with Firestone, the first in 82 years, and it was signed the next month. The agreement included a 24 percent wage increase for rubber tappers, a 20 percent reduction in the daily tree quota, and the provision of powered transport to bring the latex to weigh stations (workers had been lugging 150-pound loads on their backs). Since then, the union has concentrated on implementing the agreement, and President Johnson-Sirleaf has met with them to discuss future reforms.[12]

Healing and Human Rights

Reintegrating thousands of unemployed former child soldiers and other ex-combatants into their communities poses another huge challenge. Although remarkably little violence has occurred so far, the explosive potential of such a large number of poor and jobless former fighters is obvious, and the funds to support their reintegration have largely run out. However difficult to achieve in the current global economic environment—prices for Liberia's key rubber, timber, and iron exports are all down—continued social and economic progress will be essential to buttress peace and democracy.

Underneath the country's tranquil surface, social inequality and injustice persist, and the trauma of the civil war remains vivid in many minds. The most sensitive cleavage is the old one that divides Americo-Liberians from the indigenous or "Country" people who make up 90 percent of the population. Although both Johnson-Sirleaf and Taylor are sometimes identified with the Americo-Liberians, they both have sought to distinguish themselves from that group and to identify with the Country majority. Considerable integration of the native peoples into government and other institutions such as the education system has taken place, but discrimination still occurs, and the Americo-Liberians remain a privileged group. Many Johnson-Sirleaf ministers and staffers are Americo-Liberians, inevitably creating suspicion and resentment. Tensions also remain between ethnic groups such as the predominantly Muslim Mandingo, who along with the Krahn, were favored by Doe (a Krahn), and the "pagan" Gio and Mano, who were Taylor's core supporters. Disputes usually break out over women or land, a problem exacerbated by returning refugees. Despite lingering grievances from the civil war and its accompanying atrocities, most communities have accepted the return of ex-combatants. Revenge killings have been mercifully few. Judicial resolution of communal disputes is often infeasible, but local groups dedicated to conflict resolution have stepped in to help fill the gap.

Liberians' current will to reconcile seems virtually as powerful as the bitter fighting of the civil war, providing a favorable social environment for democratic development. The Truth and Reconciliation Commission's report, published in July 2009, recommended war-crimes prosecutions for more than two-hundred individuals. Remarkably, it even recommended that President Johnson-Sirleaf be barred from running again for public office for thirty years due to her past support for Charles Taylor. The report also called for institutional reforms, conflict-resolution forums, and reparations to victims of rights abuses. Prince Johnson, one of several national legislators named in the report, threatened to mobilize his old fighters if the Commission pursued his case. Although suspicions abound that arms remain hidden, groups that campaign against arms proliferation have been able to find evidence of only a few weapons caches, and few take Prince Johnson seriously: After the report came out, civil society groups criticized him and other ex-warlords loudly and fearlessly, in keeping with Liberians' newfound general (and solidly democratic) habit of sounding off freely about public issues and persons of all sorts. In the meantime, the legislature has tabled the report.

As is often the case elsewhere in Africa, the judicial system suffers the most from neglect. The rule of law remains imperfectly enforced. Judges and magistrates are ill paid, too easily corrupted, and thin on the ground outside Monrovia. Public confidence in them is low: In one poll, 80 percent of respondents said that they had no faith in the judiciary, and the few who did complained that it took too long to act.[13] Prison conditions can be awful; prisoners may languish behind bars for months and even years on petty charges, or without even knowing what they have been charged with. According to an October 2008 report by Rescue Alternatives Liberia, only 104 of the 882 prisoners held in Monrovia's Central Prison had been convicted; the rest were awaiting trial.[14] Police are now unarmed, mass jail breaks occur from time to time, the crime rate is rising, and citizens have resorted to vigilante killings of suspected criminals.

The armed forces have been completely revamped, downsized, and retrained at great expense by the U.S. security contractor, DynCorp. According to a 2009 International Crisis Group report, Liberia's army of 2,000 enlisted soldiers and 110 officers has been vetted in perhaps the best process anyone has witnessed anywhere in the world.[15] Although former soldiers who have been forced to retire have protested their meager pensions, the army no longer appears to be a threat to democracy.

Freedom of Association and the Press

Liberia's media sector is robust and well organized, despite its weaknesses, and government infringements on press freedom have met with staunch challenge. Press coverage of government officials has been an important check on corruption, and the media's alliance with civil society has protected and expanded the democratic space that Liberians enjoy. A report by the Center for Media Studies and Peace Building, "The Triumph of Impunity: Attacks on Freedom of Expression in Liberia 2008," provides a comprehensive account of unpunished threats and abuses, such as the closure of a radio station by a local official, the brief detention of some journalists for taking pictures, the beating of other journalists by police, the seizure of a journalist's camera by the Chief Justice, and an apparent government attempt to manipulate the Press Union of Liberia. Yet compared to the report for 2006 and 2007, when many more beatings of journalists occurred and the minister of information attempted to close a newspaper for publishing pictures of Presidential Affairs Minister Willis Knuckles having sex with two women, the media environment in Liberia is clearly improving.[16]

As in many African countries, Liberia's many newspapers are too expensive for most citizens and have small circulations, yet there has been progress. A 2007 report documents 38 newspapers, approximately 15 of which publish with any regularity. Leading papers such as the

Inquirer, which is published five times a week, have grown in circulation from 500 daily copies in 2003 to as many as 2,500 copies of eight pages reaching four of Liberia's 15 counties in 2007. Journalists are poorly paid at perhaps $20 a month and are thus susceptible to payments from those they are writing about. Most advertising comes from the UN mission, and papers struggle to make ends meet. Radio reaches a much larger audience. There are currently 15 private FM stations operating in Monrovia, as well as the state-owned Liberia Broadcasting System, and as many as 50 community radio stations operating throughout the country, although the quality of their programming remains uneven.[17]

Liberian civil society was tempered by the civil war and is still maturing. Its sustainability is in doubt, however, as the country normalizes and international donors shift their priorities. Because civil society is such a broad sector, including trade unions, religious bodies, professional associations, women's and youth groups, human-rights organizations, and think tanks, it is useful to focus on function more than structure. In the context of Liberia's democratic development, some NGOs emerged with essentially political objectives, such as promoting the rule of law, providing voter education, increasing media freedom, or fostering reconciliation and conflict resolution. Others, such as women's and youth groups or the unions and professional societies, are not primarily political, but occasionally become active in ways that have political implications, as when they become involved in a public issue seen as affecting their members' interests.

As a case study, Liberian civil society deserves close scrutiny. Civil society has been a feature of Liberian life from the beginning, as the Americo-Liberians—perhaps inspired by their roots in the association-happy United States described by Alexis de Tocqueville—introduced churches and Masonic societies. Women's groups and the YMCA have long been fixtures; and traditional secret societies such as the Poro might even be considered incipient foundations for civil society. The Press Union of Liberia (founded 1965) and the Federation of Liberian Youths (founded 1979) belie claims that civil society is artificial or a recent import. Since the war, hundreds of NGOs have emerged, some due to generous donor funding, some merely as "briefcase" NGOs, of course; but many undoubtedly have sprung from authentic individual and collective initiatives.

Liberian civil society's relative density may be among Liberian democracy's most important foundations. In comparison with neighboring Guinea, Liberia has many more independent NGOs, and the correlation with a stronger democratic culture seems more than accidental. It is a virtuous circle. The stronger civil society grows, the better it becomes at countering government attempts to restrict democratic space or resist reform, and the more room civil society then has to operate and grow. For example, Liberian NGOs effectively blocked a proposed NGO law as too restrictive. Among other dubious provisions, the law originally would have required domestic NGOs to submit their plans for checks on their conformity with the government's own development plans. Liberian NGOs not only stopped this, but also won improvements that gave them greater freedom for their work. Currently, NGOs and some in the press are campaigning for a Freedom of Information Act, a Human Rights Commission, and acceptance of the Truth and Reconciliation Commission report (which was researched and prepared with considerable NGO help).

The contributions of civil society to conflict resolution, rights promotion, the fight against corruption, and the election process have been notable, although the efforts of the UN and other international agencies are more obvious. As an independent evaluation of the civil society program supported by the National Endowment for Democracy found in 2008:

> Many grantees claim that the human rights situation in the country is improving and attribute this to their own efforts. The reality is more nuanced. Several factors contribute to these gradual improvements in human security—a primary condition for an active civil society and a hallmark of solid democratic institutions. The default provider[s] of security and protection are the United Nations Mission in Liberia (UNMIL) forces, more than 17,000 strong. This is the highest civilian to peacekeeper ratio in Africa. . . . Within such a context determining the appropriate degree of responsibility for the overall improvement of human rights in Liberia to national human rights groups is difficult. The gains won by UNMIL are palpable and real, but unless government can rapidly scale up capacity and take over UNMIL activities, then nothing sustainable will have been achieved.[18]

In fact, it is this very challenge of sustainability that underscores the critical and increasingly neglected role of civil society. Liberian civil society has made a conscious shift from the heroic mode of the years during which it struggled for human rights and democracy in the face of Taylor's violent misrule. Currently, a more pragmatic engagement with the Johnson-Sirleaf government is the order of the day. Civil society groups are using democratic openness to press for more reforms. As has not always been the case in Africa, no one can say that the state has coopted Liberian civil society, which continues to write the most encouraging chapter in the larger story of Liberia's real but uneven democratic development.

The National Coalition of Civil Society Organizations of Liberia (NACCSOL), the largest civil society network in the country, unites 120 CSOs promoting a culture of advocacy, social mobilization, solidarity, and the exchange of information and skills. A tally of its membership list shows 29 human-rights organizations, 21 democracy-promotion organizations, 9 professional organizations, 22 trade and labor unions, 18 women's organizations, 14 youth organizations, 10 community-based

organizations, 3 business groups, 6 faith-based organizations, and a traditional group, the National Traditional Council of Liberia. Many of
these groups are indisputably serious organizations, and there are certainly many more Liberian NGOs and CSOs that are not members of
NACCSOL. But NACCSOL clearly represents a formidable power as
its members work to lobby for the public officials' Code of Conduct, an
oversight body for security agencies, passage of the proposed Security
Reform and Intelligence Bill, the Freedom of Information Act, and the
establishment of an NGO council. Civil society does not have the resources to take the place of government, but once the UN leaves, civil
society will play a more crucial role than ever in promoting a democratic culture, holding the government accountable, and providing services
such as conflict mediation and access to justice—in short, in providing
the enabling environment that democracy will need in order to thrive.

In its search for leaders capable of taking on such tasks, civil society finds itself facing an ironic "problem of success": Civil society has
done such a good job of cultivating democratic leadership that many of
its brightest lights are now working for the new government. Sam Kofi
Woods, former director of the Justice and Peace Commission (JPC) and
the Foundation for International Dignity, became minister of labor, and
later, public works. Tiawan Gongloe, a colleague of Woods's from the
community of lawyers concerned with human rights, took over when
Woods took the public-works job. Jerome Verdier, former executive director of Liberia Democracy Watch, became chairman of the Truth and
Reconciliation Commission. Frances Morris-Johnson, also a former director of the JPC, heads the Anti-Corruption Commission. Gabriel Wil-
liams, a former Press Union president, is serving in a prominent role as
Assistant Minister of Information. Although some critics assail NGOs
as mere launching pads used by ambitious and charismatic individuals,
it might be fairer to say that the NGO world serves as a place where
Liberians with talent and commitment can prove themselves ready for
public responsibility.

The international community's role has been decisive—it helped to
end the war and start the rebuilding. Yet questions continue to swirl
around matters of sovereignty, sustainability, and repeatability. Liberian
exceptionalism cannot be denied. In no other country in Africa has the
United States been more important, whether socially, politically, dip-
lomatically, economically, or symbolically. Liberians often call their
country a U.S. "stepchild," founded as it was by former slaves from
the United States who named the capital after a U.S. president, adopted
a flag resembling the Stars and Stripes, modeled their government on
the U.S. Constitution, and yet have always felt neglected by the mother
country. At times when a relatively modest yet decisive action might
have saved Liberia from grave trouble, Washington has declined to
intervene. Doe's bloody coup, which came as President Jimmy Carter

was preparing his failed run for reelection, met with little response. The badly flawed elections that Doe staged in 1985 were accepted by the administration of Carter's successor Ronald Reagan. Prince Johnson's gunmen besieged Monrovia without much opposition from Washington. Later, when anti-Taylor insurgents were attacking in 2003, Monrovians piled heaps of corpses before the U.S. Embassy as a plaintive appeal for help while U.S. Navy warships floated offshore. Many Liberians thought that the mere presence of a handful of U.S. troops on the ground could have ended the fighting.

Liberia has long accommodated U.S. strategic interests. During the Cold War and after, it hosted the Voice of America listening post that served much of the mid-Atlantic. In 2007, Liberia was one of the few African countries to express a willingness to have facilities of the new U.S. Africa Command based on its territory. The relationship has not been all one way. The United States helped to undermine Taylor's bloody misrule by refusing him economic support and orchestrating sanctions. Since Johnson-Sirleaf took office, U.S. aid to Liberia—whose current population is thought to be roughly 3.5 million—may be unprecedented in Africa on a per-capita basis. Direct U.S. support totaled $102 million in 2007, $161 million on 2008, and an estimated $190 million in 2009. Approximately $70 million of this each year was for development assistance, economic support, and food aid. Support for peacekeeping operations averaged $50 million a year.[19] According to President Johnson-Sirleaf, the total donor assistance that Liberia has received since her accession to office at the start of 2006 has averaged $500 million a year.

The U.S. government provided support to the Liberian elections through groups such as the National Democratic Institute, the International Republican Institute, the International Foundation for Election Systems, and Search for Common Ground; to GEMAP through IBI International, and to Mercy Corps for civil society development. Funds supported security-sector reform through Dyncorp, and renovation of the airport through Pacific Architecture Engineering. Foundations such as the National Endowment for Democracy, the Norwegian Fund for Human Rights, the Open Society Institute, and the Global Fund for Human Rights have been the main supporters of Liberian civil society organizations promoting democracy and human rights, and their total donations have averaged an estimated $2 million a year over the last several years.

Civil society across Africa has been accused of being an artificial creation of international donors focused on external priorities, as opposed to something that springs spontaneously from local concerns. Although Liberian civil society is in many respects dependent on donor support, the funding that it receives pales in comparison to what the Liberian government (and especially the security sector) is getting. Most support for democracy promotion has been channeled through international NGOs, and UN support has tended to come in the form of technical advice and sponsorship of workshops and publications, as opposed to the direct, institutional support that indigenous NGOs require if they are to function autonomously.

Philosophical Questions

The philosophical questions raised by the arc of events in Liberia are troubling and instructive. Those who advocate democracy are often fond of piously declaring that it cannot be imposed by force. In Liberia's case, however, one might well argue that this is precisely what occurred. The story has odd twists. Charles Taylor won a democratic election in 1997 (albeit only after he had made himself a national player by dint of an armed rebellion). His repressive rule was ended six years later essentially through force of arms. The guns that sent him packing, moreover, were those of yet another indiscriminately violent insurgency—this one calling itself Liberians United for Reconciliation and Democracy (LURD)—that hardly qualified as a popular movement of any sort. It killed thousands of innocent Liberians, and the scant appeal of its warlord headmen and minority support base was laid bare in the 2005 elections when its chief, Sekou Conneh, and the Progressive Democratic Party that he had jerry-built as his political vehicle garnered a vanishingly small 0.06 percent of the vote. Yet without the intense military pressure that LURD brought to bear on Taylor, it is unlikely that he would have fallen from power and in doing so made way for the transitional government—and the massive armed peacekeeping presence—that rendered possible the elections of 2005 and the democratic progress which followed. Was the sacrifice necessary? Was the violence justifiable? Or was Liberia's democratic outcome simply a result of making the best of a bad situation?

The level of residual support for Taylor and the populist appeal of politicians such as George Weah evident in the 2005 election suggest that many Liberian voters continue to harbor older tastes—leanings that favor the "big man" style of governance that has long been the bane of African political life. Liberia's political class has shown a greater propensity for the old patterns of corruption, ethnic appeals, and an authoritarian style of politics than for the new stress on good governance and liberal democracy.

Yet for all its populist dangers, an appeal to the grassroots, to traditional values, to basic needs such as food, housing, and employment, must understandably resonate with voters more than the abstract jargon of international criminal courts and World Bank targets. President Johnson-Sirleaf seems to be striking the balance, but it will be difficult to maintain. Democratic culture seems to be taking root in Liberia, but it may yet wither. The nation is at peace, but the reconciliation process has miles to go. Taylor is still on trial, and the Liberian legislature will likely keep putting off approval of the Truth and Reconciliation Commission's report. Liberians are tired of war, but the deep tensions that fueled the strife are still present just under the surface. With the right provocation, they could erupt into violence again. Instability in Guinea and Côte d'Ivoire could spill over the border into Liberia, and Charles Taylor proved well how a small fighting force might gain the support of unemployed and disaffected youth. Liberia has an abundance of former warlords who might be tempted again by that option. As is the case also in Congo (Kinshasa), Kenya, Sierra Leone, Somalia, and Sudan, the question continues to be raised whether it is better to end impunity and prosecute warlords (with the hope of deterring future warlordism), or whether prudence dictates overlooking past crimes for the sake of preserving a peace that was restored only at great cost and which remains all too fragile.

Economic development and the reform of government have taken place, but much of this has been due to international pressure and massive financial assistance. The Liberian government must still prove that it has the political will and commitment to continue implementing sound policies with much less outside support. There is no doubt that GEMAP was an unprecedented international intervention into the sovereignty and governance of a nation. Yet it produced tangible results. Sierra Leone has also stabilized and democratized after massive international assistance. Yet Sierra Leone also shares with Liberia high levels of corruption, high levels of youth unemployment and disaffection, and an uncertain level of political stability. Such international interventions might be appropriate in the case of similarly failed states such as Congo (Kinshasa) and Somalia, but a proportionate financial commitment would likely be prohibitive in cost, given their size. Although a continuum might be formulated along which states and governments become more or less legitimate, more or less democratic, more or less abusive, and therefore more or less in need of intervention, the truth is that intervention seems to be a function of the relative size of the problem, its strategic and political importance, and its economic cost. Liberia was clearly a failed state, it is small in both land area and population, and it has a coastline and a modern port—intervention thus seemed affordable, at least in the days before the global recession. Larger states such as Congo (Kinshasa), Ethiopia, Nigeria, and Sudan are less susceptible to such efforts.

Liberia's independent press and civil society have promoted democratic culture, helped to keep the government accountable, and provided a sound grassroots basis for an engaged citizenry. Although Liberian civil society has deep historical roots, talented and dedicated leaders, and a growing presence throughout the country, it continues to rely on international assistance. How sustainable will civil society be when this assistance inevitably begins to dwindle? Perhaps, much as happened in South Africa, civil society in Liberia will shrink as leaders go into government and groups close down due to lost funding or missions that are either accomplished or no longer relevant. Yet in Liberia as in South Africa, civil society has earned respect and created a legacy that will affect Liberian life far into the future, even if not every currently constituted civil society organization survives. Groups are learning to cooperate, to conduct strategic activities at minimal expense, to raise money in new ways, to both engage the government and build grassroots support, to share experiences across national borders, and to preserve a role and fight for survival. Liberia has set forth anew on the road to democracy. The way has been paved with international help and Liberian blood and toil. It is an uncertain road. There are still many checkpoints. But it looks much better than it did less than two decades ago.

NOTES

1. Justice and Peace Commission, "The Liberian Crisis," Monrovia, July 1994.

2. "Liberian Legislators Push for Referendum, Seeking to Reduce Presidential Term," FrontPageAfrica, 26 February 2009.

3. "Liberia Improved Budget and Assets Management Project: A Summary of Achievements to Date," IBI International, 8 June 2009.

4. Bob Davis, "Liberia Cuts Foreign Debt by $1.2 Billion," *Wall Street Journal,* 17 April 2009, A6.

5. Available at *www.globalintegrity.org/reports/2006/liberia/scorecard.cfm.*

6. Available at *www.heritage.org/index/country/liberia.*

7. Available at *www.transparency.org/policy_research/surveys_indices/cpi/2008.*

8. "Liberian Leader Threatens to Sack More Ministers," *Agence France Presse,* 9 September 2009.

9. Thomas Doe Nah, "Issues and Challenges Facing the Civil Society Sector in Liberia," available at *http://cental.org/CSO%20Issues%20and%20Challenge%20-%20Liberia.pdf.*

10. "Sirleaf Commissions Justice Team," *All Africa,* 27 August 2009.

11. "IRI Poll Finds Liberians' Concerns Go Unmet by Legislature and Political Parties: Food and Hunger Top Concerns," available at *www.iri.org/newsreleases/2008 -10-03-Liberia.asp.*

12. "USW Congratulates Liberian Rubber Workers on Landmark Labor Agreement," PR Newswire, 7 August 2008, available at *www.newscom.com/cgi-bin/prnh/20080131/DC12982LOGO.*

13. Center for Law and Human Rights Education, "Human Rights Situation Report," Monrovia, July 2009.

14. Rescue Alternatives Liberia, "Criminal Justice Outlook, Vol. 1, No. 1: The Prison Sector Must Be Autonomous," Monrovia, October 2008.

15. International Crisis Group, "Liberia: Uneven Progress in Security Sector Reform," Africa Report No. 148, 13 January 2009, 12. Available at *www.crisisgroup.org/home/index.cfm?id=5867&l=1*.

16. Center for Media Studies and Peace Building (Monrovia), "The Triumph of Impunity: Attacks on Freedom of Expression in Liberia 2008," and "The Perennial Tragedy of Democracy: Attacks on Freedom of Expression in Liberia 2006 – 2007," available at *www.cemesp-liberia.org.*

17. Partnership for Media and Conflict Prevention in West Africa, "Strengthening Liberia's Media: A Review of Media Support in the Post-Conflict Transitional Period and Recommendations for Future Actions," April 2007, available at *www.i-m-s.dk/publication/strengthening-liberias-media-2007.*

18. Edward Rackley, "An Evaluation of the National Endowment for Democracy's Grants Program in Liberia (2001–2006)," National Endowment for Democracy, Washington, D.C., April 2008, 7.

19. These figures are from the 2008 budget request of the U.S. Agency for International Development, available at *www.usaid.gov/policy/budget/cbj2008/fy2008cbj_highlights.pdf.*

III

East Africa

14

KENYA: BACK FROM THE BRINK?

Michael Chege

Michael Chege is an advisor on international development policy in Kenya's Ministry of State for Planning and Development. He obtained his doctorate from the University of California, Berkeley, and most recently served as a professor and director of the Center for African Studies at the University of Florida, Gainesville. This essay originally appeared in the October 2008 issue of the Journal of Democracy.

On New Year's Day 2008, the world awoke to news of horror and mayhem in Africa. In a scene reminiscent of Rwanda in 1994, 39 people seeking refuge burned to death in a church torched by ethnic mobs from a rival political party. Yet this was Kenya—East Africa's economic powerhouse, normally considered a stable, peaceful haven on an otherwise troubled continent. Following the hasty announcement of incumbent president Mwai Kibaki's reelection on the evening of December 29, strongholds of the opposition Orange Democratic Movement (ODM)—certain that their candidate Raila Odinga had been cheated out of victory—erupted in protest demonstrations that soon degenerated into rape, looting, and indiscriminate murder by machete. The actions were aimed against the Kikuyu, Kibaki's ethnic group, and locals suspected of voting for Kibaki's Party of National Unity (PNU). For nearly three weeks, there was no letting up. During this period, Kenyan police, in their efforts to put down the violence, were accused of shooting innocent demonstrators in ODM strongholds in Nairobi and Kisumu.

Kikuyu reprisal attacks broke out in late January in Nairobi and its satellite towns, targeting ethnic groups who formed the bedrock of ODM support—the Luo, Luhya, and Kalenjin. A Luo family of eight was burned to death in the lakeside town of Naivasha. The *New York Times* echoed the widely held view that Kenya's electoral violence seemed to "to have tapped into an atavistic vein of tribal tension that always lay beneath the surface in Kenya but until now had not produced widespread mayhem."[1] The nature and degree of the postelection violence fed pessimistic observers' belief that African societies have an inherent propensity for fratricide, cynicism, and economic nihilism.

But that perception is false. As that *Times* article appeared, Kenyan leaders from different ethnic groups were already at work on a peace formula. Mediation led by former UN secretary-general Kofi Annan furthered the process, and with critical high-level support from the United States, Britain, the European Union, and the African Union, calm was restored. Most credit, however, goes to the two party leaders, who saw sense in compromise and shook off extremists who, in the case of the ODM, were urging a break-up of the country along party lines and, in the case of the PNU, the use of more force to overcome opposition resistance. In February, the parties reached an agreement on a PNU-ODM coalition government with Kibaki as president, Odinga as prime minister, and an equally shared cabinet reflecting Kenya's ethnic diversity. The new government was sworn in two months later.

The political tools used to end the conflict are well known. They include a "grand coalition government" of all major parties and leaders; "power-sharing" between ethnic-based factions; and allocation of executive positions so that all major groups are fairly represented. Such practices represent important elements of the "power-sharing" or "consensus" model of democracy that Arend Lijphart prescribes for conflict-prone plural societies like Kenya.[2] The agreement, however, left out three important pillars of his full-consensus model—autonomy and federalism, the mutual veto, and the electoral system of proportional representation (PR). It was not a perfect solution, and Kenya is still at risk given the level of political animosity generated by the disputed election and subsequent ethnic killings.

Still, Kenya may find salvation in the ashes of this disaster. As Fareed Zakaria reminds us, mature democracies in the past have themselves suffered—and learned—from lapses into authoritarianism and violence directed at resented minorities by movements claiming majority support.[3] For Kenya to recover politically, Kenyans must now renegotiate the foundations of a democratic state (disputes about which lay at the heart of the violence). These basics include the right to change government through free and fair elections, the entitlement of all Kenyans to own property and vote as they wish anywhere in the country, and the banning of hate speech as a political campaign tool. These reforms must be complemented by other measures of a consensus model of democracy—devolution with autonomy, a bicameral legislature, a PR electoral system, and a parliamentary government. All this depends on an enhanced capacity to maintain law and order, which were the first casualties of the crisis.

The Context of Conflict

Kenya's population, estimated at nearly 38 million, is composed of 42

African ethnic groups and significant minorities of Arab, South Asian, and European descent. The Kikuyu (with the closely related Embu and Meru), whose traditional homeland is in Central and Eastern provinces (see map below), constitute the largest of the groups but only about 22 percent of the total population. The Luhya, located mainly in Western Province, follow with 14 percent; the Luo, who reside predominantly in Nyanza Province, comprise 13 percent; and the Kalenjin, living mostly in the Rift Valley, account for 12 percent.[4] The Kikuyu lost significant landholdings to British colonists in the early twentieth century, and as a result many migrated to white-owned farms in the Rift Valley and elsewhere as traders, also leading the way in adopting modern education and market agriculture.

MAP—KENYA'S PROVINCES

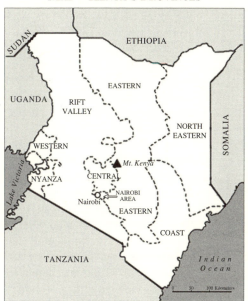

Kenya gained independence from Britain in 1963 after a violent anticolonial struggle—the Kikuyu-led Mau Mau uprising (1952–59)—and its first two decades of independence were generally considered a success. Under President Jomo Kenyatta (1964–78), an ethnic Kikuyu, and his Kenya African National Union (KANU), the market-driven economy grew impressively, a rarity among the many failed state-run economies of Africa. Freedom House rated the country Partly Free over this period, a remarkable achievement for a de facto one-party state that reflected Kenya's robust press, competitively elected parliament, and active civil society. The closing years of Kenyatta's rule, however, were marked by rising intolerance, corruption, high-level political assassinations, and widespread discontent over the dominance of Kikuyu in business and among senior political appointees.

The shine continued to fade under Kenyatta's successor, Daniel arap Moi (1978–2002) of the Kalenjin ethnic group. Despite a good start, in 1982 his regime took an authoritarian turn, imposing legislation making Kenya a de jure one-party state and persecuting dissidents seeking political competition. In 1988, the government banned secret balloting for legislative elections, and voters were required to line up publicly behind the candidate of their choice. In 1989, Freedom House downgraded Kenya's aggregate ranking to Not Free. Corruption escalated as the regime methodically dodged economic and political reforms. Annual economic growth declined significantly between 1990 and 2000, and poverty levels soared.

In this environment, demands for multiparty democracy escalated, especially following the assassination in February 1990 of Foreign Minister Robert Ouko, a known opponent of official corruption. Faced with combined local and international pressure, in December 1991 the Moi government yielded (in letter but not in spirit) to demands for democratization and multiparty politics. Two controversial general elections followed in 1992 and 1997, in both of which Moi's KANU party was declared the winner with a plurality of the vote. Given the high level of electoral malpractice, Kenya during these years could at best be described as a competitive authoritarian regime rather than a democracy. Political space, however, was gradually opening up.

In Kenya's December 2002 elections, the National Alliance Rainbow Coalition (NARC)—a broad multiethnic reform coalition that included Kibaki's National Alliance of Kenya (NAK) party and Odinga's Liberal Democratic Party (LDP)—prevailed, ending the monopoly of President Moi and KANU. The country earned international accolades for conducting a peaceful transition of power from one party to another, a critical marker of democratic progress. Only three African countries—Ghana, Senegal, and Benin—had previously managed this feat.

When NARC came to power in 2003 with a 63 percent mandate, there was widespread relief and hope in the new government, which had campaigned on ending corruption, jump-starting the economy and creating 500,000 jobs a year, improving public services, and making constitutional reforms that would redistribute power from the all-powerful presidency. The Kenyan people expected an end to the culture of impunity and corruption that characterized the Moi years and the prosecution of the malefactors; they expected fair public appointments "that reflected the face of Kenya" and renewed efforts to reclaim Kenya's international reputation for stability and hospitality to tourists and foreign investors.

In its first term, the Kibaki administration presided over a stunning economic recovery underpinned by macroeconomic discipline, reduced deficit spending, a doubling of tax revenue as a result of stricter enforcement of regulations, an improved business environment, and the privatization of failing state-operated enterprises. Multinational firms such as General Electric, Hewlett Packard, Google, Virgin Atlantic, and Radisson Hotels came to invest. Economic growth rose from 3.4 percent in 2003 to 7 percent in 2007, raising per capita incomes for the first time since the 1980s. National poverty levels fell from an estimated 56 percent in 1997 to 46 percent in 2006. On a visit to the country in April 2007, *New York Times* columnist Thomas L. Friedman detected some signs of an East Asian–style newly industrializing economy in the making,[5] and many well-informed Kenyans thought the same.

Not all the high expectations for the new government, however, would be met. The Kibaki administration's political stewardship of Kenya failed to match its economic record, particularly with regard to prosecution and conviction of high-level corruption before and after 2003, despite having laid the legal and institutional framework to do so. A prime example of this disappointment was its reaction to the so-called Goldenberg scandal, a US$800 million Moi-era scam involving government rebates for fake diamond exports. In 2004, the government appointed a judicial commission to investigate the scandal. It released its findings in February 2006, implicating top leaders in government and in the opposition. But despite high-level prosecutions of a few of them—including the current security minister, George Saitoti—nobody has been convicted or jailed for the Goldenberg scandal.

Even worse, in early 2005 news broke of the Anglo Leasing Scandal, a series of security contracts with official payoffs that were in part intended to finance the 2005 constitutional referendum and 2007 PNU campaign. John Githongo, permanent secretary for governance and ethics, conducted an exhaustive investigation and concluded that top members of the government were involved.[6] As a result, Githongo received death threats and ultimately resigned and fled to the United Kingdom. Two cabinet ministers who were forced to resign in connection with Anglo Leasing were subsequently reappointed. Again, no convictions have resulted.

While some ministers were fighting accusations of graft, others took to intimidating the press. In March 2006, hooded policemen raided the pro-opposition daily the *Standard* and its television station, threatening staff and shutting both down for a time. The bad old ways seemed to have returned.

An Alliance Crumbles

Kibaki's first-term government clearly had a mixed record—it had delivered on the economy but disappointed in national governance. In the long run, however, its failure to honor a power-sharing agreement with its coalition partners was to become its greatest political liability. NARC's interethnic coalition was based on a memorandum of understanding (MoU) between Kibaki's NAK and Odinga's LDP, providing for an equal share of cabinet positions and most other high-level appointments and consensus-based decision making. In addition, NARC formed a "summit" of its top six figures, who exercised leadership over Kenya's main ethnic groups.

Kibaki's closest aides, most of them Kikuyu, had other ideas, however. Unable to countenance the idea of the head of state sitting in a body of political coequals, they shot down all attempts to shore up the

NARC "summit." Instead, they hoped to combine strong presidential authority and a growing market economy in the mode of the Kenyatta regime.[7] Mateere Keriri, the president's former chief of staff, acknowledged that he had advised Kibaki to trash the MoU because, he asserted, power sharing would have divided Kenyans along ethnic lines.[8] In doing so, the group betrayed Odinga, who had proposed Kibaki as the NARC presidential standard-bearer in 2002 and also campaigned for him with more vigor than anyone else. As a result of the presidential camp's maneuvers, the LDP received less than an equal share of seats in the cabinet and complained loudly about it.

While vacationing in the resort city of Mombasa in December 2004, Kibaki proposed an end to coalition-building and the dissolution of NARC's constituent parties in order to form one strong governing party to face the KANU opposition in parliament. Rather than consensus, Kibaki was proposing a two-party adversarial system based on the first-past-the-post electoral system that has brought so many African countries to grief because, in the context of deep ethnic mistrust and ethnic-based parties, one side's victory will always arouse fear if not outright hostility among the losers.[9] Predictably, the LDP vigorously objected to the idea of dissolving the NARC's constituent parties. Once certain that the coalition as envisioned in 2002 was beyond salvage, the LDP began casting about for alternatives, including an alliance with the discredited KANU opposition, which was soon consummated. And with that, the die was cast.

The face-off between the rump-NARC under Kibaki and the combined LDP-KANU opposition came during the November 2005 referendum on a new constitution. The independence constitution, which provided a federalist structure with a bicameral legislature, had been whittled down under Kenyatta to produce a strong presidency with enormous power (including the right to detain dissidents without trial)—a trend that intensified in the Moi years. As political liberalization expanded after the reintroduction of multiparty politics, there was a spirited civic-led campaign in favor of a new constitution that would guarantee individual liberties and reduce presidential power by restoring checks and balances. To achieve that, Odinga and others advocated a split executive (closer to the French model), with a president and executive premier, and a federalist devolution of power to the regions.

But there was also a strong constituency that saw the new constitution as a charter that would guarantee a fairer distribution of tax revenues ("national resources") among Kenya's ethnic homelands, which roughly coincide with the provinces. With the Mount Kenya region's economic edge in mind, this strategy was intended to bring about more equitable development through the devolution of state functions from the center to the provincial level, known in Kenya as *majimbo* government. These demands received unexpected support from a 2004 donor-funded report on inequality in Kenya, which concluded that urban areas and the Kikuyu districts had superior economic and social indicators as a result of high-level patronage from previous governments that had discriminated against less-developed regions.[10] The allocation of public monies dominated the political debate from 2004 up to the 2007 elections.

In its twilight years, the Moi government, bowing to a strident civic campaign for a new constitution, had agreed to hold a national constitutional conference. A new body, the Kenya Constitutional Commission, composed of eminent lawyers and personalities, was formed to consult public opinion on proposals for debate and approval by the constitutional conference. Its chairman, Kenyan constitutional lawyer Yash P. Ghai, in the end acknowledged that the commissioners had a greater appetite for money than work, and that "some were not particularly knowledgeable about constitution-making."[11] The commission nevertheless received political and financial reinforcement from the Kibaki administration as soon as it came to office, but soon ran into trouble with Kibaki's inner circle, who opposed the proposal for a split executive. Finally, however, victory on the floor of the Constituent Assembly went to advocates of devolution and a new position of prime minister.

The "Bomas Draft Constitution" (named for the conference's venue) was a federal constitution and a highly complicated one at that. It proposed four layers of government and the devolution of most functions (except defense and foreign affairs) to the provincial, district, and community level. In addition, it contained numerous entitlements based on "second-generation" human rights—health, housing, food, and clean water—without stating how they were to be financed. Debates ensued that led to doubts about the political and fiscal feasibility of the Bomas Draft.

Kibaki and his advisors got an excellent opportunity to reach a deal with Bomas enthusiasts when legislators from all parties met in Naivasha in November 2004 and hammered out what would have been a functional compromise: devolution to the district level only, enhanced local-development funding, and a prime minister appointed by the president and answerable to him. The Kibaki power faction, however, still fixated on a strong presidency, again squandered the opportunity and disowned the agreement. Opponents of Kibaki saw this obstinacy as further evidence of the arrogance of a moneyed Kikuyu elite keen to consolidate wealth and executive power on its side.

Soon after, the government, with Attorney General Amos Wako in the lead, drafted another constitution, which borrowed heavily both from the Bomas Draft and the Naivasha agreement. It contained two tiers of government and a prime minister nominated by the president. More controversially, however, it brought under the constitution the already operational Muslim Kadhi Courts that handled intra-Muslim civil disputes. This outraged many on the Christian right in Kenya, who denounced the inclusion of the Kadhi Courts as a move toward the Islamization of the country, and they therefore joined the LDP in opposing the new draft constitution. The government's naïve attempt to placate the Christian right by introducing Christian and Hindu courts into the constitution failed to mollify its opponents. Despite stiff opposition from Odinga and his supporters, parliament passed what came to be known as the "Wako Draft" in July 2005 and presented it to the public in a constitutional referendum in November.

The government lost the referendum (57 to 43 percent) to the LDP-KANU opposition alliance, which had now united as the Orange Democratic Movement. The referendum's outcome made it clear that, although Kibaki still had widespread backing, his base of support had narrowed to the Mount Kenya region—the Kikuyu homeland. The government had thus worked itself into a corner. The Wako Draft, which was in many ways a sensible compromise, lost largely because of anti-Kikuyu rhetoric targeted at various ethnic constituencies. For pastoralist groups like the Maasai, a proposed national land commission was portrayed as a ruse through which Kikuyu would grab their pastures. For the densely peopled farming communities in Western Kenya, the Wako Draft was flayed for proposing equal land-inheritance rights for sons and daughters—an idea that was anathema to the tradition-bound groups. Notably, both articles had been extracted directly from the Bomas Draft, which ODM had championed. To all non-Kikuyu, the Wako Draft, with its high threshold for amendments, was depicted as a Trojan horse for continued Kikuyu dominance.

Kibaki accepted the defeat of the referendum graciously, and his erstwhile LDP allies expressed hope of reconciliation and a return to the 2002 reform agenda. Such a rapprochement would have split the Orange alliance, thereby isolating KANU and reunifying NARC to the advantage of the Kibaki government. Instead, the president dissolved the cabinet and, after a month, announced a new one that excluded the LDP but took on board some legislators from KANU and other smaller parties. ODM leaders, now free of ministerial responsibilities and nursing grievances of exclusion from a government that some of its top brass had fought hard for, proceeded to build the party into a strong nationwide machine. Many of these leaders were bitter at what they saw as an increasingly pro-Kikuyu bias in high-level government appointments, especially in the ministries of finance and education and the Office of the President. The battle lines of the 2007 election campaign had now been drawn.

"Forty-One Tribes Against One"

A backlash against the perceived favored status of the Kikuyu—already the country's strongest economic force—found its way into ODM's campaign platform, consolidating ethnic support in the non-Kikuyu regions. The reinvigorated opposition launched its campaign against the Kibaki government, criticizing it over inequalities in "national resource distribution" that reinforced trends going back to the Kenyatta years.

On 22 July 2006, a widely read column by Barrack Muluka in the

Standard asserted that Kenya faced a serious problem of regional economic inequality because Central Province, the Kikuyu homeland, took more in development projects from the Treasury than it contributed. The article broke down Kenya's total tax revenue of 23.7 billion shillings by province, and claimed that Central Province contributed less than all the others except for the hardscrabble North Eastern Province.[12] In effect, the Kikuyu area was accused of fleecing the less-developed provinces—a charge that was raised throughout the campaign.

Yet none of the figures was true. The Kenya Revenue Authority does not even record taxation by internal administrative boundaries. Moreover, the country's total revenue for 2005, which was available to the public at the time, was in actuality about twelve times the amount cited in the article. Finally, 55 percent of government revenue was culled from trade-based taxes and drawn mainly from Nairobi, the Mount Kenya region, Mombasa, and the smaller cities. The balance came from personal and corporate taxes, primarily in the same regions. Thus there is a clear correlation between the level of commercial activity (which the Kikuyu were believed to dominate) and the level of taxation. Yet government services such as education and health care, which serve all Kenyans alike, account for the greatest part of public expenditures.

Nonetheless, the bogus figures gained additional currency among the public, particularly when some ODM presidential-primary candidates began to cite them while campaigning in late-March 2007.[13] The press began reporting the tax figures as fact, with the *Standard*'s opinion columnists agitating for *majimbo* as the path to regional economic equality. The government, meanwhile, did nothing to refute the charges. Many voters in the ODM regions were convinced that devolution would lead to retention of the revenues they remitted to Nairobi.

Following the pattern of electoral campaigns all over the world that have won by targeting "economically dominant minorities,"[14] politicians stoked ethnic tensions with an effective campaign of disinformation in the run-up to the elections, pitting the Kikuyu against Kenya's other African ethnic groups. Building on the rhetoric of the 2005 referendum, the ODM grassroots campaign turned the election into a contest of "forty-one tribes against one" and "Kenya against the Kikuyu." The campaign highlighted Kikuyu domination in banking, government, trade, out-migration, education, and commercial farming, and Kikuyu success was blamed for the marginalization suffered by the other groups.

The Kikuyu are widely accused of having taken an economic lead as a result of political patronage under Kenyatta's presidency. Kenyatta himself has been bitterly attacked for his alleged role in "pouring" the Kikuyu into the Rift Valley (home to the Maasai and Kalenjin) from central Kenya soon after independence in order to make room in Central Province for the large estates of the Kenyatta family and the propertied Kikuyu class, said to be "home guards" who fought on the British side during the

Mau Mau uprising. It is widely believed that the Kikuyu obtained pref-
erential treatment in government-financed settlement schemes for previously white-owned farms in the Rift Valley. ODM militants interviewed
for this article in the Rift Valley cited the same arguments to explain their
anger, and foreign correspondents in Nairobi have repeated these views,
adding (wrongly) that the British colonialists had favored the Kikuyu in
business and education.[15] The end result was a reinvented history in which
the Kikuyu had set themselves up for resentment and retaliation.

In reality, however, there were already an estimated 150,000 Kikuyu in
the Rift Valley in the 1930s as a result of British expropriation of Kikuyu
lands. By the time of the first African-population census in 1948, Kikuyu
accounted for 26 percent of the region's inhabitants,[16] and already constituted a majority in Nakuru District, the epicenter of anti-Kikuyu electoral
violence since 1992. Even with the loss of Kikuyu lives incurred during
the Mau Mau rebellion (estimated at 50,000), their share of the Rift Valley population had changed little by the time of the last colonial census
in 1962.[17]

Horace Njuguna Gisemba has identified three ways in which the Kikuyu acquired land in the Rift Valley after independence: 1) British and
World Bank settlement programs at the end of colonial rule; 2) state-fi-
nanced transfers of British-owned land to groups of Kenyan buyers; and,
most important of all, 3) market transactions.[18] The land in dispute was
predominantly Maasai-owned prior to colonial rule, and although other
farming communities—such as Luhya, Kisii, and even Kalenjin—were
beneficiaries of the three programs, the Kikuyu purchased more and in
larger numbers.

It is important to note that ODM ran on more than simply redressing
ethnic inequalities. The Orange Movement attacked the Kibaki administration for tolerating corruption and failing to prosecute those associated
with it, some of whom were in ODM, before and after the 2002 election.
Additionally, Odinga was emphatic about revamping Kenya's creaky
infrastructure through privatizing construction, and he rightly compli-
mented Kibaki for having revived the economy. Furthermore, Odinga
pledged to accept defeat if the election was fair.

Activists at the precinct level, meanwhile, drove home the promise of
redressing inequality. In parts of the Rift Valley, Kikuyu received orders
to leave for good. In Nairobi and its environs, some Kikuyu landlords
were threatened with expropriation and told that they themselves would
become the tenants. Furthermore, ODM had promised its youthful constituency a new world with free schooling, jobs, cash for the poor, roads,
hospitals, and more. Odinga, in his September 2007 speech accepting
the presidential nomination, stated that ODM would end Kenya's "economic apartheid," under which one black group had all the privileges.
In December 2006, prior to these populist appeals, Kibaki led Odinga in
the polls by 42 to 14 percent. In those conducted after Odinga's nomina-

tion as ODM standard-bearer, he led Kibaki by 42 to 38 percent. Odinga would maintain that narrow lead up to election day.

Contrasting Campaigns

Kibaki and his supporters were late in cobbling together a political party to take charge of his campaign. With the NARC now in tatters, and its nominal leader, health minister Charity Ngilu, edging closer to the ODM, Kibaki and his advisors dithered and then launched the Party of National Unity on 30 September 2007—three months before election day. The PNU campaign lacked all political flair, not to mention a clear message to counteract the opposition's rhetoric of ethnic inequality, and it was launched too late to build a strong grassroots network. It had no braintrust to counter the *Standard*'s anti-Kikuyu articles, and Kibaki's gentlemanly demeanor failed to mesh with younger PNU activists who wanted to mobilize the disenchanted youth and communities outside the Mount Kenya region. In addition, its campaign headquarters was unwieldy and underfunded.

Ultimately, PNU based its campaign on trust in Kibaki's competent economic stewardship, which it asserted would ensure a better quality of life for the Kenyan people, as opposed to the "empty rhetoric" *(domo)* of the ODM. Accordingly, "Kibaki Aendelee" (let Kibaki continue) served as the PNU's campaign anthem and slogan. Forced to react to each ODM move, the PNU failed to neutralize the ODM's alluring message. The ODM was appealing to people's hearts with passionate reminders of economic exclusion, while the PNU appealed to their minds with dry statistics depicting a promising economic future; the ODM campaign was lively and colorful, while the PNU's was bland and businesslike.

Running on the government's outstanding economic record and Kibaki's leadership was the PNU's best hope. This message appealed especially to the business class. Share prices on the Nairobi Stock Exchange fell during the first quarter of 2007, and the PNU seized on this, blaming the drop on fears of an Odinga victory at the polls. Odinga, appealing to politically and economically marginalized peoples, proffered a populist platform; not surprisingly, the better-off and better-represented Kikuyu feared that such policies would jeopardize the current favorable business environment and re-create the awful Moi years. Many non-Kikuyu—in Western Kenya, Eastern Province, and the Coast—had the same concerns. This accounts for the narrow gap between the two parties as the finish line drew close. Kibaki and the PNU, however, did not anticipate how easily the ODM could turn the PNU platform upside down by pointing out that the benefits of economic growth had accrued only to a privileged few. The ODM thus pledged greater and faster economic redistribution, and this resonated with the crowds.

On the campaign trail, Kibaki acquitted himself with both vigor and dignity, surprising his advisors and the opposition. He shed his business suit for an open-necked shirt, walked through the crowds, shook hands, and promised new administrative districts, schools, and hospitals. Some of his most vocal defenders, however, made the mistake of attacking Odinga's leadership credentials, even likening him to terrible African dictators such as Idi Amin. Kikuyu bigots boasted that a Luo could not govern Kenya. Because many of those leveling such charges had themselves accepted Odinga's help to win the election in 2002, their criticisms rang hollow and instead actually helped Odinga, even among the youth in Kikuyu areas.

The PNU campaign also had a seamy side that preyed on ethnic fears. Rumors were circulated alleging that the United States and Britain were backing Odinga in retaliation against Kibaki and the Kikuyu for reducing Kenya's dependence on U.S. and British aid. Following the distribution of anti-Kikuyu leaflets in the Rift Valley and threats of residential-property seizure in and around Nairobi, rumors began to spread that the ODM, if it should win the elections, planned to perpetrate a Kikuyu genocide. People in the Mount Kenya region and in the Kikuyu diaspora took this threat seriously, as illustrated by the powerful grassroots networks that arose to get out the vote on election day. Shops and bars even pledged not to open until everyone had voted. Turnout in the Kikuyu districts was estimated at over 80 percent. Mount Kenya voters saw the contest more as a matter of their survival than of Kibaki's victory.

Violence Breaks Out

Although election day, December 27, was remarkably calm, there had been some unrest and even violence beforehand. Party primaries for legislative nominations, if one can call them that, often degenerated into brawls and fistfights. The polarizing ethnic rhetoric turned into hate speech, getting mass circulation via FM Radio in the mother tongues of Kenyan ethnic groups. In mid-2007, after the government injudiciously nominated replacements to the Electoral Commission of Kenya (ECK) without consulting the opposition parties (as had been the convention since 1997), the ODM warned that there was a plot to rig the election. The ODM instructed its enforcers to keep an eye out for ballot-rigging at all stages. When the government started assigning administration policemen to ODM strongholds in Western Kenya, some of the ODM's young supporters got jittery. Five policemen were subsequently murdered, and several buses owned by Kikuyu companies were set afire in the Rift Valley, Kisii, and Nairobi. Additionally, there were isolated reports of looting and eviction of families.

While election day itself was calm, it was the calm before the storm. The first two days after the election were tense. As results began to come in, initially from ODM strongholds in Western Kenya and the Rift

Valley, Odinga had a clear lead. ODM also led in parliamentary elections in those regions. As the results from Central Kenya and Eastern Province were tallied, however, Odinga's lead narrowed and PNU parliamentary candidates gained some victories. With television and radio stations fixed on the ECK headquarters in downtown Nairobi, though, it became clear that there were delays in announcing the results.

Two incidents explain much of what followed. First, late in the afternoon on December 29, when everyone was expecting the final results of the presidential tally, Samuel Kivuitu, the head of the ECK, publicly stated his suspicion that districts near the capital had delayed reporting results because "they were being cooked." Most pro-ODM demonstrators cited this as the first sure sign that election fraud was afoot. Next, there was a full day of arguments among top ODM and PNU officials, all faithfully aired on television, on the accuracy of the tally coming in from constituencies in Nakuru, Central Kenya, Eastern Province, and the Coast. After some time, the police were called in to empty the hall and then suddenly, with only the state television station present, Kivuitu announced that Kibaki had won the presidential election with 4,584,063 votes to Odinga's 4,352,993. Within the hour, Kibaki was sworn in at the State House. Rioting began immediately.

ODM leaders maintain that the violence was spontaneous, and to some extent it was—but not entirely. As demonstrators in Nyanza, Western Province, and the Coast have attested, anger sparked by a stolen victory quickly erupted into wholesale attacks on Kikuyu and Kisii properties, which were looted and gutted. Some residents were murdered; others fled. In Kericho and the northern Rift Valley (both of which are predominantly Kalenjin), however, the violence was different. Human Rights Watch "interviewed members of several pro-ODM Kalenjin communities who described the ways in which local leaders and ODM party agents actively fomented violence against Kikuyu communities."[19] The perpetrators did not hide their intentions, which were to cleanse the area of "black dots" *(madoa doa)* and recover their patrimony in land free of Kikuyu. According to Human Rights Watch, "The end result in most rural communities . . . surveyed was the complete destruction of every Kikuyu home and the displacement of every Kikuyu family. Hundreds of people were killed in the process."[20] Rape, as often happens, became a weapon of war, and neighbors who had lived in peace for years turned their backs on one another. The level and nature of the violence were such that Jendayi Frazer, U.S. assistant secretary of state for African affairs, labeled it ethnic cleansing.

As refugees from the Rift Valley began pouring into Central Province, reprisal attacks, apparently orchestrated by wealthy Kikuyu, broke out against ODM supporters near Nairobi. At this point, Kenya was spiraling toward civil war, and the police and army, seemingly overwhelmed, were unable to stem the bloodbath fully. The scare, as noted above, brought Kenyan statesmanship to the fore, and Kenya has for the time being been saved.

The country is now at a watershed moment. Will it be able to transform this tragedy into opportunity by reforming and strengthening its enfeebled democratic institutions as older democracies have? Or will it unravel like many of its neighbors? With the tragedy averted, supporters of democratic governance in Kenya must take lessons from the recent events and all that led up to them. The highest priorities must be the restoration of law and order and the prosecution of those guilty of violent acts. These must be followed by the thorough reform of the ECK, which failed to confront electoral malpractice as it had in 2002. Changing the electoral system from a wholly majoritarian one to a mix of party-list proportional representation and majority voting should be the next priority. All this must be accomplished before the next election in 2012.

These and the other important reforms, however, will require a new constitution better suited to Kenya's ethnically pluralistic nature. The core challenge is greater decentralization—a democratic federalism capable of enforcing basic citizenship rights across the country while giving political space to competing provincial interests. The problem so far has been that advocates of *majimbo* equate it with ethnic purity and the denial of property rights to "outsiders," while proponents of a centralized state consider regional autonomy to be a ruse for ethnic cleansing. This dichotomy is, in a nutshell, what the electoral violence in Kenya was all about. Effective democratic governance, however, should make it possible to have both local autonomy and cast-iron guarantees of individual rights, including secure property ownership and the entitlement of all citizens to vote for a party of their choice. Kenya now has a window of opportunity to adopt reforms and build the democratic structure that befits it best. But that window may not be open long.

NOTES

1. Jeffrey Gettleman, "Disputed Vote Plunges Kenya Into Bloodshed," *New York Times,* 31 December 2007.

2. Arend Lijphart, *Democracy in Plural Societies* (New Haven: Yale University Press, 1977); see also W. Arthur Lewis, *Politics in West Africa* (New York: Oxford University Press, 1965), 64–90.

3. Fareed Zakaria, *The Future of Freedom: Illiberal Democracy at Home and Abroad* (New York: W.W. Norton, 2003), 59–69.

4. U.S. Central Intelligence Agency, *The World Factbook; www.cia.gov/library/publications/the-world-factbook/geos/ke.html,* updated 24 July 2008.

5. Thomas L. Friedman, "The African Connection," *New York Times,* 4 April 2007.

6. See Githongo's report, available at *http://news.bbc.co.uk/1/shared/bsp/hi/pdfs/09_02_06_kenya_report.pdf.*

7. Joel D. Barkan, "Kenya After Moi," *Foreign Affairs* 83 (January–February 2004): 87–100.

8. "Keriri Tells Why Kibaki Trashed Coalition's 2002 MoU," *Standard* (Nairobi), 11 September 2007.

9. Larry Diamond, *Developing Democracy: Toward Consolidation* (Baltimore: Johns Hopkins University Press, 1999), 104.

10. Society for International Development (SID), Eastern Africa Regional Office, *Pulling Apart: Facts and Figures on Inequality in Kenya* (Nairobi: SID, 2004). The report controversially argued that Kenya was among the most unequal societies in the world, and also touched on gender inequalities.

11. Yash Ghai, "Dishonest and Incapable CKRC," *Standard*, 26 July 2004.

12. Barrack Muluka, "Devolution Can Cure Skewed Distribution of Nation's Wealth," *Standard*, 22 July 2006; see also Muluka, "Federalism Could Bridge Current Development Gaps," *Standard*, 29 July 2006.

13. *Standard*, 24 March 2007; and *Sunday Nation* (Nairobi), 25 March 2007.

14. See Amy Chua, *World on Fire: How Exporting Free Market Democracy Breeds Ethnic Hatred and Global Instability* (New York: Random House, 2003).

15. See Jeffrey Gettleman, "Kenya Kikuyus, Long Dominant, Are Now Routed," *New York Times*, 7 January 2008; Greg Mills, "Defusing the Ethnic Time-Bomb," *International Herald Tribune*, 12 February 2008; Stephanie McCrummen, "Ethnic Fault Lines Emerge in Kenya's Post-Election Turmoil," *Washington Post*, 1 January 2008; Sarah Childress, "Violence in Kenya Exposes Tribes' Widening Wealth Gap," *Wall Street Journal*, 30 January 2008; and Michela Wrong, "Who Are the Kikuyu? And Why Do Kenya's Other Tribes Resent Them So Much?" *Slate*, 8 February 2008; available at *www.slate.com/id/2184031*.

16. East African Statistical Department, *African Population of Kenya Colony and Protectorate* (Nairobi: 1950). The figures apply to the Rift Valley Province as presently constituted.

17. Republic of Kenya, *Kenya Population Census, 1962, Volume II* (Nairobi: Ministry of Economic Planning and Development, 1966). Kikuyu made up 27 percent of the Rift Valley population in 1962; a third of Kikuyu had by then migrated out of Central Province.

18. Horace Njuguna Gisemba, "The Lie of the Land: Evictions and Kenya's Crisis," *Africa Policy Brief No. 2*, Africa Policy Institute, February 2008.

19. Human Rights Watch, "Opposition Officials Helped Plan Rift Valley Violence," 23 January 2008; available at *www.hrw.org*.

20. Testimony of Chris Albin-Lackey to the U.S. Senate Committee on Foreign Relations, Subcommittee on African Affairs, 7 February 2008.

15

THE CRISIS IN KENYA

Maina Kiai

Maina Kiai *currently makes documentaries on social justice and is the Strategic Advisor of the Movement for Political Accountability in Kenya, and is the former chairperson of the Kenya National Commission on Human Rights. This essay draws on his keynote address at the Fifth Assembly of the World Movement for Democracy in Kyiv on 6 April 2008.*

I am indeed privileged to have this opportunity to share some thoughts today on the question of democracy, especially after the flawed and disputed presidential elections in Kenya in December 2007. For the first two months of this year, Kenya grabbed headlines all over the world as the country descended into chaos and violence that left more than a thousand dead in less than a month and 300,000 others displaced from their homes. In much of that international coverage, one could discern the unspoken thoughts of "here we go again, yet another African country descending into tribal violence."

But many longtime observers were shocked and alarmed that Kenya could go this "typical African way." For years, Kenya had come to be regarded as perhaps the one African country that was "a little different." After all, Kenya had avoided military coups, major armed conflicts, and international wars. It had served as the hub for humanitarian assistance efforts and other international interventions in East Africa. It was the country that hosted refugees, not one that generated them. It was the home of the only UN headquarters in the global South.

The tourism industry in Kenya had been booming, and tourism can only thrive amid stability. Kenya was a major exporter of flowers to the West—and what more powerful symbol of peace is there than a flower? Moreover, Kenya had a significant population of expatriates who had left their own stable countries and chosen to settle there. This was the land of amazing wildlife, contrasting landscapes, and white beaches—the land of exotic people such as the Maasai. This was the country of the award-winning film *Out of Africa*.

Yes, Kenya has had its share of massive grand corruption and klep-
tomaniacs in powerful positions, and it has suffered occasional ethnic
conflicts. Yes, it has had all-powerful presidents who have made major
public-policy pronouncements in off-the-cuff roadside speeches. Yes,
it has had difficulties allowing freedom of expression and association.

But it was one of very few African countries that had managed to
hold regular elections since gaining independence in 1963, no matter
that the outcomes of many of those elections were predetermined. Kenya had all the trappings of democracy. It had a functioning parliament,
complete with a wigged speaker bedecked in flowing red robes, just as
they have in Great Britain. And it had a judiciary whose judges wore
heavy white wigs and were deferentially addressed as "Your Lordship,"
just as in Great Britain. It had a vibrant civil society that had managed
to muscle concessions from the state, especially after the Berlin Wall
fell. It was the base for foreign reporters always ready to jump on a
plane to cover the incessant conflicts across Africa.

With all that then, how could things have gone so wrong? How could
the world fail to read and predict the inherent instability? How could
a population, long used to predetermined elections, now rise up and
reject them so violently?

Clearly, one of the most important lessons from Kenya is that we
must look beyond the forms and façades of democracy to the substance
of it. Democracy must mean more than having legislators who simply
endorse the wishes of the executive or who, when they do differ, do
so merely to advance their personal interests. Democracy must mean
more than having judges who sit on a raised bench all decked out, but
are afraid to make decisions that upset the executive. And it must mean
more than holding periodic elections.

A wise man once said that democracy is more about what happens
between elections than the elections themselves. And by this standard,
Kenya and many other countries—Zimbabwe, for example—fall flat.
Also failing are the international support programs that approach elections as events rather than as processes.

Kenya's constitution provides for an imperial presidency in which
the officeholder can run the country as a personal fiefdom. It is a country where the president doles out public lands and forests to anyone
he fancies. He alone decides who becomes a judge. He alone appoints
members to the Electoral Commission. He can create any public office
and staff it with anyone he wants at whatever salary he wishes. He can
fire almost anyone at will. He decides if parliament will sit for thirty
days in a year or 180. He decides which regions will be given resources
for development and which ones will remain marginalized.

Between elections, it is the legislature's job to hold the executive
accountable. And if it cannot or will not make the executive change
its decisions and policies to fall in line with public interest and public

opinion, the legislature becomes irrelevant in making democracy work. For democracy to be effective, legislatures must be responsive to their voters and intent on serving the public rather than themselves.

In Kenya, our legislature has been remarkably effective at serving itself. Legislators have, for example, granted themselves a mostly untaxable salary of US$150,000 a year; interest-free mortgages; subsidies to buy $50,000 cars; generous lifetime pensions of up to $4,000 a month after serving five years; and a gratuity payment of $22,000 at the end of each five-year term (perhaps to help fund their reelection campaigns).

The sum effect of these perks is that our legislators—among the highest paid in the world—are so comfortable that they lose touch with the voters. For the majority seeking elective office, it is about the money, not about serving the public. Let us not forget that Kenya has a GNP of about $600 per person per year and that more than 40 percent of all Kenyans live on less than a dollar a day. Kenya ranks in the bottom 25 countries in the Development Index of the United Nations Development Programme (UNDP), while its legislators' perks rank among the top five countries in the world.

Further undermining the integrity and efficacy of our parliament is that it serves as the sole pool from which the cabinet is drawn. In Kenya, not only is a minister's status significantly above that of ordinary legislators but his earnings are almost double. Additionally, as ministers, legislators have the ability to dispense favors, award contracts, and exercise influence—and all for money. It is therefore the rare person who enters parliament without desiring a ministerial appointment. As a result, Kenya will soon have a cabinet composed of forty ministers and fifty assistant ministers out of the 222-member National Assembly—in other words, more than 42 percent of the legislature will be in the executive. Clearly, other countries should not adopt this Kenyan model unless their desire is to discredit representative government.

The Scourge of Corruption

Compounding the fragility of democracy is Kenya's other major problem—endemic, chronic corruption that uses public office as a vehicle to loot coffers, with little risk of being held accountable. Corruption has become a way of life for the political and civil-service elite, and it is a main reason why cabinet positions and high-level public-service positions are in such demand in Kenya. Despite the many official perks that come with these offices, the money one can make from corruption is far greater. It is no accident that the wealthiest Kenyans today have been or still are in some form of "public service," whether as politicians, civil servants, or officials of public companies. Elected on a platform of zero-tolerance for corruption in 2002, President Mwai Kibaki's handling of his first major test on a matter of grand corruption within his regime—the Anglo Leasing scandals—dashed the hopes of Kenyans and forced his special anticorruption advisor to flee into exile in 2005.

Kenya's inability to confront deep-seated grievances and historical injustices has played a role in intensifying the postelection crisis. Since independence, there have been underlying issues of inequality along individual, regional, and ethnic lines. For example, there have been land-ownership issues, and those communities that have had greater access to presidential power and its attendant patronage are seen as beneficiaries of favoritism. Finally, there have been serious human rights violations, committed both by state agencies and by powerful people, that have for too long been swept under the rug.

The lesson here is that ignoring our problems does not work. In 2004, a Presidential Task Force recommended the formation of a Truth, Justice, and Reconciliation Commission to address past state-instigated and state-sponsored conflicts in the Rift Valley, among other major injustices. President Kibaki declined to implement the group's recommendations because at the time he needed the support of the province's leaders to shore up his fledgling political alliance. But the net effect is that the Rift Valley again was the epicenter of some of the worst violence in the present crisis—in some cases with state support and in some without—as it did not take much to reactivate the 1990s-era militias. Simply put, the message to perpetrators was clear: You can get away with murder if you are close enough to the government.

And through all this, where have Kenya's international "friends" been? Rather than confront the problem, Kenya's allies abroad decided to accept the regime's promises and continue with business as usual. So even after the pathetic handling of grand corruption, World Bank lending to Kenya has doubled since 2005. UNDP-Kenya touted the country as a success story and championed partnership with the government on the basis of its rhetoric, not to mention a perverse aim of increasing core budget support no matter the credibility of the regime. This created an intimacy between the leaders of the UNDP and the regime that precluded objectivity when it was needed most.

Bilateral donors have lined up to offer assistance both for development and recurrent expenditures. A significant part of our free primary education program, for example, is funded by the international community, even though we could probably fund it ourselves if we cut down on obscenely high public expenditures. Of the many bilateral programs, the most absurd is the Governance, Justice, Law and Order Sectors Reform Programme. Intended to improve governance, this was a well-intentioned program at its inception. But even when it became clear—after the regime failed to stem corruption, after it sent in masked police led by mercenaries to attack a private media station, and after the justice minister ratcheted up his hard-line rhetoric against independent voices and critics—that the regime lacked the political will needed for reform, the program continued as usual, focusing on modernization rather than reform. The current crisis in Kenya is in fact a crisis of governance, making the program and its donors look ridiculous.

But what then explains Kenyans' rejection, manifested in a repugnant form of violence, of the flawed elections? Since none of these issues is new, why now and not before? I believe that that the answer is rooted in Kenyans' desire to protect their hard-won freedoms. Kenya has been on a forward democratic trajectory since 1992, when multiparty politics was restored. Democratic space has been painstakingly and painfully expanded each year since, and exploded wide open with the defeat of President Daniel arap Moi's party in the 2002 elections.

But many politicians on all sides would prefer to shrink this space, which has led to more vocal criticism, has exposed wrongdoing, and has prepared the citizenry to challenge political leaders in ways never before imagined. The media have played a significant role in empowering Kenyans, and it is therefore not surprising that they have been the first targets in efforts to reduce this democratic space. Kenya's broad and vibrant civil society (from NGOs to religious groups) has also played a critical role in the expansion and protection of this space—legitimizing the culture of protest born in the 1990s; mobilizing the public around issues such as constitutional reform and accountability; providing safe havens and alternative viewpoints; and giving voice to the voiceless.

It is also important to note that Kenyan elections have gotten progressively better and fairer since 1992, culminating in the 2002 elections (which were Kenya's best so far and resulted in regime change) and the 2005 constitutional referendum that the government lost. The effect of these last two ballots was that Kenyans finally believed in the power of the vote as a way to resolve differences peacefully and as a legitimate means to change leaders, as illustrated by the recent parliamentary elections, which saw almost 70 percent of incumbents lose their seats. When this sense of empowerment was subverted in the fraudulent 2007 presidential elections—watched on live television by voters—and legal spaces for peaceful protests were prohibited, it was not surprising that frustrations boiled over and violence ensued.

The Need for a Full Accounting

Let me emphasize that I do not support the violence that occurred. Along with most Kenyans, I mourn the lives of those who perished—whether from police fire in the west of the country or at the hands of rioting mobs and militia actions in the Rift Valley. There must be full accountability—no sacred cows. It is for this reason that the Kenya National Commission on Human Rights, together with local and international partners, is documenting and gathering evidence that at present suggests complicity at very high levels on both sides.

In conclusion, I would suggest that, if we are to make democracy work anywhere in the world, a paradigm shift is necessary. We must turn our efforts from the forms of democracy to the substance of it. And it is here that structures such as competent independent election bodies are indispensable. It is here that competent and nonpartisan (both in structure and personnel) anticorruption bodies are vital. It is here that a functioning and effective parliament must be created. It is here that a proper justice system, from policing to prisons to the judiciary itself, is critical. And it is here that legitimate spaces for independent media and civil society are necessary. All these structures depend on sustainable and sensible constitutional and legal frameworks that have at their core the people they serve, rather than the political elite.

But while structures and systems are crucial, we must never forget that democracy is about people. It is about shifting power from leaders to the people themselves, especially in the periods between elections. This is the time to invest in the people and in their empowerment. This is the time to invest in bottom-up strategies that give ordinary people the guts, ideas, and power to hold their leaders accountable and to force their leaders to listen. This is the new challenge for the prodemocracy movement—a challenge that we must urgently embrace and address as creatively as possible. There are many lessons to learn from around the world, and greater effort must be made to encourage an exchange of the ideas, strategies, and techniques used to empower people in other societies.

As for Kenya, I believe that its people will prevail in this continuing struggle for democracy, respect, and development. There is a wind of change at the back of the Kenyan people, impelling them to demand respect from the leadership on both sides, even though these leaders seem deaf to their calls.

At present, Kenyans are ahead of their leaders. It is the Kenyan people—regardless of political or ethnic affiliation—who have championed and demanded a lean cabinet rather than a bloated one. And though it currently looks as though the political class has triumphed with one of the world's most swollen cabinets, I am optimistic that this struggle will not end here and that the Kenyan people—who with their taxes bear the cost of the many ministers, even as the regime seeks international assistance for recovery and reconstruction—will keep voicing their discontent.

In these struggles, we expect support from our international friends for a pro-people approach to democracy assistance—an approach that is not about meeting funding targets, which often results in propping up regimes if their rhetoric is on point. Rather, democracy assistance should focus on the realities on the ground and on ensuring that the leaders' actions are indeed geared toward bettering the lot of the citizenry rather than enriching themselves. Why give financial support to a regime that pays its leaders more than the leaders of donor countries? Why support a regime that refuses to reclaim funds siphoned off by corruption and stashed abroad? Why support a regime that uses tax revenues to build mansions and buy limousines for its leaders, yet turns around and begs for assistance to buy food for its hungry children?

This is the challenge of our times and we must be ready to meet it. We must and we will succeed.

16

TANZANIA'S MISSING OPPOSITION

Barak Hoffman and Lindsay Robinson

Barak Hoffman is the executive director of the Center for Democracy and Civil Society at Georgetown University. Lindsay Robinson is a master's student at Georgetown University in the Department of Government's Democracy and Governance program. This essay originally appeared in the October 2009 issue of the Journal of Democracy.

Just before the announcement of the results of Tanzania's 1995 elections—its first multiparty contest in more than thirty years—the soon-to-be president-elect, Benjamin Mkapa of the long-ruling Revolutionary Party of Tanzania (Chama Cha Mapinduzi—CCM), proudly boasted that the party "didn't need to cheat because it was quite certain that CCM was going to win."[1] Such swagger is characteristic of the CCM's electoral campaigns. In the nearly fifteen years since Tanzania inaugurated multiparty elections, the CCM has not faced any serious opposition to its rule.

What explains the chronic weakness of opposition parties in Tanzania? The easy explanation is a combination of uninspiring leadership and little popular demand for change, a line of reasoning that also defines the CCM as a relatively benign hegemon acceptable to the vast majority of Tanzanians. Although this argument is based on a significant amount of truth, it overlooks the CCM's deliberate attempts to suppress those who contest its near-monopoly of power, including its willingness to resort to coercion when other methods fail. Such realities raise serious questions about the ruling party's benevolent reputation.

Many of the hurdles that CCM opponents face are self-imposed, but that explanation alone does not suffice. Instead, the marginal status of rival parties results in large measure from the CCM's intentional methods of silencing them. The CCM employs three strategies to impede its competitors: 1) regulating political competition, the media, and civil society; 2) blurring the boundary between the party and state; and 3) the targeted use of blatantly coercive illegal actions. Before considering these measures in greater detail, however, we must first take a look at the country's history and the background to its transition toward democracy.[2]

The United Republic of Tanzania was formed in 1964 as a union between two newly independent ex-British colonies, Tanganyika (mainland Tanzania) and the People's Republic of Zanzibar (comprising the islands of Zanzibar and Pemba). The unity agreement granted Zanzibar a fair degree of autonomy, allowing it to keep its own president and parliament in addition to its national representation. Julius Nyerere, the leader of Tanganyika's liberation movement and its president since independence in 1962, became president of Tanzania in 1964.

The mainland and Zanzibar possess sharply different demographics. The mainland of Tanzania has a population of approximately forty million, primarily black African with no dominant majority ethnic group, and it is fairly evenly split between Christians and Muslims. Zanzibar, by contrast, has a population of about one million, divided mainly between Arabs and black Africans, and is almost entirely Muslim. While there are few ethnic tensions on the mainland, there are tensions between Africans and Arabs on Zanzibar, deriving from the long history of Arab economic and political dominance over Africans on the islands. Overall, however, the country has remained peaceful and united despite its diversity, in part because of Nyerere's advancement of Swahili as the national language.

In 1967, guided by Nyerere, Tanzania became a socialist state. Ten years later, with a new constitution and the formation of the CCM—a merger of Nyerere's Tanganyika African National Union and the islands' Afro-Shirazi Party—it became a de jure one party-state as well. In the mid-1970s, however, the country's economy began to atrophy, and by the middle of the next decade, it had become clear to the CCM leadership that socialism was not viable. Thus they began to move toward a more market-oriented system.

Although the CCM undertook Tanzania's economic transition to capitalism from a position of weakness, it initiated political changes from a posture of strength. The party began to move the country toward democracy in the early 1990s, largely due to the influence of former president Nyerere, who had voluntarily left office in 1985. When Nyerere commenced discussions on a political transition, neither an organized opposition to the CCM nor a demand for a multiparty democracy existed. On the contrary, in a 1992 public-opinion survey 77 percent of respondents claimed that they preferred the country to remain a one-party state with the CCM in control.[3]

Nyerere advocated a democratic transition in Tanzania not because of internal opposition but because external donors, who provided more than 30 percent of the country's GDP in aid from 1985 to 1993, were pressuring the government to open its political system. In addition, Nyerere and his supporters believed that the growing number of democratic transitions elsewhere in sub-Saharan Africa would inevitably catalyze pressures for similar changes in Tanzania. CCM leaders who supported moving to a multiparty system understood that if they initiated changes before calls for them grew strong, they would be able to shape the new democratic rules in their favor. In this the party has largely succeeded, and Tanzania today is not a democracy, but a one-party hegemonic regime under CCM rule.

Tanzania's transition toward democracy corresponds to what Gerardo Munck and Carol Leff term "transition from above" and what Samuel Huntington calls "transplacement."[4] These terms refer to a ruling power that initiates a transition in the context of a weak opposition so that the ruling power can establish rules favorable to its retention of political control. The CCM's actions correlate closely with Munck and Leff's argument that the mode of transition and the balance of power among agents of change strongly affect posttransition political institutions. The CCM took full advantage of being the sole agent of change, putting in place a set of policies that significantly impedes the development of an effective political opposition.

Lack of Demand for Democracy

One of the simplest explanations for the weakness of opposition parties in Tanzania is lack of demand for them, and a reading of selected survey data can support this contention. According to the 2008 Afrobarometer survey, 56 percent of respondents in Tanzania claimed to trust opposition parties either not at all or only a little bit, while 51 percent claimed to trust the CCM a lot. Along the same lines, of the 81 percent of respondents who said that they felt close to a political party, 90 percent responded that the party they felt close to was the CCM.[5] Similarly, 79 percent responded that if an election were held tomorrow, they would vote for the CCM. In addition, Tanzanians are overwhelmingly pleased with the way in which democracy is functioning under CCM rule. Seventy-four percent of respondents considered Tanzania to be a full democracy or nearly so, far above the mean of 59 percent in the nineteen countries included in the 2008 Afrobarometer survey. Moreover, 71 percent claimed to be satisfied or fairly satisfied with democracy, the third-highest level of satisfaction (behind Botswana and Ghana) and 22 percentage points above the mean for all the countries surveyed. Given these results, one might surmise that Tanzanians either do not desire multiparty competition or do not understand the concept of democracy.

This reading of the data, however, presents a skewed picture of Tanzanians' beliefs and knowledge about democracy. First, demand for multiparty democracy is strong. In the 2008 Afrobarometer survey, 72 percent of Tanzanian respondents preferred democracy to any other form of government, and 63 percent rejected one-party rule. In addition, 61 percent did not believe that party competition is likely to lead to conflict.

Moreover, Tanzanians largely understand the concept of democracy.

The Afrobarometer survey described three hypothetical countries and asked respondents to what extent each was a democracy. Eighty percent of respondents claimed that a country with many political parties and free elections is a full democracy or a democracy with minor problems. By contrast, 76 percent claimed that a country which has one dominant political party and a feeble opposition, and where people are afraid to express their political opinions, is not a democracy or is at best a democracy with major problems. Finally, only 20 percent responded that a country that has one major political party and many small ones, and where people are free to express their opinions (the situation that most resembles Tanzania today), is a full democracy. Thus it is difficult to accept the argument that Tanzanians do not desire multiple political parties or understand the concept of democracy.

The aforementioned data are difficult to interpret. While the vast majority of Tanzanians prefer multiparty democracy to any alternative form of government, they express no strong desire to elect any party other than the CCM. Although reconciling these divergent preferences is challenging, they are understandable given the CCM's conduct compared to that of opposition parties, especially during elections.

CCM campaigns are highly sophisticated, and the party spends lavishly on them. In the 2005 election, now-president Jakaya Kikwete attended approximately nine-hundred rallies and spoke to an estimated 70,000 people each day. Most rallies were highly orchestrated affairs, combining political speeches with entertainment and widespread distribution of CCM paraphernalia, such as t-shirts, hats, and posters. Moreover, in a recent by-election for the parliamentary seat from Busanda in Mwanza Region, the CCM dispatched twenty top leaders to election rallies, including regional MPs and three ministers, and raised approximately US$1.5 million (about $12 per voter) for the campaign. Because such organizational capacity and resources greatly exceed those of any other party, it is not surprising that voters continue to choose the CCM over the alternatives. In addition, while the CCM's campaigns highlight the party's achievements, those mounted by opposition parties often advertise their weaknesses.

Opposition parties in Tanzania need little assistance in marginalizing themselves: They fight each other constantly and consistently fail to work together, and their leaders behave in ways that do not inspire confidence, thereby discouraging all but their most loyal adherents. The Civic United Front (CUF) is the only opposition party that consistently wins a respectable level of votes in parliamentary elections, largely due to its strength in Zanzibar, its home base.[6] CUF supporters, however, have attacked CCM members and destroyed their property, primarily in Zanzibar, thus gaining a reputation for violence that has harmed CUF efforts at widening its narrow regional appeal. During campaigns, CUF partisans frequently tussle with CCM supporters, and they are the most likely perpetrators of a number of assaults against the CCM and state property—stoning CCM cars, attacking campaign meetings, vandalizing CCM branch offices, and bombing government buildings. The CUF also acquired a reputation for ineptitude after failing to negotiate a power-sharing agreement with the CCM in Zanzibar following the 2000 election (which many, including international observers, suspect that the ruling party had rigged).

The most promising opposition figure outside the CUF has been Augustine Mrema, formerly of the National Convention for Constitution and Reform–Mageuzi (NCCR-Mageuzi) and now the leader of the Tanzania Labor Party (TLP). Mrema's actions, however, make it difficult for voters to support him, as he has managed to wreck both opposition parties to which he has belonged. Prior to joining opposition forces, Mrema had held three ministerial posts, including deputy prime minister, under various CCM governments and acquired a reputation for integrity and fighting corruption. After being dismissed as minister of labor and youth development in early 1995, however, Mrema left the ruling party to become the NCCR-Mageuzi's presidential candidate.

At the time, Mrema was the great hope of anti-CCM forces, and the ruling party considered him a real threat. Despite CCM harassment during the campaign, Mrema still managed to win 28 percent of the vote. Yet after the election, he accused a number of NCCR-Mageuzi leaders of being CCM infiltrators, causing a major rift in the party. In 1999, Mrema quit NCCR-Mageuzi, stealing its property on his way out, and then joined the TLP, where his embarrassing and reckless behavior escalated. Besides fragmenting the TLP's leadership, he used members' dues to purchase a home and, while campaigning for the 2005 election, helped himself to $98,000 from the party's coffers for ethically dubious expenditures—$83,000 to buy alcohol for voters and $15,000 to hire a monkey to attract people to his rallies. Not surprisingly, Mrema's popularity imploded. In the 2005 election, he received less than one percent of the vote.

Finally, the opposition has consistently failed to work together. The planned unity ticket between NCCR and CUF in 1995 collapsed because they were unable to agree on a running mate for Mrema. In 2000, both the CUF and the Party for Democracy and Progress (Chama cha Demokrasia na Maendeleo—known as Chadema) backed the CUF's Ibrahim Lipumba as their presidential candidate, but other opposition parties did not. And a coalition was never seriously considered in 2005, because CUF leaders suspected that their counterparts in the smaller opposition parties were CCM plants and refused to collaborate with them.

Suppressing the Opposition

Although the CCM's opponents are weak and the demand for their point of view is low, these factors alone do not account for the party's continued dominance in the multiparty era. In fact, opposition parties have been more effective than many realize, especially considering the methods—both legal and illegal—that the CCM employs to ensure that those who oppose it do not achieve meaningful representation. Thus the opposition parties' electoral performance tells only part of the story.

The ruling party has developed sophisticated legal mechanisms to ensure its continued control through the regulation of political competition, civil society, and the media. Groups seeking to oppose the CCM routinely confront policies that regulate political competition in ways that make them appear even weaker than they are. These include biases in the electoral formula that allot the CCM more than its proportional share of seats in parliament, an electoral commission that lacks independence, campaign-finance rules that overwhelmingly favor the CCM, and onerous party-registration procedures.

The most critical institutional design favoring the CCM is that of the electoral system, which has guaranteed an overwhelming CCM majority in parliament even though the party's share of the vote has not always been equally large. Tanzania uses a single-member, first-past-the-post (plurality) electoral system for presidential, parliamentary, and local elections—the same electoral system utilized prior to Tanzania's return to multiparty competition. The plurality system means that parties failing to receive a majority of votes can still win office.

Plurality voting has permitted the CCM to win a share of parliamentary seats exceeding its share of the popular vote by 20 percent in each of the three parliamentary elections since the country's transition toward democracy: In 1995, the CCM received 59 percent of the vote and 80 percent of the seats; in 2000, it received 65 percent and 87 percent, respectively; and in 2005, 70 percent and 90 percent.[7] As a result, the CCM has kept the two-thirds majority needed to pass constitutional amendments in the National Assembly, even though its vote share reached that level only once, in 2005.[8] The margins have been similar in local elections.

The CCM has also used the design of the ballots to discourage voters from supporting opposition parties. In the 1995 and 2005 national elections, ballots provided a space for voters' registration numbers or had serial numbers printed on them that connected the ballot to the voter's identity. Despite opposition protest, the National Electoral Commission (NEC) refused to change the ballot designs, and the NEC director defended the system by saying that it was necessary to "assist when queries arise through petitions after the polls and results are announced."[9] The NEC also allowed the CCM to use the Tanzanian national emblem as its ballot picture in 2005, a clear suggestion that a vote for the party was a vote for the country, while a vote for the opposition was not. It is not surprising that the NEC allows ballots compromising secrecy and portraying the opposition as anti-Tanzanian. While officially the commission is independent, de facto it is not. The president has the sole authority to appoint and remove all commissioners, and the commission's funding is dependent on the CCM-dominated parliament.

Campaign finance is another major built-in hurdle for the opposition. Campaigning in Tanzania is expensive and difficult. Much of the country's population lives in rural areas. Villages typically lie miles apart on unpaved roads, making it difficult and expensive to visit voters. In the 1995 election, the government granted subsidies to all candidates for presidential or parliamentary office (approximately $10,000 and $1,000, respectively, per candidate), because it did not fear any real threat, wished to appear supportive of democratic competition, and wanted to divide its opponents' vote share by attracting more candidates. But when the opposition captured more of the popular vote that year than the CCM expected—roughly 40 percent in the parliamentary and presidential races—parliament passed a new subsidy law strongly favoring the CCM.

The new statute disburses half the subsidy in proportion to a party's popular vote share in the previous election and the other half according to how many seats a party holds in parliament and local governments.[10] Since the distribution of seats in parliament and in local councils is skewed heavily toward the CCM, the formula benefits the party disproportionately even after accounting for the CCM's massive margins of victory. Take, for example, the 2005 election subsidies: The CCM received more than seven times the amount of the next largest party, the CUF, even though the CCM received only five times as many votes. Moreover, this money often finds its way directly into the hands of the electorate, as the law permits candidates to distribute gifts, including money, to voters.[11]

Opposition parties must also overcome burdensome party-registration procedures. In addition to fulfilling certain ideological conditions, such as secularity and acknowledgment of the union, parties must produce proof of a membership that includes at least two-hundred people from ten or more of the country's 26 regions; two of these regions must be in Zanzibar. Thus parties that have a limited support base geographically, but in their own localities are stronger than the CCM, are not allowed to compete. This policy also makes it costly to form a new party because registration requires proof of a nationwide presence. In addition, the statute prohibits existing parties from forming official coalitions without registering as a new party.

Regulating Civil Society and the Media

The CCM actively thwarts not only aspiring opposition parties and politicians but also civil society and the media. The Non-Governmental Organizations Act of 2002 is major roadblock that keeps civil society from playing an active role in politics. This statute requires that NGOs must serve "the public interest," defined as "all forms of activities aimed at providing for and improving the standard of living or eradication of poverty of a given group of people or the public at large."[12] Since the law defines the public interest in terms of economic development, the government can and has prohibited NGOs from undertaking political activities, thereby keeping groups unable to register as political parties from forming NGOs as an alternative way to address political concerns. The law also prevents NGOs whose interests might be aligned with opposition parties from campaigning on their behalf.

The NGO legislation permits the government to regulate all aspects of civil society, not just restrictions on political activities. Once an NGO has registered, the government monitors it via a required annual report. If at any time the organization oversteps its mission as outlined in its state-approved constitution, the government has the authority to suspend the group.[13] Choosing not to register as an NGO, however, is risky. Any member of a group that attempts to evade government regulation by not registering faces criminal charges and hefty fines (sometimes up to $400), a year in prison, or both, plus a ban on joining another NGO for five years.[14] The CCM has wielded the NGO law against organizations that it perceives to be a threat. For example, when HakiElimu (Education for All) broadcast a series of advertisements in 2005 criticizing the government for failing to improve primary education as it had promised, the government prohibited the NGO from undertaking studies or publishing information on the education sector, and enforced the ban for eighteen months.

The ruling party has also imposed a legal framework inimical to freedom of the press. In 1993—two years before the country's return to multiparty elections—the CCM passed a broadcasting law that established state-owned radio and television, prohibited stations without a state-issued license from operating, and allowed the government to regulate media content.[15] Since most Tanzanians get their news by radio, the law allowed the CCM effectively to monopolize the dissemination of information to the vast majority of the electorate. As a result, the CCM receives far more media exposure than opposition parties. During the 2005 election cycle, it received almost thirty hours of radio coverage—as much as the next thirteen largest parties combined and more than three times the coverage of the CUF, the largest opposition party.

Legislation also deters journalists from criticizing the ruling party or the government, and enables the government to keep the media from exposing information that it would rather keep under wraps. The president has "absolute discretion" to prohibit the broadcasting or publishing of information that is not in "the public interest or in the interest of peace and good order."[16] In addition, sedition and libel clauses are often vague and give the judiciary wide discretion over their interpretation. For example, defamation need not be "directly or completely expressed." Rather, speech must stay within the bounds of what is "reasonably sufficient" to make a point, and judges have the authority to determine what constitutes gratuitous criticism.[17] Consequently, in 2004 there were more than eighty libel suits pending in high courts,[18] and in 2008 the weekly *Mwanahalisi* was suspended for three months for publishing a story alleging a rift in the CCM leadership.

The press's fight against these regulations has succeeded in persuading the ruling party to relax their enforcement, but not to change them. This limited achievement is due in part to the rapid expansion of the media: Between 1992 and 2006, the number of newspapers with more-than-local readerships increased from 7 to 42; radio stations from 1 to 47; and television stations from 0 to 15. These media outlets have joined together to form a lobby powerful enough to impose a four-month-long blackout on coverage of the minister of information, culture, and sport after he suspended *Mwanahalisi* without what the media considered to be just cause. The media also played an active role in exposing corruption scandals that led to the resignation of former prime minister Edward Lowassa and the firing of former Bank of Tanzania governor Daudi Ballali.

. During Tanzania's transition to a de jure multiparty system, the CCM made no moves to separate the party from the state. Rather, its leadership deliberately created a set of political institutions that blurred the distinction between the two in order to keep its position and power secure. This strategy is twofold: First, the CCM's rigid organizational structure ensures members' compliance with the prerogatives of the party leadership. Second, the CCM's control over civil servants allows the party to use government institutions to inhibit the opposition.

In most Tanzanian cities and towns, CCM offices are typically open, party officials are working hard, and their knowledge of the party's policies is strong. The CCM leadership set in motion this machine-like efficiency by aligning its own goals (winning elections) with incentives (advancement through the party) for the party's branch-level workers. CCM branch-office staffers are responsible for bringing citizens to party rallies and for securing their votes. Senior CCM officials can easily verify how effectively the branch worker has carried out these tasks—the former by turnout, the latter by election results. Those who perform well advance in the party hierarchy. In other words, ambitious junior party officials have every incentive to give the CCM leadership what it wants. In addition, since any elected official who votes against the party can be expelled, the party structure allows CCM leaders the freedom to adopt whatever policies they desire.

As a result of this impressive structure, the CCM has the capacity to implement far-reaching social changes without losing political control. Socialism *(ujamaa)* may have led to disastrous economic consequences, but creating a one-party state, nationalizing the economy, and implementing collective farming nonetheless required a highly organized political structure. This institutional setup has proven extremely useful and resilient, and has allowed the party to change policies radically when necessary without losing political control. For example, when in the late 1980s it became clear that socialism was causing an economic catastrophe, the party was able to restructure the economy along capitalist lines without suffering any loss of political authority.

The CCM's structure is as useful for suppressing opposition as it is for implementing policy. This is most evident at the regional and district (local) levels. The highest regional and district authorities—the regional commissioner (RC) and the district commissioner (DC)—are appointed directly by the president rather than elected.[19] At the same time, the CCM constitution explicitly states that the RCs and DCs are the party's representatives in the region and the district, thus obscuring where the party ends and the state begins.[20]

RCs and DCs use their power—especially control over the police—to promote CCM activities and interfere with those of the opposition. For example, holding any large gathering, demonstration, or rally requires police permission—due to public safety concerns, according to the government. Moreover, permit applications require that the applicant list every topic on the agenda, and if an allowed rally strays from that program, the police can break up the meeting.

The police frequently reject permit applications for rallies where popular opposition leaders will be speaking—as happened in the run-up to the 2000 elections. In late 1999, Mrema, running for the TLP, was repeatedly refused permission to hold rallies in his home region of Kilimanjaro. The following year, CUF's Ibrahim Lipumba was barred from speaking in the Kagera and Kigoma regions. By hiding behind the defense of public safety, the state can claim that its decisions are for the common good rather than for narrow partisan purposes. But the pattern of bans belies these claims: Although opposition candidates consistently run afoul of complex campaign procedures and laws, CCM candidates seem to avoid these problems entirely.

RCs and DCs have final approval over not just the police, but all government employees in their jurisdiction. Civil servants are accountable to the district executive director (DED), who reports to the DC. DEDs have employed numerous tactics to ensure that civil servants help the CCM to maintain political control, including:

• Allowing the CCM to use public facilities (stadiums, schools) for campaigning, but denying such use to opposition parties;
• Having tax collectors target opposition supporters as well as business owners who fail to support or vote for the CCM;
• Threatening to revoke the licenses of business owners who do not support the CCM;
• Ordering police to shut down businesses during the CCM rallies to boost attendance;

• Telling public-school teachers to encourage their students to attend the CCM rallies and to discourage them from going to opposition gatherings;

• Telling citizens that basic services are contingent on a ruling-party victory in their area;

• Threatening civil servants with firing if they fail to mobilize the electorate for the CCM;

• Placing civil servants on fundraising committees for CCM candidates.

Typically, these legal means of controlling political competition, containing civil society and the media, and blurring the lines between party and state are effective at suppressing opposition movements quietly, and hence the party has a reputation for benign hegemony. When these tools fail to eliminate a particular threat, however, the CCM has employed clearly coercive and illegal measures to win elections.

Skirting the Law

As the ruling party, the CCM can for the most part act with impunity. Because it controls the police and security services, it can even operate outside the bounds of the law, jailing or beating opposition supporters at will. And when campaign funding runs dry, the governing party can dip into state coffers, stealing public monies so that it can keep campaigning.

The police have jailed opposition-party leaders and members, members of NGOs, and journalists under numerous pretexts in order to prevent an unwanted activity, in retaliation for something, or to intimidate other activists. The CCM will go to great lengths when it perceives a political threat. For example, during the 1995 presidential campaign, the minister of home affairs wrote to the inspector-general of police, requesting him to find some reason to arrest Mrema, the leading opposition figure at the time, and to ban his party's rallies. When the private weekly *Shaba* printed the letter making this demand, its editor and director were arrested. The state did not deny the letter's veracity; instead, it claimed that the pair had been detained for revealing official secrets.

The CCM plot to end Mrema's campaign was not an isolated occurrence. Before each election, opposition parties find that they are banned from holding campaign events, and their presidential candidates spend an inordinate amount of time in jail. Mrema was arrested on sedition charges twice before the 2000 election and once before the 2005 election. CUF's Lipumba was detained without charge twice in the run-up to the 2005 election. Christopher Mtikila, the outspoken leader of the unregistered Democratic Party, has been arrested at least eight times over the years. Yet only one conviction resulted from all these arrests—

Mtikila's for sedition in 1999—and most cases never went to trial. The police have never arrested a CCM presidential candidate.

The CCM has also frequently resorted to violence against its opponents and critics. During the 2005 campaign, Lipumba received death threats via cell-phone text messages and was beaten and robbed in Bukoba. In 2004, a popular opposition MP representing the Moshi Rural constituency, who had already been arrested five times while campaigning for a by-election, was run off the road, beaten, and robbed the night before the poll. In January 2008, shortly after *Mwanahalisi* published a list of corrupt officials, two of the paper's editors were disfigured when an assailant threw acid in their faces. In October of that same year, police employed heavy-handed tactics against Chadema in a by-election for the Tarime District's parliamentary seat. The deceased Chadema MP had been popular in the area, thus the CCM leadership saw his death as an opportunity at last to capture the seat. Prior to the election, police broke up a Chadema rally using tear gas and rubber bullets and arrested 29 people, including Chadema's parliamentary candidate. In response to the attack, the head of police special operations said, "In a war anything can happen," and accused the Chadema supporters of attacking police.[21]

The highest levels of violence that the CCM has countenanced have occurred in Zanzibar. The October 2000 election, in particular, exposed the willingness of the island's CCM faction to use force to retain control. While harassment, violence, and intimidation occurred before the election, the greatest brutality came afterward—once voters realized that the CCM had rigged the poll. The blatant theft of the election led CUF members to demonstrate. In retaliation, police fired on a group of three-hundred or so CUF protestors, and there ensued a massive wave of repression featuring the arbitrary arrest, torture, and murder of suspected CUF supporters. The violence continued to escalate until January 2001, when police killed at least 35 CUF supporters and wounded hundreds at a party demonstration. It is important to recall, however, that because of the semiautonomy of the CCM branch in Zanzibar, we cannot directly attribute its actions there to those of the overall party.

Subjecting the opposition to physical violence and incarceration is not the only unequivocally illegal measure that the CCM uses to stay in power. Party members have also conspired to steal state resources to finance electoral campaigns. Most egregious was the 2005 theft of $111 million from the Bank of Tanzania. Those under investigation for the crime claim that high-ranking CCM officials ordered them to do it, and a Ugandan newspaper traced at least $20 million of this money to CCM campaign expenditures in the competitive 2005 parliamentary races in Songea Urban and Kigoma Urban constituencies.

A decade and a half after Tanzania's transition to a multiparty system, a viable opposition still does not exist, nor is there evidence to suggest that one will materialize in the near future. On the contrary, the opposition's vote share has declined with each election, as has their representation in parliament. Not surprisingly, public opinion about Tanzanian politics mirrors this pattern. While we can attribute the opposition parties' failure to win over the public in part to their own insalubrious behavior, that alone does not explain why opposition parties remain feeble in Tanzania. The ruling party's sophisticated and ruthless techniques have largely kept the opposition ineffective and unpopular. The CCM has overwhelmingly succeeded in utilizing its vast spheres of control to ensure its continued dominance. To repress opposition quietly, the CCM manipulates the rules that govern political competition, civil society, and the media, and consciously obscures the division between itself and the state. If those methods fail, the party takes other actions, often coercive and illegal, to guarantee that it will prevail at the polls.

Although it would be inaccurate to say that the CCM silences all opponents—opposition parties do win seats in parliament, and the CUF is a powerful political force in Zanzibar—there are nonetheless troubling signs of political suppression. The international community has long known that elections in Zanzibar have never been free and fair, but the situation on the mainland also is far from perfect. The mainland CCM has mobilized, sometimes violently, to squelch political threats. Beneath the CCM's image as a benign hegemon lies a merciless force. Relentless in its quest to extend its reign, the CCM employs a deliberate strategy to repress opposition. Thus, while the ruling party currently allows for generally free and fair balloting, it is an open question how the party will react if a nationally competitive opposition party should manage to emerge.

NOTES

1. "Future Tanzanian President Rejects Election Fraud Claims," *Agence France Presse,* 20 November 1995.

2. Although the term "transition toward democracy" is awkward, it better characterizes recent political changes in Tanzania than "transition to democracy," as the country still is not one.

3. Amon Chaligha et al., "Uncritical Citizens or Patient Trustees? Tanzanians' Views of Political and Economic Reform," Afrobarometer Working Paper 18, March 2002; available at *www.afrobarometer.org/papers/AfropaperNo18.pdf.*

4. Gerardo Munck and Carol Skalnik Leff, "Modes of Transition and Democratization: South America and Eastern Europe in Comparative Perspective," *Comparative Politics* 29 (April 1997): 343–62; Samuel P. Huntington, *The Third Wave: Democratization in the Late Twentieth Century* (Norman: University of Oklahoma Press, 1991).

5. Excluding those whose responses were coded as "not applicable."

6. The CUF consistently receives approximately 40 percent of the popular vote in Zanzibar and controls about 40 percent of the seats in the Zanzibar House of Representatives. The party's base of support is the islands' non-African population.

7. Electoral Institute of Southern Africa, "Tanzania: Election Archive"; available at *www.eisa.org.za/WEP/tanelectarchive.htm.*

8. One can argue that since single-member districts are the systems most likely to create two parties, the electoral system will not benefit the CCM in the long run, as it will hasten the creation of a national opposition. While this is certainly a possibility, so far it has magnified CCM's victories, not caused the opposition to coalesce.

9. "Opposition Party Threatens to Pull Out of Election Over Defective Ballot Papers," Radio Tanzania, via BBC Summary of World Broadcasts, 16 October 1995; "Tanzanian Poll Body Defends Ballot Paper Design," *Guardian* (Dar es Salaam), 15 October 2005.

10. If a candidate runs unopposed, he or she is deemed to have won 51 percent of the vote for purposes of subsidy allocation; see Government of Tanzania, Act No. 11 (1996) to Amend Political Parties Act No. 5 (1992), secs. 16, 17, and 18.

11. Benson Bana, "A Framework Paper for Studying Political Parties on Issues Related to Party Conduct and Management," Research and Education for Democracy in Tanzania Working Paper, 2007. Recently, the High Court judged the practice to be illegal, although it is not yet clear whether it will be allowed in the 2010 election.

12. Government of Tanzania, Non-Governmental Organizations Act, 2002, part I, sec. 2.

13. Global Integrity, "2006 Country Report: Tanzania"; available at *www.globalintegrity.org/reports/2006/pdfs/tanzania.pdf.*

14. Non-Governmental Organizations Act, 2002, part IV, section 35.

15. Government of Tanzania, Broadcasting Services Act, 1993.

16. Government of Tanzania, Newspapers Act, 1976, sec. 27 (2).

17. Newspapers Act, 1976, sec. 40 (2) and 43.

18. U.S. Department of State, Bureau of Democracy, Human Rights, and Labor, "Tanzania: 2004 Country Report on Human Rights Practices," 28 February 2005; available at *www.state.gov/g/drl/rls/hrrpt/2004/41630.htm*; we were unable to find more recent data.

19. Government of Tanzania, Regional Administration Act, 1997, part II, sec. 5 (2).

20. CCM Constitution, secs. 5 and 6.

21. "Opposition Party and Police Spar in By-Election Campaign," *Citizen* (Dar es Salaam), 8 October 2008.

17

PERSONALIZING POWER
IN UGANDA

Andrew M. Mwenda

Andrew M. Mwenda has been political editor of Uganda's Daily Monitor *and host of a prime-time radio talk show. He is a founding fellow at
the Advocates Coalition for Development and Environment (ACODE),
a public-policy research group in Kampala. This essay originally appeared in the July 2007 issue of the* Journal of Democracy.

Throughout the 1990s, the international donor community hailed Uganda
as Africa's leading postconflict success story.[1] The country's achievements,
so it was said, were both economic and political. Economically, the government of guerrilla-leader-turned-president Yoweri Museveni had taken giant
steps away from state control and toward a more liberal and market-friendly
system. Politically, the Museveni administration was praised for ensuring
stability, respecting human rights, and putting in place a democratization
process in a land still deeply wounded by the murderous dictatorship of
General Idi Amin (r. 1971–79) and the years of bloody strife that followed
his fall and flight into Saudi Arabian exile.

Overlooking the Museveni government's many unsavory deeds, observers invested further hopes in a constitution-making process that led
to the adoption of a new basic law in 1995. With all its flaws—such as
banning normal political-party activities—the 1995 constitution did set
up a number of democratic guarantees as well as a few checks and balances against arbitrary uses of power.

A dozen years after the adoption of the new constitution, however,
the democratization process has been thrown into reverse. Uganda today
is sliding backward toward a system of one-man rule engineered by the
recently reelected President Museveni, who has now been in power for
more than two decades. Perhaps more disturbingly still, the stakeholders whom one would naturally expect to arise to denounce Museveni's
sapping operation against free and open government—Uganda's oppositionists, civil society groups, middle-class citizens, and foreign donors
and creditors—have been virtual no-shows.

Why has this been happening? The answer lies in Museveni's use of force and intimidation on the one hand, and his manipulation of patronage—much of it funded from abroad—on the other. The backsliding has gathered momentum over the last few years. In 2004, Museveni's administration proposed sweeping constitutional changes. These included a removal of the two-term limit on the president; a reduction in the number of years it takes for a lawyer to qualify for a seat on the High Court; the ending of Parliament's powers to vet the president's ministerial appointments and to censure ministers for corruption or incompetence; the granting to the president of new power to dissolve Parliament; a cutback in the authority of the Inspector General of Government, Uganda's national ombudsman; and abolition of the Uganda Human Rights Commission.[2] In an effort to direct attention away from these changes, Museveni's government proposed to reintroduce multiparty political competition.

The point of the changes was to strengthen the presidency while enfeebling the institutions that might act as a check upon it. The very manner in which the government pushed the measures, moreover, was subversive of democracy. In order to get the 322-member Parliament to lift the limit on presidential terms, for instance, Museveni's lieutenants made free use of bribery, blackmail, and naked intimidation. With the skids thus greased, the amendment glided through easily, opening the door for the president to run again and again. Given that elections in Uganda—as in most of Africa—are invariably marred by executive-orchestrated irregularities, this amendment is tantamount to a license for the creation of a presidential monarchy. With Museveni, a hale 63-year-old, set to stay in office indefinitely, the future of democracy in Uganda looks bleak.

The amendments were just the icing on the cake. The government had long been engaging in practices both official and unofficial that rendered constitutional guarantees impotent. President Museveni had been chipping away at Parliament's power since the late 1990s. In 1996, he expanded his cabinet from the constitutionally prescribed 40 members to 67. Since most cabinet officers are Members of Parliament (MPs), and since the army has ten seats in the legislature, this has meant that nearly a quarter of all MPs belong to the executive branch. More direct ways of keeping legislators in line exist as well: In October 2004, soldiers arrested and brutally beat four northern MPs for trying to hold a political rally in one of their constituencies.

Cowing the Judges, Muzzling the Press

Museveni has targeted Uganda's judiciary too. In 2001, the opposition brought before the Court of Appeal a suit challenging the constitutionality of the June 2000 referendum that had endorsed the president's

favored "no-party system." In early 2005, the Court ruled that the referendum had indeed violated the 1995 constitution. Museveni's response
was to don his general's fatigues and go on national television to warn
judges against crossing his government. The next day, the National Resistance Movement (or NRM, Museveni's political party) sent a mob
into the court buildings, forcing judges to flee their chambers and bringing judicial business to a standstill. After this outrage, the hooligans
were treated to a sumptuous, taxpayer-funded party in the court gardens
to reward them for a "job well done."

With Parliament weakened through bribery, brutality, and manipulation, and the judiciary cowed through intimidation, the president then
turned on the independent press—the last bastion of dissent against his
increasingly absolute rule. In August 2005, the government closed KFM,
Uganda's most independent radio station, for a week and threw me—a
KFM talk-show host—in jail on charges of "sedition" and "promoting
sectarianism." Journalists from the independent *Weekly Observer* faced
similar treatment. On 13 November 2005, the government demanded the
shutdown of the *Daily Monitor,* the country's only independent daily
newspaper. After a two-week standoff, the decision was dropped.

By October 2005, the president had subdued all internal opposition
to his efforts to create a one-man authoritarian government. Dissenters
from his own party either kept an enforced silence or else sat licking their
wounds while exiled to the ranks of Uganda's perennially ineffective
opposition parties. What passed for civil society was no better than the
feckless opposition politicians at stopping the slide toward one-man rule.
Official intimidation hung over the independent press like the sword of
Damocles, with Museveni threatening to revoke the publishing rights of
any media enterprise that dared to carry criticism of his rule.

Uganda's foreign donors and creditors—who pay for nearly half the
government's budget—have also done little to rein in their man in Kampala. After Museveni blatantly disregarded an agreement that his administration had made regarding the 2005 transition from "no-party" (read:
one-party) politics to multipartism,[3] only the British, Dutch, and Irish
governments—funders of Uganda for more than two decades—made
even the token gesture of cutting off small amounts of aid.

As the 23 February 2006 presidential election began to draw near, it
seemed that Museveni would face almost no competition. That changed
on 26 October 2005, when former presidential candidate Kizza Besigye
suddenly and unexpectedly returned from exile in South Africa.[4] Opposition forces were galvanized. Voter registrations shot up, with a stunning two million people (Uganda's total population is only 28 million)
signing up in just three days until the Electoral Commission declared
the time for new registrations expired even as long queues of excited
aspiring voters snaked through city streets and village byways. Within
two weeks of his arrival, the energetic Besigye had toured almost fifteen

of Uganda's then-56 districts, drawing huge and welcoming crowds as worried administration officials looked on.

On November 14, the government jailed Besigye. When his supporters attempted a peaceful demonstration, soldiers crushed it with tanks and armored personnel carriers, leaving three people dead. Kampala looked like a war zone; newspaper headlines began comparing it to Baghdad. Besigye was taken before the High Court and charged with treason plus a rape allegedly committed in 1997. When the High Court granted bail, the military accused Besigye of terrorism and placed him in the custody of a court martial. Foreign diplomats whom the minister of internal affairs had accredited to attend the trial found themselves ejected and locked out of the courtroom by soldiers.

In one especially macabre incident, the government sent hooded gangs sporting sunglasses and brandishing automatic weapons into the High Court to kidnap 21 of Besigye's codefendants in the event that they received bail. Looking on as the thugs waved their guns at jurists and diplomats, the terrified detainees decided to remain in custody. The courts later released Besigye himself, but only after almost two-thirds of the campaign period had gone by.

On election day, the *Daily Monitor* opened a tally center to monitor results, which the paper's radio affiliate KFM began to broadcast. As this independent effort was starting to make it clear that Museveni would not get the 50 percent required to avoid a runoff, the president's men moved in to close the tally center, jam its radio signal, and block its website. It was amid circumstances such as these that the Electoral Commission announced Museveni's first-round reelection with 59 percent of the vote.

A Taste for Violence

Looking back over Museveni's career, it is fair to say that he has never been a friend of liberty. He scorns the rule of law, shuns due process, and is always willing to run roughshod over people's rights. He believes in violence as a legitimate instrument to bring about "revolutionary" political change and in the army as an important pillar of political power. At the University of Dar Es Salaam in Tanzania, Museveni wrote a bachelor's thesis defending Frantz Fanon's calls for the use of violence. Both before and since Museveni became president, the themes of violence and the military have played central roles in his speeches and writings.[5]

After claiming that President Milton Obote had stolen the 1980 election from them, Museveni and his party took to the bush as the National Resistance Army (NRA). Their goal was always to seize power by force of arms. In order to keep itself in funds and supplies, the NRA robbed banks, looted stores, and raided hospitals. Nor did it shrink from terrorism, blow-ing up petrol stations and mining roads in order to destroy ambulances. Impunity thus lies at the very foundation of its bid for power. Can anyone seriously think that a group which seeks to rule by the gun and stoops to pillaging hospitals will, once it captures the state, stay its hand from plundering the public fisc or brutalizing political foes?

From its inception, Museveni's army-turned-party has been informed by the logic of authoritarianism. The leader wears all the hats and pulls all the strings. During his time in the bush, Museveni was the chairman of the NRM as well as commander of the NRA, sitting atop both the Army Council and the High Command. He also presided over the legislative National Resistance Council, all the while acting as his movement's chief theoretician and philosopher. Checks and balances to guard against the abuse of power can mean but little when so many levers rest in one pair of hands. When in January 1986 Museveni's forces took Kampala and made him president, he gained the resources of a state to help him rent or if need be coerce political support from the distressed body of his wounded country.

At first, the authoritarianism did not seem so bad. Museveni's forcefulness helped to promote economic reform. The various organs of the shadow state that he had created as a guerrilla had the potential to become partners in an internal debate. Yet Museveni never truly tapped that potential. Instead, he adeptly manipulated these organs to project the illusion that consultation was occurring even as he was effectively ruling by decree. A close look at what was happening could often reveal the sham. Many times in the late 1980s and early 1990s, for example, if Parliament was slow to pass some measure that Museveni saw as important, he would put on his uniform and chair a closed legislative session until his bill had been rammed through.

The desperate situation that Museveni inherited in 1986 required a strong and dynamic leader. Amin's depredations—he had killed somewhere between 80,000 and a half-million people and had expelled the country's Indo-Ugandan merchant class *en masse* in 1972—were followed by seven years of savage infighting that came in the wake of his ouster. Uganda was on its knees, its government and economy alike in ruins. Iron-fisted tactics appeared necessary—and even legitimate— since the country needed a leader who could take quick and decisive decisions where institutions were too slow or inept. Thus did Parliament swiftly approve Museveni's plans to restore the traditional local monarchies, privatize state enterprises, allow Indo-Ugandans to return and reclaim their property, cut back on the civil service, and the like. Yet as institutions recovered and fresh economic growth produced new interest groups, Museveni's penchant for informal methods and arbitrary decision making became increasingly counterproductive.

In 1986, not long after it seized power, Museveni's government restricted political-party activities on national-healing grounds. At the time, this sounded reasonable. Museveni appeared magnanimous as he invited leaders of other parties to join him in a national-unity (or as the president called it, a "broad-based") government. Yet even as the situation improved, Museveni held fast to the ban on parties, letting go of it only under considerable pressure in 2005. With the benefit of hindsight, we can understand the subjective motives for his seeming magnanimity.

The NRA was the strongest armed force in the country by the mid-1980s. But Museveni's political vehicle, the NRM, was unseasoned and rested on a narrow, unsteady base. Museveni, a brilliant student of Uganda's politics, reasoned that the no-party, "broad-based" approach offered several advantages, including: 1) a viable alternative to the counterproductive expedient of open military rule; 2) a boost to his own NRM's political appeal nationwide; and 3) the means to make rivals and potential rivals from other parties serve at his beck and call.

To improve his chances for success, Museveni not only used his soldiers, police, and security agents to stop other parties from organizing, but also exploited local councils to build the NRM's organizational infrastructure, cajoled leaders from other parties to join the NRM, and systematically rid official ranks of all those who remained loyal to their old parties. The decentralization of the budget process gave local officials reason to work with the NRM; the continued use of armed coercion made them fear what would happen if they broke with the president's movement.

Evidence that Museveni never had any intention of building a democracy may be gleaned from the NRM regime's conspicuous refusal to repeal any of the many repressive laws—including some of the worst of Idi Amin's decrees—that remained on the books in 1986. In fact, Museveni's time in power has seen draconian statutes hampering freedoms of organization, expression, assembly, and publication not only retained, but reinforced. The only signs of nascent democratization appeared in the constitution-making process. Even there, however, enabling acts to give effect to many of the 1995 basic law's provisions were not forthcoming, and activists from opposition groups, civil society, and the media had to sue in court in order to have repressive laws struck down.

The worst obstacle to democratic development in Uganda has been the personalization of the state. Arms and money are essential to this malign process. The arms belong to the military and security services, which the regime deploys selectively in order to suppress dissent. The money sluices through a massive patronage machine that Museveni uses to recruit support, reward loyalty, and buy off actual and potential opponents. In his efforts to personalize the state, Museveni has skilfully undermined formal institutions of governance, preferring as he does to use highly arbitrary and informal methods of recruiting and rewarding officials. The destruction of Parliament's will and ability to check executive power has been a keystone of his approach. Not surprisingly, the personalization of the state has gone hand in hand with its increasing arbitrariness.

Building a Patronage Empire

Museveni has always sought to use the army to build his personal (less so the NRM's) political base. He employs violence sparingly and selectively—as an instrument of last resort when the political process fails to yield before his requirements or the opposition appears to need whipping into submission. Patronage, typically in the form of government contracts, tenders, and jobs, is his preferred tool and the one that he used to render Parliament ineffective.

Museveni's success at consolidating his power and stifling democracy flows from his knack for integrating large chunks of the political class into his vast patronage empire. To grasp how he has achieved this feat, it is crucial to examine how he has conducted Uganda's reconstruction process over the last two decades.

Discussions of Uganda's reconstruction over the last two decades have generally focused on "what" has been done, with lists of fairly tangible but often short-term political and economic accomplishments reeled off like an athlete's statistics. My intention is to shift the emphasis from "what" has been done to "how" it has been done, with special mindfulness of how the process of reconstruction has failed to help build up the crucial mediating institutions *between* the state and the individual citizen upon which democratic governance must so often depend.

By shifting the focus from "what" to "how," I hope to highlight the inherent fragility, over the longer term, of the short-term achievements—chiefly political stabilization and minimal economic recovery—for which President Museveni so often receives credit. By personalizing power and undermining the development of democratic institutions of governance, Museveni has mortgaged his country's future without securing the basics that will be needed to make that future work. A degree of stability and growth has been bought, at least for a time, but at a price that is no bargain.

In his 1997 study of Ghana, Daniel Green argues that the logic of structural adjustment

> promotes a system of political and administrative praxis that depoliticizes economic governance, allows autonomy of the economic sphere and eschews rent-seeking. This implies non-interference in the workings of markets, with policy making that reflects economic rationality and a fundamental concern for enhanced economic efficiency and productivity.[6]

Green further claims that the logic of adjustment is therefore "fundamentally antipatrimonial in both the economic and political spheres." Museveni's record shows that theories such as this are mistaken. In

Uganda, the process of economic reform has meant not fewer but *more* opportunities for patronage. To implement many of the key components of the reform program, donors and the government chose to rely not on the traditional civil service, which was widely seen as inept and poorly motivated, but on purpose-built, semi-autonomous bodies that recruited employees by offering better terms and conditions of service than could be had in the old-line bureaucracies.

In the name of improving tax collection, attracting investors, and moving forward with privatization and decentralization, the early 1990s saw the creation of such semi-autonomous agencies as the Uganda Revenue Authority, the Uganda Investment Authority, the Privatization Unit, and the Decentralization Secretariat. The opening of the economy created a need for institutions to regulate the newly liberalized sectors. From the ashes of the old marketing boards for commodities such as cotton, coffee, and tea rose "development authorities" for these crops and tobacco as well. Similarly, the tasks of liberalizing the telecommunications, power-generation, and broadcasting industries fell to new regulatory bodies, all with major officers and boards appointed by the president and his lieutenants. These new arrangements brought the regime immense patronage opportunities while sapping the strength of a civil service that was now honeycombed by small, easily manipulated institutional pockets.

According to an audit conducted by Uganda's Ministry of Finance, Planning, and Economic Development, as of 2003 the country had 95 semi-autonomous government agencies, mostly created with donor support. Almost four-fifths of these agencies revealed their budgets at the auditors' request, though nearly all refused to submit figures on the numbers of people that they employ. The audit found that the total budget allocated to these bodies had been growing by 30 percent every year, and that as of 2003 it was US$280 million. This is a huge sum in Uganda, whose entire Gross Domestic Product (GDP) for 2006 is estimated to amount to only slightly more than $8.5 billion.

Adding to the fragmentation of the central government was the emergence within individual ministries of project monitoring and implementation units. Again, international donors encouraged the growth of these units within ministries as part of their overall strategy to bypass the incompetence of the civil service. Because regular pay in the civil service is so low, enterprising bureaucrats with an eye on career enhancement turned to proposing projects to donors. Since writing a project that donors approve normally entails being placed in charge of it, this tactic was a passport to officialdom's elite ranks.

In this fashion, Museveni's reforms sparked a proliferation of special projects within ministries. These projects meant not only increased institutional fragmentation but still worse, wider opportunities for what amounts to a new form of corruption. Civil servants who write projects typically set them up so that a project's main benefits go to its staffers in the form of salaries, allowances, official cars, and domestic or foreign trips complete with per-diems.

The Strange Neglect of the Central State

With so much energy diverted into self-dealing amid the frenzied spawning of new, donor-funded minibureaucracies, the institutional infrastructure of the central state went begging and failed to recover as it should have done and as Uganda still badly needs it to do. The spread of semi-autonomous agencies and special-project units also raised huge policy-coordination challenges. The situation bred gridlock and then, however unintentionally, personalism as the seemingly readiest solution to gridlock. In this way, institutional fragmentation has become an ally and reinforcer of personal rule as the fragmentation ensures that there will arise no large and effective institution to form a center of power.

In addition to fragmentation around and within the central government, there has emerged under Museveni an onset of fragmentation at the local-government level as well. The driver here has been the president's policy of decentralization. As of 2002, local governments taken together were spending nearly 40 percent of the national budget. The dollar figure for local spending in 2006 was US$1.2 billion. Because Uganda was a one-party state in all but name, this placed vast sums in the hands of local regime functionaries. They decided where to build a new dispensary, which clinic to renovate, which primary school to rebuild, or which road to repair.

The incentive for local notables across Uganda was to join the NRM in order to become eligible for posts in local administrations. Districts and municipalities in Uganda receive over 95 percent of their budgets from Kampala, which in turn receives close to half its budget from foreign aid. Such aid thus became the grist that the mills of Museveni's neopatrimonialism learned to grind. Decentralized budgeting caused every community to agitate for its own autonomous district (the basic unit of local government) in order to be surer of getting its share.

In the political sphere, this meant that every ethnic group in a country with a history of communal strife and fragmentation had fresh incentive to seek its own district. In the rush for local autonomy, elites even began to allege ethnic and clan tensions where none had previously existed. In 1990, Uganda had 33 autonomous districts to cover its 236,000 square kilometers. By 2006, the number of such districts had risen to 81. With each new district came a raft of government jobs, each one a patronage opportunity. The coherence of regional and local governance suffered as these small geographical units, like the minibureaucracies with which the central government teemed, were easy targets for presidential manipulation.

With so many of Uganda's "best and brightest" in both Kampala and the regions now integrated into the government, it has become increasingly difficult to find educated people to lead civil society and the opposition. Reform may have led to 5 percent annual economic growth, but at the same time it has weakened democracy by allowing the government to buy off the political class and by shattering both the central and local governments into shards that a personalistic president can easily arrange and direct as he wishes.

Among the most important consequences of Museveni's relationship with donors was that once he gave them nearly free rein over the policy- and budget-making processes, the donors left him a free hand (and sometimes even gave him a helping hand) with his military plans. These included operations against the long-running insurgency of the Lord's Resistance Army (LRA) in northern Uganda as well as invasions of Sudan (1997) and the Democratic Republic of Congo (1998). Donors did consistently urge Museveni to restrain his military spending, but on technical rather than ethical grounds: They were content to warn that directing more than 2 percent of GDP to the armed forces might hamper growth, but never asked Museveni about the moral wisdom of his taste for violence as an instrument of politics.

Like many an authoritarian ruler before him, Museveni seems to grasp that the best way to control his armed men is to make it so that they cannot cohere. By instigating the emergence of many hostile informal factions in the military, and by promoting the proliferation of both formal and informal security outfits, Museveni has turned the strategy of fragmentation to his own purposes in this sector of the state as well as in its more sedate organs. "Divide and rule" are the watchwords that allow the president to sustain his personal control.

Over Museveni's two decades in power, Uganda has bubbled with a veritable alphabet soup of formal security organizations. There is the UPDF, the CMI, the ISO, the ESO, the CID, and the SB, as well as the more euphoniously named Uganda Police and Prison Services. For good measure, the president has also encouraged the proliferation of nonstatutory coercive units including the Civic Defence Team, the Popular Intelligence Network, the Special Operations Unit, the Joint Anti-Terrorism Taskforce, the Presidential Guard Brigade, the Violent Crime Crack Unit (VCCU), and the exotically monikered Kalangala Action Plan and Black Mamba Urban Hit Squad. To round out the picture, in every district or ethnic community that has faced a rebel group, the government has trained and armed a local ethnic militia as a response.

The founding of many of these armed groups was justified at first by immediate necessity. Some even enjoyed public support for fighting crime, as did the VCCU when it crushed (albeit not without extrajudicial killings) an alarming outbreak of armed robberies in 2001 and 2002. Yet irregulars with guns have seldom been noted for exemplary discipline, training, and professionalism, and a number of these groups have overstayed whatever welcome the public was once prepared to accord them.

As is the case with the other proliferating organs in Museveni's para-state, these armed units are a source of jobs that the president can hand out to his political hangers-on. Moreover, they allow him to sap the power of the formal security organizations even as he boosts his capacity to use deniable force against his opponents without having to worry about official state sanction. The sad and predictable upshot for the rest of the country outside Museveni's charmed circle has been that hopes for democracy have suffered and the underpinnings of personal rule have taken on added strength as these informal security outfits have learned that they can act with impunity.

Armed conflicts continue in various parts of Uganda, and Museveni exploits these as excuses and justifications for clampdowns on individual freedoms in general and those of his opponents in particular. Newspapers and radio stations have been closed illegally, while journalists have suffered detention and harassment. Opposition politicians and supporters whom Museveni finds threatening have been targeted for ill treatment and jailed or forced into exile. "Security" has been the regime's cry in all cases, the most notorious of which has been the imprisonment and trial of Kizza Besigye on charges of treason and terrorism. The use of former LRA commanders as state's witnesses against him has been arguably the most blatant token of the degree to which justice has been perverted.

How does Museveni do it? What has made it possible for him to undermine Uganda's democratic prospects so successfully? Uganda's two uninterrupted decades of what has been by regional standards highly robust economic growth make Museveni's dubious "achievement" seem at first glance inexplicable.

Conventional political economy, after all, teaches us that sustained economic growth—especially the kind driven by the private sector—nurtures constituencies with a vested interest in enlightened government. The World Bank and the Ugandan government tell us that this has been the case with Uganda over the last two decades. After twenty years of growth, why has Uganda descended into one-man rule? As the foregoing account suggests, all evidence points not to the strength but to the terrible weakness of the democratic impulse in Uganda.

Hide-Away Peasants and Walk-Away Professionals

Possible explanations begin to suggest themselves once one takes a closer look at the country. To begin with, 88 percent of all Ugandans live in rural areas, mostly as small farmers. Whenever governments have oppressed them, as for example via the extortionate agricultural taxes that were common across Africa in the 1970s and 1980s, the continent's peasants have tended to react not by demonstrating but rather by withdrawing into subsistence agriculture or leisure—putting out no more effort than it takes to feed themselves and their families, and preferring a mute idleness to either loud complaints or the dire prospect of working for the taxman.[7] In other words, instead of confronting a burdensome state, they have simply done their best to avoid it.

In other regions of the world, the educated middle class has formed the foundation for a democratic order. The crisis that besets Africa's middle classes has been akin to that which has burdened the continent's peasantry. When dictators have plundered their countries, the middle classes in all but a few places (Malawi, Kenya, and Zambia) have failed to stand up for the cause of enlightened government. Rather than fight, Africa's middle classes often choose flight: They take the exit option and go into exile. In Uganda, President Museveni's foreign-aid–funded state has integrated huge sections of the elite class into the government's patronage network. Those Ugandan professionals without the luck to be thus coopted have mostly left the country, leaving Museveni largely unopposed as he consolidates his personal rule.

A related problem is actually a development of the 1990s, and has been occasioned by the spread of the global nongovernmental-organization (NGO) movement. The growth of such groups has handed Ugandan and other African elites chances to build prosperous careers as NGO staffers in their own countries even when their governments are crumbling under the weight of corruption, mismanagement, and authoritarianism. After government, the fastest-growing employer in Uganda is the NGO sector. The middle-class know-how and energy that might have gone into democratizing the state have instead been diverted into the work of NGOs that carry out "policy advocacy," "humanitarian relief," and bureaucratized human rights activism.

The international donor community has made Uganda's case even worse than it might otherwise be. By pouring in huge sums to pay for state spending on infrastructure as well as free and universal primary schooling and basic health care, international donors have been helping Museveni's government to win legitimacy and popularity while undermining the opposition. Moreover, the subsidies from donors allow the government to direct more of its own revenues into expanding its huge patronage schemes, which in turn attract more foreign aid as they grow.

Many donors now realize that they have been shoring up a corrupt system, but find it hard to step away. Having long hailed Uganda as a great success story, they have made their claims to run effective aid programs depend on the country's perceived fortunes. Conversely, Museveni has come increasingly to depend for his political survival on continued financial and diplomatic support from his foreign donors. Out of this nest of codependency have sprung incentives for donors to keep propping up what would otherwise be the unsteady edifice of Museveni's regime.

Why has Uganda's much-touted private sector not become the backbone of the democratic struggle in the country? To answer this question, we must again point to the political pathology that afflicts Africa generally. Whenever things have gone badly in various African countries, the private sector has chosen not to defend enlightened government by confronting the state and demanding better policies and more accountability, but has instead looked for ways to work around the problem.

From the 1960s through the 1980s, for example, many African states laid down laws and regulations so hostile to business and enterprise that multinational capital mostly just threw up its hands and withdrew. Indigenous private enterprises, by contrast, saw much more opportunity than threat in this trend. Africa's poorly institutionalized states could declare many more rules than they could enforce. Their efforts at regulation served mainly to spur the growth of sprawling black markets and informal sectors in which African entrepreneurs with the right know-how could and did prosper. From Ghana to Uganda, the age of foreign-capital flight was also the golden age of indigenous private enterprise.

The Silence of the Business Classes

One might have thought that liberalization, deregulation, and privatization in Uganda would have nurtured a private sector with a vested interest in democratic governance. But as the NRM's antidemocratic train has gathered momentum, Uganda's business classes have mostly stood by and left the struggle for democracy to politicians, jobless (and perhaps unemployable) young people, and a tiny handful of professionals and academics. More disturbing still, even if an opposition thus composed should somehow displace Museveni, it would most likely end up merely reprising his patrimonial and antidemocratic politics: The nameplates on the doors would change, but what went on behind them would remain much the same.

Even after all of Museveni's much-discussed liberalization and privatization, the government remains Uganda's largest consumer of goods and services as well as its biggest formal employer. The nature of the reconstruction process, driven as it has been by foreign aid, has much to do with this. So much aid money goes through the government's hands that the high road to the best profits for domestic and even foreign business interests is to deal with the state. Such a state-dependent private sector cannot be relied upon to become a voice for democracy.

Besides, the strongest business interests are those underwritten by multinational capital and the capital of the Indo-Ugandans who returned to the country after Amin fell. But these interests lack deep and dense ties with the larger corpus of Ugandan society, and so have scant political heft. (Indeed, for these interests to support the prodemocracy struggle would be to risk dispossession.) As for the rest of the business class, most of it is too thoroughly dependent on state patronage ever to challenge the status quo, while those few businesspeople who are independent are too thin on the ground to venture jumping into the political fray.

Yet there is a ray of hope in this seemingly hopeless situation. The regime's corruption,[8] violence, and vast patronage eat away economic resources, leaving almost nothing for investment. This undermines its ability to reproduce itself in the long term because it destroys the economic foundation of the regime's political survival. To date, the regime has been saved from this grim prospect by foreign-aid donors stepping in to pay for investments in roads, free primary and secondary education, and health care. If international donors pulled the plug, the regime would no longer be shielded from the consequences of its own misdealings and would have to bend to democratic pressures.

In fact, even if donors keep the aid coming the regime will be growing increasingly vulnerable. By premising its survival on handing out massive state patronage to certain elites, the regime has corrupted their souls. Thus it has become increasingly obvious that the regime cannot even buy support, but must *rent* it, so weak and tenuous is the loyalty that the regime commands. It is impossible to integrate all or even most elites into the state-patronage system—especially given the explosion in the number of educated Ugandans, who now simply number too many for state payrolls ever to accommodate. Amid this climate of discontent, large and not always peaceful demonstrations began breaking out in Ugandan cities in early 2007. Where they will lead remains of course uncertain, but they cannot be counted as good news for the Museveni regime.

Finally, the regime's core support in rural areas is also coming under increasing strain. Over the last three years, the agricultural sector has grown at an annual average rate of only 0.9 percent, even as population growth has been reaching a record 3.5 percent. The regime's response to this agrarian crisis has been to extend welfare (free basic health care and primary education) and tax relief (by abolishing market dues and the poll tax). Such measures, however, only relieve symptoms and offer no long-term solution to the growing discontent of Uganda's rural majority.

The future of democracy in Uganda lies in the ability of the opposition to take advantage of these developments and convert them into votes. The recent spate of demonstrations signals that this is beginning to happen, and there may be at least a chance for an opening after all.

NOTES

1. For example, see *The World Bank Experience with Post-Conflict Reconstruction, Volume VI: Uganda Case Study* (Washington, D.C.: World Bank, 2000); and *Uganda: Post-Conflict Reconstruction, Country Case Study Series* (Washington, D.C.: World Bank, 1998).

2. *Government White Paper on Constitutional Review and Political Transition* (Entebbe, Uganda: Government Publishing House, 2004).

3. Parliament had voted in May 2005 to hold the referendum on multipartism at the end of July. On 28 July 2005, voters went to the polls and ended the "no-party" era. For more background on Uganda's political history plus a guardedly optimistic analysis of the shift from Museveni's original "no-party" or "broad-based" government to multiparty competition, see Edward Kannyo, "Change in Uganda: A New Opening?" *Journal of Democracy* 15 (April 2004): 125–39. A more skeptical diagnosis may be found in Anne Mughisha's comment entitled "Museveni's Machinations," *Journal of Democracy* 15 (April 2004): 140–44.

4. Besigye, a former officer in Museveni's army who had become a critic of the "no-party" system, had won 28 percent to Museveni's 69 percent in the 12 March 2001 election.

5. Yoweri K. Museveni, *What Is Africa's Problem?* (Minneapolis: University of Minnesota Press, 2000); and *Sowing the Mustard Seed: The Struggle for Freedom and Democracy in Uganda* (New York: Macmillan, 1997).

6. Daniel Green, "Ghana: Structural Adjustment and State (Re)formation," in Leonardo Villalon and Philip Huxtable, eds., *Critical Juncture: The African State Between Disintegration and Reconfiguration* (Boulder, Colo.: Lynne Rienner, 1997), 189.

7. Robert Bates, *Markets and States in Tropical Africa: The Political Basis of Agricultural Policies* (Berkeley: University of California Press, 1984); and Goran Hyden, *Beyond Ujamaa in Tanzania: Underdevelopment and an Uncaptured Peasantry* (Berkeley: University of California Press, 1992).

8. Examples of the regime's misuse of funds are not lacking. For instance, since 1998 President Museveni has had the use of a luxury jet aircraft that costs US$22,000 in public funds per day to maintain and operate. According to estimates from Uganda's Ministry of Education, the average cost of building a primary-school classroom is $4,200. Assuming that a classroom seats fifty students, this means that money which could have given schoolrooms to 728,000 Ugandan children (many of whom now study under mango trees) has instead gone to finance the rarefied travel habits of a single man. Other examples might include Museveni's bloated cabinet and squadrons of presidential appointees, which cost altogether $370 million per year; or the $40 million per annum that goes into the pockets of dishonest generals as pay for "ghost soldiers" who exist only as names on military payrolls.

18

THE REMARKABLE STORY OF SOMALILAND

Seth Kaplan

Seth Kaplan *is a business consultant to companies in developing countries as well as a foreign-policy analyst. His book* Fixing Fragile States: A New Paradigm for Development *(2008) critiques Western policies in places such as Congo (Kinshasa), West Africa, Syria, and Pakistan, and lays out a new approach to overcoming the problems they face. For more information, see* www.sethkaplan.org. *This essay originally appeared in the July 2008 issue of the* Journal of Democracy.

The sorry state of Somalia has been regularly in the headlines in recent years. Reports have chronicled the rise to power in Mogadishu of a group of Muslim extremists calling themselves the Islamic Courts Union (ICU), their subsequent ejection by Ethiopian troops, and the repeated failures of peace conferences to reconcile the country's many factions. As media across the world also reported, the fighting and chaos in late 2006 and early 2007 even prompted U.S. military intervention.

The attention paid to the violent drama in the south of Somalia is perfectly understandable, but both the media and the international community are missing an equally important—and more peaceful—story in the north, where a remarkable political transformation is under way. Inattention to this northern success story is ironic given that it offers important lessons for the governments, scholars, and analysts who have made democratization the centerpiece of efforts to combat extremism in the Muslim world and to promote better governance in developing countries.

The Republic of Somaliland, the secessionist northwestern slice of Somalia that declared independence in 1991, has a far better democratic track record than any of its neighbors despite—or, perhaps, because of—a dearth of assistance from the international community. Abutting the Gulf of Aden just south of the Red Sea, across the water from Yemen and Saudi Arabia, and bordered by Ethiopia and the rest of Somalia, this strategically important territory is not even recognized by the international community but undoubtedly has the most democratic political system in the entire Horn of Africa. In contrast to the chaos and extremist threats that continue to plague much of the rest of Somalia—and unlike the authoritarian regimes that throng its neighborhood—Somaliland has held three consecutive competitive elections since its constitutional referendum in 2001, has a parliament controlled by opposition parties, and boasts a vibrant economy dominated by the private sector.

Somaliland has achieved these successes by constructing a set of governing bodies rooted in traditional Somali concepts of governance by consultation and consent. In contrast to most postcolonial states in Africa and the Middle East, Somaliland has had a chance to administer itself using customary norms, values, and relationships. In fact, its integration of traditional ways of governance within a modern state apparatus has helped it to achieve greater cohesion and legitimacy and—not coincidentally—create greater room for competitive elections and public criticism than exists in most similarly endowed territories. Far too many poor states are held back by administrative and political systems built separately from the societies that they are meant to serve, thus rendering those systems illegitimate, ripe for exploitation, and a major hindrance to democratization and development. Although Somaliland's fledgling state institutions are still fragile and have many weaknesses, if properly nourished they can become robust champions of a democratic system that is actually reflective of and integrated into the society that it is meant to represent—giving the country a far better chance to develop toward greater freedom and prosperity in the years ahead.

Somaliland thus offers important lessons, both for its neighbors and for other postcolonial states in the Middle East and Africa. The success of its society-led, bottom-up process of democratization stands in sharp contrast to the repeated failure of international attempts to construct a Western-style state in the rest of Somalia—and calls into question the fundamental assumptions underlying the top-down, unitary state-building exercises so commonly attempted in fragile states.

"The Very Definition of a Failed State"

Somalia embodies one of postcolonial Africa's worst mismatches between conventional state structures and indigenous institutions. Although a shared ethnicity, culture, language, and religion might seem to offer an excellent basis for a cohesive polity, in reality the Somali people are divided by clan affiliations, the single most important component of their identity. Traditional, customary methods of governance are ill suited to the centralized bureaucratic governing structures that colonizers and Westernized elites have repeatedly attempted to impose on the country. Those attempts have brought only chaos and conflict, creating what the Council on Foreign Relations has characterized as "the very definition of a failed state."[1]

Anthropologists typically describe traditional Somali society as stateless, characterized by a wide dispersion of power among clans and subclans. So-

MAP—SOMALILAND AND SOMALIA

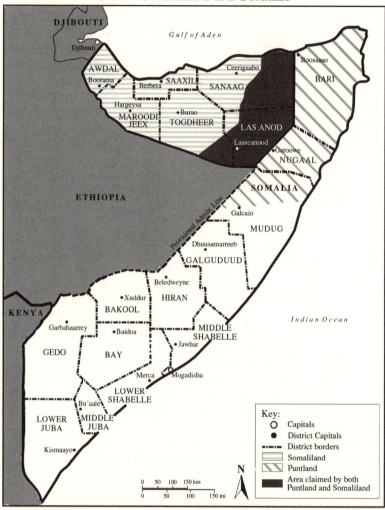

malis' long history as pastoral nomads has made them fiercely independent, but also well accustomed to a variety of democratic practices.

The Somali population (some 13 to 14 million people, including those now living in neighboring states) is divided into six major clans and a number of minority groups. Each of the clans consists of subclans that join or split in a fluid process of "constant decomposition and recomposition."[2] These "clan-states" typically work through a diffuse and decentralized decision-making process that culminates in a community meeting open to all adult males—a *shir*—at which major economic, political, and social policies are determined. These societal institutions, and the customary law (*xeer*) that governs behavior within the community, are deeply ingrained and function independently of modern state structures. Although

Islam plays a major role in the lives of a socially conservative people, it is subordinate or complementary to clannism in shaping their outlook.

Starting in the 1880s, European colonialists divided Somalis among the British Somaliland Protectorate (today's Somaliland), Italian Somalia (the rest of Somalia), and French Somaliland (now Djibouti), as well as parts of Ethiopia and Kenya. This launched a process whereby outsiders and Westernized elites tried to create new, modern institutions that completely ignored traditional societal norms and relationships. In trying to marginalize long-established patterns, these modernizing efforts ended up permanently disconnecting the state, such as it was, from the society that should have been its foundation.

Somalia came into being on 1 July 1960, when the British Somaliland Protectorate, having gained its formal independence on June 26 of that year, joined with what had been its southern neighbor, Italian Somalia. Initial euphoria rapidly soured as signs of state dysfunction mounted. Corruption worsened, electoral politics became increasingly chaotic, and state programs delivered little public benefit. Clannism infected politics and administrative organs as each group sought to maximize the spoils that it could loot from the system.

This high level of disenchantment led many to welcome Mohamed Siad Barre's armed coup in 1969. Siad Barre's socialist regime made some popular reforms in the areas of education, health, and the status of women, but suffered a humiliating defeat by Ethiopia in the Ogaden War of 1977–78, and encountered growing dissatisfaction with one-party rule. Siad Barre fell back on members of the Daarood subclans linked to him by birth or marriage; all other groups were pushed out. He eventually came to depend on repression and foreign aid (development assistance peaked at a stunning 57 percent of annual GNP) to prop up his highly centralized and socially isolated state.[3] Siad Barre's fall in 1991 left Somalia in the hands of warlords and militias whose grip was challenged but not broken by the ill-fated UN- and then U.S.-led military intervention that culminated in the October 1993 "Black Hawk Down" incident in Mogadishu.

In the 1990s, disaffected clans began to carve up the country. The Haarti grouping (a subset of the Daarood) created a semi-autonomous region in the east called Puntland, while in the northwest the Isaaq clan led the effort to build Somaliland.

The international community has launched at least fourteen peace initiatives since Siad Barre's dictatorship collapsed, yet Somalia remains divided and without a functioning central government—the longest-running example of state failure in the postcolonial period. If anything, the authority and cash that outsiders have repeatedly tried to give some central body have distorted the traditional relationships that undergirded a robust society for centuries, while helping to entrench warlords and their private armies. The Transitional Federal Government (TFG)—a reed-thin affair produced by a 2002 regional initiative and based mainly on a clique from the Daarood clan—had never controlled more than a small area around one city near the Ethiopian border before Ethiopia's 2006 invasion. The TFG, nonetheless, receives recognition from the international community as Somalia's legitimate government.

The ICU, which won armed control of large areas of southern Somalia in 2006, naturally also had strong clan ties. The Hawiye group, never fond of the Daarood-dominated TFG, is a close ICU supporter. The Islamists were able to expand so rapidly both because of their ability to supply a measure of order—something prized by residents weary of years of chaos and strife—and because they coopted various subclans by giving them significant stakes in local administrations. Even though scattered in the wake of Ethiopia's assault, the ICU and its Islamist leaders have vowed to fight on via an Iraq-style guerrilla campaign. Ethiopian forces have faced suicide attacks and remotely detonated bombs, making Mogadishu dangerous enough to deter foreign states from sending peacekeepers. The current anarchy resembles the one out of which the ICU first grew, suggesting that the group's prospects can by no means be called bleak.

Ordinary Somalis have paid the highest price for these repeated failures at state formation. They are among the world's poorest and hungriest people, with an average life expectancy of only about 42 years and a mortality rate for children under five that exceeds 25 percent. The adult literacy rate may be lower than 20 percent in some parts of the state.[4]

Another Model in the North

While the south has been caught up in the cauldron of competing factions, a different model has emerged in Somaliland. Whereas attempts to build stable state structures in Mogadishu have mostly been top-down, with outsiders in the lead, Somaliland has constructed a functioning government from the bottom up, on its own, with little outside assistance.

When Somaliland broke away, it took with it six of Somalia's eighteen regions, encompassing slightly more than a fifth of Somali territory and between a quarter and a third of the total population.[5]

Northern discontent goes all the way back to the formation of Somalia in 1960. Subsumed into the larger, southern-dominated state structures, in which unfamiliar Italian laws and colonial-era elites predominated, northerners felt like a people apart. When the new administration discriminated against them in sharing out top posts and other state resources, the northerners' sense of grievance grew larger still.

Serious challenges to the union began as Siad Barre's grip weakened in the late 1970s. No fewer than ten clan-based resistance movements sprang up across the country. The most notable among them was the Somali National Movement (SNM), a group formed in 1981 and closely affiliated with the Isaaq clan that makes up some 70 percent of Somaliland's population.[6] In 1988, civil war erupted. Siad Barre bombed Somaliland's two largest cities to rubble, killing an estimated fifty-thousand people and making refugees of a million more. This brutality convinced northerners that they should find their own solution to the challenge of state-building.

Somaliland has profited from a unity conferred by its comparatively homogeneous population, modest disparities in personal wealth, widespread fear of the south, and a lack of outside interference that might have undermined the accountability that has been forced on its leaders.[7] This cohesiveness—which makes Somaliland sharply distinct from both Somalia and most other African states—has combined with the enduring strength of traditional institutions of self-governance to mold a unique form of democracy.

From the onset of Somaliland's independence movement, traditional democratic methods have predominated in efforts to create governing organs. The SNM was notable for its internal democratic practices, changing its leadership no fewer than five times in the nine years that it spent fighting the Siad Barre regime. A Council of Elders established during this time to resolve disputes and distribute food among the refugees quickly gained legitimacy. When the war ended, it came to play a key role in promoting a process of representative decision making. Within two years of the SNM's victory, it had turned power over to a civilian administration.

From the time independence was declared, a wide-ranging and inclusive process of national dialogue sought to construct a consensus on the system of political representation that should govern Somaliland. Between 1991 and 1996, interclan dialogue went on despite conflicts and interruptions, eventually yielding the broadly legitimate government that has delivered security and growing prosperity since 1996.

Of the many interclan meetings, all financed by local businesspeople and community leaders, the 1993 Boorama *shir beeleed* (clan conference) was the most important. From it came a Peace Charter—based on the traditional law of social conduct between clans—that established the basis for law and order, and a National Charter that defined the political structures of government. The Boorama gathering, attended by five-hundred elders, religious leaders, politicians, civil servants, intellectuals, and businesspeople, set the pattern of institutionalizing clans and their elders into formal governing bodies, something that is now referred to as the *beel* (clan or community) system of governance.

This "dynamic hybrid of Western form and traditional substance"[8] formalized the role of elders in an upper house of elders (known as the Guurti) responsible for security and managing internal conflicts, and allocated seats in the legislature based on clan numbers. A conference in 1996–97, after the war, increased the number of seats available to non-Isaaq clans. The 2001 Constitution, approved by an overwhelming majority of the population in a national plebiscite, sought to minimize clannism and entrench consensus-based decision making by limiting the number of political parties to three and requiring them to have significant support in each of Somaliland's six regions.

Mohamed Haji Ibrahim Egal, who had been Somalia's prime minister before the 1969 coup and who became Somaliland's president in 1993, provided inspired leadership during the breakaway state's formative years. His government negotiated with the relevant subclan in order to gain access to revenue from the port of Berbera, rebuilt government buildings, reopened the central bank with a new currency (the Somaliland shilling), created a new civil service, melded militiamen into a national army, and removed roadblocks and informal "taxes" from major roads. Somaliland now has many of the trappings of modern statehood, including not only its own currency, army, and cabinet ministers, but also license plates and even a national air carrier, Daallo Airlines.

The Uses of Tradition

This remarkable process of bottom-up state-building using traditional forms, now reinforced by three successful democratic elections, has yielded a system in which the public feels it has a strong stake together with a robust sense of national identity and patriotic pride. It has produced

> [A]n unprecedented degree of interconnectedness between the state and society . . . in stark contrast to the past when previous regimes received enormous infusions of external assistance without which they could not survive, and as a result became completely divorced from the economic foundations of their own society.[9]

The success of this bottom-up state-building process is evidenced by the high sense of security that Somaliland's people feel, and by the growing buoyancy of their economy. Hundreds of thousands of refugees have returned home and tens of thousands of landmines have been removed and destroyed. The capital city of Hargeysa, reduced to a mere ten-thousand people in 1991 by Siad Barre's bombings, is now home to more than half a million. Its peacefulness and economic vitality draw migrants from Ethiopia and southern Somalia. Markets throughout Somaliland are filled with products from around the world; telephone charges are among the cheapest in Africa; and the private sector, not the government, provides electricity, water, education, and health care. Three new universities have been built, privately funded hospitals and schools proliferate, and a number of nongovernmental organizations are working to improve administrative capacity. Members of the Somali diaspora, more than a hundred thousand of whom live in the United States and Europe, support these efforts with extensive international networks, expert knowledge of how modern societies operate, and monetary contributions thought to be worth US$500 million a year.[10]

Although many of its governing structures need work and many of its politicians, bureaucrats, and judges lack experience, Somaliland has already passed a number of democratic milestones that few states in Africa and the Middle East have reached. Altogether, the country has successfully managed the May 2001 constitutional referendum, the December 2002 local elections, the 2003 presidential campaign, and the September 2005 legislative poll. (The next round of voting includes local and presidential elections, scheduled at the time of this writing for October and December 2008, respectively.) The 2005 House of Representatives elections saw 246 candidates contest 82 seats in an undertaking that involved 982 polling stations, 1,500 ballot boxes, 1.3 million ballot papers, 6,000 party agents, 3,000 police, 700 domestic observers, and 76 foreign observers. The latter "were fairly unanimous in their views that [the elections] were, on the whole, the freest and most transparent democratic exercises ever staged in the Horn of Africa."[11]

The National Electoral Commission (NEC) has rightly been widely praised as the most competent of Somaliland's government institutions. In dealing with the many challenges of running an election in a poor, war-scarred, and semiliterate country—one that lacks not only electoral rolls, but even reliable estimates of the number of eligible voters—the NEC has repeatedly chosen a highly transparent method of engaging political parties and other key stakeholders in decision making, has debated problems and possible solutions openly and at length, and has sought outside assistance. The use of indelible ink on voters' fingers to prevent double voting, the presence of representatives from all parties at every site where votes are cast or counted, and the participation of a significant number of observers have ensured elections that are remarkably free and fair.

Somaliland's democracy has repeatedly surprised outsiders with its robustness. When, in May 2002, President Egal died abroad, power was smoothly passed to Vice-President Dahir Riyale Kahin, even though Riyale is from the small Gadabursi clan and had fought for Siad Barre against the Isaaq. The April 2003 presidential poll was possibly the closest ever fought in Africa, with Riyale winning by only the slimmest of margins—just eighty votes out of almost half a million ballots. The opposition contested the result in the courts, but when its judicial appeals failed, it accepted the outcome peacefully.

Constitutional governance has not been completely free of glitches and has deteriorated to some degree over the past two years. The Guurti election scheduled for August 2006, the last stage of the democratic transition begun in 2001, was postponed in May 2006 because Parliament could not agree on issues such as how to distribute seats and choose members—tricky issues in an institution based on traditional structures and delicately divided among the clans. Extending the term of the current Guurti to October 2010 provoked fierce controversy. Similarly, the Guurti's unilateral April 2008 attempt to extend the president's term for a year, supposedly because of security concerns, was highly controversial. (At the time of this writing, it is unclear when this election will actually take place.) In 2007, three politicians were jailed for almost five months for attempting to form a new political party. Although women have the same rights to vote and run for office as men, only 2 out of 379 municipal councilors and 2 out of 82 members of parliament are female. Some legislative, executive, and judicial procedures have not been followed according to the letter of the law. The electoral-management system, despite its relative success, contains much room for improvement.[12]

The country also suffers from many of the maladies common to all poor, underdeveloped states: The rule of law and civil society are weak, corruption is rife, nepotism and clannism sway many official appointments, the executive towers over the other branches of government, Parliament lacks the power to initiate legislation, the poorly trained and underfunded judiciary can do little to check the administration, and competent officials of all kinds are in short supply. As in many countries—underdeveloped and developed alike—the government has shown itself tempted to sacrifice civil liberties in the name of security. Somaliland's print media are relatively free and criticize the government, but a weekly magazine that dared to discuss the idea of Somaliland reuniting with Somalia (a particular sore point for the government) was banned, and in early 2007 the chairman of Haatuf Media Network and two of his journalists spent two months in jail for having written about presidential corruption. Meanwhile, the executive branch continues to operate a Security Committee that has sweeping powers of arrest and sentencing despite calls from the legislature, judiciary, civil society, and the diaspora to disband the body.

The *beel* system of government, though responsible for bringing peace and democracy to Somaliland, also places significant limits on the development of a fully representative and effective democracy. As Somalilanders who advocate fuller modernization have complained, clan elders hold disproportionate power. People from powerful lineages have an edge in obtaining government posts, and clannism has hobbled efforts to make the civil service more meritocratic. Compromises intended to ensure that the smaller clans are fully included in the system have given them a disproportionately high number of seats in Parliament. The government has been unable to finalize the delineation of regional and district boundaries because these are closely associated with traditional clan territories. Women remain excluded from traditional governing structures, and hence from the regime that is built on them.

Despite these problems, however, Somaliland has achieved much with very little outside assistance. In fact, the dearth of external involvement has been in many ways a blessing, for it has kept foreign interference to a minimum while fostering self-reliance, self-confidence, and a distinct Somaliland identity.

Needed: International Recognition

Notwithstanding Somaliland's success at building a stable democracy in a region better known for instability and authoritarianism, the international community continues to refuse to recognize Somaliland as a state. Although this lack of recognition did not significantly hamper (and as noted above, may even have helped) Somaliland in its formative years, its hopes of consolidating and expanding its political and economic gains hinge now on winning international acceptance as a sovereign state, with all the rights and benefits that such a status confers.

Somaliland's isolation hurts in a number of ways. Governing organs cannot receive bilateral technical assistance from other countries; the World Bank, the International Monetary Fund, the African Development Bank, and bilateral development agencies cannot offer it loans and financial aid; banks and insurance companies will not set up branches within the country; the cost of living is higher because local firms cannot directly import goods without local banks to issue letters of credit; international investors (and the jobs that they would create) stay away because insurance and other investment protections are lacking. Many diaspora professionals—whose return would help to invigorate Somaliland's legal, accounting, health, and educational systems—are reluctant to come home for fear of Somaliland's uncertain legal status. The threat of continued unrest and even factional fighting or an increase in terrorist activities in the south will continue to hamper Somaliland's development as long as its future is held hostage to events in Somalia.

Somaliland can make a strong case for recognition on a variety of grounds. It existed as a separate territory with internationally recognized borders during more than seven decades of colonial rule, and even its brief interlude of independence at the end of June 1960 was enough to garner it recognition by thirty-five sovereign states. Somaliland's authorities argue today that they are dissolving an unsuccessful marriage rather than seeking secession, and that therefore their case is analogous to the breakup of Sénégambia (Senegal and Gambia) and the United Arab Republic (Syria and Egypt). They also draw parallels with Eritrea, their neighbor to the north, which was originally a colony separate from Ethiopia and which gained its de jure independence in 1993.

The political case rests on widespread dissatisfaction with and even rejection of the union from its inception in 1960, the discrimination that northerners faced within it, the brutality that the Mogadishu government showed during the civil war, and the Somaliland people's repeated expressions of its desire to live independently of Somalia. The May 2001 constitutional referendum was effectively a plebiscite on independence.

Although opponents in Sool and eastern Sanaag refused to participate, 97 percent of those who did vote approved the document in a ballot widely deemed to have been free and fair.

Somaliland actually—and ironically—does a far better job than Somalia of meeting the criteria of the 1933 Montevideo Convention on the Rights and Duties of States, which include having a permanent population, a defined territory, a functioning government, and the capacity to enter into relations with other states. Since 1991, Somalia has not come close to having a functioning administration able to assert its control over a significant part of the country's territory.

Although de jure recognition remains elusive, Somaliland has achieved de facto recognition in a number of ways. In January 2008, Somaliland's president led a delegation to Washington and London and met with officials in both capitals.[13] Egypt, Ethiopia, France, Kenya, Italy, and Yemen have also welcomed official visitors from Somaliland. Ethiopia, the state that has worked most closely with Somaliland, has a quasi-embassy in Hargeysa with a staff of twelve.[14] Ethiopia and Djibouti accept Somaliland passports. Britain, the European Union, and the United States have financed programs to help train parliamentarians and conduct and monitor elections. The UN and many international aid agencies operate programs throughout Somaliland's territory and deal with its government. All of this suggests a "creeping informal and pragmatic acceptance of Somaliland as a political reality."[15]

The biggest internal challenge to the state's legitimacy stems from problems that it has had in gaining the loyalty of two eastern subclans. Each belongs to the Haarti grouping that dominates neighboring Puntland and supports a unified Somalia. On 1 July 2007, the subclan that controls the disputed area in eastern Sanaag proclaimed the semi-autonomous state of Maakhir in order to distance itself from both Hargeysa and Mogadishu. That October, Somaliland captured Las Anod, the capital of the Sool region, from Puntland forces, consolidating Hargeysa's control over most of this province, at least for now. Although the restive eastern subclans are not enough to derail independence, Somaliland authorities would strengthen their case for recognition if they could entice discontented local leaders to join the administration and thus extend Hargeysa's formal authority over all of what was once British Somaliland. Offering a handful of central-government posts to the leaders of these groups and making a greater effort to redress whatever inequities they perceive in the services that they receive might prove a good start.

Given its strong case, why has no country recognized Somaliland? The argument most often heard is that recognition would set a bad precedent in a region where weakly cohesive states struggle to hold together. Some fear that international recognition of Somaliland will trigger the balkanization of the rest of Somalia. Others mention the possibility that any change in the status quo will derail peace efforts in the south or may ignite conflict between the two states, as has happened in the case of Ethiopia and Eritrea. However, Somaliland's history as a separate state with recognized boundaries gives it a status that few other territories (and no other territories within Somalia) can claim, reducing the chances that others could use its independence as a precedent. Somaliland's refusal to participate in any post-1991 peace conference means that its permanent withdrawal should not hamper the prolonged and unsuccessful venture of bringing peace to Somalia. In fact, the rise of the ICU in the south led some security analysts to argue before the Ethiopian invasion that Somaliland's independence could avert what threatened to become a civil war between the former British protectorate and southern Somalia.[16]

The African Union (AU) reviewed many of these issues during a fact-finding mission in 2005 and concluded that Somaliland's case was "unique and self-justified in African political history" and that "the case should not be linked to the notion of 'opening a Pandora's box.'" It even admitted that a "plethora of problems confronting Somaliland [are in part] the legacy of a political union with Somalia, which malfunctioned, [and] brought destruction and ruin."[17]

Rwanda, South Africa, Zambia, and several other African states support Somaliland's independence, yet the AU has been paralyzed because of opposition from Somaliland's neighbors, each of which has a vested interest in the country not gaining recognition. Ethiopia, for example, concerned about the irredentist claims of its own Somali population, has tried to divide and weaken Somalia since the Ogaden War three decades ago, and considers any attempt to strengthen Somaliland as inimical to Ethiopian interests. Tiny Djibouti sees Somaliland as a threat to the port that powers the economy of that former French colony. Western countries have tended to see the whole matter as an internal African affair. Arab countries—especially nearby Egypt and Saudi Arabia—have vehemently opposed independence; the Saudis have even sought to sabotage Somaliland's economy by refusing to import any of its livestock since 1997. Many of these neighboring countries would prefer a united Somalia acting as a counterweight to Ethiopia, a Christian-majority country that is the Horn of Africa's predominant local power.

Success and Its Lessons

Somaliland's success so far in building its region's most accountable and open political system holds important lessons about how states can develop and democratize—and why most countries in its region have not.

First, Somaliland's evolution shows that states should look inward for their resources and institutional models and adopt political structures and processes that reflect the history, complexity, and particularity of their peoples and environment. Instead of mimicking a Western-style top-down system of governance, which typically ignores or suppresses indigenous traditions and customs, Somaliland has been forced by its isolation to build a state enmeshed in its surrounding society. Far too many postcolonial regimes have looked outward for their governance models and resources—often becoming dependent on foreign aid and advisors and ensuring that their domestic roots will never run deep enough.

This means not that Western political models have no relevance to non-Western societies, but rather that those models must be adapted to accommodate local political, economic, and societal customs and conditions. Robust states are unlikely to be built with centralized regimes, Western-style laws, and a democracy defined solely in terms of regular elections; instead, capable, inclusive, participatory, responsive, and accountable governments should be promoted no matter what form they take.

In a similar vein, international assistance efforts are more likely to succeed if they bolster rather than distort local capacities and institutions. Undisciplined injections of foreign money all too often undermine or overwhelm local processes, especially given the tendency of many international programs to focus on easily quantifiable targets for financial aid or poverty reduction and to promote the importation of generic, centralized state models. Helping underdeveloped countries should not be about propping up the state from outside, but rather about connecting it—and making it accountable where possible—to its surrounding society.

A second lesson to be gleaned from Somaliland's experience is that a population's cohesiveness and the success of democratization efforts are closely related. States made up of competing ethnic, religious, and clan groups—Iraq, Kenya, and Nigeria come to mind—are often torn asunder by zero-sum battles over who will control the state and its resources. By contrast, cohesive societies such as Somaliland's, with its strong sense of common history, identity, and destiny, are more likely to reach consensus as to how the government should work, how changes in that government should come about, and how the state should spend its resources. The governments that such societies produce are also much more likely to appear legitimate and representative in their citizens' eyes. Moreover, recent studies have shown that homogeneous populations are more likely to invest in public goods such as roads, schools, and health centers—all necessary for development.[18] These cohesive states' social glue is far more likely to accommodate the competitiveness intrinsic to democracy; the fractured societies common to divided countries are more likely to break down—perhaps violently—in the face of electoral combat.

Of course, Somaliland is not entirely free of such divisions. The country's difficulties in negotiating a fair distribution of seats in its Parliament, in demarcating the boundaries between regional and district administrative territories, and in limiting the political space to a set number of actors all show the challenges that it must meet in order to reconcile competing clan interests. It has similarly experienced problems (reflected in disagreements over acceptable levels of media freedom and political activity) in trying to strike a balance between individual rights and group rights—a perennial problem for young states as they strive to craft the terms under which multiple identity groups can live together. Somaliland's struggles with secessionist groups, moreover, remind us that even those new countries where most people support the national idea will face opposition to the whole state-building notion.

A third lesson that Somalia offers the international community is the importance of institutional design. Because cohesiveness figures so largely in the building of robust and democratic countries, the international community needs to do more to foster such governing bodies and systems as will best promote cohesiveness in a given context. A good first step would be for the international community to stop insisting on political models that are clearly unable to advance cohesion—or that even undermine it. Persistent efforts to reequip Somalia with a centralized state—carried out despite the repeated failures of such efforts in the past—show a lack of appreciation for the informal institutions that drive Somali society. Bolivia, Congo (Kinshasa), Iraq, Sudan, and other divided countries are unlikely to build successful democracies unless and until they shift governmental resources and responsibilities away from the center and toward local bodies that are more likely to be responsive to relatively cohesive groups of people. In practice, this will usually best be accomplished by adopting some form of federal arrangement and by accommodating diverse forms of self-government. In a few instances, however, the only way to leverage local capacities and loyalties to build a strong state may be secession.

The standard development paradigm gives "little thought . . . to the possibility that existing state structures might . . . be the cause of instability" in many postcolonial countries, even when "state-like entities such as Somaliland are more viable in terms of their ability to manage their own territory, to provide basic services, and in terms of their internal cohesiveness."[19] Such an approach to state building disregards the many vast differences between countries, and ignores the people's desire to choose not only their leaders but also their institutions. The international community would do better if it focused on retailoring and leveraging traditional forms of governance that have evolved to suit local conditions instead of trying to squeeze societies into inappropriate Western models of what a modern state is supposed to look like. Development and democratization work best when a state's institutions are genuine reflections of an organic historical process.

NOTES

The author thanks Lulu Farah-Todd for her help in organizing his trip to Somaliland.

1. See *www.cfr.org/publication/10781/somalias_terrorist_infestation.html*.

2. My description of the clan system of governance owes much to Virginia Luling,

"Come Back Somalia? Questioning a Collapsed State," *Third World Quarterly* 18 (June 1997): 292.

3. Ken Menkhaus, "Somalia: Political Order in a Stateless Society," *Current History*, May 1998, 220.

4. Roland Marchal and Ken Menkhaus, *Somalia Human Development Report 1998* (Nairobi: UN Development Programme, 1998), 12.

5. There is no census data for either Somaliland or Somalia, but Somaliland's population is generally estimated at between 2.5 and 3.5 million. See International Crisis Group (ICG), "Somaliland: Time for African Union Leadership," *Africa Report,* No. 110, 23 May 2006, 4.

6. Asteris Huliaras, "The Viability of Somaliland: Internal Constraints and Regional Geopolitics," *Journal of Contemporary African Studies* 20 (July 2002): 158.

7. This last point was mentioned repeatedly in interviews conducted by the author in Hargeysa in September 2006. See also Matt Bryden, "The Banana Test: Is Somaliland Ready for Recognition?" (unpubl. ms.), 6; and Mark Bradbury, Adan Yusuf Abokor, and Haroon Ahmed Yusuf, "Somaliland: Choosing Politics over Violence," *Review of African Political Economy* 30 (September 2003): 462.

8. Academy for Peace and Development (APD), "A Self-Portrait of Somaliland: Rebuilding from the Ruins" (unpubl. ms., APD, Hargeysa, 2000).

9. Carolyn Logan, "Overcoming the State-Society Disconnect in the Former Somalia: Putting Somali Political and Economic Resources at the Root of Reconstruction," USAID/REDSO, September 2000, 20.

10. Huliaras, "The Viability of Somaliland," 162.

11. Bradbury, Abokor, and Yusuf, "Somaliland: Choosing Politics over Violence," 475.

12. For a specific list of how this might be done, see APD and International Peacebuilding Alliance (Interpeace), *A Vote for Peace: How Somaliland Successfully Hosted Its First Parliamentary Elections in 35 years* (Hargeysa: APD, 2006), 49–52.

13. See Ann Scott Tyson, "U.S. Debating Shift of Support in Somali Conflict," *Washington Post,* 4 December 2007, A17.

14. Author's interview with Somaliland's foreign minister, Abdillahi M. Duale, Hargeysa, 17 September 2006.

15. Bradbury, Abokor, and Yusuf, "Somaliland: Choosing Politics over Violence," 458.

16. This discussion borrows from ICG, "Somaliland: Time for African Union Leadership," 19–21.

17. African Union Commission, "Resume: AU Fact-Finding Mission to Somaliland, 30 April to 4 May 2005," Addis Ababa, 2005.

18. Eduardo Porter, "The Divisions That Tighten the Purse Strings," *New York Times,* 29 April 2007.

19. Ian Spears, "Reflections on Somaliland and Africa's Territorial Order," *Review of African Political Economy* 30 (March 2003): 94.

IV

Southern and Central Africa

19

AN ACCIDENTAL ADVANCE? SOUTH AFRICA'S 2009 ELECTIONS

Steven Friedman

Steven Friedman, *director of the Centre for the Study of Democracy of Rhodes University and the University of Johannesburg, teaches politics and international relations and has written for numerous South African publications. This article originally appeared in the October 2009* Journal of Democracy.

Democratic advances are often achieved in spite of the politicians who trigger them. Thus South Africa's April 2009 parliamentary and provincial elections, despite a largely unedifying campaign that culminated in the naming of a president who only days before had dodged having to defend himself in court against corruption charges, may yet prove an important democratic breakthrough.

In the April 22 balloting, the ruling African National Congress (ANC) won 66 percent of the vote and 264 seats in the 400-seat National Assembly—down 15 seats from 2004, and the party's first-ever decline in vote share. The Democratic Alliance (DA), the official opposition party, won 16.7 percent of the vote and 67 seats. The Congress of the People (COPE), the ANC splinter party formed in the fall of 2008, won 7.4 percent and 30 seats, and the Inkatha Freedom Party (IFP) won 4.6 percent and 18 seats. The remaining seats were allotted to nine smaller parties, each with less than 1 percent of the vote. (South Africa has a closed-list proportional-representation system that awards seats to any party able to win a quarter of one percent of the vote.) Two weeks after the polling, parliament elected ANC leader Jacob Zuma as president of the republic.

If the election does become a turning point, it will be so not because high-minded leaders sought to deepen democracy, but because competition for power and influence opened new democratic avenues. This is hardly a uniquely South African development. Dankwart Rustow's pioneering study of democratic transitions argued that democracy is born not when leaders wish it, but when conflicts resolve themselves in ways that make it the most pragmatic option.[1] This holds not just for the birth of democracy but also for the ways in which it becomes broader, deeper, and more enduring.

Understanding the prospects for and threats to democracy in South Africa that stem from the election therefore requires us to look beyond the proclivities of the politicians embroiled in power struggles to the processes that these political battles may be creating and influencing. Before discussing how the election may reshape politics, however, it is necessary to place it in context.

If we understand democracy purely as a set of "negative" freedoms that protect individuals from arbitrary government power, South Africa's democracy has done much better than expected since its inception in 1994.[2] Overall, civil liberties have been respected,[3] and the country's 1996 constitution is enforced by a constitutional court that has periodically overturned legislation and rejected government decisions. A vigorous national debate provides a platform for divergent voices, many of them highly critical of the government.

The country's racial divisions ensure that predominantly black political officeholders must contend with a white minority that is deeply skeptical of majority government, well-resourced, and well-connected, and thus able to express its misgivings whenever government performance is seen to be lacking—which is almost always. Regular national, provincial, and local elections have produced results that are largely accepted as an accurate reflection of the voters' will. The relative ease with which society has moved from an authoritarian racial oligarchy to a functioning democracy remains remarkable, even though it is often taken for granted, particularly by many in the white minority.

But if we see democracy also as positive liberty—as a regime of popular sovereignty in which law and policy are meant, as far as practicable, to reflect the will of an actively participating citizenry—then progress is far more modest. Since 1994, elections have been marked by vigorous campaigning, much public debate, and, until this year, the election of the ruling ANC with an ever-increasing share of the vote (see Table on page 270). By 2004, the ANC also controlled all nine provincial legislatures and all but one of the local councils in metropolitan areas. The ANC has for almost a century represented the majority identity in the country and has thus been assured of growing support.[4]

Electoral contestation within the ANC has also been limited. While the party's constitution provides for regular contested elections at all levels, its political culture—which stems from its long period as an outlawed resistance movement—has deterred internal competition, branding those who vie for office as selfish and overambitious. Until late 2007, there were some internal ANC elections, but the party leadership was for the most part chosen by conclaves of party elders.

These realities contributed to a conspicuous lack of government accountability and responsiveness. Political leaders, confident that they would lead and govern for as long as they wished, felt no great pressure to account to the electorate and respond to its concerns. Elections, of course, are not the only source of democratic accountability. The country's racial dynamics, as well as a diversified economy that made resources available to independent citizens' organizations, ensured far greater accountability than we might expect if we focused solely on election results.[5] But the seemingly inevitable electoral arithmetic limited the impact of attempts to hold government to account and also allowed the government to keep the vast majority of poorer citizens at arm's length.

The result was evident in both the government's style and performance. The administration of President Thabo Mbeki, who took office in 1999, relied heavily on centralized decision making that placed a premium on technical expertise rather than the concerns of the electorate. While this initially appeared to offer a more managerial and more efficient style of government, by 2007 it had become clear that the administration's efficiency was largely illusory, as illustrated by a much-discussed electricity crisis, continued high crime levels, and only mixed success in addressing poverty despite the devotion of substantial resources to this task.[6] The gulf between what policy makers felt was needed and what a welter of research evidence revealed about preferences and dynamics among the poor hurt the government's antipoverty policies.[7] In short, government remained largely insulated from the need to respond to the people and take action on their concerns; thus the depth and breadth of democracy and government effectiveness remained weak.

The Palace Rebellion

Mbeki's government was also largely insulated from his own party, a reality that became apparent in December 2007, when he failed to win re-election for a third term as ANC president, losing to the party's deputy president, Jacob Zuma. Mbeki loyalists likewise lost the contests for every other senior ANC leadership post that year. This was the first time that an incumbent president had been defeated in an ANC election since 1949, and it signaled to its leaders that they could no longer rely on party activists to re-elect them. Because ANC leaders can no longer assume victory, they are now more likely to feel accountable to the rest of the party.

Within a few months of the Mbeki camp's losing control, the ANC was transformed from a party in which contested elections were seen as a symptom of indiscipline to one in which all posts were hotly contested. An ethos that might have been appropriate for a movement fighting racial domination has proven inadequate to managing competition among ambitious politicians hoping to secure status and privilege. Moreover, the coalition that backed Zuma was diverse and divided, held together by little more than a common desire to defeat Mbeki. Since that task has now been accomplished, the divisions have grown and, if not managed effectively, could prompt another split in the ANC.

But while the pressures forcing ANC leaders to respond to party members (who constitute only a fraction of its voters) have increased since the ANC election, the need to show the same concern for voters has not, as the ruling party faced no threat at the polls. On the contrary, the politics of 2008 were dominated by the preoccupations of politicians, not the concerns of voters. To take but one example, the ruling party disbanded a special investigative unit that is deeply unpopular among ANC politicians without consulting a public worried about high crime rates. While the constitution mandates that the public must be consulted on legislation through parliamentary hearings, ANC legislators made it clear before the first hearings that they would be voting to abolish the unit, signaling to the people that their opinion on this issue was irrelevant.[8]

Still, as the election approached, there were indications that the ANC would need to pay more attention to the electorate than had been the case in previous campaigns. The ANC leadership's call for Mbeki to step down as party president led to the formation of COPE—the first serious competition that the ANC has faced for its traditional voter base. At the same time, press reports revealed that internal ANC opinion polls showed a significant drop in public support—probably a reflection of voter disenchantment with a politics which seemed to ignore their concerns entirely. The ANC also faced a challenge in the Western Cape from the DA, which seemed set to benefit from a shift away from the ANC by many of the province's voters. (The DA is a union of the Democratic Party—the official opposition since the 1990s and a descendant of earlier white progressive parties, including the party to which Helen Suzman belonged—and a section of the New National Party.)

All this suggested that 2009 could be the first election in which the ANC vote would shrink. The prospect of greater competition, along with a sustained voter-registration campaign mounted by nongovernmental organizations, heightened interest in the election in a society whose levels of electoral participation were already high—especially for a country where election results are not in doubt. In all, some three-million new voters registered.[9] The election, South Africa's fourth since it became a democracy, was thus widely thought to be the most important since the first universal-franchise ballot in 1994. To what extent did the result vindicate these expectations?

There is a certain irony about the election. While it may well have broken the mold of electoral politics, it did so not because voters behaved differently but because they acted in much the same way as they had for the past decade and a half.

The ANC did lose some ground. Its share of the national vote dropped

by almost 4 points, a result that deprived it of the two-thirds majority—
and thus the right to change the constitution at will—that it had enjoyed
since 2004. This seemingly modest loss in support would have been
far greater had it not been for an outcome unlikely to be repeated: The
ANC scored a decisive victory (63 percent) in KwaZulu-Natal (KZN)
Province at the expense of the IFP, which in 1994 had won a majority there but gained only 22.4 percent of the province's vote this time
around. Some analyses attributed the ANC's enormous gains to Zuma's
being a Zulu who shared an ethnic identity with most KZN voters. While
Zuma's embrace of Zulu tradition surely helped, his ability to break the
link between the IFP and traditional Zulu leaders, which previously had
ensured it much of the rural vote, may have been decisive.

Regardless, the effect was to gain the ANC hundreds of thousands
of votes—one analysis estimates that without the swing in KZN, the
ANC's national vote would have dipped below 60 percent.[10] Although
this figure exaggerates the likely decline, the ANC did lose ground in
every other province. Thus there was a far more decisive move away
from the ruling party than the national poll numbers suggest.

The DA did even better than expected in the Western Cape—it won
a narrow absolute majority, better than the plurality that most had predicted. Together with an enhanced turnout of its traditional supporters
elsewhere in the country, this gave the DA a 5-point increase in its national vote share.

Both COPE leaders and media commentators had believed that the
new party's roots in the ANC—most COPE leaders had been ruling-
party politicians (former defense minister Mosiuoa Lekota and former
premier of Gauteng province Mbhazima Shilowa, for example)—would
enable it to supplant the DA as the official opposition. With COPE winning only 7.4 percent of the vote, however, these expectations were disappointed. Smaller parties, representing an array of racial, religious, and
ethnic constituencies, all lost ground, as their supporters defected to the
DA and COPE in the hope of strengthening opposition to the ANC.

One of the more remarkable features of the campaign was something
that did *not* occur—significant election-related violence. The heightened competition did spark some violence, including at least two deaths
in KZN, and there were reports of political intolerance and coercion,
ranging from attempts to exchange public services for votes to attempts
to deprive parties of meeting venues. Some traditional leaders allegedly
told their subjects to vote for specific parties. Overall, however, levels
of violence and intolerance were much lower than had been feared.[11]
Moreover, since the 1994 elections—when the country was divided into
"no-go areas," party-dominated zones that were hostile to campaigning
by rivals—it has become progressively easier for the parties to campaign on one another's territory.

It is unclear whether this improvement was due to enhanced toler-

TABLE—PARLIAMENTARY ELECTION RESULTS, 1994–2009

PARTY	2009		2004		1999		1994	
	% OF VOTE	SEATS	% OF VOTE	SEATS	% OF VOTE	SEATS	% OF VOTE	SEATS
ANC	65.9	264	69.7	279	66.4	266	62.6	252
DA[1]	16.7	67	12.4	50	9.6	38	1.7	7
COPE	7.4	30	-	-	-	-	-	-
IFP	4.6	18	7.0	28	8.6	34	10.5	43
Independent Democrats	0.9	4	1.7	7	-	-	-	-
United Democratic Movement	0.8	4	2.3	9	3.4	14	-	-
Freedom Front Plus[2]	0.8	4	0.9	4	0.8	3	2.2	9
African Christian Democratic Party	0.8	3	1.6	7	1.4	6	0.5	2
United Christian Democratic Party	0.4	2	0.8	3	0.8	3	-	-
Pan Africanist Congress of Azania	0.3	1	0.7	3	0.7	3	1.2	5
Minority Front	0.2	1	0.4	2	0.3	1	-	-
Azanian People's Organisation	0.2	1	0.3	1	0.2	1	-	-
African People's Convention	0.2	1	-	-	-	-	-	-
New National Party[3]	-	-	1.7	7	6.9	28	20.4	82
Federal Alliance	-	-	-	-	0.5	2	-	-
Afrikaner Eenheids Beweging	-	-	-	-	0.3	1	-	-

Notes:
1. Contested as the Democratic Party in 1999 and 1994.
2. Contested as Freedom Front in 1999 and 1994.
3. Contested as the National Party in 1994.

ance or simply the lack of incentive for parties to campaign outside their strongholds. Residential segregation was a key feature of apartheid, and elements of past settlement patterns remain today. Thus there is often a strong coincidence between identity and geography, which tends to determine where a party will dominate: the ANC in urban townships where the black poor live, the DA in the suburbs where most residents are racial minorities, and the IFP in the rural areas of KZN in which traditional leaders dominate. In many cases, local party leaderships have entrenched themselves and muscled out their challengers.[12] As a result, parties (particularly larger ones) have focused on mobilizing their own supporters rather than on competing for votes in their rivals' areas. Elections were free and fair, but largely uncompetitive.

The 2009 election challenged this pattern. The emergence of the breakaway COPE meant that for the first time there was serious competition for the votes of ANC supporters. At the same time, in KZN the ANC targeted the rural areas traditionally dominated by the IFP, while the latter tried to win support in the urban areas where the ANC has held sway. And in the Western Cape, the DA rallied voters who had backed the ANC in the previous election.

This posed a significant risk of violence and the possibility that local party leaderships would force their opponents out. As the contenders arguably had never experienced vigorous electoral competition, there was no guarantee that they would allow opponents to campaign in their territory. While national party leaderships urged tolerance and signed a code of conduct, there was a real danger that local leaderships would not feel bound by these national commitments. The relatively low levels of intolerance and violence in 2009 therefore represented an important breakthrough, since they suggest that society has a more robust capacity to cope with enhanced electoral competition than the history just sketched would suggest.

The Power of Identity

Electoral choices in South Africa are shaped by identities: Voters across the spectrum tend to remain loyal to parties that represent their identity group, defined by a complex mix of race, language, and culture. Although the 2009 election was the most competitive in the country's history, the shifts in voter sentiment were far from a break with the past. The outcome was not a product of voters' abandoning identity voting. On the contrary, the swings occurred because identity voting was given new expression.

Evidence suggests that most ANC voters who told pollsters that they would bolt the party in fact stayed with it. Identity voting means that party loyalties are particularly strong, so many voters who swear months ahead of time that they will stay at home or switch parties instead return to their political base by election day. Polls taken months before the ballot may be interesting measures of trust in political leadership, but they are weak predictors of voting patterns.

One reason that the ANC lost support was the feeling of some voters that their ANC identity was best expressed through COPE. Most of the new party's vote seems to have been gleaned from ANC supporters upset by Mbeki's removal or dismayed at Zuma's perceived threat to traditional ANC values (in addition to the corruption charges against him, he had stood trial for rape, which alienated some voters despite his acquittal). Still loyal to the roots of the ANC, these defectors believed that by voting against the party's new leadership they were supporting its traditional values.

Given the strength of party loyalties, then, it seems inevitable that if any party ever bests the ANC at the polls, that party will prove to have been one that emerged from within ANC ranks and managed to convince most ANC voters that it represented the ethos and tradition of the movement better than did the ANC itself. That is why COPE's formation prompted such excitement among both opposition parties and commentators—they sensed that the promised split in the ANC support base had arrived.

That judgment was premature. COPE's leaders may have emerged from within the ANC, but they were not senior enough to make the case to voters that they were representing ANC tradition rather than breaking with it. The COPE leadership was composed almost entirely of politicians who had fought apartheid from within the country and had gravitated to the ANC from rival resistance movements or from the trade unions. None of the senior exiled or jailed ANC figures joined the new party, in some cases despite intense antipathy to Zuma and his supporters. COPE, then, was directed not by seasoned ANC veterans but by more recent leaders whose authenticity could be questioned. The party also blundered in its choice of Bishop Mvume Dandala—a respected clergyman, but one with no history of ANC activism—as its presidential candidate.

The DA, with its victory in the Western Cape and its improved performance in some other provinces, also drew voters away from the ANC. But this too stemmed from the tenacity of traditional political identities. A chief reason for the DA's success was that many of the "coloured" voters in the Western Cape who had voted ANC in 2004 switched back to the DA.[13] They did so in response to the province's ANC leadership, which they felt gave priority to the interests of black Africans and which they found culturally and politically foreign. Disillusioned, they concluded that the ANC was not a party for people like them, and they returned to the opposition. Moreover, the DA's supporters among racial minorities turned out in droves, hoping to keep a Zuma-led ANC from winning two-thirds of the vote. This boosted the DA's vote share, even in provinces that it lost. The DA remains a home for minority identities. It reached out to black African voters in this campaign, but without noticeable success.

The drop in support for smaller parties was not a decisive endorsement of a three-party system. Many of these parties' supporters switched to the DA or COPE because they were convinced by the argument that voting for these parties was more likely to strengthen the opposition than their traditional vote (even though voting for smaller parties does little to weaken the opposition in South Africa's PR system). Again, a key factor was identity-based antipathy toward the new ANC leadership. But the result was not to wipe out smaller parties—they simply won fewer seats. As long as the electoral system remains as it is, smaller parties will remain viable because they will offer a vehicle for particular identities to enjoy a voice in parliament.

Finally, the dramatic swing away from the IFP was also identity based. Some voters probably did vote ANC because Zuma is Zulu. Just as important, however, are voters' ties to traditional institutions—the more closely connected the voters are to the Zulu chieftaincy, the more likely they are to vote IFP. The party has lost votes in each successive election because voters drift from it to the ANC as they reduce their ties to the rural areas. It follows that KZN voters will desert the IFP if their chief changes sides or if they sense that the power of traditional leaders is waning. Both factors played a role in the 2009 contest.

The April election did not signal that South Africans are beginning to abandon identity politics in favor of voting their economic interests. Nor is there any reason why such a change would enrich democracy. Although academic commentators in South Africa tend to see identity voting as a symptom of political primitivism, identity politics plays a role in well-established democracies as well. There are numerous regional and religious parties across Western Europe, for example, and even in countries where parties do not overtly represent identities, voters may nonetheless choose their party allegiance based on identity—"red" and "blue" states in the United States, for instance, or Scotland's dependable support for Labour and southern England's backing for Conservatives— whatever the state of the economy or the perceived performance of the party.

That South Africans continue to vote their identities does not make them abnormal or backward; rather, it places them firmly in the democratic mainstream. What is worth noting about the 2009 elections, however, is the possibility that, by casting its votes based on the same criteria as before, the electorate may have opened up previously stifled democratic potential.

The Election and Democracy

Because the swing away from the ANC was not decisive enough to cause the party great alarm, the decline in its vote will not automatically induce ANC leaders to be more accountable and responsive to voters. Its reduced share of the vote was still higher than the 63 percent that it won in 1994's founding election. Politicians wishing to see the result as an ANC victory can cite most media observers in their support. Much of the reportage and commentary during the campaign had created the expectation that the ANC would lose far more ground than it actually did. Accordingly, instead of characterizing the outcome as a setback for the ruling party, the media dubbed it a triumph.[14]

The ANC's first-ever electoral retreat was thus portrayed as an advance, and the first sign that the ruling party was losing touch with some voters was instead presented as a confirmation of its near-organic connection with the electorate. Similarly, some ANC strategists keep comparing the result not to the previous election but to the outcome predicted by its early polls. Furthermore, neither the media commentary nor the ANC's understanding of the election takes into account that, months before the election, many voters said that they would not vote for the ANC but did so in the end. These voters were not expressing allegiance to the current leadership; they were expressing loyalty to the party in spite of that leadership.

It is therefore not clear that the ANC will view the results as a sign that it needs to take voters more seriously. Already there are indications that the warning is going unheeded. Like the Mbeki administration, the first Zuma cabinet is hoping to achieve more efficient government not by strengthening citizens' ability to hold it to account, but through central planning and coordination, to be exercised through a planning commission and a ministry for monitoring and evaluation, both located in the presidency.

While shifts in voting trends were far less dramatic than expected, the outcome may nonetheless prove crucial to the country's immediate economic and political future. Although COPE failed to meet its own exaggerated expectations, it will be a presence in both the National Assembly, with its 30 seats, and the provincial parliaments. (It won at least 4 seats in five of the nine provinces, including roughly a sixth of the seats in the Eastern Cape and Northern Cape.) This should increase the pressure on the ANC to show voters that it cares about them, because this opposition, unlike earlier rivals, competes for the ANC's own vote pool.

This change may yet prove to be the most important product of the election and the events preceding it. If COPE manages to survive—it has been plagued by internal problems but has enough seats nationally and provincially to make it a going concern—a new dynamic making for more vigorous democracy seems likely, as the votes of the vast majority of the electorate will be subject to contest.

The effect may not be immediate, especially if the ANC interprets voter loyalty in the face of all the pre-ballot warnings of disaffection as a mandate to continue business as usual. Such an interpretation would, of course, ignore the extent to which many ANC voters supported the party in spite of its governing style. Moreover, if the ANC believes that it will always win no matter what, it would probably see little reason to resolve its internal divisions. If the party follows this path, government will remain far less accountable than citizens want, but the result may be new splinter parties and more voter support for ruling-party rivals. The ANC could, however, choose to take this poll as a message to mend its internal fissures and reconnect with its voters. Citizens would then enjoy better government, and the ANC would prolong its appeal to the electorate.

There is evidence that the latter interpretation enjoys some support within the ANC leadership. While Mbeki's stock response to government failure was to centralize and insulate the regime from the criticism, the current leadership seems at least somewhat aware that it cannot get government to work unless it is more accountable. During the campaign, Zuma stressed citizens' role in holding officials to account and promised mechanisms making it easier to voice dissatisfaction with government officials and politicians who are not providing adequate public service.[15] Thus far, the only concrete attempt to implement the promise has been the creation of a "hotline" that people can call to lodge complaints (which will obviously be accessible only to those who have telephones). The mere acknowledgement, however, that government has a duty to report and respond to citizens is in itself important.

The change in leadership may also augur well for a foreign policy that supports human rights. During its tenure on the UN Security Council, South Africa protected the Burmese junta, but the new government has called for the release of opposition leader Aung San Suu Kyi.[16] While South Africa continues to support Zimbabwe's unity government, it now presents this as a strategic path to democracy and no longer defends Robert Mugabe. The 2009 elections may not have produced a dramatic or swift shift to deeper democracy, but it may have set in motion trends that will yield more democracy in the future, and thus may well prove a watershed in the country's democratic development.

Breaks in the political logjam are essential if democracy is to advance. But, while a more fluid politics opens opportunities, it also creates threats. There is no guarantee that the new government will continue to respect the constitution. The institutions that could be imperiled in this case are the judiciary, the media and, perhaps, the academy.

Zuma's legal problems, which were made to dissolve just days before the election, have triggered tension between ANC leaders and judges. The party seemed to regard kindness to Zuma as the sole test of whether the courts were executing their constitutional mandate: Judges were accused of being "counterrevolutionary" or hostile to democracy if they were hostile to Zuma.[17]

Immediately after national prosecutors withdrew charges against Zuma, Blade Nzimande, minister of higher education and South African Communist Party (SACP) general secretary, insisted on action to reform the judiciary. Although he claimed to support measures that would strengthen judicial independence, South Africa has a long history of politicians professing to extend freedoms when they plan the opposite—for example, universities were, under apartheid, strictly segregated by the Extension of University Education Act—and critics feared that Nzimande's goal was instead to control the courts. When Zuma used the same language in his State of the Nation address some weeks after the election, anxiety among ANC critics rose further.

Moreover, it is possible to undermine checks on government without changing the constitution, simply by appointing the right people to key posts. The chief justice and several Constitutional Court judges are due for mandatory retirement soon, and the government's choice of replacements will be an obvious indicator of its intentions. For example, some in the new leadership dislike Deputy Chief Justice Dikgang Moseneke because he delivered a speech promising to rein in ANC politicians who were not acting constitutionally.[18] If he is appointed chief justice, there will be reason for confidence that judicial independence will be respected. Should someone else take the position—particularly if it is someone close to Zuma—anxiety will mount.

For some time, the ANC has been calling for a media tribunal. ANC leaders, including Zuma, have groused about what they see as the public's limited ability to seek redress from newspapers that treat the public unfairly. Academic independence may be threatened if the University of South Africa caves in to demands by ANC-aligned youth organizations that the head of the school, Barney Pityana, be removed. These groups claim that calls for Pityana's removal stem from administrative issues and have nothing to do with his being a prominent member of COPE, but the coincidence is too great to be credible.

It remains to be seen whether these threats are serious—whether there is an ANC consensus on its approach to the judiciary, the media, and the academy, and what the party's intentions are. There are signs that the threat has been exaggerated: Concerns about the media seem to have translated into a plan to enhance ANC communication with the Fourth Estate. And Nzimande, the minister most likely to press the university to fire Pityana, has told him on behalf of the government that his job is safe. The animus against these bodies is not ideological but rather a reaction to institutions perceived as unsympathetic to Zuma. Support for Zuma among the new leaders is anything but unanimous, however, which may lessen the likelihood of new controls. Ultimately, the outcome will depend on debate among the leadership and the nature of the public's reaction.

The Economic Crisis and Accountable Government

South Africa has not been immune to the global economic downturn. While the major banks operate without state backing, the country has been affected by declines in investment and exports and is experiencing its first recession in seventeen years.[19] Because Zuma's election was supported by the ANC's leftwing allies, the Congress of South African Trade Unions (COSATU) and the SACP, the change in leadership was watched with some anxiety by the business community.

Expectations or fears of a shift leftward were always exaggerated, but they have also been rendered far less relevant by the economic crisis.[20] Like other market economies, South Africa must adjust to current realities by expanding fiscal policy to take up the slack of declining public investment. The more active role for the public sector sought by the left is now the subject of a consensus supported even by business. A task force of business, labor, and other key private actors has recommended actions designed to address the crisis. Thus the issue now is not whether the government will intervene—all key interests agree that it must—but whether it will do so effectively.

During the past few years, the government often has been ineffective. Changed economic circumstances mean that it needs to perform much better over the next few. To this end, technical expertise is important, but the chief requirement is greater government accountability. Without demands to account for its actions, government is unlikely to seek out the needed technical competencies. Likewise, if the government is to make any strides in terms of poverty reduction, it must begin to report and respond to the needs and concerns of the poor themselves. That was not the case under Mbeki, and the government's aloofness proved to be an enormous hindrance to any progress on this front.[21]

The election—and how the ANC chooses to respond to it—will potentially have great bearing on the prospects for more accountable government. Thus far, the ANC's response has been mixed, but it is more open to taking citizens seriously than the Mbeki administration. The planning commission and monitoring ministry may be inappropriate approaches, but are born of a recognition that voters want better government service. Zuma, knowing that his administration will be judged in part by its ability to protect citizens from economic hardship, signaled in his acceptance speech that addressing the economic crisis would be his priority.[22]

Nevertheless, it is too early to predict that the 2009 election will compel the government to rise to the challenge of providing the services that citizens need and want. In addition to other divisions within the ANC leadership, some in the new government are former Mbeki supporters, adding to the diversity. The next election for party president will be in 2012, and Zuma has said that he does not want a second term. Some press reports have claimed that the battle to succeed him has already begun and is stirring even more infighting among ANC leaders. COSATU, meanwhile, has claimed that Zuma does in fact want another term; if true, this would sharply reduce the incentives for further internecine squabbles. But should Zuma definitively bow out of the 2012 race, they would surely flare again.

These matters of internal party politics have potential consequences beyond the ANC. If party leaders are too absorbed with power struggles to address national priorities, divisions within the new government could stymie effective governance. The danger is that a great deal of attention will be paid to the concerns of politicians, but little or none to those of citizens. The Zuma cabinet is the biggest in the country's democratic history because of the need to accommodate many factions and individuals to prevent conflict in the party. This inclusive approach could make for more productive government by reducing resistance to official plans. It could, however, also mean that government is being structured to ensure that politicians are catered to at the expense of voters.

Most likely, the next five years will see an uneven combination of greater accountability mixed with continued concern for politicians over voters—real politics is usually more messy and uneven than the neat explanations of commentators would suggest. Inevitably, different ANC leaders will interpret the mandate conferred by the election differently, adding to the unevenness. What does seem clear, however, is that, in light of the economic crisis, effectual government performance will be the key issue of Zuma's presidency. In the end, South Africa's ability to weather the storm will depend in part on whether governing-party politicians take the election result as a cause for self-congratulation or as a warning.

NOTES

1. Dankwart A. Rustow, "Transitions to Democracy: Towards a Dynamic Model," *Comparative Politics* 2 (April 1970): 337–64.

2. Isaiah Berlin, "Two Concepts of Liberty," in Berlin, *Four Essays on Liberty* (London: Oxford University Press, 1969).

3. One exception has been harsh police treatment of grassroots protest movements, which, while not ordered by the government, has not been prevented by it. See "Bishop Rubin Phillip's UnFreedom Day Speech," 27 April 2008; available at *http://antieviction. org.za/2008/04/30/bishop-rubin-phillips-unfreedom-day-speech.*

4. Steven Friedman, "Who We Are: Voter Participation, Rationality and the 1999 Election," *Politikon* 26 (November 1999): 213–24.

5. Steven Friedman, "Voice for Some: South Africa's Ten Years of Democracy," in Jessica Piombo and Lia Nijzink, eds., *Electoral Politics in South Africa: Assessing the First Democratic Decade* (New York: Palgrave Macmillan, 2005), 3–22.

6. According to Minister of Finance Trevor A. Manuel, at the turn of this century, the government was allocating 57 percent of its spending to the poorest 40 percent of the population, and under 9 percent to the wealthiest 20 percent. Budget speech, 23 February 2000; available at *www.finance.gov.za.*

7. Steven Friedman, "South Africa: Globalization and the Politics of Redistribution," in Joseph S. Tulchin and Gary Bland, eds., *Getting Globalization Right: The Dilemmas of Inequality (*Boulder, Colo.: Lynne Rienner, 2005), 11–49.

8. "Let's Pretend to Consult," *City Press,* 2 August 2008; available at *http://jv.news24. com/City_Press/Features/0,,186-1696_2368908,00.html.*

9. Nthambeleni Gabara, "Voters' Roll Grows to 23-Million," *South Africa Info,* 11 February 2009; available at *www.southafrica.info/about/democracy/elections-110209.htm.*

10. Adam Habib, "Election Analysis: South Africa's 2009 Elections," *The Thinker,* May 2009, 12–14.

11. Election Monitoring Network, press statement, 20 April 2009; available at *www.idasa.org.za/index.asp?page=programme_details.asp%3FRID%3D75.*

12. "AEC Members Tear Gassed, Beaten and Arrested; Residents Lay Blame on ANC," Western Cape Anti-Eviction Campaign, Gugulethu AEC Press Update, 9 February 2009; available at *http://antieviction.org.za/2009/02/09/aec-members-tear-gassed-beaten-and-arrested-residents-lay-blame-on-anc.*

13. People classified as "coloured" under apartheid were of mixed race, Malay, or a residual category for those who were neither white, black African, nor Indian.

14. See, for example, *Sunday Times* (Johannesburg), 26 April 2009.

15. Amy Musgrave, "South Africa: Zuma Appeals for Joint Effort to Fix Hurdles," *Business Day* (Johannesburg), 20 April 2009.

16. "South Africa Calls for the Immediate Release of Aung San Suu Kyi," *Weekly Mail* (Cape Town), 22 May 2009; available at *www.mg.co.za/article/2009-05-22-sa-calls-for-immediate-release-of-aung-san-suu-kyi.*

17. Mohau Pheko, "If You Must Insult Judges, Mr. Mantashe, Raise Your Standard of Propaganda," *Sunday Times,* 19 July 2008.

18. "ANC Does About-Turn Over Moseneke Comments," *Mail and Guardian Online,* 17 January 2008; available at *www.mg.co.za/article/2008-01-17-anc-does-aboutturn-over-moseneke-comments.*

19. Mariam Isa, "Shrinking Factory Output Points to Rates Cut," *Business Day,* 13 May 2009.

20. Steven Friedman, "The Person May Change, But the Policy Lingers On," Thought Leader, *Mail and Guardian Online,* 11 December 2007, *www.thoughtleader.co.za/stevenfriedman/2007/12/11/changing-the-person-not-the-policy.*

21. Steven Friedman, "South Africa: Globalization and the Politics of Redistribution."

22. Parliament of South Africa, "Zuma Promises Five Years of Hard Work," statement, 6 May 2009; available at *www.info.gov.za/speeches/2009/09050810551001.htm.*

20

THE ILLUSION OF DEMOCRACY IN BOTSWANA

Kenneth Good

Kenneth Good *is adjunct professor in global studies at RMIT Univer-sity in Melbourne, Australia, and was professor of politics at the University of Botswana for fifteen years. He is the author, most recently, of* Diamonds, Dispossession, and Democracy in Botswana *(2008).*

Ketumile Masire, Botswana's longest-serving president (1980–98), wrote in his memoires that Botswana—in its combined record of economic growth, governance, and "democratic development"—was "un-matched in the developing world."[1] Since gaining independence from Britain in 1966, Botswana has regularly held multiparty elections that are deemed free and fair on the day, and its perceived level of corruption, as measured by Transparency International (TI), is lower than elsewhere in Africa. Yet the country's much lauded political stability is little more than ongoing ruling-party predominance, supported by a disempowered Parliament, a weighted electoral system, and a weak and divided opposition.

Over the course of almost three decades, Botswana enjoyed the highest rate of economic growth in the world, as its cumulative GDP per capita (GDPpc) quintupled. Diamonds fueled this rapid growth in the sparsely populated country, accounting for at least half the GDP, three-quarters of export earnings, and more than half of state revenue in the early-twenty-first century. This booming economy facilitated in-frastructure development in transport and communications and social investment in education and health, as the country moved from abject underdevelopment at independence to upper-middle-income (UMI) status and a GDPpc of US$6,180 in 2005. Substantial government spending (36 percent of GDP in 2005) rather than foreign aid and loans funded these achievements.

Botswana's government eagerly proclaims its broad success—in growth, governance, and democracy. Indeed, Freedom House has con-sistently rated Botswana as a Free country and a relatively liberal democracy since 1974. But for all the confidence of this assertion, the country's democracy has always been illusionary. Power is concentrated in the hands of the president, who is chosen by the ruling party rather than elected by the people, and since 1998 gains office in automatic succession from his predecessor. He is constitutionally empowered to act alone, enjoys sweeping powers of appointment, and holds in his hands all civil, military, and surveillance powers.

The 57-seat Parliament is popularly elected, but four additional MPs with full voting rights are appointed by the president. Parliament's independence and autonomy are limited. It is dependent on the presidency for its finances and administration, and while the president is entitled to prorogue or dismiss the legislature, the legislature has no power of impeachment. About 40 percent of the MPs in mid-2008 were either ministers or assistant ministers, while some 50 percent were mainly former civil servants or military personnel, who were either unable or disinclined to voice dissent. Parliament has never vetoed an executive decision or plan.[2]

In the 44 years since independence, elections have never resulted in a change of government. Polling in Botswana, moreover, has been notable for a turnout of well below 50 percent of eligible voters. The ruling Botswana Democratic Party (BDP) enjoys all the advantages of incumbency—in funding, transport, and communications, as well as access to the media—while the opposition, effectively the Botswana National Front (BNF) and Botswana Congress Party (BCP), is financially and organizationally weak and divided.

The simple-majority electoral system also disadvantages opposition parties. In 2004, for example, when opposition parties won 48 percent of the vote, they received only 23 percent of the parliamentary seats, while the BDP with barely 4 percent more of the popular vote gained 77 percent of seats. This hardly qualifies as a structural democracy, let alone a substantive one. Moreover, there appears to be some correlation between low voter turnout and ruling-party parliamentary strength: For example, when voter turnout was 32 percent in 1969, the BDP won 77 percent of the seats; when turnout dropped to 24 percent in 1975, the BDP won 84 percent; and when turnout jumped to 46 percent in 1994, BDP seats amounted to only 67 percent.[3] Officialdom expresses a ritual concern about voter apathy, but the low rates of electoral participation in Botswana might be better seen as rational, positive disengagement from a sterile and static political system.

Respect for the rule of law and for established institutions and processes declined after Lt. General Ian Khama became vice-president in 1998, and worsened when he automatically succeeded to the presidency on 1 April 2008. Power has become highly centralized and personalized around Khama, who remains simultaneously Kgosi Khama IV (paramount chief of the Bamangwato) and actively engaged with the Botswa-

TABLE—PRESIDENTS AND VICE-PRESIDENTS OF BOTSWANA, 1966–PRESENT

TENURE	PRESIDENT	VICE-PRESIDENT	PARTY
2008–present	Lt. Gen. Ian Khama	Lt. Gen. Mompati Merafhe	BDP
1998–2008	Festus Mogae	Lt. Gen. Ian Khama	BDP
1980–1998	Ketumile Masire	Festus Mogae (1992–98) Peter S. Mmusi (1980–92)	BDP
1966–1980	Seretse Khama	Ketumile Masire	BDP

na Defense Force (BDF); he is commander-in-chief and regularly operates military aircraft. Khama's government is highly militaristic, and
state agencies have even carried out extrajudicial killings. Respected
figures speak now of widespread fear among the people and of incipient
anarchy. In a year's time, governance and democracy have been so cor-
roded by Khama's idiosyncratic rule that even the country's diamond-
dependent economy is threatened.

Rising Wealth, Increasing Inequality

Botswana's first decade of independence was one of path-finding,
and was also characterized by government probity. As opportunities
arose in the mid-1970s for individuals—especially those well placed in
the BDP and the government—to amass wealth through intensified cattle production and corporate diamond extraction things began to change.
In 1975, the government launched the misnamed Tribal Grazing Land
Policy, which privatized communal land resources and in the process
offered big opportunities for ambitious cattlemen. Inside a decade, between seven-hundred and a thousand cattle ranches were established.
More than 12 percent of tribal land was zoned for commercial ranches,
while almost no land was reserved for the rural poor.

As the government implemented pro-growth policies that favored
the rich, inequalities widened along with the expanding economy.
Consultations with non–cattle owners about their land needs were cursory. Of the 4,500 San (also known as Bushmen or Basarwa) living in
Ghanzi as impoverished squatters, the district commissioner said that
they should be moved so that cattle owners could fence their land. By
the mid-1970s, large cattlemen, totaling at most 15 percent of the population, owned 75 percent of the national herd, while founding president Seretse Khama himself held about 30,000 cattle. Although such
policies hastened the growth of inequality, the impact of the widening
gap was delayed and muted as infrastructural development brought
broad benefits.

When in the 1980s economic growth reached world-record levels
under Ketumile Masire, Seretse Khama's successor, the fruits went directly to those at the top. The private-business activities of public servants were accorded legal recognition in 1982, allowing them to engage

in commercial agriculture, to own land and other property, and to hold shares in private companies. In 1990, senior bureaucrats' salaries were raised. At the same time, the government rejected proposals to raise the minimum wage for impoverished unskilled agricultural and domestic-service workers. Accordingly, income inequality widened over the subsequent decade: The poorest 40 percent of the population saw their income share drop from a total of 11.6 percent in 1993–94 to only 5.8 percent ten years later, while the share of the richest 20 percent rose from 59.3 percent at the start of the period to 70.9 percent in 2002–2003.

Despite years of high growth and wealth pouring into the country, successive BDP presidents failed to achieve structural economic development. Diamonds were used to invest in cash assets and for public expenditure and consumption. Diversification did not take place. In 2005 and 2006, manufacturing was still only 3.3 percent of GDP, and agriculture had collapsed to below 2 percent of GDP. Thus as diamond output slowed, so did economic growth. Moreover, gross capital formation and foreign direct investment were simultaneously declining.[4]

The social consequences of these limitations were severe. Unemployment in the early-twenty-first century was officially put at 24 percent, but unofficially assessed at closer to 40 percent. Poverty remains serious, with 49 percent of the population living on $2 a day in 2007, and Botswana's Human Development Index (HDI) scores were also inconsistent with its status as a relatively rich African country. The country's infant-mortality rate is invidious—more than four times the rate among most other middle-income countries. And its Global Hunger Index (GHI) scores have also worsened—declining during the same period in which poorer Ghana's scores were improving.[5] The country has also had one of the world's worst rates of HIV infection, although it was one of the first to provide antiretroviral drugs to infected citizens, helping to check the spread of the virus.

High economic growth stimulated greed among the ruling elite, and subsequently led to deteriorating probity and governance. The first signs of corruption came in 1986 with the Leno Affair, a quickly suppressed scandal involving high-ranking politicians and bureaucrats in the sale of prime government-owned property in the booming capital, Gaborone. The linkages between growth, spending, and graft soon escalated. Beginning in 1991, a series of corruption scandals burst into public view—huge sums squandered on a fraudulent contractor for the supply of books to primary schools; illegal land acquisitions in fringe areas of Gaborone; and fraud and misappropriation in the Ministry of Local Government and the Botswana Housing Commission (BHC). The most flagrant, however, was the near collapse of the National Development Bank (NDB) in 1994, brought about by government ministers. According to then–minister of finance (and future president) Festus Mogae, the NDB was owed millions in arrears. Among the bank's major debtors were Minister of Commerce and Industry Ponatshego Kedikilwe, Minister of Labor Patrick Balopi, and President Masire himself.

By 1994, however, the independent press was more active, making suppression of the scandal impossible, and the public was paying close attention. Early that year, when half the NDB staff were declared redundant, a list naming the bank's ministerial debtors and its top fifteen borrowers was circulated around Gaborone. Students demonstrated in support of the workers and against the debtor ministers. Three presidential commissions of inquiry into the textbook affair, the BHC, and illegal land sales were established in advance of the October 1994 elections, and their reports made public. Yet no inquiry was made into the NDB scandal. President Masire said that the NDB events had to be placed in the context of a country where "agricultural pursuits" were risky, and where the future depended on "people who venture." He also denied that there was anything wrong with his being "a successful farmer" while "holding the office of President" and determining the government's agricultural policies.[6]

Between 1985 and 1991, commercial-bank lending expanded by more than 30 percent a year, and state developmental expenditures by more than 35 percent. Credit was available at interest rates lower than the rate of inflation, and employment in the construction industry tripled. Masire claims that during these years the country saw little corruption, which he attributes to a "long-standing practice of open discussion" in Botswana that "encouraged transparency."[7]

Ex-minister David Magang, however, notes that Botswana's rulers have never welcomed divergent opinions, "especially when the subject is the president or his deputy."[8] Magang has stressed Masire's instrumental role in the corruption and mismanagement of the growth period, and how close it came to undermining the stability of ruling-party predominance. Easy money and cronyism were "the hallmarks of [Masire's] presidency." Ministers failed to service loans that they had awarded themselves because they expected their debts to be canceled, as they were on at least three occasions in the late 1980s.[9]

The high degree of elite corruption could not escape the public eye, however, and in 1994, people—among them school children, university students, and trade unionists—for the first time intervened in politics in significant numbers. The BNF's slogan for the elections that year was "Time for a Change," and the 1994 balloting did indeed mark a shift, as voter turnout improved and the opposition's parliamentary representation rose from 3 to 13 seats.[10]

Both the electoral results and the scandals involving the president and ruling party were highly problematic for the BDP and gave rise to factionalism within the party. One camp, headed by BDP secretary-general Daniel Kwelagobe and Kedikilwe, opposed the introduction of anticorruption measures, while the other main group, which included

Magang and Mogae, believed that reform was necessary in order for the BDP to hold on to power. President Masire took no steps to mend these divisions, and the discord thus "festered and became malignant."[11] Masire has since written that the factionalism was "not philosophical" but rather focused on personal gain—on whether, for instance, a new diamond-cutting factory should be located in Kwelagobe's hometown or in a rival's base. According to Masire, such divisions became "unbridgeable" and "greatly weakened the party and its ability to govern effectively."[12]

Between 1995 and 1998, a series of maneuvers meant as short-term palliatives to corruption and factionalism elevated Mogae and then Khama, both nonparty men. (Up to that point, Mogae had been a financial technocrat, above the party fray.) The stratagem involved a 1998 constitutional amendment enshrining the automatic succession of the vice-president to the presidency on completion of the president's term, his resignation (as in Masire's case), or death in office. This move protected Vice-President Festus Mogae from the Kwelagobe-Kedikilwe camp when Masire stepped down in March 1998, as the new arrangement denied Parliament any role in determining Masire's successor.

Mogae chose Ian Khama, the son of Botswana's first president, as his vice-president. Khama was expected to bring a new dynamism to the flagging, unprincipled BDP and to bring the party back together. Yet Mogae's example—for instance, disregarding laws that prohibited the vice-president from operating military aircraft—served to show Khama that the president is above the law. The vice-president took the lesson to heart. And although the level of corruption may have diminished somewhat as economic growth began to slow, there have been continuing legal and governance problems stemming from earlier excesses.

How Transparent?

Although Transparency International has given Botswana good marks, the country is obviously far from clean. It is true that there is an Ombudsman, but its powers are weak and limited. The Directorate on Crime and Economic Corruption (DCEC) was established by Mogae as a response to the major corruption in the 1990s. It has strong investigatory powers, but cannot prosecute without presidential approval. Botswana has no Freedom of Information legislation, no whistleblower-protection laws (instead it has punitive Confidence Laws to protect state agencies from public disclosure), and no register of the assets and incomes of MPs and ministers. And Parliament is unable to enforce accountability upon the executive.

Furthermore, Botswana dissociates itself from continentwide efforts against corruption. In 2006, it failed to ratify the African Union's (AU) Convention on Preventing and Combating Corruption. Likewise, despite the urging of its four representatives to the Pan-African Parliament (the legislative body of the AU), Botswana has remained outside the voluntary African Peer Review Mechanism intended to help AU member states improve governance and accountability.

Mineral dependency seems to promote economic and social inequality, corruption, and a lack of accountability. This has been widely recognized in oil-rich countries such as Saudi Arabia or Nigeria, but less so with regard to diamond wealth. In Botswana, the source of corruption, inequality, and domination is diamond production. The country's wealth has been reliant on the De Beers corporation's ability to maintain a world market based on the illusion of the high value, scarcity, and permanency of the gems. The De Beers Botswana Mining Company (Debswana) works in a close duopolisic relationship with the government—the chairman of Debswana's board of directors is also the permanent secretary in the Office of the President, and Debswana's managing director from 1992 to 2004 was a close friend of President Mogae and was described on his retirement as probably "one of the most powerful individuals in the country."[13]

The establishment in late 2006 of the Diamond Trading Company (DTC), a joint processing and marketing venture between the government of Botswana and DeBeers, has had major consequences. The country's acute dependency on the gems has deepened, although the possibilities for diversification within this sector have grown. At the same time, the government of Botswana is now responsible for the integrity of the luxury, essentially illusionary, gems. It was one thing for a secretive corporation to perform this task, but another for a formally democratic country to do so.

The agreement establishing the DTC was tied to a secret 2006 leasing arrangement for Jwaneng, the world's most profitable diamond mine. Diamond output in Botswana was expected to drop in two stages, and, if no new sources were found, to cease around 2029. Diamond beneficiation and aggregation—the main role of the new DTC—were uncertain and problematic, and the labor costs of jewelry making in Botswana were around five times higher than in India. In addition, although sixteen "sightholders" (authorized bulk purchasers of rough diamonds) had been accredited to DTC at the end of 2007, all were actually De Beers clients, and no independent companies were accredited to DTC in 2008. Near the end of that year, De Beers announced the indefinite postponement of aggregation processes in Botswana.

Finally, the diamond industry has taken a drubbing as consumers have become more conscious of "conflict diamonds"—rough diamonds illegally traded in conflict situations. Thus the Kimberley Process Certification Scheme (KPCS) was put into place in 2000 in order to regulate the trade in rough diamonds. The KPCS has been a partial success, but illegal trade and attendant violence continues in some countries—notably, in recent months and to a shocking extent in Marange in neighboring Zimbabwe. Although President Khama has voiced occasional criticism of Zimbabwean president Robert Mugabe's human-rights violations, he has not backed up his words with any proposed action against the entry of toxic Zimbabwean diamonds into the world market.[14]

The Ethnic Factor

Just as government policies favored the rich at the expense of the poor during the boom years, they had an equally pernicious effect on Botswana's ethnic minorities. For decades, the government has portrayed the country as ethnically homogenous—an assertion that is credible only when contrasted to the extreme tribalism that exists elsewhere on the continent. Yet the guise of ethnic harmony was easily maintained for many years, as Botswana's census does not collect data on ethnicity, despite repeated pleas for their inclusion from national and international agencies.

The Tswana is Botswana's predominant ethnic group, officially comprising about 80 percent of the population. Of the minority groups, the largest is the Kalanga, which officially accounts for roughly 10 percent of the population. Although ethnic strife is absent in Botswana, the country's minority groups have suffered discrimination and oppression. In the 1990s, educated professional elites of the Kalanga and Wayeyi groups organized to confront the prevailing ethnic relations, speaking out against minority government policies of "cultural genocide," and challenging official census numbers.

Tswana domination has come under attack from international organizations as well. The UN's Committee to End Racial Discrimination (CERD), for example, has noted significant human-rights violations in discriminatory legislation (in particular against the Wayeyi and San peoples) as well as in the preferences accorded to Setswana speakers in the workings of the court system and in education. In 2002, CERD criticized the "on-going dispossession of San people" in the Central Kalahari Game Reserve (CKGR).[15]

The subordination of the San has been the most extensive of any group. They confront discrimination on the issues of land, income, health, education, autonomous political organizations, and even their very identity. They are a people without a self-given name; the names that are attached to them are those used by their masters. Their official names are Basarwa and Remote Area Dweller (RAD)—the former carries the connotation of worthless fellow and is used as an epithet, while the latter replaces emotive ethnicity with the cooler but inexact factor of geography. The San's history was appropriated by outsiders and replaced by stereotypes of backwardness, ignorance, incapacity, and landlessness—all justifications for their subordination. Given the absence of census data, even their size is uncertain. Official estimates have remained unchanged over decades, numbering them at some 40,000. Informed scholarly estimates, however, suggest that in the 1990s San and other contiguous communities in the Kgalagadi and Ghanzi districts numbered about 120,000.

The San alone have no secure land rights in Botswana, and they are also the poorest people in the country. When they acquired access to small plots on RAD settlements beginning in the mid-1970s, the land was commonly of poor quality, and resources like water and good grazing—where they existed—were appropriated by outside cattle-men. Detailed scholarly studies indicate that the top monthly wages for San laborers in Ghanzi and surrounding areas during a decade of high growth was an eighth of the statutory minimum wage—itself dwarfed by top public servants' earnings, which were 35 times greater than the minimum wage and more than 270 times greater than the wages of a San laborer.

Enforced or coerced relocation—in order to make way for commer-cial farming and mining as well as ecological and tourism interests—has been the repeated experience of most San communities in Botswana. Most recently, some three-thousand people were evicted from the CKGR in two waves in 1997 and in 2002. According to the African Commis-sion on Human and Peoples' Rights (ACHPR), the evictions testified to "the refusal of the government of Botswana to recognize that the inhabitants of the area [had] ancestral rights to the territory." The gov-ernment's tactics—the withdrawal of vital hunting licenses, the closure of equally vital boreholes and the spillage of water tanks, the splitting up of families, and the spreading of rumors— had, according to a 2006 Botswana High Court ruling, "wrongfully and unlawfully" dispossessed the residents of the CKGR of their land.[16]

The First People of the Kalahari (FPK), founded in 1991, was the first San advocacy organization in Botswana. When its cofounder addressed the Botswana Society in Gaborone in 1992 on the problems his people were facing, he met with incomprehension and hostility. He was then summoned to police headquarters and told: "We own you. Don't think the [aid] donors will be here forever, and when [they] leave it will be just you and us."[17] FPK's call for recognition of the San's cultural rights was denounced as separatist, backward, and foreign-inspired.

The country's presidents have been consistent in their refusal to coun-tenance San concerns. For President Masire, the Basarwa were "the most unwilling [of all groups] to avail themselves of the opportunities for edu-cation, health care, and participation in the modern economy."[18] Mogae's views were worse, referring to the San as "stone-age creatures" doomed to extinction if they did not toe the government line.[19] And in December 2008, President Khama told San representatives that their hunting way of life was an "archaic fantasy."[20] And despite the 2006 High Court ruling in favor of the CKGR residents, the government has yet to provide them with the water sources and hunting licenses essential for their survival.

Extrajudicial Killings

On 13 May 2009, John Kalafatis, a longtime Gaborone resident, was shot dead in a hail of bullets while sitting in a car parked at a shopping center in the capital. The incident elicited no direct response from the government, but it stimulated good investigative reporting by Botswana's independent press. It soon emerged that the shooting was carried out by members of Military Intelligence (MI—a unit within the BDF), and the Directorate of Intelligence and Security (DIS)—a new organ with extraordinary powers.[21] The Kalafatis incident may be the most flagrant, but it is not the only instance of questionable killing.

At a press briefing shortly after Vice-President Lt. General Mompati Merafhe returned from accepting the "Best African Country of the Year" award in New York (the same week of the Kalafatis killing), he declared that "the integrity of this country cannot be determined by one or two shootings."[22] Ramadeluka Seretse, the minister of defense, justice, and security, had stated in Parliament that there had been twelve shootings involving police since April 2008, resulting in eight deaths. Dumelang Saleshando, a BCP parliamentarian, stated publicly that Kalafatis had been killed by the BDF and DIS, and that the latter was "a law unto itself." The DIS Tribunal—supposedly there to ensure the accountability of the Directorate—is actually composed of Khama's "political cronies," who are loyal first and foremost to the president.[23]

Government officials held a press conference shortly thereafter (though no private media were invited), during which they focused on exonerating the president rather than expressing any condolences or regrets to Kalafatis's family or to the country. Two days later, the Law Society of Botswana accused the government of shielding Kalafatis's killers. These events generated "immense fear" throughout the country, which appeared to be sliding toward anarchy.[24]

From there, the scandal escalated, as President Khama decided to sue the *Sunday Standard* for linking his name to the Kalafatis killing. This move elicited the ire of many, including former special advisor to President Mogae, Sidney Pilane, who accused Khama of ruling through fear and patronage. The public was weary, he said, of "a President who places himself at the centre of everything," and demanded that Khama ensure an independent and credible investigation into all the killings over the past year.[25] Attorney Dick Bayford, acting on behalf of the Kalafatis family, pointed out that "public perceptions" of the president were harsh: Khama "is nepotistic, corrupt and misuses government resources for personal and family gain"; as vice-president "he was contemptuous of parliament"; and under his presidency, security agents had killed unarmed citizens, and the

DIS had spied on people "because [the president] is paranoid about being displaced as leader of the ruling party."[26]

Media investigations uncovered information about the relationship between the security agencies: MI and the DIS often worked hand-in-hand in the planning and execution of operations. DIS agents operated under the "implicit assumption that they [had] . . . orders to shoot." When a suspect was killed by the DIS, the Police Service had the task of explaining the incident to the public and protecting the DIS from scrutiny.[27] Finally, details began to surface about a possible relationship between Khama and a businessman who may have been authorized to give orders to the DIS, BPS, and BDF.[28] In answer to a parliamentary question on the deaths of people at the hands of security agents since April 2008, Ramadeluka Seretse declared on June 30: "I do not see the need to set up an independent inquiry as a measure to restore confidence in the law enforcement agencies." If there had been any drop in confidence, he said, it was "due to the general increase in the rate of crime."[29]

The Power of the Presidency

President Ian Khama has exercised personal rule to an extreme. This may in part be due to the narrowness of his qualification for political leadership in a democracy. Prior to assuming the vice-presidency, his experience had been limited to the military and to chieftaincy and dynastic politics. His education appears to have peaked at the Sandhurst Military Academy in Britain (1972–74).

In 1977 when Ian Khama was 24 years old, his father, President Seretse Khama, appointed him Brigadier in the new BDF, bypassing more experienced and better-educated officers in what was then the Police Mobile Unit. Four years later, the younger Khama became the paramount chief of the Bamangwato people. On 31 March 1998, he formally resigned as commander of the BDF and registered as a member of the BDP. He was appointed minister of presidential affairs the next day. The day after, Mogae nominated him to be vice-president.[30]

Khama made clear from the outset that he was a *kgosi* (chief) first and foremost. He would move into high office only on his own terms. He refused to abdicate his chieftaincy, as the law and political practice required. He also brought with him his close attendants from the BDF, for whom new positions had to be created. Khama knew that the BDP, riven by factionalism and scandal, needed him more than he needed them. Thus he made his own rules and assumed far greater power than had previous vice-presidents.

Two further characteristics of Khama's personalized rule stand out: reliance on directives and decision making by caprice. In late 1998, a new bill passed restricting the serving of alcohol in restaurants to specific midday and evening hours. It was widely believed that Khama had influenced these regulations out of his aversion for alcohol. Later, president Khama established further restrictions. In 2008, he imposed a 30 percent alcohol tax and shortened the operating hours of liquor outlets without any regard for the impact of these measures on production, sales, and employment at Kgalagadi Breweries (one of the country's biggest manufacturers) or on the entertainment sector.

In March 2009, the president addressed social behavior by issuing a directive establishing a detailed dress code for bureaucrats. Declaring that it was "mandatory for public employees to dress in a manner that reflects credit on the Public Service," the instructions threatened punishment and job loss if employees came to work in tight skirts or pants, sleeveless tops, or clothing that exposed cleavage, backs, stomachs, or underwear. The measures were clearly directed more at women than men.

The state extended its control over personal communications, planning to install by December 2006 a high-tech surveillance network to intercept all cell-phone and electronic mail entering and leaving Botswana. When the system encountered problems, the government called for the registration of all cell-phones in the country. Those who failed to record their identity details by the end of 2009 would be disconnected.

Khama has frequently insisted that democracy demands discipline, and the latter appears to override the former in his thinking. He likewise seems convinced that moral weakness abounds in Botswana. Vice-President Merafhe has voiced his agreement, noting that there is "moral decay in society," and that if people failed to follow the country's leadership, the leadership would "borrow some disciplinary measures from the military."[31]

While Khama is agitated about what he perceives to be Botswana's shaky morality, the Afrobarometer found in October 2008 that the people themselves voice greatest concern over economic problems, with unemployment at the top, followed by poverty and rising food prices. A significant majority—67 percent—of respondents felt that the government had failed badly in tackling job creation. And while 64 percent of respondents were unhappy with the government's handling of inflation in 2003 and 2005, no less than 87 percent were displeased in 2008.[32] Other reports, however, suggest strong public support for Botswana's democracy.

Meanwhile, Batswana's rejection of one-party rule, one-man rule, and military rule remained strong, and in the case of the latter two had grown even more firm, perhaps as a result of Khama's "propensity to act alone and rule by decree." Popular dislike for rule by one man rose from 86 percent of respondents in 1992 to 92 percent in 2008. People strongly disliked military rule, with 89 percent rejecting it. The Afrobarometer noted the growing public perception that the military had been "making inroads into the civil service."[33]

Such perceptions accorded with the facts. The entry of the military into government had begun in April 1998, but it increased after April 2008. Lt. General Merafhe became vice-president, former captain Kitso Mokaila became minister for the environment, and Ramadeluka Seretse, minister of justice, defense, and security, was a BDF brigadier. Seretse's ministry includes the BDF, the police, the DIS, the Office of the Attorney General, public prosecutions, and the DCEC. The appointment of military men reportedly cascaded downward as well, with Colonel Moakohi Modisenyane at the Central Transport Organization, and Colonel Silas Motlalekgosi becoming head of the prisons service. Colonel Duke Masilo became deputy senior private secretary to the president, and Tefo Mokaila became private secretary to Khama.[34]

President Khama's inner circle of advisers has included his nephew, his former brother-in-law, his cousin by marriage, and various trusted friends—some of whom serve in the government, some in the media, some in the business community, and some of course in De Beers.[35] The president's reliance on a band of relatives and trusted loyalists has diminished the role of established institutions and processes. To hold the office of vice-president, for example, one must be elected to Parliament. Khama won uncontested the safe BDP seat of Serowe North in 1998 after the incumbent became high commissioner in London. When Khama prepared to relinquish the seat to assume the presidency (the president holds no elected office), he publicly declared that his younger brother Tshekedi would inherit the electorate directly from him without the usual practice of a primary election. Tshekedi duly gained the seat unopposed. Since Tshekedi has a twin brother, Anthony, and his own ambitions, the chain of dynastic preferment may not end there.

President Khama has never addressed a press conference. In July 2009, he rebuffed an invitation from the Botswana National Youth Council to participate in a face-to-face debate with other political leaders in preparation for national elections in October. The BDP soon followed up his rejection with a preemptory order instructing the Youth Council to terminate its debate program immediately. In sum, Khama's governmental style is "reclusive, divisive, secretive [and] isolationist," and "contemptuous of such other organs as the media, civic society and the opposition."[36]

Curbing presidential excess is no easy task constitutionally. People have expressed a distaste for unelected militaristic government, and reputable figures warn of anarchy. But the capacity of the constitutionally based autocracy for self-perpetuation is strong, as was seen in the late 1990s when Masire was able to survive despite corruption, popular reversals, and factionalism. Nonetheless, Khama's rule stands out for the heavy stress that he has placed on centralizing power and his comparative neglect of socioeconomic development.

Although he was brought in by Mogae to cure factionalism and revive the BDP, Khama's failures were on full public display in July 2009 as the BDP nearly split in two—with one faction backed by Khama himself and the other (vehemently denounced by the president) by Kwelagobe and Kedikilwe. When delegates chose the Kwelagobe-Kedkilwe camp at the party congress in July, Khama tried to nullify the results. National elections were then three months away. Socioeconomic problems remain sharp, and Khama seems unable or unwilling to address them. The viability both of the diamond economy and of presidentialism are threatened. The president's autocratic tendencies may intensify, but with collapsing legitimacy. The likely trajectory of the country is a downward spiral.

NOTES

1.Quett Ketumile Joni Masire, *Very Brave or Very Foolish? Memoirs of an African Democrat,* ed. Stephen Lewis (Gaborone: Macmillan Botswana, 2006), vii.

2. Jonathan Kaunda, *The Progress of Good Governance in Botswana 2008* (Gaborone: BIDPA, 2008), 31, 43.

3. Mpho Molomo and Wilford Molefe, "Voters and Electoral Performance of Political Parties in Botswana," and Adam Mfundisi, "Civil Society and Voter Education in Botswana," in Zibani Maundeni, ed., *40 Years of Democracy in Botswana* (Gaborone: Mmegi, 2005), 102, 165. Note that not all eligible voters bother to register, hence this figure exaggerates turnout.

4. Kaunda, *The Progress of Good Governance in Botswana 2008,* 51, 54.

5. Von Grebmer et al., "Global Hunger Index: The Challenge of Hunger 2008," International Food Policy Research Institute, Washington, D.C., 2008, 36–37.

6. For details see Kenneth Good, "Corruption and Mismanagement in Botswana: a Best-Case Example?" *Journal of Modern African Studies* 32 (September 1994): 499–521.

7. Masire, *Very Brave or Very Foolish,*166–67 and 239.

8. David Magang, *The Magic of Perseverance* (Cape Town: Centre for the Advanced Study of African Societies, 2008), 459–60.

9. *Botswana Gazette,* 30 March 1994.

10. For an account of the protest action against corruption, authoritarianism, and state suppression, see Kenneth Good, "Towards Popular Participation in Botswana," *Journal of Modern African Studies* 34 (March 1996): 53–77.

11. Magang, *Magic of Perseverance,* 478–79.

12. Masire, *Very Brave or Very Foolish?,* ix, 134–35.

13. Kenneth Good, *Diamonds, Dispossession, and Democracy in Botswana* (Oxford and Johannesburg: James Currey and Jacana Media), 17–18.

14. See, for example, Human Rights Watch, *Diamonds in the Rough: Human Rights Abuses in the Marange Diamond Fields of Zimbabwe,* June 2009.

15. Good, *Diamonds, Dispossession, and Democracy in Botswana,* 108–09.

16. See Good, *Diamonds, Dispossession, and Democracy in Botswana,* ch. 5; and *Sesana and Others v. Attorney General* (52/2002) [2006] BWHC 1 (13 December 2006), available at *www.saflii.org/bw/cases/BWHC/2006/1.html.*

17. Good, *Diamonds, Dispossession, and Democracy in Botswana,* 125.

18. Masire, *Very Brave or Very Foolish,* 235.

19. Quoted in Good, *Diamonds, Dispossession and Democracy,* 124.

20. Quoted in Survival International, *Press Release,* 24 September 2009.

21. Republic of Botswana, Intelligence and Security Bill, 2006, *Government Gazette Extraordinary,* 3 November 2006. The DIS was established to combat "subversive activities from the country's detractors"; its officers could use firearms when "necessary and reasonably justifiable"; they had wide powers of arrest and detention without warrant; their powers were undefined and threatening; and they were appointed on terms and conditions chosen by the president.

22. *Mmegi Online,* 19 May 2009.

23. Saleshando's letter to the editor, *Mmegi Online,* 20 May 2009. Brigadier Seretse is first cousin to Ian Khama. The members of the Tribunal were Isaac Seloko, a member of the Central Committee of the BDP as chair; Tsetsele Fantan, cousin to Khama; and Adolf Hirschfeldt, a former police officer. At the top of the DIS was Isaac Kgosi, who had been a close associate of Khama during his long years as BDF Commander and was later personal secretary to Khama during his tenure as vice-president.

24. *Mmegi Online,* 15 May 2009.

25. *Sunday Standard Online,* 7 June 2009.

26. *Sunday Standard Online,* 31 May and 1 June 2009.

27. *Sunday Standard Online,* 7 June 2009.

28. *Mmegi Online,* 19 June 2009, and *Sunday Standard Online,* 21 June 2009.

29. *Mmegi Online,* 2 July 2009.

30. His installation in Serowe constituted the resurrection of the Khama dynasty. Monageng Mogalakwe, in *Mmegi Online,* 10 July 2009 (reprinted from 2003), and Mike Mothibi, *Mmegi,* 10 April 1998.

31. *Sunday Standard Online,* 22 February 2009.

32. "Perspectives on Economic Management in Botswana: Jobs and Widespread Wealth Elude Even a Well-Managed Economy," Afrobarometer Briefing Paper No. 62, March 2009.

33. "Demanding Democratic Rule: Batswana Support Democracy and Reject Non-Democratic Alternatives," Afrobarometer Briefing Paper No. 61, March 2009.

34. *Mmegi Online,* 2 April 2008.

35. "Of the Khama's, by the Khama's, for the Khama's," *Mmegi Online,* 27 February 2009. See also Gideon Nkala, "Khama's Kitchen Cabinet," *Mmegi Online,* 27 March 2008.

36. The Watchdog, *Sunday Standard Online,* 2 February 2009.

21

ZAMBIA: ONE PARTY IN PERPETUITY?

Kate Baldwin

Kate Baldwin *is a doctoral candidate in political science at Columbia University. She is writing a dissertation on clientelism and redistribution based on field research in Zambia.*

On 2 November 2008, Rupiah Banda was sworn in as Zambia's fourth president. The death of his predecessor Levy Mwanawasa less than three months earlier had triggered an unanticipated presidential election, and Banda had run as the candidate of the ruling party, the Movement for Multiparty Democracy (MMD). His election was not as smooth as the party had hoped it would be. The installation ceremony was hastily arranged just hours after the official results were announced, a full five days after polling was supposed to finish. The final margin of victory was razor slim, a mere 35,209 votes out of 1,791,806 ballots cast. In spite of these blemishes, however, the event was significant, as it was the first time an African country had selected a new leader peacefully through the ballot box following the death of a president.[1] In addition, the MMD became the first African party in a multiparty presidential regime to transfer power between three different elected leaders without losing office.[2]

The conventional wisdom is that incumbent governments in Africa rarely lose elections, and the overall empirical trends support this idea. In the past twenty years, incumbent parties in sub-Saharan Africa have won 80 percent of elections that they have contested.[3] However, the conventional wisdom needs to be qualified slightly to distinguish between incumbent presidents and incumbent parties. Although incumbent presidents win 86 percent of elections they contest, incumbent parties win only 57 percent of the presidential elections they contest following leadership transitions. Second-generation parties, formed after a country's independence, are particularly unlikely to survive a leadership transition. Within this category, only the People's Democratic Party (PDP) in Nigeria and the MMD have maintained power after leadership transitions, and the PDP victory was severely tainted by electoral fraud.

Why has the MMD enjoyed such a long run in office? The party's grip on power is not due to the inability of politicians and civil society groups to mobilize opposition. Zambians have demonstrated both the willingness and the capacity to throw individual "big men" out of power. During the 1991 elections, political leaders and civil society groups coordinated to defeat independence leader Kenneth Kaunda. In 2001, politicians and a coalition of non-governmental organizations thwarted the MMD's first president, Frederick Chiluba, in his bid for a third term. Individual big men have been removed from the Zambian political scene on more than one occasion, but the MMD has hung onto power across two different leadership transitions. In 2001, the party survived the transition of power from Chiluba to the MMD's second leader, Levy Mwanawasa, and in 2008, it successfully managed the unexpected transition to Banda's leadership following the death of Mwanawasa.

The MMD's unusual success at managing leadership transitions has not been the result of an ingenious master plan. Instead, a series of small decisions and unplanned events have allowed the party to avoid the campaign challenges and internal fractionalization that typically befall parties following leadership transitions. Two factors have been particularly important in explaining the MMD's success. First, during both transitional elections, the man in the president's office believed that he had a personal stake in the election outcome. President Chiluba thought that he could pull strings from behind the scenes following the election, and acting President Banda knew he would be installed as president provided that the MMD won the polls. In both election campaigns, the individual with access to the enormous resources and influence concentrated in the president's office was firmly on board.

However, the party's enormous abuse of power in the 2001 and 2008 elections is not sufficient to explain its longevity. After all, politicians and civil groups successfully prevented Kaunda from returning to office and Chiluba from seeking a third term in spite of the vast resources each of these leaders spent trying to remain in office. The second key factor is the MMD's practice of rotating leadership between different ethnic groups. This has created a situation in which politicians and voters from across Zambia see opportunities for achieving their goals within the governing party, and it has prevented a broad opposition coalition from coalescing against the MMD. The same individuals concerned by the prospects of a "president for life" are less alarmed by the idea of a "party in perpetuity" because they believe that they or their representatives may be the next to lead the MMD.

Before the MMD

Zambia achieved independence from the British crown on 24 October 1964. The challenges of governance were high in this landlocked,

MAP—PROVINCES AND MAJOR LINGUISTIC GROUPS IN ZAMBIA

scarcely populated, and multiethnic country. Zambians commonly cite the fact that their country has 73 tribes, though the census contains only 61 tribal identities. These tribes divide into five main linguistic groups—the Bemba speakers in the north, the Tonga speakers in the south, the Lozi speakers in the west, the Nyanja speakers in the east, and the Northwestern linguistic group in the region of the same name. Bemba speakers are the largest group, with about 30 percent of Zambians speaking Bemba as their first language.

At independence, Zambia adopted a presidential system, with a parliament and an executive president elected directly by citizens. Multiparty competition was permitted in the first two elections in 1964 and 1968, but the United National Independence Party (UNIP) and its leader Kenneth Kaunda had no serious challengers in either contest. By the early 1970s, support for the opposition parties had grown, and the president decided it would be prudent to declare the country a one-party state prior to the third elections in 1973. Over the next eighteen years, the country continued to hold elections, but all parliamentary candidates were required to be members of UNIP, and Kaunda was the only candidate on the presidential ballot. The country's economy also began a steady downward decline, due to a combination of falling copper prices

TABLE 1—ELECTION RESULTS BY PARTY, 1991–2008

PARTY	PRESIDENTIAL VOTE SHARE (%)					ELECTED PARLIAMENTARY SEATS (%)			
	1991	1996	2001	2006	2008	1991	1996	2001	2006
MMD	75.76	72.59	29.15	42.98	40.63	83.33	87.33	46.00	50.00
UNIP	24.24	--	10.12		--	16.67	--	8.67	
UPND	--	--	27.20	25.32*	19.96	--	--	32.67	17.33*
FDD	--	--	13.17		--	--	--	8.00	
PF	--	--	3.40	29.37	38.64	--	--	0.67	28.67

*These percentages are for the UDA, an electoral alliance formed by the UPND, FDD, and UNIP prior to the 2006 election.

and economic mismanagement. Bread riots and a failed coup in 1990 provided the impetus for a coalition of civil society groups to come together to lobby for the reintroduction of multiparty democracy. Facing increasing social unrest, Kaunda changed the constitution in December 1990 to reintroduce multiparty politics.

Since the global political opening that began in 1989, Zambians have shown that they will not tolerate presidents for life. Politicians and civil society organizations have mobilized against individual big men trying to bend the rules to prolong their stay in power. However, these groups have not shown the same level of opposition when rules are breached to keep the governing party in power. Furthermore, the individuals mobilizing against the big men who breached the rules of the game often had an extremely instrumental commitment to protecting the law from encroachment.

Given an opening, Zambians were quick to mobilize against Kaunda in 1991. Leaders of labor unions, business organizations, and the bar association joined the opposition movement. This motley coalition registered as a political party, the Movement for Multiparty Democracy, in January 1991, and it elected Frederick Chiluba, a trade-union leader, as its presidential candidate. Although some MMD members may have been motivated by a normative commitment to democracy, many simply viewed the party as an alternative conduit to power. The opposition contained large numbers of individuals with personal grievances against Kaunda's leadership; according to Carolyn Baylies and Morris Szeftel, more than a fifth of the new MMD candidates had suffered "dismissal from office, exclusion from election, arrest and detention without trial, and public humiliation" during the Kaunda era.[4]

The results of the 1991 elections indicated that voters were committed to a change in leadership. The playing field disadvantaged the MMD. The ruling party flew Kaunda around the country in an army helicopter and distributed T-shirts and food at its campaign events. Even so, the MMD managed a resounding victory, as the figures in Table 1 above indicate. However, this remarkable success may have reflected excitement about ousting an unpopular leader, rather than voters' commitment to democracy or the rule of law. The fact that many citizens had turned out to dance in the streets following false rumors of a coup against Kaunda in 1990 suggests that Zambians may have been committed to turnover by any means.[5]

Zambians' opposition to "presidents for life" was demonstrated again during the 1996 presidential election. International observers made much of the fact that Chiluba disqualified Kaunda from running by amending the constitution to require Zambian ancestry of all presidential candidates. UNIP subsequently boycotted the election and called for its supporters to do the same. However, most Zambians were unbothered by the constitutional amendment. According to Michael Bratton, "by largely ignoring the boycott and granting the MMD a second term, most Zambians indicated that they hoped that the 'old man' (Kaunda) would quietly step aside from politics."[6] The return of a previous "big man" was prevented, but at the expense of the constitution.

In 2001, politicians and civil society thwarted the new "big man" attempting to impose himself as "president for life." As Chiluba's second term came to an end, a number of his supporters lobbied to change the constitution to allow a third term. This triggered a highly coordinated response from politicians and civil society. Although Chiluba used his access to resources to encourage some media sources, NGOs, church leaders, and traditional chiefs to support his bid, he was ultimately unable to silence his critics. Approximately eighty politicians signed an anti-third-term petition, including many senior cabinet ministers. When this failed to stop Chiluba's bid, more than a third of parliamentarians signed a petition calling for the impeachment of the president on grounds of corruption and abuse of office. Again, personal political ambitions played an important role in this campaign. Although the rhetoric surrounding these petitions emphasized the sanctity of the constitution, a number of the ministers who spoke out against the third term harbored presidential ambitions and subsequently ran for president on opposition tickets.

At the same time, a coalition of non-governmental organizations, church groups, and the Law Association of Zambia organized a campaign against the third term from outside parliament. Between February and May 2001, a number of cities held public demonstrations, and citizens wore green ribbons to show their opposition to the amendment. In rural areas, some traditional chiefs voiced their disapproval. Ultimately, Chiluba was forced to take notice of this widespread opposition and called off his bid for a third term.

The extraordinary mobilization of politicians and civil society groups in 1991 and 2001 indicates that these groups have the commitment and the capacity to ensure that individual big men step down. Yet these actors have been less persistent and less effective in demanding turnover of the governing party. Although opposition parties have consistently challenged the MMD, the party has not lost a single presidential election since it first entered the political scene in 1991.

The MMD faced multiple challengers in the transitional election in 2001. The United Party for National Development (UPND) had formed in the late 1990s and was led by well-known businessman Anderson Mazoka. During Chiluba's failed bid for a third term, a number of MMD members broke away to form the Forum for Democratic Development (FDD) and the Heritage Party. UNIP also fielded candidates in almost every constituency, and numerous smaller parties had significant support in particular regions. At the end of a hard (and unevenly) fought campaign, Mwanawasa beat Mazoka by just 33,997 votes. The president won less than 30 percent of the popular vote, hardly a strong result but sufficient to claim victory under the country's plurality rules. The MMD also formed a minority government in parliament, having won only 68 of the legislature's 150 elected seats.[7]

The MMD won cleaner presidential and parliamentary elections in 2006. The death of Mazoka just a few months before the balloting to the elections made the UPND less of a threat, in spite of the alliance it had formed with the FDD and UNIP prior to elections. Although former MMD minister Michael Sata and his party, the Patriotic Front, mounted significant opposition to the MMD in the north of the country, Mwanawasa won the three-way race by a comfortable margin, and the MMD secured half of the elected parliamentary seats. The party's victory in the 2008 presidential by-elections was less assured, given the death of Mwanawasa less than three months earlier. Mwanawasa's vice-president, Banda, faced the same major competitors that Mwanawasa had faced in 2006, and just barely edged out Sata this time around.

The MMD has now been in power continuously for eighteen years through five elections. Although the last three elections have been very competitive, the MMD has always eked out victories. Most remarkably, the party has held onto power through two leadership transitions. This is a feat few other parties have accomplished in presidential regimes.

Why Are Leadership Transitions So Difficult for Parties?

Although incumbent presidents rarely lose elections in Africa, incumbent parties have much worse odds of retaining power following leadership transitions. In Benin, Kenya, Ghana, Mali, Liberia,[8] and Sierra Leone, incumbent parties have been rejected at the ballot box after adopting a new leader. Across sub-Saharan Africa, incumbent parties who have adopted new leaders lose power about half of the time. This is due to the fact that posttransition elections tend to be both *more competitive* and *fairer* than elections with incumbent presidents.

Posttransition elections are typically more competitive because the process of choosing a new leader divides the incumbent party. The concentration of power in the president's office encourages ambitious politicians to aim for this position, and vacancies at the top of the incumbent party often attract a dozen contenders. These candidates mobilize groups of supporters around them, and since only one of these factions ultimately wins the party leadership, the losing groups frequently break away and form their own parties. In Mali, Adema presidential candidate Soumad'la Cissé lost the 2002 elections after a number of senior Adema leaders splintered off and ran against him. The Sierra Leone People's Party lost a large section of its traditional support base and, consequently, the 2007 presidential election when Charles Margai, the son of the party's founder, formed a new party upon losing the leadership race. Similarly, Raila Odinga precipitated the downfall of the Kenya African National Union by leading the "Rainbow Alliance" out of the party after President Daniel arap Moi imposed Uhuru Kenyatta as his successor in 2002. Malawi provides a slight variation on this theme in that the United Democratic Front largely held together during the 2004 campaign but then lost power due to fractionalization immediately after the election.

In addition, posttransition elections are typically fairer than elections with incumbent presidents. This is because incumbent parties depend heavily on presidents using the prerogatives of their office to help them win elections. African presidents have access to vast amounts of discretionary resources. They control slush funds, vehicles, and other resources that facilitate the campaigning process. They can also use presidential directives to pass populist policies that will increase support for their parties. Finally, presidents generally exert significant control over electoral commissions, the courts, and other state institutions. Presidents usually control appointments to these institutions and, as a result, the individuals heading them are often partial to the president's interests. In contrast, political parties and individual legislators in Africa typically control minimal resources, have limited policy-making influence, and enjoy less direct influence over key state institutions. As a result, incumbent parties depend on the president to tilt rules, resources, and policies in their favor.

The stakes of personally holding office are high in Africa, and this encourages presidents to abuse their offices to ensure their own reelection. In contrast, presidents who *truly* anticipate standing aside after an election may not benefit particularly from keeping their party in power, and they are probably less willing to bend the rules in their party's favor. Admittedly, the number of politicians in this group is small. Wherever possible, presidents facing term limits attempt to handpick a successor. However, in places where presidents are unable to enforce their choices due to institutionalized party procedures, they appear less willing to twist rules and redirect public resources. In Mali, Adema held party primaries to select its candidate, and outgoing president Alpha Oumar Konaré was uninvolved in the 2002 election campaign. In Ghana, the New Patriotic Party selected its presidential candidate for the 2008 election at a party convention; outgoing president John Kufuor backed one of the losing candidates and subsequently played a limited role in the general campaign. In Benin, Mathieu Kérékou had only a loose relationship with any of the parties in his "Presidential Movement," and he refused to endorse any candidate in the 2006 elections. Given that the president, not the party, controls the lion's share of the resources in these countries, it is not surprising that international and domestic observers judged each of these elections to be very clean.

Although incumbent parties in presidential regimes have a difficult time navigating the more evenhanded and competitive elections that follow leadership transitions, they have had greater success following leadership changes in parliamentary regimes. Parliamentary constitutions typically contain greater provisions for changing government leadership between elections, allowing incumbent parties to avoid entering elections immediately following fractious leadership races with lame-duck heads of government who may not be willing to abuse their office for the party's gain. The country of Botswana and its ruling party, the Botswana Democratic Party, have each had three leadership changes, all in off-election years. Similarly, the African National Congress was able to remove Thabo Mbeki from the South African presidency seven months in advance of the 2009 elections. Incumbent parties in presidential regimes do not typically have this option.

So how has the MMD in Zambia managed to avoid the hazards involved in leadership transitions not once but twice? In order to stay in power, the party has had to keep the electoral playing field skewed in its favor, while reining in the growth of splinter parties. By good fortune, the individual in charge of the president's office in both 2001 and 2008 felt personally invested in the election outcome and was willing to push the limits of legality to facilitate the MMD's re-election. However, this in itself was not sufficient to ensure MMD victories. Politicians and civil society groups in Zambia have ousted presidents in spite of their vast power. The second key component has been the MMD's practice of rotating leadership between different ethnic groups. Consequently, politicians and voters from all regions of the country perceive opportunities for advancement within the party, reducing their incentives to mobilize against the MMD.

The Power of the President's Office

During the 2001 and the 2008 Zambian elections, the president's office managed the MMD's campaign, providing the party with access to resources and influence over the electoral process that it could not have managed on its own. After Chiluba's quest for a third term had been routed, he handpicked Mwanawasa to succeed him and subsequently became highly invested in Mwanawasa's electoral campaign. Chiluba is thought to have selected Mwanawasa in order to balance change with controllability. The MMD needed to offer evidence of a leadership change to the groups who had opposed Chiluba's third term bid so forcefully, but at the same time, Chiluba hoped to continue to control power from behind the scenes.

Mwanawasa's differences from Chiluba were both ethnic and substantive. While Chiluba is a Bemba-speaking Lunda whose family is from Luapula province, Mwanawasa was a Lenje whose family was from Central province. Chiluba's regime was believed to be extremely corrupt, but Mwanawasa had a reputation for honesty. He had been Chiluba's first vice-president from 1991 until 1994 when he resigned, citing corruption within the government. However, Mwanawasa lacked charisma, and he did not have strong grassroots support, leading Chiluba to believe he could control him. In addition, a serious car accident in 1991 left Mwanawasa with a permanent speech impediment, and his political opponents cruelly referred to him as "the cabbage" to suggest a lack of mental acumen. Chiluba needed to personally lobby NEC members to ensure that his pick was selected over more high-profile politicians who had indicated an interest in the presidency, including longtime minister and fellow Bemba-speaker Michael Sata.

Convinced that he would be able to pull strings from behind the scenes after the election, Chiluba managed the entire 2001 campaign for the MMD. Mwanawasa was conspicuously absent from many of the MMD's rallies and campaign meetings; instead, Chiluba took the lead, bringing the full power of the president's office to the campaign. He instituted programs to sell government-owned houses to tenants at favorable prices and to fund new homes for traditional chiefs. In addition, the Office of the President mobilized large amounts of government funds for the MMD's campaign. According to testimony provided to the Supreme Court, the Office of the President used about US$4 million from government bank accounts in Lusaka and London to bribe former president Kenneth Kaunda and traditional chiefs, and to purchase 158 vehicles, 1500 bicycles, and 300 bales of second-hand clothes for campaign use.[9] Chiluba's influence over the electoral commission may also have adversely affected the ability of opposition members to register to vote. Zambian citizens require a National Registration Card (NRC) prior to registering to vote, but the NRC registration drives began suspiciously late in opposition strongholds, and they were overseen by political appointees loyal to Chiluba.[10]

Chiluba's maneuvering allowed the MMD to squeak back into office. Although observers noted some irregularities in the tabulation process, the main problems were due to the president's manipulation of resources and rules prior to election day. Chiluba was ultimately wrong in his prediction that he could control Mwanawasa. The latter encouraged parliament to lift Chiluba's immunity from prosecution in 2002, and the former president was put on trial for corruption. However, Chiluba's miscalculation was crucial in ensuring the MMD's victory through the leadership transition.

In 2008, the MMD selected Mwanawasa's vice-president, Banda, as its presidential candidate, thereby ensuring the person with the greatest incentive to secure an MMD victory was also the person with the greatest influence over the electoral process. The Zambian constitution provides for the vice-president to take over in the event of the president's incapacitation, and Banda had been acting as president for two months prior to Mwanawasa's death. Banda was considered an MMD outsider, brought in by Mwanawasa to increase the profile of Easterners in the party after voters in this region shifted their support to the MMD in the 2006 election. When the president died, Banda faced stiff competition from 14 other MMD members hoping to be the party's candidate in the special presidential election. However, the MMD's National Executive Committee overwhelmingly backed Banda, suggesting that they appreciated the electoral importance of access to the president's office.

The acting president subsequently used his policy-making power, his access to state resources, and his institutional connections to facilitate an MMD victory. He accelerated a program to provide traditional chiefs with cars, and he gave former president Kaunda a new mansion. In addition, Banda travelled around the country with two helicopters and an international team of "image consultants," and he was criticized for handing out mealie meal (a staple food) at campaign events. The acting president also selected the date for the election, a decision with significant consequences for the electoral process. The chosen date was three weeks prior to the date required by the constitution, and the electoral commission decided not to conduct any new voter registration, citing time constraints. This disenfranchised the 500,000 Zambians who had reached voting age in the two years since the 2006 election. Probably not coincidentally, Sata's strongest support came from young people. Polls show that this group preferred Sata to Banda by a two-to-one margin, suggesting that their disenfranchisement could have been sufficient to sway the election result.[11]

The Advantage of Ethnic Balance

The fact that both the 2001 and the 2008 election campaigns were managed by the acting president helps explain why the MMD was able to tilt the playing field in its favor. But it remains unclear why Zambian political and civil society allowed the party to get away with this abuse of power. After all, Chiluba and Kaunda also abused presidential resources during the 1991 elections and the third-term debate but were ultimately unsuccessful in their campaigns. The groups that mobilized so forcefully against Kaunda's presidency for life and Chiluba's third term managed only limited resistance to the MMD's manipulation of policy, resources, and rules during the 2001 and 2008 elections.

The overriding concern of politicians and voters with maintaining access to political power explains the different reactions to presidents-for-life and parties-in-perpetuity. Presidents-for-life obviously block the access of other actors to the highest political position; however, parties-in-perpetuity are not necessarily as exclusive. The MMD's practice of including all ethnic groups in its upper echelons has helped defuse mobilization against it. The party's leadership has rotated between three different ethnic groups during the past decade, and both Mwanawasa and Banda went to great lengths to ensure that their cabinets were ethnically "balanced." This has led Zambians of diverse backgrounds to believe their aspirations can be met through the MMD. Politicians see room for career advancement and voters suppose their region will eventually receive its fair share of resources.

The practice of building inclusive multiethnic coalitions has historic precedent in Zambian politics. Kaunda was a Bemba-speaker (though his parents were from Malawi), but he rotated the position of prime minister between individuals from Eastern, Southern, Western, and Northwestern provinces.[12] In a country like Zambia, where no group or region makes up a majority of the population, a certain amount of ethnic balancing would also appear politically advantageous following the introduction of competitive elections. Yet the practice declined in the 1990s under Chiluba, who appointed more cabinet ministers from Bemba-speaking areas. This lead to vocal opposition from non-Bembas and encouraged the formation of splinter parties, particularly during the third-term debate when it became unclear if Chiluba would ever step down.

However, since 2001, the MMD has pursued an ethnically inclusive strategy, which has prevented further fractionalization of the party and has helped heal some of the divisions that occurred during the Chiluba era. Although Chiluba marginalized many ethnic groups during his tenure in office, he made a last-ditch effort to extend the MMD's ethnic appeal by selecting Mwanawasa as his successor. This decision extended the appeal of the party on the margins. It appeased a number of non-Bemba politicians, who were unwilling to accept "yet another Bemba" as president.[13] Many community leaders and citizens were also pleased that a politician from a smaller tribe had been selected; a local chief commended the MMD for proving the presidency "was not only for Bembas and Ngonis" (an Eastern tribe).[14] There were strong regional voting patterns in the 2001 election, with the MMD faring well in the North, the UPND dominating in the South and the West, and UNIP maintaining support in the East; however, the MMD won more of the popular vote outside of its core areas than the opposition parties did outside of theirs.

The MMD's commitment to "ethnic balancing" also assisted the party in defusing anger after the election about its abuse of resources during the campaign. Given that the MMD did not have a parliamentary majority, it is remarkable that the opposition parties did not do more to hold the MMD accountable for its corrupt practices during the 2001 elections. Following the elections, three opposition candidates, Mazoka of the UPND, Christian Tembo of the FDD, and Godfrey Miyanda of the Heritage Party, filed a lawsuit challenging the electoral results. However, a number of international observers remarked that the opposition parties pursued their challenge half-heartedly and without devoting significant effort to collecting evidence.[15] Furthermore, by the time the court verdict validating the election was reached in 2005, a number of members of the UPND, FDD, and Heritage Party had joined Mwanawasa's government, fragmenting the opposition.

In the immediate aftermath of the 2001 elections, Mwanawasa prioritized extending the MMD's support base to encompass a wider range of ethnic groups. The interaction of regional voting patterns with a first-past-the-post electoral system left the MMD with no elected members of parliament (MPs) from some regions. Since cabinet ministers must also be MPs, this limited the amount of regional balance that could be created if Mwanawasa limited himself to appointments from within the MMD. Undeterred, Mwanawasa diversified his cabinet by appointing opposition members. This strategy was partly a political necessity, as Mwanawasa sought to build a majority coalition in the face of opposition from some of Chiluba's (predominantly Bemba) supporters in the MMD. However, his equitable sharing of the spoils among different tribes had incidental effects, encouraging further defections to the MMD.

Opposition members belonging to small ethnic groups were particularly likely to decide their chances for political advancement would be better within the president's party. For example, one outspoken politician from Western province left the UPND for the MMD in 2006, claiming she had been "used" by the "narrow, tribal, and ethnic" party.[16] During campaign rallies outside the Bemba and Tonga areas of Zambia, MMD politicians frequently reminded voters that they were the only party that had embraced all tribes in the country. Voting patterns in recent elections reflect the MMD's increasingly diverse support base; although the MMD has made few inroads into the UPND's core support group in Southern province, in all other provinces the MMD won at least a quarter of the votes in both the 2006 and the 2008 elections.

Alternative explanations of the MMD's longevity emphasize the failure of the opposition to unite, and indeed, opposition disunity has been crucial in keeping the MMD in power.[17] However, one of the main causes of opposition disunity has been the MMD's strategy of ethnic inclusiveness. The MMD has managed to offer sufficient room for advancement within the party to pick off key opposition leaders. In addition, the alternative option of joining the government has made opposition leaders less concessionary with each other in negotiations over status in electoral alliances. For example, the electoral alliance that formed between the UPND, the FDD, and UNIP prior to the 2006 elections collapsed in 2008, with the leaders of the two smaller parties deciding they were better off backing Banda.

Even after Mwanawasa had control over the MMD and a firm majority in parliament, he continued his strategy of ethnic inclusiveness. His appointment of Ng'andu Magande as finance minister provided Southern representation in the cabinet, and his selection of Banda as vice-president appeased Easterners. After the 2006 election, the party also coopted key members of the northern-based Patriotic Front, encouraging them to join the Constitutional Review Commission over objections from their party leader Sata.

Since the death of Mwanawasa, the MMD has continued its commitment to "ethnic balancing." During the process of selecting a new leader in 2008, the MMD national secretary explicitly invited members from all ethnic groups to apply, insisting that "no member, no family, no occupation, no religion, no region, no tribe, no gender should be intimidated in their aspirations to be considered as candidates for [the] Republican presidency under the MMD ticket."[18] Interestingly, the two frontrunners in the leadership race, Banda and Magande, were both from areas that were opposition strongholds in 2001. Following the 2008 election, Banda has continued Mwanawasa's strategy of building broad multiethnic cabinets. Although he bypassed his rival, Magande, for finance minister, he appointed another Southerner, Situmbeko Musokotwane, in his place. Northwestern province received five cabinet ministers, the most of any province, but Western and Eastern province were not far behind, with four ministers each.

The MMD's efforts at inclusiveness have not totally undermined the opposition. Zambia still has two opposition parties with significant bases of support, the UPND and the PF, and the consistent competitiveness of elections indicates the limits to the MMD's popularity. However, the MMD leadership has been adroit in managing elections, always winning just enough defectors and manipulating the playing field sufficiently to guarantee a victory. In addition, the party's practice of rotating power among different groups has given opposition leaders and voters less incentives to unite against it.

Time to End the Party?

The MMD's success at surviving leadership transitions has been due to a combination of chance and calculation. It is difficult to ensure simultaneously that the acting president believes he will be in charge after the election, and that citizens believe power is being rotated among different groups. In the 2001 election, these conflicting goals were rectified only through a miscalculation on Chiluba's part. In the 2008 election, the death of Mwanawasa and the MMD's selection of the person constitutionally entitled to act as president until the election made these goals compatible. This difficult balancing act may explain why so many incumbent parties do not stay in power in the aftermath of leadership transitions.

What are the implications of these partial turnovers, in which leaders rotate but the party in power does not, for the quality of democracy in Zambia? The rotation of the presidency is an important first step in ensuring democracy and good governance. Leadership cycles may limit the damage any particular leader can do in office, and presidents that do not expect immunity for life may curb some of their worst abuses of power. In addition, Zambia's experience of selecting new leaders via elections has created an expectation among politicians and voters that future alternations of power will be peaceful and rule-bound. These are significant achievements.

However, the current status quo in Zambia has important democratic deficits. Most obviously, the steps the MMD has taken to remain in power are decidedly undemocratic. The abuse of the president's office during campaigns has been irresponsible and costly to the country. Furthermore, in spite of the MMD's efforts at inclusiveness, its long stay in power has reduced politicians' accountability to the electorate. Politicians whose fates depend more on their position within a particular party than on the possibility of losing an election have little incentive to address their constituents' concerns. Zambians should reject not only "presidents for life" but also "one party in perpetuity."

NOTES

The author wishes to thank Alex Scacco and Toby Moorsom for comments on earlier drafts.

1. Togo also held presidential elections following the death of long-time president Gnassingbé Eyadéma, but only after the army's attempt to install Eyadéma's son by force failed.

2. Two parties in parliamentary systems have accomplished this, the BDP in Botswana and the ANC in South Africa.

3. These calculations are from a data set of multiparty elections in Africa assembled by the author for the period 1989–2008, using Staffan Lindberg's dataset of African elections as a starting point for creating this dataset.

4. Carolyn Baylies and Morris Szeftel, "The Fall and Rise of Multi-Party Politics in Zambia," *Review of African Political Economy* 54 (July 1992): 84.

5. Michael Bratton, "Zambia Starts Over," *Journal of Democracy* 3 (April 1992): 92.

6. Michael Bratton, "Second Elections in Africa," *Journal of Democracy* 9 (July 1998): 62.

7. The Zambian president may appoint eight additional MPs.

8. The head of the transitional government in Liberia, Gyude Bryant, was the chairman of the Liberian Action Party (LAP).

9. "Former Intelligence Chief Chungu Spills the Beans," *Times of Zambia,* 1 February 2003.

10. Peter Burnell, "Zambia's 2001 Elections: the Tyranny of Small Decisions, 'Non-Decisions' and 'Not Decisions,'" *Third World Quarterly* 23 (December 2002): 1103–1120 and Carter Center, *Observing the 2001 Zambia Elections: Final Report* (Atlanta: The Carter Center, 2002).

11. I am grateful to Steadman International for sharing their data with me.

12. "Tribal Politics," *The Post* (Lusaka), 19 November 2001. On Kaunda's ethnicity, see Daniel Posner, *Institutions and Ethnic Politics in Africa* (Cambridge: Cambridge University Press, 2005), 98.

13. Karolina Hulterström, "The Logic of Ethnic Politics: Elite Perceptions about the Role of Ethnicity in Kenyan and Zambian Politics" in *Political Opposition in African Countries: The Cases of Kenya, Namibia, Zambia and Zimbabwe* (Uppsala: Nordiska Afrikainstitutet, 2007), 26.

14. "Senior Chief Puta endorses Mwanawasa," *Times of Zambia,* 9 October 2001.

15. See Burnell, "Zambia's 2001 Elections," and Carter Center, *Observing the 2001 Zambia Elections: Final Report.*

16. "Chiluba Has Destroyed My Beauty—Nakatindi," *The Post* (Lusaka), 11 June 2006.

17. Lise Rakner and Lars Svåsand, "From Dominant to Competitive Party System: The Zambian Experience 1991-2001," *Party Politics* 10 (January 2004): 49–68.

18. "Katele Clarifies on Presidency," *Times of Zambia,* 27 August 2008.

22

VOTING FOR CHANGE IN THE DRC

Herbert F. Weiss

Herbert F. Weiss *is emeritus professor of political science at the City University of New York and senior policy scholar at the Woodrow Wilson International Center for Scholars in Washington, D.C. This essay originally appeared in the April 2007 issue of the* Journal of Democracy.

On 30 July and 29 October 2006, less than a year after a December 2005 constitutional referendum, the vast and strife-wracked Democratic Republic of the Congo (DRC) held its first multiparty elections since 1965. The second of the two elections was a runoff for the presidency between Joseph Kabila, the sitting transitional president, and runner-up Jean-Pierre Bemba, one of four transitional vice-presidents and the leader of the rebel-group-turned-political-party known as the Movement for the Liberation of Congo (MLC).

Kabila won the runoff by 58 to 42 percent—Bemba charged fraud but the Supreme Court held the result valid on November 27—and was inaugurated as president on 6 December 2006. He named the third-place finisher from the first round, 81-year-old Antoine Gizenga of the Unified Lumumbist Party (PALU), to the post of premier on December 30. The two have since named a cabinet comprising some sixty ministers and have the backing of a comfortable majority in the newly elected 500-member National Assembly. While no single party holds a majority of the seats in the National Assembly, the alliance backing Kabila and Gizenga numbers about 300 legislators. There are 267 registered parties in the DRC, 70 of which won at least one seat in the National Assembly. Independent candidates hold a fifth of all seats.

The geographic pattern evident in the presidential vote—especially during the first round, when Kabila carried the east while Bemba and Gizenga dominated the west—was not present to the same degree in the National Assembly vote. Kabila's Party of the People for Reconstruction and Democracy (PPRD) won 111 seats, while Bemba's MLC took 64 and Gizenga's PALU garnered 34 seats.

Although ethnic solidarity is assumed to be an ever-present variable in DRC politics, in these elections that factor cannot be coupled with political-party results. Depending on how one counts them, there are anywhere from two-hundred to six-hundred ethnic groups in the DRC. In the past, the major ethnic groups tended to vote in homogeneous blocs. The latest election is a break with this pattern and seems to have been replaced by regional and perhaps *lingua franca* solidarity. In other words, while the electorate tended to vote for "sons of the land," these sons belonged to a variety of different parties and party alliances. Even though there are many election constituencies that are by and large ethnically homogeneous, very few of them elected candidates to the National Assembly who all belong to the same party. Despite various institutional attempts to give women a greater role in governance, the elections resulted in women winning less than 10 percent of the seats in the National Assembly.

Given the DRC's tragic recent history—including the 1998 to 2003 conflict whose toll of three to four million human lives makes it the worst the globe has seen since World War II—the holding of a successful national election stands as a major positive accomplishment. The voting itself appears to have been mostly orderly and peaceful (though factional violence did break out between rounds), and turnout was impressive at 70 percent during the first round and 65 percent during the second. Yet the divisions born of ten years of war, foreign occupation, and humanitarian disaster remain, and have manifested themselves in the behavior of voters who used their ballots to reject whichever political faction ruled their portion of the country during the years of war and division (see map below).

The 2006 balloting was preceded by what may well have been the most vigorously contested campaign period ever seen in Africa. The marquee race was for the new presidency created by the 2005 constitution. Most diplomats, foreign and domestic experts, and Kabila himself viewed the sitting transitional president as the clear favorite to carry away 50 percent and hence the prize without need for a second round. That did not happen.

In the July 30 first round, voters also chose among nearly 10,000 candidates in order to fill the new 500-member National Assembly. In the October 29 second round, voters elected the members of the eleven provincial assemblies (fifteen more are to be added by subdividing most of the existing provinces before the end of February 2009). In addition, by the end of January 2007, each of these eleven provincial assemblies had voted to select its quota of national senators and its province's governor.

The large number of candidates signaled the high level of interest that the elections aroused. Even though each aspiring presidential contender had to make a nonrefundable deposit of US$50,000 just to get on the ballot, 33 persons presented themselves. In addition to the 10,000 National Assembly aspirants, nearly 14,000 more competed for the 690 seats available in the eleven provincial assemblies.

The election process received immense support from the international community. The transitional government had established an Independent Electoral Commission (CEI) that successfully organized the structure of the election, but DRC authorities could neither pay the bill nor ensure the physical security of participating citizens. Contributions from foreign donors—mainly West European states—amounted to about half a billion U.S. dollars. In addition, MONUC (the UN peacekeeping force in the DRC), provided crucial help. MONUC is currently the largest UN mission in the world, with more than 15,000 military and civilian personnel. It employed its massive transport system to help the CEI deliver election materials to polling stations, and then helped with the collection and counting of ballots—no small matter in an infrastructure-starved country with more than 50,000 voting sites. The European Union sent a force of more than a thousand troops (EUFOR) in order to supplement MONUC in seeing to it that the capital city of Kinshasa would be peaceful on and around election day.

Following procedures agreed upon by most political and military factions in the 1999 Lusaka Ceasefire Agreement and subsequent accords, the journey toward an elected and therefore legitimate government began with the establishment of the transitional government in 2003. This involved a presidency composed of a president and four vice-presidents, plus a transitional legislative assembly of 500 appointed members and a transitional senate of 100 appointed members. Kabila was the transitional president and Bemba was one of the four vice-presidents. The Lusaka Agreement stipulated that the transition would produce a new constitution and then organize democratic elections leading to an elected government. The electoral process started with a vast voter-registration campaign in the second half of 2005. The campaign was a surprising success, registering just over 25 million voters, or perhaps 90 percent of those over 18 and hence eligible to vote (the DRC's estimated total population is around 60 million). Many have argued that the hunger of Congolese for voter cards as forms of general identification (such necessary papers are hard to come by in the DRC) played a role in the registration drive's success, but participation in the two rounds of the election was also very high. Registration might have mounted even higher had not one of the most important political leaders, veteran oppositionist Etienne Tshisekedi of the Union for Democracy and Social Progress (UDPS), urged his followers to boycott the registration process.

Ratifying the Constitution

With voter registration accomplished, the next item of business was to ratify the new constitution that the transitional government had devised. The 18–19 December 2005 up-or-down vote on the document drew 67 percent turnout. Of the more than 15 million who cast ballots, 84 percent approved the constitution. Turnout was lowest (33 percent) in the UDPS stronghold of the two Kasai provinces (Occidental and Oriental), which together are home to about 16 percent of the DRC's people. Elsewhere, UDPS boycott calls had fallen mostly on deaf ears, and on New Year's Day 2006 Tshisekedi reversed himself and listed a number of conditions under which his party would join the electoral process. The most important was the demand that the registration process be reopened. The CEI rejected this demand on grounds of equity, feasibility, and cost. The Commission's head, Catholic clergyman Abbé Apollinaire Malu Malu, suggested a compromise solution, but the UDPS considered the offer insufficient and rejected it. Whatever the merits, the controversy left many Congolese feeling that the CEI and its chief were biased in favor of Kabila.[1]

The referendum revealed the presence of strong regional differences that the subsequent elections showed to be profound, important, and politically dangerous. Kinshasa's huge population—arguably the most politically sophisticated in the DRC—split over the constitution, approving it with only a narrow 51.5 percent majority. Behind this result lay a dynamic "no" campaign led in part by the UDPS. Other regions where the "no" vote was important were Bas Congo, northern Bandundu, southern Equateur, and the Kasais, especially Occidental. Eastern provinces such as Orientale, Maniema, North Kivu, South Kivu, and Katanga voted massively in favor of the constitution. This voter split turned out to be a foretaste of the presidential election seven months later, when the east would prove to be a Kabila stronghold.

Foes of the constitution listed a number of objections, calling the document too given to centralism, beyond the transitional government's legitimate scope, and the product of a process that had shut out groups such as the UDPS. But far more important than any specific misgiving was the underlying mood of suspicion. Growing numbers of Congolese were coming to fear that the whole process was for the sole sake of legitimating the leaders who had held power in Kinshasa during the years of war, division, and transition, and enjoyed the backing of Europe, the United States, MONUC, and South Africa. This mood would spread to include the DRC's highest Catholic Church authorities, the supporters of Jean-Pierre Bemba, probably the vast bulk of the Congolese diaspora, and a large share of Congolese intellectuals.

The referendum, then, was a great technical success, but its passage also marked the beginning of a mood of deep dissatisfaction and suspicion aimed at the people who had made up the Kinshasa authorities prior to reunification, at the international community, and very specifically at the CEI and its top official.

With the new constitution ratified, the next steps were the passage in

March 2006 of an electoral law consistent with the new constitution, and then the holding of the elections for the presidency and the National Assembly on July 30. In addition to the abovementioned 50-percent-or-runoff rule in the presidential election, the new system featured a party-list, proportional representation (PR) system with no runoff provision as the means of filling both the National Assembly and the provincial assemblies.

The Election Law determined that the geographical constituency for both the national and provincial assembly elections would be the administrative subdivision called a "territory." The country has 189 such legislative constituencies (including urban communes). The share of the National Assembly's 500 seats apportioned to each territory depended on the number of voters registered there. About a third of the 189 territories received only a single seat due to their low population density or low registration percentage. In such de facto single-member districts, the victor would be whichever candidate was "first past the post" with the largest vote total.

In both the National Assembly election and the provincial assembly races, each voter could choose one and only one candidate (whether an independent or a member of a party list). In a territory with more than one seat, any individual on a party list who received more votes than were required for election would automatically have his or her "surplus" votes redistributed to the next most successful candidate on his or her list. Independents could not form lists and hence could not benefit from this rule. As a result, some party candidates beat independents despite having gained fewer raw votes than their nonparty rivals.

Provincial assembly elections were held at the same time as the presidential runoff, on October 29. In January 2007, each provincial assembly chose its province's governor as well as senators to represent the province in the national Senate. Each province is apportioned two senators for each provincial district (the district is the administrative unit between the province and the territory). According to the 2005 constitution, each of these districts is to become a province with two senators by February 2009. The large northeastern province of Orientale, for instance, will become four provinces.

Patterns of Voter Behavior

There are two fundamentally different ways to interpret the first-round election results. One can ask, "Who did the Congolese citizenry vote *for?*" Or one can ask, "Who did the Congolese citizenry vote *against?*"

The answer to the first question leads to the conclusion that the DRC is a deeply divided country. The division largely overlaps with the geographic areas where two of the four Congolese *lingua franca*—Lingala and Swahili—predominate. Kabila won the lands where Swahili is spoken, while Bemba and Gizenga carried the Lingala-speaking regions. Under

Mobutu Sese Seko's 32-year dictatorial rule (1965–97), Lingala-speakers from Equateur Province tended to dominate the political arena. Under Joseph Kabila and his father and predecessor as president Laurent Kabila (1997–2001),[2] Swahili has, to a considerable degree, become dominant.

The answer to the question of who the Congolese voted *against* leads one to conclude that the citizenry by and large all voted with a single voice, especially during the first round. Who did they all vote against? They voted against the people and authorities who had ruled them during the years from 1998 to 2003, when the DRC was divided between areas controlled by the Kinshasa authorities and areas run by various rebel groups. If one looks at the map of this division, it largely overlaps with the areas that voted for Kabila, on the one hand, and either Bemba or Gizenga on the other. In other words, in the Kinshasa-controlled areas, the vote went *against* Kabila and in favor of Bemba or Gizenga. In the areas controlled by one or another rebel authority during those years, the vote went *against* Bemba (and other former rebel leaders such as Transitional Vice-President Azarias Ruberwa) and in favor of Kabila.[3]

National Assembly results support the thesis that almost everywhere in the DRC the first round was a protest vote against former rulers. Voters sent only 45 members of the 500-seat Transitional National Assembly—a body wholly appointed by the Kinshasa authorities, rebel groups, political parties, and so on—to the new, fully elected National Assembly. Does this not further suggest that the major theme of this election was "Let's throw out the particular set of rascals who have been ruling us"?

The notion that July 30 saw a wholesale but criss-crossing protest vote against personalities that had led different parts of the DRC during the years of war and division has yet to gain much recognition in the DRC. But then again, a linguistic interpretation of the split that the elections produced is far more comforting to the DRC's political elite than one which argues that their fellow citizens have in effect rejected them all.

The worst moment of the entire electoral process came just as Malu Malu was about to release the first-round presidential results on August 20. That day and the next, deadly fighting raged in central Kinshasa between Kabila's presidential guard and Bemba's militia, the latter of which had stationed several thousand armed men in Kinshasa under the agreement that had created the transitional government. When the combat was over, 23 people lay dead and 43 were wounded. The entire electoral process might have collapsed had not intense international pressure, directed at both camps but especially at Kabila's, made the two sides steer clear of further violent showdowns. Significantly, there was virtually no civilian or popular involvement in the confrontation. For the representatives of the international community, the lesson learned was that establishing security in Kinshasa would take more effort. The EUFOR and MONUC forces filled this role successfully.

Map—Democratic Republic of the Congo

In the first round of the 2006 presidential election, Joseph Kabila won Katanga, Maniema, Province Orientale, North Kivu, and South Kivu; Jean-Pierre Bemba won Bas Congo, Kinshasa, Equateur, Kasai Occidental, and Kasai Oriental; and Antoine Gizenga won Bandundu.

In the first round, it was possible to vote "for"—or in spirit "against"—any one of 33 candidates. Indeed, 35 percent of the electorate voted for candidates other than Kabila and Bemba. In the second round, voters had three choices, Kabila, Bemba, or abstention. Participation nationwide dropped from 70 percent in the first round to 65 percent in the runoff, but in some provinces the participation decline was steeper and therefore more significant. Despite the differences across provinces, some of which will be discussed below, it is nonetheless a fact that the vast majority of the Congolese who had voted for candidates other than Kabila or Bemba chose to vote in the second round, and this substantially raised the legitimacy of the election.

Even though neither candidate was, in my view, highly popular, the country split between staunch, even passionate, supporters of each. In other words, antagonism toward "the other guy" was probably a stronger motivator than enthusiasm for the chosen candidate. Kabila did little personal campaigning, meeting few voters and preferring instead to mobilize support via intermediaries such as elites from different groups, parties, regions, and the like. He also had some success using television interviews and was favored by the state television stations. Bemba took a more populist approach.

MAP—DEMOCRATIC REPUBLIC OF THE CONGO, 1998–2003

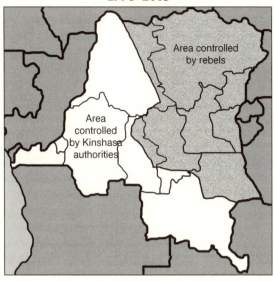

He had a considerable amount of personal charisma and attempted to create a direct link to the masses of voters. He also employed television effectively and indeed owned two television stations.

The sad absence of survey data from the campaign period as well as exit-poll data from election day makes it hard to know exactly what drew voters to one or the other of the two candidates. Analysts must do their best with subjective interviews and a dose of intuition.

Kabila's great appeal in the east seems to have been twofold. First, he brought peace and reunification—though not an end to ongoing violence. His campaign slogan was "momemi maki aswanakate" (he who carries eggs does not start a fight), meaning "I brought peace and will not put it at risk." Second, from 1998 onward, first his father and then he himself had aided the struggle against the forces of Rwanda and its Congolese ally, the rebel Rally for Congolese Democracy, based in the North Kivu town of Goma (RCD/Goma). Kabila gave arms to the Mai Mai (a catchall name for various loosely organized anti-Rwanda and anti-RCD/Goma militias in the eastern DRC), and accorded their leaders high military rank and major posts in the transition. Many in the east saw the Mai Mai campaigns against the Rwandans and their RCD/Goma allies as heroic and patriotic, even though the cost in lives was disastrously high and the Rwandans left as a result of international pressure and negotiations rather than force. Astonishingly, the accusation that Joseph Kabila is not a genuine Congolese but rather a Rwandan Tutsi whom Laurent Kabila adopted did not seem to hurt Joseph Kabila in precisely that part of the country—the intensely anti-Tutsi and anti-Rwandan Kivu provinces—where its impact should have been greatest.

In the DRC's southern and western regions, Kabila seems to have been judged on the basis of how the Kinshasa authorities performed between 1997 and 2006. Unlike the east, the western DRC was not burdened by ongoing local war and endless violence. Yet standards of living kept dropping, the legal and judicial systems were corrupt and closed to the poor, unemployment broke all records, and the political elite kept postponing the end of the transition while hundreds of appointed legislators and officials continued to enjoy good pay and perquisites. Bemba benefited from the resulting voter disaffection, running on the claim that he—unlike Kabila—was a true "bwana mboka" (son of the land). At the same time, distrust of the CEI and the whole electoral process was mounting—and proving a key driver of Bemba's support. Criticism of the electoral commission as favoring Kabila, as untrustworthy, and as a tool of "foreigners" and "imperialists" came not only from the UDPS and its immediate allies but crucially, and with ever-wider resonance, from influential Catholic prelates. The late Frédéric Cardinal Etsou, the archbishop of Kinshasa till his death in January 2007, was the most outspoken among them.

The first round's third-place finisher, Antoine Gizenga, won 13 percent. His vote came mainly from Bandundu Province and Kinshasa, both of which had been under central-government control during the period of war and division. Gizenga had been Patrice Lumumba's[4] vice-premier in 1960 and had spent most of the years since the mid-1960s in exile. Gizenga was in many ways the most consistent and loyal representative of the Lumumbist tradition in Congolese politics and was the long-time president of PALU. Although he never joined Tshisekedi in rejecting the electoral process, Gizenga had been critical of the transition process and had stayed out of the transitional government. It makes sense to see his first-round support as a protest vote against the Kinshasa authorities as well as a token of the esteem in which this uncorrupted standard-bearer for Lumumbist nationalism is held in Bandundu.

The Runoff

When both Kabila and Bemba fell short of 50 percent on July 30, Gizenga became the most likely kingmaker. He consulted numerous intellectuals, politicians, and diplomats before deciding to support Kabila in the runoff. In exchange, Kabila promised to give the post of prime minister in the new government to PALU—that is, to Gizenga. Kabila named Gizenga to the post on 30 December 2006.

Shortly before the runoff, Gizenga explained that he was throwing his support behind Kabila in order to help bridge the DRC's grave east-west split.[5] A number of other reasons probably actuated Gizenga as well. Kabila's first-round 45 percent made him the likely winner anyway, and for the octogenarian Gizenga it was "now or never." His party had been in opposition since the early 1960s; this was the first chance that its activists had ever had to gain power without abandoning the party or its principles. Then too, Gizenga had been closely associated with Angola during his long exile, and Angola was a major Kabila backer. Finally, joining the son of Laurent Kabila—who had cut his political teeth as a Lumumbist guerrilla leader in the mid-1960s—was in a sense reestablishing a latter-day Lumumbist alliance. For PALU that was not insignificant.

With PALU and its "patriarch" Gizenga on board, Kabila found other allies eager to jump on his bandwagon. One of these was the late President Mobutu's son Nzanga Mobutu, who had gained some support in the first round largely at Bemba's expense. Joseph Kabila had of course been a leading officer in the 1997–98 military campaign that had ousted Mobutu from power. In the politics of the DRC, however, ten years is a long time.

Virtually all international observers have concluded that the runoff was well organized, proceeded mostly without incident, and benefited from the great devotion shown by polling-station officials and voters. Serious problems that had hampered the collecting and tallying of ballots in the first round had mostly been solved by runoff day. Of course, observers could be present at only a small percentage of the more than 50,000 polling stations, and those visited were overwhelmingly in urban centers or easily reached villages. The only authorities or monitors at the vast majority of polling stations were the five officials detailed to each, plus witnesses sent by various parties and in some cases Congolese civil society observers. Since so many Congolese have complained that there was cheating, it makes sense to discuss how fraud could have occurred.

Prior to entering the delicate question of possible chicanery, two issues will have to be visited. The first has to do with differences in participation rates across provinces, while the second involves the impact of alliances formed after the first round. A quick comparison shows that in the provinces which Kabila won, second-round turnout averaged 76 percent, while pro-Bemba provinces managed only 56 percent turnout on runoff day. Thus, a principal reason why Bemba lost may have been the low participation rate of his potential voters. This weak turnout was at least partly explained by low registration and participation rates in the UDPS stronghold in the two Kasai provinces, as well as by a severe tropical rainstorm that hit Kinshasa and Bas Congo provinces on election day. All four of these provinces had been in the Kinshasa-controlled areas during the conflict years and favored Bemba. More broadly, Kabila's campaign managed to turn the tide of rejection during the first round in the west sufficiently to add significantly to his support. In the six provinces that Kabila lost on both July 30 and October 29, his average vote share rose from 13 percent in the first round to 26 percent in the second. The cognate figures for the five provinces that Bemba lost on both days were by contrast just 2 percent and 7 percent. The significance here is how very low Bemba's support was in both rounds of the election

TABLE—DEMOCRATIC REPUBLIC OF THE CONGO, 2006 PRESIDENTIAL-ELECTION RESULTS

PROVINCE	ELIGIBLE VOTERS	RATE OF PARTICIPATION (IN PERCENTAGES)		VALID VOTES (IN PERCENTAGES)		VOTES FOR KABILA (IN PERCENTAGES)		VOTES FOR BEMBA (IN PERCENTAGES)	
		First round	Second round	First round	Second round	First round	Second round	First round	Second round
Kinshasa	2,913,313	72.14	57.71	96.37	98.16	14.73	32.00	49.07	68.00
Bas Congo	1,227,775	76.03	51.59	91.41	96.33	13.91	25.86	36.21	74.14
Bandundu	2,925,126	68.77	50.63	96.31	97.87	2.65	39.45	9.71	60.55
Equateur	2,923,680	74.37	84.45	93.66	98.90	1.86	2.85	63.67	97.15
Kasai Occidental	2,010,405	45.31	51.42	94.09	97.68	11.42	23.30	31.93	76.70
Kasai Oriental	1,975,430	39.19	42.67	94.29	97.86	36.09	32.59	14.56	67.41
Province Orientale	3,241,470	77.59	63.84	93.58	95.74	70.26	79.48	5.20	20.52
North Kivu	2,451,475	80.99	77.05	93.21	97.51	77.71	96.45	0.77	3.55
South Kivu	1,651,262	90.16	84.06	94.98	98.27	94.64	98.31	0.28	1.69
Maniema	626,327	84.97	80.24	95.11	98.85	89.80	98.33	0.38	1.67
Katanga	3,473,936	71.58	75.58	94.81	98.51	77.97	93.76	3.37	6.24
Total	25,420,199	70.47	65.36	94.46	97.84	44.86	58.05	20.03	41.95

Source: Independent Electoral Commission, *www.cei-rdc.cd.*

in the provinces where he lost and therefore how insignificant the difference between 2 percent and 7 percent is.

After the first round came a flurry of negotiations as both Kabila and
Bemba scrambled for allies. The focus for each camp was to build a runoff majority that would carry over to the new National Assembly so that
winning the presidency could be accompanied by the ability to govern. In
this regard, the many supporters of Antoine Gizenga in his home base of
Bandundu Province and in Kinshasa faced a conundrum. They had, in my
view, supported him in the first round not only out of respect for him, but
also as a protest against Kabila, whom Gizenga was now asking them to
support! Many appear to have stayed home or not listened on October 29,
as turnout in Bandundu dropped from 69 percent on July 30 to 51 percent
on the later date, while Bemba carried the runoff there by 61 to 39 percent.
In other words, most of Bandundu's voters, like their counterparts in nearly
all the areas that Kinshasa had controlled during the war, refused to vote
for Kabila and either abstained or voted for Bemba.

Was There Cheating?

As the votes were being counted, Bemba was confident that he was
winning. When the CEI declared Kabila the winner, Bemba insisted that
the results were false. Large numbers of Congolese agree, and are by all
indications sincerely convinced that the election was somehow stolen.
As noted earlier, their ranks include influential figures in the Catholic
Church. Could there have been manipulation in Kabila's favor?

The first occasion for suspicion is the abovementioned difference in
participation rates. Since each polling station received a number of blank
ballots roughly equal to the number of names on its voter roll, low turnout
would in practice make available numbers of unused ballots that the five
polling-station officials—assuming that they were in collusion and witnesses were absent—could fill out in any way they liked without the CEI
knowing anything was amiss. One of Bemba's legal challenges concerned
obstacles that he alleged were set up to block his party witnesses from
participating in the vote count—conducted in each polling station immediately after it closed its doors to voters. Cheating of the type described
would of course have been most likely to occur in areas that were the most
unified behind one candidate or the other. Such areas were in fact mostly
for Kabila, whose second-round support involved majorities ranging from
79 to 98 percent in Orientale, North Kivu, South Kivu, Maniema, and
Katanga. Bemba, by contrast, won a near-unanimous majority only in
Equateur, which gave him a 97 percent victory.

A second opportunity for manipulating the results concerned the so
called derogation lists. These lists were devices meant to aid the cause of
greater electoral participation. In an ad hoc manner they listed the names
of people—such as polling-station officials—whose election-day duties

prevented them from reaching the polling stations where they were registered. In principle, such a list was established in each polling station, and eligible voters had to present their valid voter-registration cards in order to add their names. There is little doubt that in some locations this authority was abused, and Bemba's camp has made charges to that effect.

Other fraud allegations held that voters had been bribed. And finally there were the widespread cries, heard even from some of his fellow Catholic clerics, that Malu Malu had falsified results in Kabila's favor. Both the man's personal qualities and the control exerted over the CEI by the various political parties (including Bemba's MLC) make the veracity of this last accusation highly unlikely.

Joseph Kabila owes his victory in no small part to his control of the transitional presidency, the longstanding support that he received from the international community, and the credit that many of his compatriots accord him for having achieved Rwandan and Ugandan military withdrawal and the reunification of the DRC. Bemba's strength was his ability to communicate directly with the Congolese masses, and his portrayal of Kabila as a foreigner who misruled the part of the DRC that he controlled prior to unification as well as during the transition.

A number of questions hang over the future of politics in the DRC. Will Kabila, with broad powers in his hands and electoral legitimation at his back, resist temptations to authoritarianism? Will Bemba's firm choice not to allow himself to be coopted, but rather to lead a parliamentary opposition, pay off—not only for himself and his followers, but most importantly for the Congolese people? Will the new constitution's division of powers between Kinshasa and the provinces be respected? Will the newfound legitimacy be used to shed Western, UN, and South African pressures for real democratization?

Another source of uncertainty—in a vast and resource-rich but poor country where central versus local power has always been a key issue—lies at the provincial level. The attention paid to the dramatic presidential runoff was so great that it completely overshadowed the eleven provincial assembly elections that took place on the same day. Kabila beat Bemba 58 to 42 percent in the nationwide popular vote, yet actually carried only five of the eleven provinces. Remarkably, however, Kabila's coalition has, at the time of this writing in February 2007, gained the majority in ten provincial assemblies as against only one (Equateur) for the Bemba camp. These results are being contested for a variety of reasons. However, they suggest that the magnetic attraction of central-government power overwhelmed electoral alliances that had been formed prior to the final presidential vote count. Provincial-assembly members must have received many incentives in order to persuade them to support gubernatorial candidates linked to the Kabila alliance in provinces that had given majority support to Bemba. One must wonder what these incentives were.

In sum, Kabila has not only won the presidential election but now heads an alliance that completely dominates the National Assembly and almost certainly the Senate, plus possibly ten of the eleven provincial assemblies (the ones that elected governors nominated by the Kabila alliance). A new cabinet has been installed comprising sixty ministers. Such a large and therefore expensive cabinet might be viewed as necessary if it involved including all political factions, but this is not the case here. No members of Bemba's alliance or the UDPS are included. Will these bodies succeed in bringing governance closer to the people's will and to their needs? Will the *centralization* of political power undermine the constitution's *decentralization* of institutional power? Finally, will this expensive election simply result in a continuation of the political practices that have operated in Kinshasa these past years? If that is the case, the group of people benefiting from the system at the top may have broadened, but ordinary Congolese will surely be disappointed.

NOTES

1. For a more detailed analysis of the 2005 constitutional referendum, see Leon de Saint Moulin, S.J., *Congo-Afrique,* February–March 2006, 12.

2. Laurent Kabila started his political career during the independence struggle as a militant supporter of Patrice Lumumba in Katanga Province. When Lumumbists organized a revolutionary movement in 1963–64, Kabila led a zone in South Kivu where Che Guevara and several hundred Cubans joined and fought in the so-called Congo Rebellion. Kabila maintained a small rebel redoubt—Hewa Bora—long after the movement was defeated elsewhere. In the 1980s, he escaped to Tanzania and did not reemerge until the Rwandan-Ugandan-Angolan invasion of the DRC (then called Zaïre) in 1996–97. With the help of these powers, he proclaimed himself president in 1997 and retained that position until his assassination on 16 January 2001.

3. The two exceptions to this criss-crossing pattern of people voting against their one-time rulers are South Katanga and North Equateur. The former had been ruled by the Kinshasa authorities yet voted for Kabila, even though his support there was thinner and more scattered than it was in the other regions where he won. North Equateur is Bemba's home base and despite the pattern described above, he carried the province.

4. Patrice Lumumba was the first elected prime minister of Congo. His party, the Mouvement National Congolais/Lumumba, won a plurality of the seats in the National Assembly in the May 1960 elections. Immediately after Congo obtained its independence from Belgium on 30 June 1960, the army mutinied, Katanga Province seceded, and law and order completely broke down. As a result, the first UN mission was sent to Congo and the country became an arena of Cold War competition. Lumumba attempted to balance Western and Soviet interests, but that led Western actors, especially the United States, to view him as a communist agent, mentally unstable, and dangerous. As a result, the U.S. Central Intelligence Agency attempted to assassinate him in September 1960. That attempt failed, but a second attempt, organized by Belgian and some Congolese actors, succeeded in January 1961. In 1963–64, his followers organized a rebellion that gained control over half the Congo.

5. Interview of Antoine Gizenga by Colette Braeckman, *Le Potential,* 26 October 2006.

23

ANGOLA'S FAÇADE DEMOCRACY

Paula Cristina Roque

Paula Cristina Roque *is a researcher with the African Security Analysis Programme at the Institute for Security Studies in South Africa, where she focuses on civil society, democracy, conflict analysis, and human security. This essay originally appeared in the October 2009* Journal of Democracy.

On 5–6 September 2008, Angolans went to the polls to elect their parliamentarians for the first time since Angola's civil war officially ended in 2002. With 82 percent of the vote, the ruling Popular Movement for the Liberation of Angola (MPLA) won in a landslide, while its historic rival and main opposition, the National Union for the Total Independence of Angola (UNITA), took a mere 10.5 percent. These were only the second multiparty elections in Angola's history and the first since 1992. Yet, paradoxically, they secured the ruling party's hegemony, the virtual elimination of the opposition, and the consolidation of a highly securitized regime. In other words, the elections served as a vehicle for the MPLA to transform Angola into a de facto one-party state while at the same time gaining long-elusive national and international legitimacy.

With its overwhelming victory, the MPLA now has 191 of the 220 directly elected seats in the National Assembly, giving the party enough power to govern and even to change the constitution without having to engage in political debate with civil society or the opposition, whose presence in the National Assembly has dropped from 91 seats to only 29. Other opposition parties fared even worse at the polls than did UNITA. The Social Renewal Party (PRS), managed to secure only 3 percent of the vote, and the National Front for the Liberation of Angola (FNLA), one of the country's three historic liberation movements along with the MPLA and UNITA, won only 1 percent (see Table on the next page). Especially given Angola's history of unaccountable governance, corruption, social and economic exclusion, mismanagement of natural re-

TABLE—LEGISLATIVE ELECTION RESULTS, 1992 & 2008

Party	1992 Legislative Elections		2008 Legislative Elections	
	Votes	Seats[1]	Votes	Seats
MPLA	1,976,940	129	5,266,112	191
UNITA	1,258,103	70	670,197	16
PRS	77,605	6	204,478	8
FNLA	84,110	5	71,600	3
ND	0	0	77,405	2

1. The National Assembly, a unicameral parliament with a four-year term, has 220 seats elected by proportional representation: 130 members are elected nationally and 90 are elected regionally.

sources, and political marginalization,[1] unchecked and unchallenged one-party rule is dangerous. Worse still, the MPLA's political stampede trampled not only opposition parties, but also civil society and the independent media, annihilating any possibility of a challenge to its rule, at least in the near future.

For nearly thirty years, Angolans suffered through one of Africa's longest and deadliest civil wars, with only a few intermittent years of tense peace. After Angola gained its independence from Portugal in 1975, the country's three liberation movements vied for control of the new republic. The two main combatants were ideological foes: The MPLA, originally a Marxist-Leninist group (though now formally social-democratic), was made up of urban elites from the capital city of Luanda, mixed-race Angolans, *assimilados,*[2] intellectuals, and whites, though its ethnic base was the Mbumbu (about 23 percent of the population). UNITA found its base in the countryside among the Ovimbundu people (37 percent of the population) of the central high plateau in the provinces of Huambo, Bié, Benguela, Moxico, and Cuando Cubango. UNITA largely represented the rural poor, portraying itself as the real "African" movement and the MPLA as elitist and exclusive—a rhetoric that resonated in a country deeply polarized along class, ethnic, and ideological lines.

As soon as the Portuguese left Angola, the MPLA, which controlled Luanda at the time, announced the establishment of the People's Republic of Angola. Three days later, UNITA and the FNLA together declared their own state—the Democratic People's Republic of Angola. Although the Organization of African Unity initially withheld recognition of either, it admitted the MPLA government to membership in early 1976. Despite the new government's official status, however, the fighting continued, ravaging the country's infrastructure and destroying its economy. Moreover, taking place at the height of the Cold War, Angola's conflict assumed international significance, with the Soviets and Cubans backing the MPLA and the United States and South Africa backing UNITA. This foreign interference helped to keep the hostilities alive for more than a decade. The first tenuous peace was not reached until 1991 with the signing of the Bicesse Accords, which called for a multiparty system.

In September 1992, Angola held presidential and parliamentary elections, organized and monitored by an international commission with the assistance of the UN Angola Verification Mission. Nearly five-million Angolans cast their votes, and the polling was peaceful. The MPLA won 54 percent of the vote in the legislative polls, securing 129 seats in parliament. UNITA won 34 percent and 70 seats. The presidential race was much closer, however, with President José Eduardo dos Santos of the MPLA winning 49.6 percent of the vote to UNITA leader Jonas Savimbi's 40 percent. Because neither managed to get a majority, a runoff was constitutionally required to be held within thirty days.

The second round of voting never took place, however, and in October 1992 eight opposition parties issued a joint declaration stating that the elections were fraudulent. The political process and attempts by the international community to peacefully resolve the impasse broke down when the government's security forces staged a brutal crackdown on UNITA's leadership and supporters in what was called the Halloween Massacre. There followed a period of political purges, revenge killings, and ethnic cleansing from both sides that eventually claimed more than 300,000 lives. These years saw the remilitarization of society, with UNITA effectively converting its guerrilla forces into a conventional army and the government arming and mobilizing civilians into the Organization for Civil Defense (ODC). In a growing climate of impunity, both sides targeted civilian populations as well.

Despite their professed will to negotiate, UNITA and the government both continued to purchase mass quantities of arms and to engage in sporadic but intense fighting.[3] Peace talks resumed in late 1993, however, culminating in the 1994 Lusaka Protocol, which called for a Government of Unity and National Reconciliation (GURN) that included members of both the MPLA and UNITA. With Savimbi repeatedly causing delays, the GURN was not inaugurated until 1997. Even then, however, the country remained divided, and Savimbi's access to diamonds and the president's to oil helped to fund the fighting, which had spun into a full-scale war again by late 1998.

In February 2002, government forces ambushed and killed Savimbi and other top UNITA leaders, and with the guerrilla leader's death came a renewed attempt at peace. On April 4, the MPLA and UNITA signed a memorandum of understanding known as the Luena Accord, which agreed on an amnesty law for crimes committed during the conflict, the integration of five-thousand UNITA soldiers into the Angolan Armed Forces, and a timetable for demobilizing the remaining UNITA military forces.

With UNITA's military defeated and its leadership either killed or left in a debilitated negotiating position, it could only comply with the government's demands. In short, the victorious MPLA had license to shape the postwar political configuration to suit its interests. The ruling party therefore set about consolidating its power and designing a strategy to manage and weaken the opposition. Facing no formidable rival, it now had even greater leeway to appropriate the country's vast resources however it saw fit, without any pressure for accountability.

The MPLA has thus shaped the transition from war to peace, from reconstruction to development, from an absence of elections to multiparty competition, without objection from the international community and without input from other segments of Angolan society. It has tightened control, harnessing state institutions and resources to ensure its political and economic hegemony, all the while extolling the virtues of peace, reconciliation, and democracy.

The Powers That Be

The MPLA, having recruited new members from old UNITA strongholds, has grown considerably since the end of the war and now has 2.8 million people on its rolls out of a population of 16 million. Moreover, MPLA-affiliated groups, such as its youth and women's leagues, have helped to cement the party's influence at all levels of society. Yet, in recent years, power has been shifting toward the presidency and away from the party, weakening the MPLA's influence and capacity to shape national politics.

In fact, although Angola in theory has a semipresidential system, in practice the presidency is by far the most powerful institution. President dos Santos is not only the head of state, he is also president of his party, commander in chief of the armed forces, and the main "advisor" on all other aspects of governance. Furthermore, he enjoys the exclusive power to nominate and dismiss the prime minister, the cabinet, and provincial governors. For the last thirty years, the president has kept the MPLA and the government in check by expanding a highly efficient system of patronage that provides incentives to a loyal elite, some of whom (politicians, family members, and the military) have amassed immense personal fortunes.[4]

After the end of hostilities in 2002, the government eased certain repressive measures that had previously been in place and reintroduced the position of prime minister. The division of power between the president and the prime minister has remained largely symbolic, however, as the ministries with real political and economic power (finance, planning, defense, interior, justice, and foreign affairs, as well as the central bank, state-owned oil company Sonangol, and national diamond company Endiama) report directly to the president. The less important ministries fall under the purview of the prime minister, who himself reports directly to dos Santos.

In Angola's hierarchy of power, the presidency is at the apex, followed by the group of presidential advisors that includes the leaders of the security and intelligence services (Serviços de Internos de Informaçaõs, or SINFO), which are currently headed by General Manuel Hélder Vieira Dias "Kopelipa." Given that the influence of these agencies in state administration and control of the population exceeds that of any ministry or provincial government, they are in essence more powerful than most of the cabinet. In this second tier of power, Sonangol and, to a lesser extent, Endiama also play crucial roles in both the management of the state and the MPLA's financial strategy, with Sonangol at the center of official corruption and the mismanagement of funds. Acting as a sovereign wealth fund, this state-owned enterprise has made several acquisitions in Portugal and the United States.

Political harassment and intimidation have been widespread since the end of the war. Through a strategy of political violence, the politics of cooptation, the persecution of opponents, and the omnipresence of members of SINFO, the MPLA has managed to neutralize any form of serious opposition. SINFO was instrumental in the 2008 elections and during the previous three years of preparation for the national polls, creating an extensive network of informers and promoting a culture of fear. In addition, the ODC civil militias (which were legalized in March 2002 and officially included in the defense ministry's annual budget) have played an active role in defending the interests of the ruling party among the rural population.

The ruling party has in its hands a wealth of resources that it can exploit in order to stay in power. Two of the most important are control over the media and control over civil society. With the coming of peace, the Angolan media should have evolved into a true forum for public debate, yet they are still widely seen as a vehicle for state propaganda. The state controls the main media outlets—the Angop news agency, the daily *O Jornal de Angola,* the public television stations Televisão Publica de Angola and TPA2, and the national radio station Radio Nacional de Angola, which serves as the MPLA's mouthpiece. The private media include only a small number of newspapers that circulate mainly in the capital city and two radio stations that are not allowed to broadcast outside the capital. In fact, only the state has outlets nationwide. In the runup to the election, these government-controlled news sources ramped up their pro-MPLA coverage without giving equal space to opponents of the ruling party, muffling any diversity of opinion. Election observers recognized that this media monopoly threatened the fairness of the entire process.

Given Angola's low literacy rates and high levels of poverty, radio continues to be the most widespread communications medium in the country. Independent radio, however, is barely surviving—many stations have been shut down or, at best, had their broadcast range restricted. In July 2008—roughly a month before campaigning was set to begin—Radio Despertar, once the voice of UNITA but now independent, was ordered off the air for six months for allegedly extending its signal 400 kilometers beyond the capital city despite being licensed for only a 50-kilometer range. The Catholic Church's Radio Ecclesia, one of the most outspoken media outlets, has fought against MPLA restrictions since 1978 in an effort to broadcast nationally and on FM. In November 2003, the Ministry of Social Communication cautioned the Church against broadcasting in the provinces, indicating that any attempt to do so would be an affront to the law and the state. Consequently, during the elections the only information circulating throughout the country was controlled and manipulated by the MPLA, touting the ruling party's new construction projects and affirming that it was the only party prepared to rule.

Civil society remains a weak public force in Angola. Before the 1992 elections, there was a significant opening of public space that allowed for the emergence of civil society groups, but that space closed as war broke out anew. In late 2002, Presidential Decree No. 82/02 introduced a new framework to regulate the activities of NGOs, one that promoted their partnership with the government rather than their role as independent actors.[5]

Wary that civil society groups could stir up popular sentiment in support of change, the government has responded hostilely to such organizations. Because Angola remains highly divided—ethnically, politically, and socioeconomically—political parties tend to view civil society organizations as either allies or enemies.[6] The MPLA regime has established policies to keep such groups under its control, even creating several official NGOs to rival independent domestic and international organizations.[7] These state-sponsored NGOs in turn function as extensions of the patronage system.

The 2008 Legislative Elections

Although the legal framework for free and fair elections was in place, the ruling party began maneuverings that threatened the opposition's fair chance at the polls. According to electoral law, campaign funding is to be provided at least ninety days before an election. It was not until late July, however, that the Council of Ministers (not the National Assembly) approved US$17 million to fund the campaigns of all the parties and coalitions for the September 5 balloting. The delay in funding gave the ruling MPLA an enormous advantage since it controlled all the state resources, including the media and the treasury. It is estimated that the MPLA's 2008 campaign cost $300 million, likely funded by donations from Sonangol and Endiama as well as from private companies and investors—a violation of regulations that prohibit political parties from accepting contributions from state-owned enterprises and foreign entities.

The regime also packed the National Electoral Commission (CNE)—a supposedly impartial body—with friends of the ruling party. Eight of the CNE's eleven members are from the MPLA or government institutions.[8] CNE president Caetano de Sousa, for example, happens also to be the vice-president of the Constitutional Court. A number of Angolan analysts have pointed out that once opposition rallies began to swell with supporters, the MPLA discreetly appointed members of SINFO, the military, and the presidency—among them former policemen and technology experts—to advise the CNE. According to some journalists, the party decided to take these actions after an August poll conducted for the MPLA showed worrying results.[9]

There was never any doubt that the MPLA would win the elections. Yet given the young electorate, the disillusionment of the impoverished majority, the increase in land conflicts between slum-dwellers and developers, and the ruling elite's visible accumulation of wealth, it was uncertain whether the ruling party would win a two-thirds majority in the National Assembly. Even many skilled workers and members of Angola's tiny middle class were disenchanted with the government. This unpredictability—especially in Luanda, where 21 percent of the electorate resides—was an incentive for the MPLA to manufacture the conditions necessary to guarantee its overwhelming victory.

On September 5, voting began across the country amid calm and order. In the capital city, however, logistical problems led to chaos. Of the 1,522 polling stations in Luanda, 320 never opened because of a lack of materials, and several others opened four hours late because they were missing ballot papers, urns, and other items. As a result, an unscheduled second day of voting took place the next day. Of the 320 polling stations that failed to open on election day, a hundred remained closed on the second day as well. And because the remaining 220 lacked sufficient materials, they were consolidated into 48 polling stations.

The chaos that ensued in the capital on election day and the unscheduled second day of voting on September 6 prompted the opposition to cry foul. UNITA called for a rerun of the polling in Luanda in eight days' time and stated that it would submit an application to the courts to overturn the capital city's election results and hold the rerun. The PRS, FNLA, and PDP-ANA also voiced their concerns, stating that the disorganization in the capital was purposely created, especially in highly populated opposition strongholds such as the neighborhoods of Quilamba Quiaxe, Sambizanga, Viana, Ramiros, Palanca, and others. UNITA likewise accused the government of deliberately cultivating chaos in areas where the MPLA was not expected to win.

Moreover, civil society, independent journalists, and members of the clergy decried the government's sophisticated and well formulated strategy to secure the rural vote. The party used intimidation and threats of war, and they coopted the Sobas, traditional leaders in each village who could deliver their village's votes. The MPLA even created an NGO—O Nosso Soba (Our Soba)—to approach the Sobas in the provinces and attract them to the party's patronage network. The ruling party successfully brought in these traditional authorities as well as local administrators and influential citizens, bribing them with money, cars, computers, motorbikes, bicycles, and promises of future benefits.[10] On election day, Sobas and unofficial elements of the MPLA stood near some polling stations, observing how people cast their votes.

The intimidation did not stop there. Civil servants and even some private-sector workers were advised to vote for the MPLA if they wanted to keep their jobs. SINFO extended its presence throughout the country and had representatives and informers in each commune of each municipality in all eighteen provinces. Some provincial representatives from the opposition claimed that SINFO operatives even queued in voting lines with ordinary citizens.

The military and the police (more than 300,000 men altogether) were told that they should vote "patriotically" and that their obedience must be to their commander-in-chief. It remains unclear whether voting in military barracks was monitored and if members of the armed forces were allowed to vote outside the barracks. In addition, the military-affairs branch of the Office of the Presidency ordered a considerable number of extra ballots, and there still has been no legitimate explanation concerning the fate of those ballots, which remain in the custody of the ministry.

The MPLA faced a particularly difficult race in the northern exclave of Cabinda, where in 1992 most voters boycotted the polls. The contest became even more difficult for the MPLA once the Front for the Liberation of Cabinda (which until 2006 had fought for the secession of the oil-rich region) endorsed UNITA, and thus the MPLA appears to have once again employed underhanded tactics to secure a win. Election observers and the opposition have accused the MPLA of bringing thousands of Congolese into the province to vote for the ruling party.

In the end, although UNITA, the PRS, and the other opposition parties had declared these elections a farce, they chose to accept the results and concede defeat rather than stoke resentment and possibly spark renewed conflict by rejecting the official outcome.

The Failure of the Opposition

Regardless of the ruling party's advantages, the opposition failed to convince voters that it could provide a credible alternative to the MPLA. Internal divisions, allegations of accepting bribes from the government, and a lack of resources made the challenge of running against the MPLA virtually insurmountable. The opposition's lack of cohesiveness, its inability to create a perception of capable leadership, and its inexperience in governing inevitably would have provided the MPLA with a win, even without any fraudulent maneuverings.

UNITA, once a mammoth movement, is today politically weak, divided, and lacking in technical and institutional capacity. Apart from its lack of cohesion and coherence, UNITA is also thought to have been intimidated, infiltrated, and coopted by the MPLA, and has suffered defections to the ruling party (which allegedly lured these defectors with government funds). Further complicating matters, UNITA had been part of the GURN since 1997, which left it in an ambiguous position—being part of the government while also playing the role of the main opposition party. This arrangement undermined UNITA's autonomy and credibility, and provided the government with an opportunity to neutralize it on both fronts.[11] Although UNITA president Isaias Samakuva managed to help the former rebel movement make the transition from guerrilla force to political party (he himself had been a diplomat and had not been active in UNITA's military structure), he failed to reconcile the provincial divisions within UNITA that had emerged over the years or to provide the party with a new guiding vision. In part because of these shortcomings, UNITA won only 16 seats at the 2008 polls.

The well-funded and well-organized PRS, the third-largest party, which had won 6 seats in 1992, was generally perceived as a credible, nationwide opposition force but won only 8 seats. The FNLA, despite its historical importance, has been reduced to a small political force, rife with divisions that were exacerbated by the death of its founder Holden Roberto in 2007. It won only 3 seats. The New Democracy Electoral Union (ND), a new coalition established only months before the election, gained the remaining 2 seats.

The Democratic Party for Progress–Angolan National Alliance (PDP-ANA) was once a promising party, but since its leader Mfulumpinga Lando Victor was gunned down in 2004 it has been divided and unable to mobilize support. Parties formed by disillusioned MPLA cadres, such as the Democratic Renewal Party (PRD) and the Party of the Alliance of the Youth, Workers, and Farmers of Angola (PAJOCA), were expected to do well, but failed to gain significant support. The Angola Democratic and Progress Support Party (PADEPA), which originated in the slums of Luanda, was considered the most likely of the minor parties to win seats because of its brave and honest campaign strategy of holding protests and rallying young people in the capital's poverty-stricken slums. Yet this party, too, was weakened by internal divisions.

After the crushing defeat of the opposition, the Constitutional Court dissolved all parties that had failed to win more than 0.5 percent of the national vote, as called for by the 2005 law on political parties. From a starting point of 108 parties during the pre-election period to the fourteen parties and coalitions that were cleared to run for the 2008 legislative elections, the country now has only six officially registered parties[12]—the MPLA, UNITA, the PRS, FNLA, ND and PDP-ANA—a number that is clearly more manageable for the MPLA. Still, the ruling party does allow opposition parties, media outlets, and civil society organizations to function—as long as they refrain from exposing inconvenient truths and do not challenge the government. Cooptation is a key tactic of the ruling party, which opens its patronage network to opposition members if they can play a useful role or if their move to the MPLA will help to demonstrate its "inclusivity" and "diversity." Such sophisticated and pragmatic practices reduce the party's need to engage in overt repression, as is illustrated by the country's small number of political prisoners.

The Veneer of Democracy

The MPLA knows that change is inevitable, and thus it aims to control the pace of change in an effort to ensure its continued rule. Government reforms, then, are more about keeping power than about creating an inclusive process that accommodates divergent opinions on matters of politics, economics, and social policy. Immediately after the elections, the MPLA stepped up its efforts to clamp down on the independent media and civil society, continuing to deny the extension of Radio Ecclesia's signal beyond Luanda and questioning the legality of local NGOs such as the Association for Justice, Peace, and Democracy. Defamation laws have been strengthened to deter any potential criticism of the president and his entourage, and many private media outlets have been transformed into official mouthpieces for the party.

The new legislative assembly was sworn in on 30 September 2008, and in January 2009 it appointed a 45-member commission, headed by MPLA parliamentarian Bornito de Sousa, to revise the constitution.[13] Although the parliament had initially agreed on a 75-day deadline to approve a new constitution, it now seems that the draft law may not be ready until later this year. Only after the Assembly passes the draft constitution will dos Santos announce a date for the presidential poll, which had been tentatively set for September 2009 but remained unscheduled at the time of this writing. This delay will cause a postponement of the local and municipal elections, which are not to take place until after the presidential election. Thus two more years will pass before Angolans can use their votes to hold local and regional governments accountable for their corruption and mismanagement of assets.

The current Angolan constitution does recognize and protect civil and political liberties, as well as social and economic rights based on the principles of equality and nondiscrimination, but there is a huge gap between constitutional theory and democratic practice. Despite the efforts to debate and pass new legislation, laws in Angola are merely ornamental—the trappings of democracy without the substance. Real power is negotiated and bargained at an extraconstitutional level, and government institutions, which have been molded to fit the personalized rule of the president, have assisted in the melding of the ruling party and the state.

Angola has a political system that is authoritarian, exclusive, and hegemonic, but that operates under the guise of multiparty electoral politics. The democratic process in Angola has brought a veneer of legitimacy to an overtly extractive, predatory, and clientelistic regime. The National Assembly will continue to serve not as a counterweight to the presidency but as a rubber stamp for the regime's policies, and President dos Santos will continue to be the ultimate arbiter of all political affairs in the country.

The constitutional commission is currently debating alternative systems of government, including a continuation of the presidential system but with a vice-president instead of a prime minister; a parliamentary system headed by a prime minister; or a parliamentary system in which the president is indirectly elected by the parliament.[14] The opposition bench strongly disapproves of the last option, as do even some elements within the MPLA, who believe that dos Santos will have greater legitimacy if he is directly elected.

In a controversial ruling in July 2005, the Constitutional Court declared that dos Santos's three presidential terms (1992–2007) do not actually count, as he was never officially sworn in. As a result, the two-term limit on the presidency was set aside and dos Santos continues to rule Angola unconstitutionally. A number of Angolan observers believe that dos Santos wants to avoid a popular election at all costs, fearing a repeat of his 1992 performance at the polls, which was far worse than his party's. If the 67-year-old president fails to secure at least 82 percent (the MPLA's 2008 legislative vote share) this time around, his position in the party hierarchy may be compromised.

The configuration of the cabinet has been changing as well. The creation of five new ministries brings the number of ministries in the new government to 33. Manuel Nunes Júnior, former chief of economic and social policy and one of the party's leading ideologists, holds the newly created post of minister of the economy. This ministry probably was created by the MPLA to check and marginalize the finance ministry and to regain control over economic policy.[15] Antonio Paulo Kassoma, the former governor of Huambo, was appointed prime minister in September 2008 after delivering a crushing electoral defeat of UNITA in its symbolic heartland.

As has always been the case, appointees who are loyal and useful to the president gain the greatest access to state funds. The president rewards his closest allies—including the top-ranking officers in the Angolan Armed Forces—with opportunities that are unavailable to others.[16] This dependence on dos Santos for access to state resources, business permissions, and favors has led to competition and factionalism within the ruling party and the elite.[17] In fact, the regime has always been and will continue to be based on two principles: control the coffers and control the security apparatus. Both are imperative for the survival of "Eduardismo"[18] and MPLA hegemony. Change in Angola will therefore come only from within the ruling party or the military.

Regime Consolidation

With the 2008 legislative elections, Angola did indeed undergo a transition, but not toward democracy. Rather than ushering in a new era of political liberalism, the recent polls helped to consolidate the MPLA's hegemony and to transform the country from a fragile state into a stable and resilient autocracy. The moment for the full enjoyment of citizenship rights, for holding the government and the elite accountable, and for the establishment of mechanisms to stop the looting of the treasury and the reign of patronage has once again been postponed.

Because of economic mismanagement and endemic corruption, most Angolans have yet to benefit from the country's rapid economic growth, which has been propelled by the oil industry and other natural resources. The oil boom, coupled with China's willingness to extend billions of dollars in loans, has enabled the government to operate without transparency. Freedom House estimates that more than a billion dollars in oil revenue disappears each year, an example of the public-finance system's inefficiency and opacity.[19] Transparency International ranks Angola 158th out of 180 countries on its 2008 Corruption Perceptions Index. Moreover, disparities in wealth make Angola one of the most unequal countries in the world, with a Gini coefficient of 0.62 in 2006, and it ranks twenty-second from the bottom (at 157 out of 179) on the UNDP's 2008 Human Development Index.

As one of the top two oil producers in sub-Saharan Africa, Angola has gained considerable diplomatic clout. The MPLA regime has skillfully wielded the country's military might and economic power, and it has adopted a pragmatic approach to diversifying Angola's development partners. Part of the government's strategy to ensure its survival and international relevance has, in fact, been to normalize relations with countries that it did not engage with historically, such as the United States and France. Angola's rich mineral resources, particularly oil and diamonds, have enabled Luanda to sign significant agreements with such diverse donors as Brazil, China, several European countries, and India. Its dealings with China, which has proven willing to invest in infrastructure projects and to extend credit lines without conditionalities, have fostered the regime's sense of invulnerability.

Unlike so many other African countries, Angola is not a major recipient of aid. Thus donors and international financial institutions can bring little pressure to bear on the regime to adhere to norms of transparency, accountability, respect for human rights, and good governance. And just as the country's oil wealth stymies international interference, it also allows Angola's government to stay detached from its own citizens. The regime relies on the offshore economy and does not depend on the population for revenues. Thus there is no reciprocal relationship between the ruling elite and the population, which creates an enormous obstacle to democratization. Unless there is a radical shift in the national economic arena, Angola's resources will continue to shape political developments and retard the process of democratization.

Although Angola's lucrative extractive economy bolsters the regime, the superficial advances that have been made in the direction of democracy, civil and political liberties, service provision, decentralization, and broad-based development may ultimately stir up popular demand for more meaningful change. If and when that happens, how will the regime navigate the path between real and façade democracy? Can it maintain international legitimacy while at the same time trying to tamp down popular movements demanding liberalization, equality, and long-overdue peace dividends?

Although Angola's oil economy has thus far protected the regime, it is not invulnerable. The current global economic crisis could result in a steep drop in the price of oil, which would force the government to reconsider its relationships with international financial institutions and limit the regime's ability to dole out patronage benefits to its supporters. Should that happen, the MPLA might have no other choice but to reopen political space to the opposition.

Even though the 2008 legislative elections helped the regime to consolidate its power, the polls were nonetheless a democratic achievement of sorts: Angola managed to hold multiparty elections in a climate relatively free of hostility and wholesale intimidation. There was an opening, albeit a narrow one, of political space prior to the voting, and the public generally accepted the opposition parties' concession to the MPLA. It is possible to view this contest optimistically as a "test-run" for multiparty politics and perhaps the beginning of the end of the MPLA's veiled autocracy. The road to real democracy in Angola will indeed be long and tortuous, but it may in one way or another have begun.

NOTES

1. See Global Witness, "Time for Transparency: Coming Clean on Oil, Mining, and Gas Revenues," March 2004, available at *www.globalwitness.org/media_library_detail. php/115/en/time_for_transparency*; and International Crisis Group, "Angola's Choice: Reform or Regress," Africa Report 61, April 2003.

2. The *assimilados* were the integrated, educated Angolans who had assimilated the Portuguese language, culture, and habits, and were a fundamental part of the urban colonial structure.

3. See Christine Knudsen, Alexander Mundt, and I.W. Zartman, *Peace Agreements: The Case of Angola,* Case Series 1 (Natal, South Africa: ACCORD, 2000).

4. See Mabel Gonzalez Bustelo, "Angola: Monarchy Supported by Oil Companies," Peace Research Center (CIP-FUHEM), 2004, available at *www.cipresearch.fuhem.es/pazy-seguridad/docs/ANGOLA%20ING%20OK.pdf.*

5. Bertelsmann Transformation Index, "Angola Country Report," 2008, *www.berteslmann-transformation-index.de/70.0.html.*

6. Augusto Santana, "Political Parties and Political Evolution in Angola," EISA Research Report No. 28, 2006, 43; available at *www.eisa.org.za/PDF/rr28.pdf.*

7. See Christine Messiant, "The Mutation of Hegemonic Domination: Multiparty Politics Without Democracy," in Patrick Chabal and Nuno Vidal, eds., *Angola: The Weight of History* (New York: Columbia University Press, 2008).

8. The CNE, chaired by Caetano de Sousa, who also chaired the 1992 elections, was composed of 2 members nominated by the president, 3 from the ruling party, 3 from the opposition parties, 1 Supreme Court justice, 1 Ministry of Territorial Administration representative, and 1 elected by the National Council of Social Communication.

9. Interviews conducted with Angolan journalists, Luanda, 2 September 2008.

10. Images of this were shown regularly on the national television station.

11. Santana, "Political Parties and Political Evolution in Angola," 23.

12. Economist Intelligence Unit (EIU), "Angola Country Profile, 2008," available at *www.eiu.com.*

13. The first vice-president of the commission is MPLA MP Ferreira Pinto, the second vice-president is UNITA MP Almerindo Jaka Jamba; of the 45 members, 35 are from the MPLA, 6 are from UNITA, 2 from the PRS, and one each from the FNLA and Nova Democracia.

14. "Constitutional Commission Members Appointed," *Angola Monitor,* Spring 2009, available at *www.actsa.org/Pictures/UpImages/Angola/Angola_Monitor_Spring_09.pdf.*

15. EIU, "Angola Country Profile 2008."

16. Many such as General "Kopelipa" hold important portfolios; he is currently the minister of military affairs in the Office of the Presidency but also heads the Office for National Reconstruction (GRN), which supervises the China Investment Fund. General Francisco Higino Carneiro, the minister of public works, controls the holding Caduta Organizações with interests in banking, insurance, tourism, and agroindustry. Angola's largest mobile-phone company, Unitel, is partly owned by the president's daughter Isabel and by the head of communications in the presidency, Brigadier General Leopoldino Fragoso do Nascimento.

17. Nicholas Shaxson, João Neves, and Fernando Pacheco, "Drivers of Change, Angola: Final Report, January 2008," available at *www.dfid.gov.uk/Documents/publications/pub_007076.doc.*

18. A term widely used in Angola to depict the monarch-like nature of Jose Eduardo dos Santos's rule.

19. See Freedom House, "Freedom in the World 2008—Angola (2008)," available at *www.freedomhouse.org/template.cfm?page=22&year=2008&country=7340.*

ZIMBABWE'S LONG AGONY

Michael Bratton and Eldred Masunungure

Michael Bratton *is University Distinguished Professor of political science and African studies at Michigan State University.* **Eldred Masunungure** *is a lecturer in political and administrative studies at the University of Zimbabwe and director of the Mass Public Opinion Institute in Harare. This essay originally appeared in the October 2008* Journal of Democracy.

The Zimbabwe African National Union–Patriotic Front (ZANU-PF) led by Robert Mugabe has held power in Zimbabwe for almost three decades. Initially hailed as a force for emancipation, this ruling party now clings to office through violent repression. What happened? How did the country's founding father become its dictator? What patterns in the party's past foretold such an adverse outcome? What are the mechanisms of ZANU-PF's enduring rule? And what do the characteristics of the Mugabe regime imply for a possible regime transition?

We address these questions from the uncertain vantage point of the political deadlock in Zimbabwe in the aftermath of the disputed 2008 presidential election. No candidate achieved an absolute majority in the March 29 first round—neither Morgan Tsvangirai, the trade unionist who leads the opposition Movement for Democratic Change (MDC) and won 48 percent of the valid votes, nor Robert Mugabe, who won 43 percent. A constitutionally mandated runoff election was therefore scheduled for June 27. In response to a vicious government crackdown that killed more than a hundred MDC officials and supporters, injured thousands in politically motivated beatings, and displaced up to 200,000 people, however, Tsvangirai withdrew from the second round. Facing no competition, Mugabe went on to score a hollow victory with 85 percent of the vote from a brutalized and shrunken electorate. But few in the West regard him as the legitimate president of Zimbabwe, and for the first time other African leaders have begun to call for either a transitional arrangement or a government of national unity. As of this writing in early September 2008, however, talks aimed at such an outcome remain stalled.

ZANU-PF's staying power hinges upon a destructive mix of ideology, patronage, and violence. The resultant regime, which we characterize as a militarized form of electoral authoritarianism,[1] has come to rest on the interpenetration of two key organs of authority: the ruling party and the security forces. Over time, as the economy collapsed, patronage resources dried up, and the rule of law and public services broke down, political elites intentionally blurred the boundaries between party and state—both at the top, between ZANU-PF structures and the security apparatus, and at the bottom, between regular military forces and informal party militias. As a result, the military became politicized and the polity became militarized.

We trace these developments to the shared origins and experiences of Zimbabwe's ruling elite. Our guiding assumption is that politicians govern principally by the methods that they first used to ascend to power. ZANU-PF's formative years were spent as a national-liberation movement dedicated to overthrowing a white-settler government by force of arms. Precedents for postcolonial rule were originally laid down during the guerrilla war of 1972–79 and revived selectively after challenges from the MDC arose from 2000 onward.

Indeed, ZANU-PF never fully transformed itself from an armed liberation movement into a democratic political party, and it has revealed its true temperament during times of political crisis.[2] In our view, five key elements constitute the ZANU-PF heritage: 1) an ideological belief in its right to rule in perpetuity; 2) a party machinery that penetrates the organs of the state; 3) a corrupted economy vested in the hands of party loyalists; 4) an institutionalized role in policy making for military commanders; 5) and a heavy reliance on violence, increasingly outsourced to auxiliary forces.

Despite the apparently dominant role played by Robert Mugabe in this model of politics, we resist reducing the future of Zimbabwe to the fate of one man. Along with his party and military colleagues, Mugabe has established an institutionalized system of authority with clear rules, structures, and incentives. Because this authoritarian regime is underpinned by extensive vested interests, it is likely to outlast the political career of any particular dictator. Indeed, the octogenarian Mugabe's authority was greatly diminished by his and the party's losses in the first round of the presidential election and in parallel legislative elections in March 2008. As a result, power in Zimbabwe effectively passed to a civilian-military junta.

Any regime transition will be conditioned by this reality. The most likely outcome is political continuity, in which Mugabe either refuses to step down or hands over the helm of the party-state to a security-minded ZANU-PF loyalist. In another widely debated solution to the current standoff, an interim administration or government of national unity would be forged between leaders of ZANU-PF and the MDC. But the degree of regime change under this scenario depends on who mediates any unity negotiations and who emerges at the head of the new order. Finally, even if, against the odds, a more democratic system is eventually installed via fresh elections, any new leader of Zimbabwe will face enormous challenges in neutralizing the power of politicized and militarized elements that have thoroughly penetrated the state.

An Ideology of National Liberation

The behavior of Zimbabwe's rulers is best understood in the context of their belief that ZANU-PF has a right to rule in perpetuity. According to this worldview, political legitimacy is determined by the ruling party's heritage as the moving force behind anticolonial liberation. Whenever necessary, party propaganda portrays the country's situation as a permanent *chimurenga* (armed struggle) and vilifies organized political opposition as a treasonous attempt to restore the colonial *status quo ante*. As in any electoral-authoritarian regime, competitive elections in Zimbabwe serve the useful purpose of demonstrating the incumbent's dominance, but only so long as the opposition can never win. Over time, it has become clear that the ZANU-PF cadres will never recognize an opposition victory at the polls or surrender control of a government that they regard as belonging indisputably to themselves alone.

The party ideology harps on several well-worn themes that are broadcast *ad nauseam* over the state-owned media. The official creed praises veterans of the liberation war as public heroes, accords them state honors at a national shrine, and memorializes their deeds in presidential speeches, street names, public holidays, political-education courses, and television shows about patriotic history. In a country where two-thirds of the populace still lives in rural areas, Zimbabwe's fertile farmland is the ultimate revolutionary symbol. Although the authorities did little to rectify racial inequalities in land distribution during the first two decades after independence, they often stirred up the issue at election time as a tool for political mobilization. Most recently, in ZANU-PF's campaign for the 2008 election, the party charged that the opposition—not just the MDC, but also the splinter group headed by former ZANU-PF cabinet minister Simba Makoni—was planning to hand back land to white farmers.

The ruling party's intolerance of political opposition was born during the liberation struggle. The two nationalist formations—ZANU with its armed wing, the Zimbabwe African National Liberation Army (ZANLA), and the Zimbabwe African People's Union (ZAPU) and its Zimbabwe People's Revolutionary Army (ZIPRA)—never achieved a unity of purpose. These rival political and military organizations operated separately and sometimes against each other. Indeed, liberation politics were marked by intense intrigue, violent purges, and leadership assassinations. These conflicts deepened an ethnic split between speakers of Chishona and Sindebele and revealed intra-Shona clan divisions that continue to drive leadership competition to this day.

Soon after independence in 1980, the supporters of Joshua Nkomo's ZAPU were portrayed in the official media as "dissidents," and their purported armed rebellion was crushed via ethnic massacres in Matabeleland between 1982 and 1987. The ruling party later hounded presidential aspirants—Edgar Tekere in 1990 and Morgan Tsvangirai in 2002 and 2008—with assassination plots or treason trials or both. In increasingly racist terms, ZANU-PF depicts the MDC as a stalking horse for regime change funded by the British, European, and U.S. governments (then–British prime minister Tony Blair was a favorite target) and for favoring liberal political and economic reforms that deny the historical contribution and socialist agenda of the guerrilla movement. Under the terms of the incongruously named Access to Information and Protection of Privacy Act (2002), which bans foreign journalists and outlaws independent publications, alternative views are restricted. Summarizing the party's position on electoral competition, a government propagandist urged that "the stampede for democracy should not undermine the gains of the liberation war."[3]

Many Zimbabweans now reject the rhetorical representation of a political world populated only by "freedom fighters" and "puppets" by turning off their televisions and radios during news bulletins on state-run broadcasting stations. In a 2005 survey, only a third of adults said that they trusted the Zimbabwe Broadcasting Corporation or the government-owned *Herald* and *Chronicle* dailies.[4] The rest of the populace sees the regime's liberation ideology as the party elite's crude attempt to hold on to power. As discussed below, the *chimurenga* ideology has become little more than a shabby cover for the personal interests of a narrow clique.

Yet recent statements by ZANU-PF barons continue to reflect a persistent sense of political entitlement. A member of the party politburo, speaking anonymously about the 2008 election, indicated that the party did not plan to surrender power through the ballot box. With reference to the presidential runoff election, he warned ominously, "We're giving the people of Zimbabwe another opportunity to mend their ways, to vote properly . . . this is their last chance."[5] Likewise, Grace Mugabe (the president's wife) publicly stated that "even if people vote for MDC, Morgan Tsvangirai will never step foot [*sic*] inside State House."[6] Mugabe himself claimed that only God, rather than a piece of paper (that is, a ballot), could remove him from the presidency.

A Politicized Party-State

A politicized party-state enforces authoritarian rule in Zimbabwe. The major prize that ZANU-PF won at independence was the apparatus of the state, including its military machinery and economic resources.

Since that time, the party has sought the vanguard role in society—as well as the supremacy over the state—historically associated with communist systems. The ruling party and public administration are fused, and organizational structures are conflated at all levels—the party is married to the state. The Constitution of Zimbabwe, however, does not explicitly recognize political parties, and thus the ZANU-PF party-state is an empirical reality rather than a legal one.

To this day, the ZANU-PF leader still thinks and acts like the apostle of the one-party state that he declared himself to be nearly two decades ago. Referring to Zimbabwe's first coalition government, ZAPU leader Joshua Nkomo complained that "the underlying problem was that ZANU ministers . . . regarded their party politburo and central committee as more important than the cabinet or parliament."[7] ZAPU was absorbed as a junior partner in the 1987 Unity Accord, Article 6 of which emphatically stated, "We shall seek to establish a one-party state." Thereafter, Zimbabwe effectively became a de facto political monopoly: The top ZANU-PF organs usurped important government decisions, and opposition parties—with three seats after 1990 and just two after 1995—were virtually eliminated from parliament.

The Movement for Democratic Change, by calling for a "people-driven" constitution, defeating the government in a constitutional referendum in 2000, and winning 57 out of 120 contested seats in parliamentary elections that year, challenged the ruling party's hegemony. A rattled ZANU-PF retaliated with repressive legislation and violence. It introduced the Public Order and Security Act (POSA), a colonial-style instrument aimed at inhibiting the opposition's political gatherings. The party also unleashed war veterans in a chaotic campaign to evict white farmers from commercial farmland, and mobilized militias under the guise of a national youth-training program. In other words, ZANU-PF signaled in physical as well as ideological terms that it would not tolerate the emergence of a democratic opposition. And by rigging elections for the presidency in 2002 and parliament in 2005, the authoritarian regime honed its strategies for hanging onto power even in the face of legitimate electoral challenges.

The project of consolidating the party-state also required a takeover of the public sector. After independence, ZANU-PF initially used demobilized war veterans and returnees from Zimbabwe's international diaspora to penetrate the civilian bureaucracy and the security agencies. Once the civil service had been Africanized, politicization of state agencies intensified. For example, in the run-up to the 1995 elections, a ZANU-PF official threatened to dismiss civil servants who might support an opposition party. In early 2001, war veterans stormed local authorities in opposition districts, locking local-government offices, closing schools, and demanding the dismissal of councilors, teachers, and other workers.

The country's judiciary—the last bastion of autonomy from the party-state—was not spared. In 2001, the authorities launched a campaign to intimidate senior jurists into retirement and to "restructure" the court system by naming a dozen new judges to the High and Supreme Courts. In December of that year, Chief Justice Godfrey Chidyausiku and three other newly appointed judges overturned a previous ruling in order to endorse the government's compulsory acquisition of white-owned farms. In short, the judiciary and other law-enforcement agencies (notably, the Zimbabwe Republic Police) were transformed into partisan instruments. Today, no state institution is impervious to the dictates of the ruling party.

An Economy of Plunder

At independence, Zimbabwe possessed a diversified economy that, in good years, fed the nation and allowed exports of surplus food to other parts of southern Africa. When ZANU-PF came to power, it put into play economic plans drawn up during the war for liberation—a strategy of growth with redistribution through provision of universal education and health services and investment in peasant farming. As a consequence, the average standard of living rose during the 1980s.

But the rot, in the form of economic mismanagement, soon set in. The ZANU-PF leadership routinely used political criteria to make economic decisions—for example, by expanding patronage jobs in public corporations and overregulating the private sector, thus slowing economic growth. Official corruption went unpunished—for example, when cabinet ministers were discovered profiting from the sale of cars from the state-run assembly plant or commandeering disability payments to which they were not entitled. The government, unable to withstand threats of violence from self-proclaimed veterans of the liberation war, broke its own budget to award gratuities and pensions, and began to print money to cover the huge costs.

Over time, however, the benefits of economic redistribution became concentrated in the upper echelons of the party-state. Cabinet ministers, senior civil servants, security-force commanders, senior judges, and ZANU-PF parliamentarians were awarded the best properties confiscated from commercial farmers. These political insiders also gained privileged access to scarce foreign-currency funds at artificially low official exchange rates. The military brass developed a taste for political plunder as they accumulated vast streams of wealth from mining concessions or trading and transport contracts secured through Zimbabwe's armed intervention in the Congo War of 1998–2003. As a result, former army commander and ZANU-PF heavyweight Solomon Mujuru is now one of the country's wealthiest businessmen. Through a holding company, the ruling party itself owns interests in motor-vehicle dealerships and garages, real estate, mining, steel, building materials, and the import and distribution of industrial machinery. These enterprises enjoy sweetheart deals to supply government departments with essential goods and services. Yet entrepreneurs who are unwilling to declare fealty to ZANU-PF find it impossible to conduct business.

Mismanagement has brought the economy close to collapse. Zimbabwe's real GDP—battered by the world's lowest growth and highest inflation rates—has shrunk by half since 2000 and increasingly operates informally on U.S. dollars and South African rands. Local-currency banknotes have long been in short supply and could soon run out. The agricultural sector—once the prime generator of jobs, foreign exchange, and inputs to manufacturing—has been largely destroyed, leaving as many as five-million Zimbabweans dependent on food relief. In a damaging brain drain, up to a quarter of the population now resides abroad, sending remittances that provide an essential lifeline for relatives back home. Despite everything, the ruling party continues to threaten nationalization of the few remaining private enterprises in the mining and manufacturing sectors.

The drastic economic decline, however, has undercut ZANU-PF's ability to distribute patronage and thereby maintain political control. The beneficiaries of the regime have shrunk to a small group of civilian and military cronies associated with the top organs of the party. Some of these self-enriched individuals who have private vested interests now regard Mugabe as a liability whose continued presence as head of state prevents the normalization of Zimbabwe's international relations and the recovery of its economy. Hence, in squabbles over dwindling resources, the personnel within the party-state institutions are fragmenting over the question of political succession. Moreover, ordinary people, including lower-ranking public servants who have seen their salaries eroded by inflation, now find appeal in the opposition's call for change.[8] At the same time, however, they model their behavior on that of the politicians. Corruption now pervades all levels of the Zimbabwean state and has spread into society at large. As parallel markets eclipse the formal sector, daily survival in Zimbabwe has become unavoidably criminalized.

Creeping Military Intervention

Civil-military relations in Zimbabwe were molded in the crucible of the liberation war. Through shared experiences in fighting for independence, civilian and military leaders developed common ideological outlooks and mutual political loyalties that survive to this day. Soldiers have long had a hand in political decision making: For example, the position of secretary of defense in ZANU's Dare re Chimurenga (War Council) has always been reserved for a senior military commander. When conflicts erupted within the liberation movements, men with guns imposed solutions. Military leaders were implicated in the controversial 1975 assassination in Lusaka of Herbert Chitepo (chairman of the Dare

re Chimurenga), the deposition of ZANU's founding president Ndaban-
ingi Sithole in 1976 (and his replacement by Robert Mugabe), and the
mysterious death of ZANLA military supremo Josiah Tongogara on the
eve of independence in 1979.

At independence, the new Zimbabwean government embarked on
the difficult and sensitive exercise of integrating into a single force
three formerly hostile organizations—the Rhodesian Security Forces
(RSF), ZANLA, and ZIPRA—each with its own ethnic base and distinct
military tradition. The government managed to subordinate the newly
formed Zimbabwe Defense Force (ZDF) to civilian political control, in
part because former ZANLA guerrillas took over most leadership and
rank-and-file positions in the integrated army. Today, ZANU-PF loyalists command the ZDF, the Air Force of Zimbabwe, the Central Intelligence Organization, the Zimbabwe Prison Service, and the Zimbabwe
Republic Police. With help from North Korean instructors, the ruling
party formed a presidential guard and the ethnically loyal Fifth Infantry
Brigade, which carried out the Matabeleland massacres of 1982 to 1987.
The subsequent unpopular military adventure in the Congo also buttressed the budget, political influence, and institutional autonomy of the
Zimbabwe Defense Forces.

The year 2000 was a turning point in civil-military relations. With the
emergence of the MDC challenge, the military's involvement in political
life became increasingly open. The party deployed state-security agencies to provide transport and logistical support to war veterans and other
land invaders. The police, increasingly infiltrated by intelligence agents
charged with enforcing loyalty to the party-state, actively harassed and
impeded the main opposition party during "the long election campaign"
between June 2000 and March 2002. In May 2001, army commander
Constantine Chiwenga toured the barracks to mobilize electoral support
for Mugabe; he warned that no soldier should ever take orders from
MDC presidential candidate Morgan Tsvangirai or any other leader who
had not fought in the liberation war. This thinly veiled coup threat was
the clearest signal yet that the Zimbabwe military was prepared to take
over the reins of power in the event of an electoral outcome it regarded
as unfavorable.

With Mugabe's controversial reelection to the presidency in 2002,
the military had already attained an enhanced role in the strategic management of national affairs. A Joint Operations Command (JOC), composed of the heads of the army, air force, police, prisons, and intelligence
agency, became the key forum for policy decisions. The Reserve Bank
governor is an ex-officio member of the JOC and its source of revenue
on demand, including direct financing of the security forces. Ironically,
the JOC originated in the colonial era as a counterinsurgency-coordi-
nation organ chaired by the Rhodesian army commander. As before,
its function today is to coordinate rapid responses to national security

threats, whose scope is now broadly defined to include the economy and elections. Policy decisions by the JOC usually ignore the parliament and bypass the cabinet, and are executed by the security services as much as by the civilian ministries. The JOC's style of governance draws upon military imagery and tactics. Operation Murambatsvina ("Clean Out Filth") was a campaign to demolish illegal urban structures and shut down informal trading; Operation Maguta charged the armed forces with responsibilities for food production, not least to ensure that the troops remained well fed; and Operation Reduce Prices forced retailers to slash consumer prices in half, leading to massive shortages.

Recent developments also confirm that early efforts to professionalize the military could not withstand counterpressures from ZANU-PF to politicize the state apparatus. In the post-2000 period, the party engaged retired and serving military officers to plan and execute party strategy by coopting them into the ZANU-PF central committee and politburo. Others were appointed to key positions in strategic state institutions such as the Reserve Bank, the Grain Marketing Board, the National Oil Company, the National Railways, and the Zimbabwe Electoral Commission (ZEC). George Chiweshe, a former judge advocate responsible for military tribunals, for example, was appointed first as a member of the delimitation committee that gerrymandered voting districts in ZANU-PF's favor in 2005 and later as the inaugural chairman of the ZEC. At the local level, active and demobilized intelligence and military personnel have been deployed to mobilize voters ahead of elections, oversee polling, and supervise the count. All election results—including the long-delayed announcement of Mugabe's loss to Tsvangirai in the first round of the 2008 election—were said to be forwarded to the JOC for approval before being sent to the national command center for release.

By all reliable accounts, Zimbabwe's military quietly seized control and subverted the democratic process in the immediate aftermath of the first round of the March 29 presidential election. There are credible reports that, on March 30, Mugabe informed his security chiefs that he had lost the presidential vote and intended to surrender power.[9] Constantine Chiwenga, now commander of the ZDF—backed by police chief Augustine Chihuri, air force head Perence Shiri, and director of prisons Paradzai Zimondi—allegedly vetoed this proposal. They insisted that Mugabe remain in office, either openly with military backing or by contesting a runoff election, the campaign for which would be run as yet another JOC operation. Code-named Operation Mavhotera Papi ("How Did You Vote?"), it would root out and target for retaliation all those suspected of casting a ballot for the MDC in the first round.

In June 2008, Tsvangirai claimed that "the country [had] witnessed a de facto coup d'etat and is now effectively run by a military junta."[10] We prefer to characterize the military's intervention as a silent coup, and the resultant hybrid as a civilian-military clique. At the time of writing, the top leadership continues to be drawn from ZANU-PF party ranks. Mugabe retains his position as national president, and Emmerson Mnangagwa, a senior politburo member and chief contender for succession, chairs the JOC.[11] Where possible, the regular military forces try to avoid overt involvement in state-sponsored violence by providing clandestine logistical support to informal paramilitary groups. In part to deflect even more international condemnation than the regime already attracts, the Zimbabwean generals prefer to present a civilian political façade.

Reliance on Violence

Regime power in Zimbabwe has always been buttressed by coercion, chillingly symbolized in ZANU-PF's trademark emblem, the fist. The political elite take as articles of faith the assumptions that violence was effective in delivering independence and that repression is the party's most effective weapon for countering real and imagined threats. As such, political intimidation is another thread of continuity connecting Zimbabwe's preindependence and postindependence eras. From the outset, Mugabe appears to have harbored a militaristic conception of political authority, proclaiming in 1976 that "our votes must go together with our guns; after all any vote . . . shall have been the product of the gun. The gun, which provides the votes, should remain its security officer, its guarantor."[12] Even in the 1980 independence elections, ZANU-PF campaigned on the slogan that it had started the war of liberation, and was the only force that could end it.

The postindependence period in Zimbabwe has been marked by at least four major periods of state-sponsored violence, all of which were accompanied by significant human rights violations. The Matabeleland massacres of the 1980s—known locally as Gukurahundi[13]—were aimed at stamping out ZAPU "dissidence" and resulted in at least ten-thousand deaths, as well as the beating, torture, rape, and disappearance of many more villagers.[14] The land expropriations of the early 2000s gave rise to the large-scale physical displacement of farm workers and their families, ostensibly because they had aligned with white farm owners in support of the MDC. In 2005, Operation Murambatsvina affected up to 700,000 city dwellers and was widely interpreted as ZANU-PF retaliation against urban voters, who had come out overwhelmingly for MDC in the 2005 presidential elections. And in every election season, especially since 2000, opposition sympathizers have suffered repression.[15] In March 2007, for instance, Tsvangirai and other MDC and civic leaders were assaulted at a prayer meeting. Mugabe's reaction to the ensuing international outcry was to announce, "If they protest again, we will bash them."

Thus the regime's recourse to violence in 2008 was new only in its desperation. Like a Cape buffalo, Mugabe has proven himself most dangerous when wounded and cornered. On the eve of the presidential election in March, he set the tone by threatening to wage war against the MDC in the event that he lost. As the election results trickled out and it became apparent that ZANU-PF had indeed lost control of the parliament and stood on the brink of losing the presidency too, the party-state launched a terror campaign of a scope and intensity never before seen in Zimbabwe. In stepping up the repression before the runoff election, ZANU-PF's apparent objective was to incapacitate, if not eliminate, the MDC as an electoral threat.

Internal ZANU-PF documents confirm that the JOC security chiefs ("with the party chairing") were in charge of logistics and operations in the runoff election of June 2008.[16] The country was divided into ten provincial command centers staffed by two-hundred serving army officers who were dispatched mainly to rural areas to supervise operations by war veterans and party youth militias, known as "green bombers" for the color of their fatigues. The JOC ordered the Reserve Bank to print money to fund pay hikes for war veterans, allowances for party youth, and payoffs to chiefs and headmen. These combined forces were instructed to invade farms, burn down houses, and incite violence. In order to conceal responsibility, auxiliaries were sometimes issued police or army uniforms, and undercover masked intelligence operatives conducted kidnappings and murders. The green bombers led all-night political education sessions—*pungwes,* a tactic from the liberation war—in which villagers were forced to chant ZANU-PF slogans and denounce "sellouts." Persons suspected of supporting the MDC were beaten in public or snatched away to secret detention centers that specialized in crude forms of torture. The police, of course, complied with orders to turn a blind eye to the abuses.

ZANU-PF's strategy for the runoff election was "electoral cleansing." The objective was to kill MDC officials and polling agents, displace qualified electoral officials such as schoolteachers, and punish known MDC supporters. The targets of intimidation were not so much the solid MDC strongholds in the cities and the southwest, but politically contested areas in the country's middle belt and northeast where, in the first round of the election, voters had swung away from ZANU-PF and toward the MDC. The object of electoral cleansing was to create "no-go zones" (note again the guerrilla-insurgency terminology) where the ZANU-PF monopoly could be enforced at the local level through the direct and demonstration effects of violence. As further punishment, the party ordered food relief to be withheld from opposition sympathizers and commercial food supplies to be distributed only to shops operated by ZANU-PF supporters or personnel. The combination of physical intimidation and the denial of basic needs to MDC supporters meant that, in the words of a Shamva villager, "only ZANU-PF people will vote. There are no opposition supporters. It will be a big advantage for them."[17]

At the center, the top MDC leaders were forced into hiding as a result of police raids on their party's Harare headquarters. Threats against the opposition leadership were rendered shockingly real when the wife of the newly elected MDC mayor of Harare was abducted and killed. Tsvangirai embarked on an international tour to African and European capitals to draw attention to the crackdown and to encourage international isolation of the Mugabe government. He returned to Zimbabwe shortly before the runoff, but, citing the unacceptable cost of the violence, ultimately withdrew his candidacy and took refuge in the Embassy of the Netherlands.

Like Burma's defensive military junta, the government of Zimbabwe limited foreign relief agencies' and international journalists' access to the hinterland. Despite the government's best efforts, however, news of the regime's brutality and the dire costs of its policy of using food as a political weapon began to trickle out. In contrast to the 1980s, when the Matabeleland massacres were hidden from public view, local and international civic actors carefully documented and publicized the 2008 crackdown.[18] Brazenly but unconvincingly, ZANU-PF tried to deflect the negative attention from the party-state by blaming the interelection violence on the MDC. Although ZANU-PF undoubtedly succeeded in raising the cost of supporting the opposition party, in so doing it laid bare its deeply antidemocratic tendencies. By blocking democratic processes and outcomes, the militarized authoritarian regime showcased for the world its own illegitimate credentials.

What Lies Ahead

Since 2000, when ZANU-PF first faced an opposition challenge from the Movement for Democratic Change, the trappings of democracy in Zimbabwe have looked increasingly threadbare. A key pitfall of electoral authoritarian regimes is that dictators desire the veneer of political legitimacy provided by managed elections and the appearance of the rule of law. They can, however, become trapped by their own façade. In March 2008, ZANU-PF lost control of the electoral process when its own electoral commission, following the letter of the existing electoral law, announced that MDC candidates had won the most seats in the parliamentary election and had outpolled Robert Mugabe in the first round of the presidential election.

This unprecedented political defeat served as a wake-up call for the generation of politicians and generals who rose to political prominence in the country's liberation war and later benefited from ZANU-PF rule, and whose past abuses now bind them in a collective quest for political survival. By seizing power on 30 March 2008, the civilian-military junta effectively blocked democracy in Zimbabwe. Moreover, democratization will be obstructed for as long as the incumbent generation remains in charge. To be sure, the imploding economy is propelling a checkmated endgame. But little in the way of positive political change can be expected if either

Mugabe or a handpicked ZANU-PF successor retains executive power, even in a government of national unity that includes MDC representation. As a seasoned commentator observed, "There is nothing to be gained by calling for a government of national unity in Zimbabwe when Mugabe makes it clear that it can only come into existence on his terms."[19]

At the time of this writing, Zimbabwe is stalled in a contested interregnum. Both Mugabe and Tsvangirai have agreed in principle to a power-sharing arrangement. The two rivals, however, each claim national leadership and have not yet arrived at agreement on a framework for national unity. Tsvangirai has indicated his willingness to assume a new position of prime minister while Mugabe retains the presidency, but only if the president's role becomes largely ceremonial. Mugabe, on the other hand, would accept Tsvangirai as a toothless premier with a limited portfolio, if the president retains all executive authority. In August, both parties attended a meeting of the Southern African Development Community (SADC) chaired by South African president Thabo Mbeki, who has for months been presiding over negotiations between the adversaries. Yet again, however, they failed to reach an agreement.

Both parties are bargaining from positions of weakness: Mugabe is increasingly isolated within and outside the country, and Tsvangirai's party, never well-organized, is in disarray as a result of state violence. The country lacks functioning political institutions because, at the time of writing, neither the parliament nor local government bodies had convened since the election. The civil service and judiciary remain severely compromised by the exodus of skilled professionals and the bias and mediocrity of the political appointees who have replaced them. In this institutional vacuum, the security forces continue to hold the strongest hand. Thus the case of Zimbabwe bears out the adage that, with respect to regime change in Africa, as goes the military, so goes the transition.[20]

The new prominence of military men in the Zimbabwean regime creates distinctive hurdles to a way ahead. First, due to the military-driven response to the March 2008 elections, it is no longer possible for a government led by ZANU-PF to win international recognition. Second, the presence in the security establishment of human rights abusers poses a difficult choice for any transition deal: Should violators be offered amnesty or prosecuted for war crimes? Until a resolution is found—no easy matter given Zimbabweans' profound emotions on this subject—the military can probably hold any transition process hostage. And third, a militarized ZANU-PF regime will always be tempted to rule by the gun, as evidenced by the persistence of violence against the opposition, violence which spread to the impoverished townships around Harare even after Mugabe's "victory" in the runoff.

So far, the common origins and destiny of the top commanders and the party elite have served to keep the military loyal. But the collapsing economy is further straining the fabric of the security forces; disgruntled elements in the rank-and-file are already going unpaid while others are being sent home because they cannot be fed in their garrisons. The greatest risk is that regular soldiers will lose the state's monopoly on violence. By relying on auxiliaries such as the war veterans and youth militias to do the party's dirty work, Zimbabwe's civilian-military junta is courting serious unintended consequences. The unemployed young people trained to intimidate the opposition owe no lasting historical or ideological allegiance to ZANU-PF. Still, these informal groups present a serious obstacle for meaningful political negotiations. If they remain intact—as ZANU-PF undoubtedly intends—they will pose threats of lawlessness and extortion that will only deepen the ruling party's bitter legacy.

Given the weak political position of Zimbabwe's civilian politicians and the prospect of a downward spiral into further violence, international intervention could ultimately go a long way in resolving the country's crisis. Already Botswana and Zambia have called on Mugabe to step aside, Mbeki and the SADC have ratcheted up negotiations, and Western nations are withholding desperately needed aid as long as Mugabe clings to power.[21] In light of the authoritarian legacy of the ZANU-PF regime, however, it remains to be seen if such political and economic pressure can succeed in bringing about a peaceful and meaningful transition.

—10 September 2008

NOTES

1. See Andreas Schedler, ed., *Electoral Authoritarianism: The Dynamics of Unfree Competition* (Boulder, Colo.: Lynne Rienner, 2006). Also Steven Levitsky and Lucan A. Way, "The Rise of Competitive Authoritarianism," *Journal of Democracy* 13 (April 2002): 51–65.

2. Goran Hyden writes of a "movement legacy" in African politics in which anticolonial resistance spawned political parties that remained loosely organized but dedicated to establishing political order. *African Politics in Comparative Perspective* (New York: Cambridge University Press, 2006).

3. Godfrey Chikowore, "Defending Our Heritage: Armed Struggle Should Serve as Guiding Spirit," *Herald* (Harare), 16 February 2002. Quoted in Terence Ranger, "Historiography, Patriotic History, and the History of the Nation: The Struggle over the Past in Zimbabwe," University of Ghent, Annual Distinguished Lecture on Africa, 2003, 3.

4. Michael Bratton, Annie Chikwana, and Tulani Sithole, "Propaganda and Public Opinion in Zimbabwe," *Journal of Contemporary African Studies* 23 (January 2005): 77–108.

5. "Violence in Zimbabwe Disrupts Schools and Aid," *New York Times,* 9 May 2008.

6. "Zimbabwe's Mugabe Will Never Step Aside for Rival: Wife," *Agence France Presse,* 29 May 2008.

7. Joshua Nkomo, *Nkomo: The Story of My Life* (Harare: SAPES Books, 2001), 223.

8. The Mass Public Opinion Institute (MPOI) reports that the expressed intention to vote for ZANU-PF fell from 41 percent in October 2006 to 20 percent in March 2008. In

the latter survey, 31 percent were undecided or refused to divulge a preference; MPOI, unpublished memo, 12 March 2008.

9. The most reliable rendition of the events leading to the JOC takeover is Craig Timberg's "Inside Mugabe's Violent Crackdown," *Washington Post,* 5 July 2008. See also Celia Dugger, "Slow Motion Coup," *New York Times,* 26 April 2008; and Allister Sparks, "Zimbabwe's Military Feels the Heat," *Cape Times,* 30 April 2008.

10. "Zimbabwe Opposition Leader Says Country Run by Military," *Voice of America,* 10 April 2008.

11. A hardliner with an intelligence background, Mnangagwa was Minister for State Security during the Matabeleland massacres. He was brought in to head Mugabe's presidential-runoff campaign reportedly because of his reputation for strong-arm tactics.

12. Robert Mugabe, "Fight Harder, Fight Harder," in *Our War of Liberation: Speeches, Articles, Interviews, 1976–1979* (Harare: Mambo, 1980), 12.

13. *Gukurahundi* is a Chishona word that means "the rain that washes away the chaff from the last harvest"; in the realm of Zimbabwean politics, it is understood to refer to the indiscriminate liquidation of perceived political enemies.

14. Catholic Commission for Justice and Peace in Zimbabwe, *Gukurahundi in Zimbabwe: A Report on the Disturbances in Matabeleland and the Midlands, 1980–1988* (Johannesburg: Jacana Press, 2007).

15. Norma Kriger, "ZANU-PF Strategies in General Elections, 1980–2000: Discourse and Coercion," *African Affairs* 104 (January 2005): 1–34.

16. "Zimbabwe Campaign: Secret Documents," *BBC News,* 12 June 2008; available at *http://news.bbc.co.uk/2/hi/africa/7450079.stm.*

17. "Zimbabwe Voices: Rural Fears," *BBC News,* 19 May 2008; available at *http://news.bbc.co.uk/2/hi/africa/7408975.stm.*

18. Human Rights Watch, *"Bullets for Each of You": State-Sponsored Violence Since Zimbabwe's March 29 Elections* (New York: HRW, 2008); Solidarity Peace Trust, *Punishing Dissent, Silencing Citizens: The Zimbabwe Election 2008* (Harare, SPT, 2008); International Crisis Group, "Negotiating Zimbabwe's Transition," ICG Africa Briefing No. 51 (2008); and Impunity Watch, *Seeking Justice for Zimbabwe: A Case for Accountability Against Robert Mugabe and Others, 1981–2008* (Washington D.C., 2008).

19. Terence Ranger, "Will Normality Return to Zimbabwe?" *East African* (Nairobi), 7 July 2008.

20. Michael Bratton and Nicolas van de Walle, *Democratic Experiments in Africa: Regime Transitions in Comparative Perspective* (New York: Cambridge University Press, 2005), 210–17.

21. *Editors' Note:* On 11 September 2008, Mbeki announced that "a unanimous agreement" had been reached between Mugabe and Tsvangirai. The power-sharing deal is set to be signed on September 15, though no specific details have yet been released.

INDEX

Yar'Adua, Umaru, xviii, 5, 11–12,
121–123, 128, 130–132, 134,
135*n*

Zaire, x, 55, 65. *See also* Congo
(Kinshasa); Democratic Republic
of the Congo (DRC)
Zambia, xi, xiii, xv, xxiv–xxv,
xxvi*t*, 8, 11, 19, 21, 24–26, 28,
40, 49, 57, 64*f*, 66, 74, 78*t*, 79,
80*t*, 81–83, 88, 90, 92, 93*t*, 95,
99, 100*t*, 102*n*, 108, 110, 111*f*,
244, 259, 295–308, 351

Zanzibar, xxii, 87*n*, 107, 220, 222–
223, 225, 230–231, 231*n*
Zimbabwe, vi, xxv, xxvi, xxvi*t*, 8,
9, 11, 14, 50–53, 55, 64*t*, 70,
72*n*, 88, 92–93, 95*t*, 100t, 102*n*,
108, 110–111, 111*f*, 113, 117*n*,
137, 143, 145, 213, 275, 287,
338–351
Zimbabwe African National Union–
Patriotic Front (ZANU-PF), xxvi,
338–351
Zuma, Jacob, xxiii, 13, 265, 267, 269,
271–278